75 Readings

An Anthology

Twelfth Edition

Santi V. Buscemi
Middlesex County College

Charlotte Smith
SUNY Adirondack

75 READINGS: AN ANTHOLOGY, TWELFTH EDITION
Published by McGraw-Hill, a business unit of The McGraw-Hill Companies, Inc.,
1221 Avenue of the Americas, New York, NY 10020. Copyright © 2013 by The
McGraw-Hill Companies, Inc. All rights reserved. Printed in the United States of
America. Previous editions © 2010, 2007 and 2004. No part of this publication may
be reproduced or distributed in any form or by any means, or stored in a data-
base or retrieval system, without the prior written consent of The McGraw-Hill
Companies, Inc., including, but not limited to, in any network or other electronic
storage or transmission, or broadcast for distance learning.

Some ancillaries, including electronic and print components, may not be available
to customers outside the United States.

This book is printed on acid-free paper

5 6 7 8 9 10 LCR 21 20 19 18 17

ISBN 978-0-07-3405896
MHID 0-07- 3405892

Vice President & Editor-in-Chief: *Michael Ryan*
Vice President & Director Specialized Publishing: *Janice M. Roerig-Blong*
Publisher: *David Patterson*
Sponsoring Editor: *Debra B. Hash*
Marketing Manager: *Kevin Colleary*
Senior Project Manager: *Melissa Leick*
Design Coordinator: *Margarite Reynolds*
Cover Designer: *Studio Montage, St. Louis, Missouri*
Cover Image: *Tinke Hamming/Ingram Publishing*
Buyer: *Susan K. Culbertson*
Media Project Manager: *Sridevi Palani*
Compositor: *MPS Limited, a Macmillan Company*
Typeface: *10/12 Palatino*
Printer: *LSC Communications*

All credits appearing on page or at the end of the book are considered to be an
extension of the copyright page.

Library of Congress Cataloging-in-Publication Data
75 readings : an anthology / [edited by] Santi V. Buscemi, Charlotte Smith. — 12th ed.
    p. cm.—(75 readings)
  ISBN 978-0-07-340589-6 (acid-free paper)
1. College readers. 2. English language--Rhetoric—Problems, exercises, etc. I.
Buscemi, Santi V. II. Smith, Charlotte, 1957- III. Title: Seventy-five readings.
  PE1417.A13 2012
  808'.0427—dc23

2011047730

www.mhhe.com

About the Authors

SANTI BUSCEMI is a professor of English at Middlesex County College in Edison, New Jersey. He teaches developmental and first-year composition.

CHARLOTTE SMITH is a professor of English at SUNY Adirondack in Queensbury, New York, where she teaches technical writing and directs the Center for Reading and Writing.

Contents

Chapter 3
PROCESS ANALYSIS   65

Chapter 4
DEFINITION   86

Chapter 5
DIVISION AND CLASSIFICATION   110

Chapter 6
COMPARISON AND CONTRAST   146

Chapter 7
EXAMPLE AND ILLUSTRATION   170

Chapter 8
CAUSE AND EFFECT 196

Chapter 9
ANALOGY 256

Chapter 10
ARGUMENT AND PERSUASION 281

Chapter 11
MIXED STRATEGIES   349

THEMATIC CONTENTS

Portraits

Rites of Passage

Aging

Learning and Education

Global Issues

National Issues

Culture and Identity

Gender Politics

Science and Technology

Health and Medicine

Uses and Abuses of Language

CONTENTS GROUPED BY GENRE AND DISCIPLINE

GENRES

Autobiography and Memoir

Biography

Satire, Parody, Humor

Letters

Speeches

DISCIPLINES

Anthropology

Arts and Humanities

Education

Ethnic Studies

Gender Studies

Government/Public Policy

History

International Studies

Biological Sciences

Philosophy/Ethics

Sociology

Preface

75 Readings: An Anthology, Twelfth Edition introduces students to a range of classic and contemporary essays. The text also exposes them to a variety of rhetorical strategies, writing styles, themes, and topics. At the same time, it retains maximum flexibility for the instructor. We have continued to include essays that provide good structural models for rhetorical techniques and that raise complex questions about current and enduring issues. Thus, the selections in this text need not be used merely to illustrate form.

For instructors who like the selections but who do not organize their classes around rhetorical modes, we have included two alternate tables of contents, which arrange selections by themes and genres. Moreover, because there is no pedagogical apparatus in the text itself to direct its use, *75 Readings* is particularly adaptable to a variety of teaching approaches. However, for instructors who desire apparatus, the online instructor's manual provides, for each selection, a brief author biography, comments introducing the essay, questions for discussion, prompts for responding to and engaging the text, and suggestions for sustained writing.

As with previous editions, we have sought the advice of many colleagues across the nation to determine changes that would make this book even more effective and appealing as a learning tool for college readers and writers. Many of these professionals have put both the new and the old selections in this book to the ultimate test by using them in their classrooms. They have also provided helpful suggestions that have enabled us to fashion a new table of contents that makes *75 Readings* both versatile and representative of contemporary American culture.

CHANGES IN THE TWELFTH EDITION

Based on reviewers' suggestions, we have included the following:

- More essays on contemporary technology; food production, distribution, and use; and cultural identity in America.
- New readings that add depth and diversity and that pique student interest:

Louise Erdrich: *Beneath My House*
Peter Elbow: *Desperation Writing*
Richard Rodriguez: *"Blaxicans" and Other Reinvented Americans*
Brandon Griggs: *12 Most Annoying Types of Facebookers*
Gary Soto: *Like Mexicans*
Maxine Hong Kingston: *Family Ghosts*
Carlo Petrini: *The Value and Price of Food*
Rebecca Brown: *Extreme Reading*
Janet Kornblum: *Tapping into Text Messaging*
Michael Rubinkam: *Texting in Class Is Rampant*
Jonathan Safran Foer: *Let Them Eat Dog*
Sherman Alexie: *Superman and Me*
John Stuart Mill: *On Liberty*

As before, *75 Readings* contains an eleventh chapter, which includes essays worth teaching because of the effective mix of rhetorical strategies they use.

SUPPLEMENTS

75 Readings offers many additional resources to Students and Instructors at: www.mhhe.com/75readings.

ACKNOWLEDGMENTS

Special thanks are due to those instructors who reviewed and helped us shape this anthology with their suggestions, particularly: William Sheldon, Hutchinson Community College; Dr. Fran

Rancourt, Granite State College; Aaron Reini, Hibbing Community College; Natasha Bauman, El Camino College, Cypress College; Alex Solis, East Los Angeles College; Portia Jeffries, Seattle Central Community College; Chris Gardner, Austin Community College; Judith Ramos, Moorpark College; Janice R. Showler, Ph.D., Holy Family University; Jane Honeycutt (nee Thorne), Austin Community College; Tim Skeen, California State University-Fresno; Bill Tigue, East Los Angeles College; and Janet Cobb, Austin Community College.

We also thank our friends at McGraw-Hill—Debra Hash, Andrea Edwards, and especially Ruma Khurana—who encouraged us and helped us continue these texts.

Santi Buscemi
Charlotte Smith

Narration

Shooting an Elephant

George Orwell

In Moulmein, in Lower Burma, I was hated by large numbers 1
of people—the only time in my life that I have been important
enough for this to happen to me. I was sub-divisional police officer
of the town, and in an aimless, petty kind of way anti-European
feeling was very bitter. No one had the guts to raise a riot, but if
a European woman went through the bazaars alone somebody
would probably spit betel juice over her dress. As a police officer
I was an obvious target and was baited whenever it seemed safe
to do so. When a nimble Burman tripped me up on the football
field and the referee (another Burman) looked the other way, the
crowd yelled with hideous laughter. This happened more than
once. In the end the sneering yellow faces of young men that met
me everywhere, the insults hooted after me when I was at a safe
distance, got badly on my nerves. The young Buddhist priests
were the worst of all. There were several thousands of them in
the town and none of them seemed to have anything to do except
stand on street corners and jeer at Europeans.

All this was perplexing and upsetting. For at that time I had 2
already made up my mind that imperialism was an evil thing
and the sooner I chucked up my job and got out of it the better.
Theoretically—and secretly, of course—I was all for the Burmese

and all against their oppressors, the British. As for the job I was doing, I hated it more bitterly than I can perhaps make clear. In a job like that you see the dirty work of Empire at close quarters. The wretched prisoners huddling in the stinking cages of the lock-ups, the grey, cowed faces of the long-term convicts, the scarred buttocks of the men who had been Bogged with bamboos—all these oppressed me with an intolerable sense of guilt. But I could get nothing into perspective. I was young and ill-educated and I had had to think out my problems in the utter silence that is imposed on every Englishman in the East. I did not even know that the British Empire is dying, still less did I know that it is a great deal better than the younger empires that are going to supplant it. All I knew was that I was stuck between my hatred of the empire I served and my rage against the evil-spirited little beasts who tried to make my job impossible. With one part of my mind I thought of the British Raj as an unbreakable tyranny, as something clamped down, in *saecula saeculorum*, upon the will of prostrate peoples; with another part I thought that the greatest joy in the world would be to drive a bayonet into a Buddhist priest's guts. Feelings like these are the normal by-products of imperialism; ask any Anglo-Indian official, if you can catch him off duty.

3   One day something happened which in a roundabout way was enlightening. It was a tiny incident in itself, but it gave me a better glimpse than I had had before of the real nature of imperialism—the real motives for which despotic governments act. Early one morning the subinspector at a police station at the other end of the town rang me up on the phone and said that an elephant was ravaging the bazaar. Would I please come and do something about it? I did not know what I could do, but I wanted to see what was happening and I got on to a pony and started out. I took my rifle, an old .44 Winchester and much too small to kill an elephant, but I thought the noise might be useful *in terrorem*. Various Burmans stopped me on the way and told me about the elephant's doings. It was not, of course, a wild elephant, but a tame one which had gone "must." It had been chained up, as tame elephants always are when their attack of "must" is due, but on the previous night it had broken its chain and escaped. Its mahout, the only person who could manage it when it was in that state,

had set out in pursuit, but had taken the wrong direction and was now twelve hours' journey away, and in the morning the elephant had suddenly reappeared in the town. The Burmese population had no weapons and were quite helpless against it. It had already destroyed somebody's bamboo hut, killed a cow and raided some fruit-stalls and devoured the stock; also it had met the municipal rubbish van and, when the driver jumped out and took to his heels, had turned the van over and inflicted violences upon it.

The Burmese sub-inspector and some Indian constables 4 were waiting for me in the quarter where the elephant had been seen. It was a very poor quarter, a labyrinth of squalid bamboo huts, thatched with palmleaf, winding all over a steep hillside. I remember that it was a cloudy, stuffy morning at the beginning of the rains. We began questioning the people as to where the elephant had gone and, as usual, failed to get any definite information. That is invariably the case in the East; a story always sounds clear enough at a distance, but the nearer you get to the scene of events the vaguer it becomes. Some of the people said that the elephant had gone in one direction, some said that he had gone in another, some professed not even to have heard of any elephant. I had almost made up my mind that the whole story was a pack of lies, when we heard yells a little distance away. There was a loud, scandalized cry of "Go away, child! Go away this instant!" and an old woman with a switch in her hand came round the corner of a hut, violently shooing away a crowd of naked children. Some more women followed, clicking their tongues and exclaiming; evidently there was something that the children ought not to have seen. I rounded the hut and saw a man's dead body sprawling in the mud. He was an Indian, a black Dravidian coolie, almost naked, and he could not have been dead many minutes. The people said that the elephant had come suddenly upon him round the corner of the hut, caught him with its trunk, put its foot on his back and ground him into the earth. This was the rainy season and the ground was soft, and his face had scored a trench a foot deep and a couple of yards long. He was lying on his belly with arms crucified and head sharply twisted to one side. His face was coated with mud, the eyes wide open, the teeth bared and grinning with an expression of unendurable agony. (Never tell me, by the way, that the dead look peaceful. Most of the corpses I have seen looked devilish.) The friction of the great beast's foot had stripped the skin from his back as neatly as one skins a rabbit. As soon as I saw the dead man I sent an orderly to a friend's house nearby to borrow an elephant rifle. I had already sent back the pony, not wanting it to go mad with fright and throw me if it smelt the elephant.

5   The orderly came back in a few minutes with a rifle and five cartridges, and meanwhile some Burmans had arrived and told us that the elephant was in the paddy fields below, only a few hundred yards away. As I started forward practically the whole population of the quarter flocked out of the houses and followed me. They had seen the rifle and were all shouting excitedly that I was going to shoot the elephant. They had not shown much interest in the elephant when he was merely ravaging their homes, but it was different now that he was going to be shot. It was a bit of fun to them, as it would be to an English crowd; besides they wanted the meat. It made me vaguely uneasy. I had no intention of shooting the elephant—I had merely sent for the rifle to defend myself if necessary—and it is always unnerving to have a crowd following you. I marched down the hill, looking and feeling a fool, with the rifle over my shoulder and an ever-growing army of people jostling at my heels. At the bottom, when you got away from the huts, there was a metalled road and beyond that a miry waste of paddy fields a thousand yards across, not yet ploughed but soggy from the first rains and dotted with coarse grass. The elephant was standing eight yards from the road, his left side towards us. He took not the slightest notice of the crowd's approach. He was tearing up bunches of grass, beating them against his knees to clean them and stuffing them into his mouth.

6   I had halted on the road. As soon as I saw the elephant I knew with perfect certainty that I ought not to shoot him. It is a serious matter to shoot a working elephant—it is comparable to destroying a huge and costly piece of machinery—and obviously one ought not to do it if it can possibly be avoided. And at that distance, peacefully eating, the elephant looked no more dangerous than a cow. I thought then and I think now that his attack of

"must" was already passing off; in which case he would merely wander harmlessly about until the mahout came back and caught him. Moreover, I did not in the least want to shoot him. I decided that I would watch him for a little while to make sure that he did not turn savage again, and then go home.

But at that moment I glanced round at the crowd that had 7 followed me. It was an immense crowd, two thousand at the least and growing every minute. It blocked the road for a long distance on either side. I looked at the sea of yellow faces above the garish clothes—faces all happy and excited over this bit of fun, all certain that the elephant was going to be shot. They were watching me as they would watch a conjurer about to perform a trick. They did not like me, but with the magical rifle in my hands I was momentarily worth watching. And suddenly I realized that I should have to shoot the elephant after all. The people expected it of me and I had got to do it; I could feel their two thousand wills pressing me forward, irresistibly. And it was at this moment, as I stood there with the rifle in my hands, that I first grasped the hollowness, the futility of the white man's dominion in the East. Here was I, the white man with his gun, standing in front of the unarmed native crowd—seemingly the leading actor of the piece; but in reality I was only an absurd puppet pushed to and fro by the will of those yellow faces behind. I perceived in this moment that when the white man turns tyrant it is his own freedom that he destroys. He becomes a sort of hollow, posing dummy, the conventionalized figure of a sahib. For it is the condition of his rule that he shall spend his life in trying to impress the "natives," and so in every crisis he has got to do what the "natives" expect of him. He wears a mask, and his face grows to fit it. I had got to shoot the elephant. I had committed myself to doing it when I sent for the rifle. A sahib has got to act like a sahib; he has got to appear resolute, to know his own mind and do definite things. To come all that way, rifle in hand, with two thousand people marching at my heels, and then to trail feebly away, having done nothing—no, that was impossible. The crowd would laugh at me. And my whole life, every white man's life in the East, was one long struggle not to be laughed at.

But I did not want to shoot the elephant. I watched him beat- 8 ing his bunch of grass against his knees, with that preoccupied grandmotherly air that elephants have. It seemed to me that it would be murder to shoot him. At that age I was not squeamish about killing animals, but I had never shot an elephant and never wanted to. (Somehow it always seems worse to kill a *large* animal.) Besides, there was the beast's owner to be considered. Alive, the elephant was worth at least a hundred pounds; dead, he would only be worth the value of his tusks, five pounds, possibly. But I had got to act quickly. I turned to some experienced-looking Burmans who had been there when we arrived, and asked them how the elephant had been behaving. They all said the same thing: he took no notice of you if you left him alone, but he might charge if you went too close to him.

9   It was perfectly clear to me what I ought to do. I ought to walk up to within, say, twenty-five yards of the elephant and test his behavior. If he charged, I could shoot; if he took no notice of me, it would be safe to leave him until the mahout came back. But also I knew that I was going to do no such thing. I was a poor shot with a rifle and the ground was soft mud into which one would sink at every step. If the elephant charged and I missed him, I should have about as much chance as a toad under a steam-roller. But even then I was not thinking particularly of my own skin, only of the watchful yellow faces behind. For at that moment, with the crowd watching me, I was not afraid in the ordinary sense, as I would have been if I had been alone. A white man mustn't be frightened in front of "natives"; and so, in general, he isn't frightened. The sole thought in my mind was that if anything went wrong those two thousand Burmans would see me pursued, caught, trampled on and reduced to a grinning corpse like that Indian up the hill. And if that happened it was quite probable that some of them would laugh. That would never do. There was only one alternative. I shoved the cartridges into the magazine and lay down on the road to get a better aim.

10   The crowd grew very still, and a deep, low, happy sigh, as of people who see the theatre curtain go up at last, breathed from innumerable throats. They were going to have their bit of fun after all. The rifle was a beautiful German thing with cross-hair sights. I did not then know that in shooting an elephant one would shoot to cut an imaginary bar running from ear-hole to ear-hole.

I ought, therefore as the elephant was sideways on, to have aimed straight at his ear-hole, actually I aimed several inches in front of this, thinking the brain would be further forward.

When I pulled the trigger I did not hear the bang or feel the kick—one never does when a shot goes home—but I heard the devilish roar of glee that went up from the crowd. In that instant, in too short a time, one would have thought, even for the bullet to get there, a mysterious, terrible change had come over the elephant. He neither stirred nor fell, but every line of his body had altered. He looked suddenly stricken, shrunken, immensely old, as though the frightful impact of the bullet had paralysed him without knocking him down. At last, after what seemed a long time—it might have been five seconds, I dare say—he sagged flabbily to his knees. His mouth slobbered. An enormous senility seemed to have settled upon him. One could have imagined him thousands of years old. I fired again into the same spot. At the second shot he did not collapse but climbed with desperate slowness to his feet and stood weakly upright, with legs sagging and head drooping. I fired a third time. That was the shot that did it for him. You could see the agony of it jolt his whole body and knock the last remnant of strength from his legs. But in falling he seemed for a moment to rise, for as his hind legs collapsed beneath him he seemed to tower upward like a huge rock toppling, his trunk reaching skyward like a tree. He trumpeted, for the first and only time. And then down he came, his belly towards me, with a crash that seemed to shake the ground even where I lay. 11

I got up. The Burmans were already racing past me across the mud. It was obvious that the elephant would never rise again, but he was not dead. He was breathing very rhythmically with long rattling gasps, his great mound of a side painfully rising and falling. His mouth was wide open—I could see far down into caverns of pale pink throat. I waited a long time for him to die, but his breathing did not weaken. Finally I fired my two remaining shots into the spot where I thought his heart must be. The thick blood welled out of him like red velvet, but still he did not die. His body did not even jerk when the shots hit him, the tortured breathing continued without a pause. He was dying, very slowly and in great agony, but in some world remote from me where not even a 12 bullet could damage him further. I felt that I had got to put an end to that dreadful noise. It seemed dreadful to see the great beast lying there, powerless to move and yet powerless to die, and not even to be able to finish him. I sent back for my small rifle and poured shot after shot into his heart and down his throat. They seemed to make no impression. The tortured gasps continued as steadily as the ticking of a clock.

13   In the end I could not stand it any longer and went away. I heard later that it took him half an hour to die. Burmans were bringing dahs and baskets even before I left, and I was told they had stripped his body almost to the bones by the afternoon.

14   Afterwards, of course, there were endless discussions about the shooting of the elephant. The owner was furious, but he was only an Indian and could do nothing. Besides, legally I had done the right thing, for a mad elephant has to be killed, like a mad dog, if its owner fails to control it. Among the Europeans opinion was divided. The older men said I was right, the younger men said it was a damn shame to shoot an elephant for killing a coolie, because an elephant was worth more than any damn Coringhee coolie. And afterwards I was very glad that the coolie had been killed; it put me legally in the right and it gave me a sufficient pretext for shooting the elephant. I often wondered whether any of the others grasped that I had done it solely to avoid looking a fool.

1936

Salvation

Langston Hughes

1   I was saved from sin when I was going on thirteen. But not really saved. It happened like this. There was a big revival at my Auntie Reed's church. Every night for weeks there had been much preaching, singing, praying, and shouting, and some very

hardened sinners had been brought to Christ, and the membership of the church had grown by leaps and bounds. Then just
before the revival ended, they held a special meeting for children,
"to bring the young lambs to the fold." My aunt spoke of it for
days ahead. That night I was escorted to the front row and placed
on the mourners' bench with all the other young sinners, who
had not yet been brought to Jesus.

My aunt told me that when you were saved you saw a light,   2
and something happened to you inside! And Jesus came into
your life! And God was with you from then on! She said you
could see and hear and feel Jesus in your soul. I believed her.
I had heard a great many old people say the same thing and it
seemed to me they ought to know. So I sat there calmly in the hot,
crowded church, waiting for Jesus to come to me.

The preacher preached a wonderful rhythmical sermon, all   3
moans and shouts and lonely cries and dire pictures of hell, and then
he sang a song about the ninety and nine safe in the fold, but one
little lamb was left out in the cold. Then he said: "Won't you come?
Won't you come to Jesus? Young lambs, won't you come?" And he
held out his arms to all us young sinners there on the mourners'
bench. And the little girls cried. And some of them jumped up and
went to Jesus right away. But most of us just sat there.

A great many old people came and knelt around us and   4
prayed, old women with jet-black faces and braided hair, old men
with work-gnarled hands. And the church sang a song about the
lower lights are burning, some poor sinners to be saved. And the
whole building rocked with prayer and song.

Still I kept waiting to *see* Jesus.   5

Finally all the young people had gone to the altar and were   6
saved, but one boy and me. He was a rounder's son named
Westley. Westley and I were surrounded by sisters and deacons
praying. It was very hot in the church, and getting late now. Finally
Westley said to me in a whisper: "God damn! I'm tired o' sitting
here. Let's get up and be saved." So he got up and was saved.

Then I was left all alone on the mourners' bench. My aunt came   7
and knelt at my knees and cried, while prayers and songs swirled
all around me in the little church. The whole congregation prayed
for me alone, in a mighty wail of moans and voices. And I kept

waiting serenely for Jesus, waiting, waiting—but he didn't come. I wanted to see him, but nothing happened to me. Nothing! I wanted something to happen to me, but nothing happened.

8   I heard the songs and the minister saying: "Why don't you come? My dear child, why don't you come to Jesus? Jesus is waiting for you. He wants you. Why don't you come? Sister Reed, what is this child's name?"

9   "Langston," my aunt sobbed.

10   "Langston, why don't you come? Why don't you come and be saved? Oh, Lamb of God! Why don't you come?"

11   Now it was really getting late. I began to be ashamed of myself, holding everything up so long. I began to wonder what God thought about Westley, who certainly hadn't seen Jesus either, but who was now sitting proudly on the platform, swinging his knickerbockered legs and grinning down at me, surrounded by deacons and old women on their knees praying. God had not struck Westley dead for taking his name in vain or for lying in the temple. So I decided that maybe to save further trouble, I'd better lie, too, and say that Jesus had come, and get up and be saved.

12   So I got up.

13   Suddenly the whole room broke into a sea of shouting, as they saw me rise. Waves of rejoicing swept the place. Women leaped in the air. My aunt threw her arms around me. The minister took me by the hand and led me to the platform.

14   When things quieted down, in a hushed silence, punctuated by a few ecstatic "Amens," all the new young lambs were blessed in the name of God. Then joyous singing filled the room.

15   That night, for the last time in my life but one—for I was a big boy twelve years old—I cried. I cried, in bed alone, and couldn't stop. I buried my head under the quilts, but my aunt heard me. She woke up and told my uncle I was crying because the Holy Ghost had come into my life, and because I had seen Jesus. But I was really crying because I couldn't bear to tell her that I had lied, that I had deceived everybody in the church, that I hadn't seen Jesus, and that now I didn't believe there was a Jesus anymore, since he didn't come to help me.

1940

Grandmother's Victory

Maya Angelou

"Thou shall not be dirty" and "Thou shall not be impudent" were   1
the two commandments of Grandmother Henderson upon which
hung our total salvation.

Each night in the bitterest winter we were forced to wash   2
faces, arms, necks, legs, and feet before going to bed. She used
to add, with a smirk that unprofane people can't control when
venturing into profanity, "and wash as far as possible, then wash
possible."

We would go to the well and wash in the ice-cold, clear   3
water, grease our legs with the equally cold stiff Vaseline,
then tiptoe into the house. We wiped the dust from our toes
and settled down for schoolwork, cornbread, clabbered milk,
prayers, and bed, always in that order. Momma was famous for
pulling the quilts off after we had fallen asleep to examine our
feet. If they weren't clean enough for her, she took the switch (she
kept one behind the bedroom door for emergencies) and woke up
the offender with a few aptly placed burning reminders.

The area around the well at night was dark and slick, and   4
boys told about how snakes love water, so that anyone who had
to draw water at night and then stand there alone and wash knew
that moccasins and rattlers, puff adders, and boa constrictors
were winding their way to the well and would arrive just as the
person washing got soap in her eyes. But Momma convinced us
that not only was cleanliness next to Godliness, dirtiness was the
inventor of misery.

The impudent child was detested by God and a shame to its   5
parents and could bring destruction to its house and line. All adults
had to be addressed as Mister, Missus, Miss, Auntie, Cousin, Unk,
Uncle, Buhbah, Sister, Brother, and a thousand other appellations
indicating familial relationship and the lowliness of the addressor.

Everyone I knew respected these customary laws, except for   6
the powhitetrash children.

Some families of powhitetrash lived on Momma's farmland   7
behind the school. Sometimes a gaggle of them came to the Store,

filling the whole room, chasing out the air, and even changing the well-known scents. The children crawled over the shelves and into the potato and onion bins, twanging all the time in their sharp voices like cigar-box guitars. They took liberties in my Store that I would never dare. Since Momma told us that the less you say to whitefolks (or even powhitetrash) the better, Bailey and I would stand, solemn, quiet, in the displaced air. But if one of the playful apparitions got close to us, I pinched it. Partly out of angry frustration and partly because I didn't believe in its flesh reality.

8   They called my uncle by his first name and ordered him around the Store. He, to my crying shame, obeyed them in his limping dip-straight-dip fashion.

9   My grandmother, too, followed their orders, except that she didn't seem to be servile because she anticipated their needs.

10   "Here's sugar, Miz Potter, and here's baking powder. You didn't buy soda last month, you'll probably be needing some."

11   Momma always directed her statements to the adults, but sometimes, Oh painful sometimes, the grimy, snotty-nosed girls would answer her.

12   "Naw, Annie. . ."—to Momma? Who owned the land they lived on? Who forgot more than they would ever learn? If there was any justice in the world, God should strike them dumb at once!—"Just give us some extra sody crackers, and some more mackerel."

13   At least they never looked in her face, or I never caught them doing so. Nobody with a smidgen of training, not even the worst roustabout, would look right in a grown person's face. It meant the person was trying to take the words out before they were formed. The dirty little children didn't do that, but they threw their orders around the Store like lashes from a cat-o'-nine-tails.

14   When I was around ten years old, those scruffy children caused me the most painful and confusing experience I had ever had with my grandmother.

15   One summer morning, after I had swept the dirt yard of leaves, spearmint-gum wrappers and Vienna-sausage labels, I raked the yellow-red dirt, and made half-moons carefully, so that the design stood out clearly and mask-like. I put the rake

behind the Store and came through the back of the house to find Grandmother on the front porch in her big, wide white apron. The apron was so stiff by virtue of the starch that it could have stood alone. Momma was admiring the yard, so I joined her. It truly looked like a flat redhead that had been raked with a big-toothed comb. Momma didn't say anything but I knew she liked it. She looked over toward the school principal's house and to the right at Mr. McElroy's. She was hoping one of those community pillars would see the design before the day's business wiped it out. Then she looked upward to the school. My head had swung with hers, so at just about the same time we saw a troop of powhitetrash kids marching over the hill and down by the side of the school.

I looked to Momma for direction. She did an excellent job of 16 sagging from her waist down, but from the waist up she seemed to be pulling for the top of the oak tree across the road. Then she began to moan a hymn. Maybe not to moan, but the tune was so slow and the meter so strange that she could have been moaning. She didn't look at me again. When the children reached halfway down the hill, halfway to the Store, she said without turning, "Sister, go on inside."

I wanted to beg her, "Momma, don't wait for them. Come on 17 inside with me. If they come in the Store, you go to the bedroom and let me wait on them. They only frighten me if you're around. Alone I know how to handle them." But of course I couldn't say anything, so I went in and stood behind the screen door.

Before the girls got to the porch I heard their laughter crack- 18 ling and popping like pine logs in a cooking stove. I suppose my lifelong paranoia was born in those cold, molasses-slow minutes. They came finally to stand on the ground in front of Momma. At first they pretended seriousness. Then one of them wrapped her right arm in the crook of her left, pushed out her mouth and started to hum. I realized that she was aping my grandmother. Another said, "Naw, Helen, you ain't standing like her. This here's it." Then she lifted her chest, folded her arms and mocked that strange carriage that was Annie Henderson. Another laughed, "Naw, you can't do it. Your mouth ain't pooched out enough. It's like this."

19   I thought about the rifle behind the door, but I knew I'd never be able to hold it straight, and the .410, our sawed-off shotgun, which stayed loaded and was fired every New Year's night, was locked in the trunk and Uncle Willie had the key on his chain. Through the fly-specked screen door, I could see that the arms of Momma's apron jiggled from the vibrations of her humming. But her knees seemed to have locked as if they would never bend again.

20   She sang on. No louder than before, but no softer either. No slower or faster.

21   The dirt of the girls' cotton dresses continued on their legs, feet, arms, and faces to make them all of a piece. Their greasy uncolored hair hung down, uncombed, with a grim finality. I knelt to see them better, to remember them for all time. The tears that had slipped down my dress left unsurprising dark spots, and made the front yard blurry and even more unreal. The world had taken a deep breath and was having doubts about continuing to revolve.

22   The girls had tired of mocking Momma and turned to other means of agitation. One crossed her eyes, stuck her thumbs in both sides of her mouth and said, "Look here, Annie." Grandmother hummed on and the apron strings trembled. I wanted to throw a handful of black pepper in their faces, to throw lye on them, to scream that they were dirty, scummy peckerwoods, but I knew I was as clearly imprisoned behind the scene as the actors outside were confined to their roles.

23   One of the smaller girls did a kind of puppet dance while her fellow clowns laughed at her. But the tall one, who was almost a woman, said something very quietly, which I couldn't hear. They all moved backward from the porch, still watching Momma. For an awful second I thought they were going to throw a rock at Momma, who seemed (except for the apron strings) to have turned into stone herself. But the big girl turned her back, bent down and put her hands flat on the ground—she didn't pick up anything. She simply shifted her weight and did a hand stand.

24   Her dirty bare feet and long legs went straight for the sky. Her dress fell down around her shoulders, and she had on no drawers. The slick pubic hair made a brown triangle where her

legs came together. She hung in the vacuum of that lifeless morning for only a few seconds, then wavered and tumbled. The other girls clapped her on the back and slapped their hands.

Momma changed her song to "Bread of Heaven, Bread of 25 Heaven, feed me till I want no more."

I found that I was praying too. How long could Momma hold 26 out? What new indignity would they think of to subject her to? Would I be able to stay out of it? What would Momma really like me to do?

Then they were moving out of the yard, on their way to 27 town. They bobbed their heads and shook their slack behinds and turned, one at a time:

"'Bye, Annie."   28

"'Bye, Annie."   29

"'Bye, Annie."   30

Momma never turned her head or unfolded her arms, but she 31 stopped singing and said, "'Bye, Miz Helen, 'bye, Miz Ruth, 'bye, Miz Eloise."

I burst. A firecracker July-the-Fourth burst. How could 32 Momma call them Miz? The mean nasty things. Why couldn't she have come inside the sweet, cool store when we saw them breasting the hill? What did she prove? And then if they were dirty, mean, and impudent, why did Momma have to call them Miz?

She stood another whole song through and then opened 33 the screen door to look down on me crying in rage. She looked until I looked up. Her face was a brown moon that shone on me. She was beautiful. Something had happened out there, which I couldn't completely understand, but I could see that she was happy. Then she bent down and touched me as mothers of the church "lay hands on the sick and afflicted" and I quieted.

"Go wash your face, Sister." And she went behind the candy 34 counter and hummed, "Glory, glory, hallelujah, when I lay my burden down."

I threw the well water on my face and used the weekday 35 handkerchief to blow my nose. Whatever the contest had been out front, I knew Momma had won.

I took the rake back to the front yard. The smudged footprints 36 were easy to erase. I worked for a long time on my new design and laid the rake behind the wash pot. When I came back in the Store, I took Momma's hand and we both walked outside to look at the pattern.

37   It was a large heart with lots of hearts growing smaller inside, and piercing from the outside rim to the smallest heart was an arrow. Momma said, "Sister, that's right pretty." Then she turned back to the Store and resumed, "Glory, glory, hallelujah, when I lay my burden down."

1970

Coming to an Awareness of Language

Malcolm X

1 I've never been one for inaction. Everything I've ever felt strongly about, I've done something about. I guess that's why, unable to do anything else, I soon began writing to people I had known in the hustling world, such as Sammy the Pimp, John Hughes, the gambling house owner, the thief Jumpsteady, and several dope peddlers. I wrote them all about Allah and Islam and Mr. Elijah Muhammad. I had no idea where most of them lived. I addressed their letters in care of the Harlem or Roxbury bars and clubs where I'd known them.

2   I never got a single reply. The average hustler and criminal was too uneducated to write a letter. I have known many slick, sharp-looking hustlers, who would have you think they had an interest in Wall Street; privately, they would get someone else to read a letter if they received one. Besides, neither would I have replied to anyone writing me something as wild as "the white man is the devil."

3   What certainly went on the Harlem and Roxbury wires was that Detroit Red was going crazy in stir, or else he was trying some hype to shake up the warden's office.

During the years that I stayed in the Norfolk Prison Colony, 4 never did any official directly say anything to me about those letters, although, of course, they all passed through the prison censorship. I'm sure, however, they monitored what I wrote to add to the files which every state and federal prison keeps on the conversion of Negro inmates by the teachings of Mr. Elijah Muhammad. But at that time, I felt that the real reason was that the white 5 man knew that he was the devil.

Later on, I even wrote to the Mayor of Boston, to the Governor 6 of Massachusetts, and to Harry S. Truman. They never answered; they probably never even saw my letters. I handscratched to them how the white man's society was responsible for the black man's condition in this wilderness of North America.

It was because of my letters that I happened to stumble upon 7 starting to acquire some kind of a homemade education.

I became increasingly frustrated at not being able to express 8 what I wanted to convey in letters that I wrote, especially those to Mr. Elijah Muhammad. In the street, I had been the most articulate hustler out there—I had commanded attention when I said something. But now, trying to write simple English, I not only wasn't articulate, I wasn't even functional. How would I sound writing in slang, the way I would *say* it, something such as, "Look, daddy, let me pull your coat about a cat, Elijah Muhammad—."

Many who today hear me somewhere in person, or on tele- 9 vision, or those who read something I've said, will think I went to school far beyond the eighth grade. This impression is due entirely to my prison studies.

It had really begun back in the Charlestown Prison, when 10 Bimbi first made me feel envy of his stock of knowledge. Bimbi had always taken charge of any conversation he was in, and I had tried to emulate him. But every book I picked up had few sentences which didn't contain anywhere from one to nearly all of the words that might as well have been in Chinese. When I just skipped those words, of course, I really ended up with little idea of what the book said. So I had come to the Norfolk Prison Colony still going through only book-reading motions. Pretty soon, I would have quit even these motions, unless I had received the motivation that I did.

11   I saw that the best thing I could do was get hold of a dictionary—to study, to learn some words. I was lucky enough to reason
also that I should try to improve my penmanship. It was sad. I
couldn't even write in a straight line. It was both ideas together
that moved me to request a dictionary along with some tablets
and pencils from the Norfolk Prison Colony school.

12   I spent two days just riffling uncertainly through the dictionary's pages. I'd never realized so many words existed! I didn't
know *which* words I needed to learn. Finally, just to start some
kind of action, I began copying.

13   In my slow, painstaking, ragged handwriting, I copied into
my tablet everything printed on that first page, down to the punctuation marks.

14   I believe it took me a day. Then, aloud, I read back, to myself,
everything I'd written on the tablet. Over and over, aloud, to
myself, I read my own handwriting.

15   I woke up the next morning, thinking about those words—
immensely proud to realize that not only had I written so much
at one time, but I'd written words that I never knew were in the
world. Moreover, with a little effort, I also could remember what
many of these words meant. I reviewed the words whose meanings I didn't remember. Funny thing, from the dictionary first
page right now, that "aardvark" springs to my mind. The dictionary had a picture of it, a long-tailed, long-eared, burrowing
African mammal, which lives off termites caught by sticking out
its tongue as an anteater does for ants.

16   I was so fascinated that I went on—I copied the dictionary's
next page. And the same experience came when I studied that.
With every succeeding page, I also learned of people and places
and events from history. Actually the dictionary is like a miniature
encyclopedia. Finally the dictionary's A section had filled a whole
tablet—and I went on into the B's. That was the way I started copying what eventually became the entire dictionary. It went a lot faster
after so much practice helped me to pick up handwriting speed.
Between what I wrote in my tablet, and writing letters, during the
rest of my time in prison I would guess I wrote a million words.

17   I suppose it was inevitable that as my word-base broadened,
I could for the first time pick up a book and read and now begin

to understand what the book was saying. Anyone who has read a great deal can imagine the new world that opened. Let me tell you something: from then until I left that prison, in every free moment I had, if I was not reading in the library, I was reading on my bunk. You couldn't have gotten me out of books with a wedge. Between Mr. Muhammad's teachings, my correspondence, my visitors . . . and my reading of books, months passed without my even thinking about being imprisoned. In fact, up to then, I never had been so truly free in my life.

1965

37 Who Saw Murder Didn't Call the Police

Martin Gansberg

For more than half an hour 37 respectable, law-abiding citizens in 1 Queens watched a killer stalk and stab a woman in three separate attacks in Kew Gardens.

Twice the sound of their voices and the sudden glow of their 2 bedroom lights interrupted him and frightened him off. Each time he returned, sought her out and stabbed her again. Not one person telephoned the police during the assault; one witness called after the woman was dead.

That was two weeks ago today. But Assistant Chief Inspector 3 Frederick M. Lussen, in charge of the borough's detectives and a veteran of 25 years of homicide investigations, is still shocked.

He can give a matter-of-fact recitation of many murders. But 4 the Kew Gardens slaying baffles him—not because it is a murder, but because the "good people" failed to call the police.

"As we have reconstructed the crime," he said, "the assailant 5 had three chances to kill this woman during a 35-minute period.

He returned twice to complete the job. If we had been called when he first attacked, the woman might not be dead now."

6   This is what the police say happened beginning at 3:20 A.M. in the staid, middle-class, tree-lined Austin Street area:

7   Twenty-eight-year-old Catherine Genovese, who was called Kitty by almost everyone in the neighborhood, was returning home from her job as manager of a bar in Hollis. She parked her red Fiat in a lot adjacent to the Kew Gardens Long Island Rail Road Station, facing Mowbray Place. Like many residents of the neighborhood, she had parked there day after day since her arrival from Connecticut a year ago, although the railroad frowns on the practice.

8   She turned off the lights to her car, locked the door and started to walk the 100 feet to the entrance of her apartment at 82-70 Austin Street, which is in a Tudor building, with stores on the first floor and apartments on the second.

9   The entrance to the apartment is in the rear of the building because the front is rented to retail stores. At night the quiet neighborhood is shrouded in the slumbering darkness that marks most residential areas.

10   Miss Genovese noticed a man at the far end of the lot, near a seven-story apartment house at 82-40 Austin Street. She halted. Then, nervously, she headed up Austin Street toward Leffers Boulevard, where there is a call box to the 102d Police Precinct in nearby Richmond Hill.

11   She got as far as a street light in front of a bookstore before the man grabbed her. She screamed. Lights went on in the 10-story apartment house at 82-67 Austin Street, which faces the bookstore. Windows slid open, and voices punctured the early-morning stillness.

12   Miss Genovese screamed: "Oh, my God, he stabbed me! Please help me! Please help me!"

13   From one of the upper windows in the apartment house, a man called down: "Let that girl alone!"

14   The assailant looked up at him, shrugged and walked down Austin Street toward a white sedan parked a short distance away. Miss Genovese struggled to her feet.

15   Lights went out. The killer returned to Miss Genovese, now trying to make her way around the side of the building by the

parking lot to get to her apartment. The assailant stabbed her again.

"I'm dying!" she shrieked. "I'm dying!"   16

Windows were opened again, and lights went on in many   17
apartments. The assailant got into his car and drove away. Miss Genovese staggered to her feet. A city bus, Q-10, the Lefferts Boulevard line to Kennedy International Airport, passed. It was 3:35 A.M.

The assailant returned. By then, Miss Genovese had crawled   18
to the back of the building, where the freshly painted brown doors to the apartment house held out hope of safety. The killer tried the first door; she wasn't there. At the second door, 82-62 Austin Street, he saw her slumped on the floor at the foot of the stairs. He stabbed her a third time—fatally.

It was 3:50 by the time the police received their first call, from   19
a man who was a neighbor of Miss Genovese. In two minutes they were at the scene. The neighbor, a 70-year-old woman and another woman were the only persons on the street. Nobody else came forward.

The man explained that he had called the police after much   20
deliberation. He had phoned a friend in Nassau County for advice and then he had crossed the roof of the building to the apartment of the elderly woman to get her to make the call.

"I didn't want to get involved," he sheepishly told the police.   21

Six days later, the police arrested Winston Moseley, a 29-year-   22
old business-machine operator, and charged him with the homicide. Moseley had no previous record. He is married, has two children and owns a home at 133-19 Sutter Avenue, South Ozone Park, Queens. On Wednesday, a court committed him to Kings County Hospital for psychiatric observation.

When questioned by the police, Moseley also said that he   23
had slain Mrs. Annie Mae Johnson, 24, of 146-12 133d Avenue, Jamaica, on Feb. 29 and Barbara Kralik, 15, of 174-17 140th Avenue, Springfield Gardens, last July. In the Kralik case the police are holding Alvin L. Mitchell, who is said to have confessed to that slaying.

The police stressed how simple it would have been to have   24
gotten in touch with them. "A phone call," said one of the

detectives, "would have done it." The police may be reached by dialing "O" for operator or SPring 7-3100.

25 The question of whether the witnesses can be held legally responsible in any way for the failure to report the crime was put to the Police Department's legal bureau. There, a spokesman said:

26 "There is no legal responsibility, with few exceptions, for any citizen to report a crime."

27 Under the statutes of the city, he said, a witness to a suspicious or violent death must report it to the medical examiner. Under the state law, a witness cannot withhold information in a kidnapping.

28 Today witnesses from the neighborhood, which is made up of one-family homes in the $35,000 to $60,000 range with the exception of the two apartment houses near the railroad station, find it difficult to explain why they didn't call the police.

29 Lieut. Bernard Jacobs, who handled the investigation by the detectives, said:

30 "It is one of the better neighborhoods. There are few reports of crimes. You only get the usual complaints about boys playing or garbage cans being turned over."

31 The police said most persons had told them they had been afraid to call but had given meaningless answers when asked what they had feared.

32 "We can understand the reticence of people to become involved in an area of violence," Lieutenant Jacobs said, "but when they are in their homes, near phones, why should they be afraid to call the police?"

33 He said his men were able to piece together what happened— and capture the suspect—because the residents furnished all the information when detectives rang doorbells during the days following the slaying.

34 "But why didn't someone call us that night?" he asked unbelievingly.

35 Witnesses—some of them unable to believe what they had allowed to happen—told a reporter why.

36 A housewife, knowingly if quite casual, said, "We thought it was a lover's quarrel." A husband and wife both said, "Frankly, we were afraid." They seemed aware of the fact that events might

have been different. A distraught woman, wiping her hands in her apron, said, "I didn't want my husband to get involved."

One couple, now willing to talk about that night, said they 37 heard the first screams. The husband looked thoughtfully at the bookstore where the killer first grabbed Miss Genovese.

"We went to the window to see what was happening," he said, 38 "But the light from our bedroom made it difficult to see the street." The wife, still apprehensive, added: "I put out the light, and we were able to see better."

Asked why they hadn't called the police, she shrugged and 39 replied: "I don't know."

A man peeked out from a slight opening in the doorway to 40 his apartment and rattled off an account of the killer's second attack. Why hadn't he called the police at the time? "I was tired," he said without emotion. "I went back to bed."

It was 4:25 A.M. when the ambulance arrived for the body of 41 Miss Genovese. It drove off. "Then," a solemn police detective said, "the people came out."

1964

The Plague

Barbara Tuchman

In October 1347, two months after the fall of Calais, Genoese trad- 1 ing ships put into the harbor of Messina in Sicily with dead and dying men at the oars. The ships had come from the Black Sea port of Caffa (now Feodosiya) in the Crimea, where the Genoese maintained a trading post. The diseased sailors showed strange black swellings about the size of an egg or an apple in the armpits and groin. The swellings oozed blood and pus and were followed by spreading boils and black blotches on the skin from internal bleeding. The sick suffered severe pain and died quickly within five days of the first symptoms. As the disease spread, other symptoms of continuous fever and spitting of blood appeared instead of the swellings or buboes. These victims coughed and sweated heavily and died even more quickly, within three days or less, sometimes in 24 hours. In both types everything that issued from the body—breath, sweat, blood from the buboes and lungs, bloody urine, and blood-blackened excrement—smelled foul. Depression and despair accompanied the physical symptoms, and before the end "death is seen seated on the face."

2   The disease was bubonic plague, present in two forms: one that infected the bloodstream, causing the buboes and internal bleeding, and was spread by contact; and a second, more virulent pneumonic type that infected the lungs and was spread by respiratory infection. The presence of both at once caused the high mortality and speed of contagion. So lethal was the disease that cases were known of persons going to bed well and dying before they woke, of doctors catching the illness at a bedside and dying before the patient. So rapidly did it spread from one to another that to a French physician, Simon de Covino, it seemed as if one sick person "could infect the whole world." The malignity of the pestilence appeared more terrible because its victims knew no prevention and no remedy.

3   The physical suffering of the disease and its aspect of evil mystery were expressed in a strange Welsh lament which saw "death coming into our midst like black smoke, a plague which cuts off the young, a rootless phantom which has no mercy for fair countenance. Woe is me of the shilling in the armpit! It is seething, terrible . . . a head that gives pain and causes a loud cry . . . a painful angry knob . . . Great is its seething like a burning cinder . . . a grievous thing of ashy color." Its eruption is ugly like the "seeds of black peas, broken fragments of brittle seacoal . . . the early ornaments of black death, cinders of the peelings of the cockle weed, a mixed multitude, a black plague like halfpence, like berries. . . ."

4   Rumors of a terrible plague supposedly arising in China and spreading through Tartary (Central Asia) to India and Persia, Mesopotamia, Syria, Egypt, and all of Asia Minor had reached

Europe in 1346. They told of a death toll so devastating that all of India was said to be depopulated, whole territories covered by dead bodies, other areas with no one left alive. As added up by Pope Clement VI at Avignon, the total of reported dead reached 23,840,000. In the absence of a concept of contagion, no serious alarm was felt in Europe until the trading ships brought their black burden of pestilence into Messina while other infected ships from the Levant carried it to Genoa and Venice.

By January 1348 it penetrated France via Marseille, and North Africa via Tunis. Shipborne along coasts and navigable rivers, it spread westward from Marseille through the ports of Languedoc to Spain and northward up the Rhône to Avignon, where it arrived in March. It reached Narbonne, Montpellier, Carcassonne, and Toulouse between February and May, and at the same time in Italy spread to Rome and Florence and their hinterlands. Between June and August it reached Bordeaux, Lyon, and Paris, spread to Burgundy and Normandy, and crossed the Channel from Normandy into southern England. From Italy during the same summer it crossed the Alps into Switzerland and reached eastward to Hungary.

In a given area the plague accomplished its kill within four to six months and then faded, except in the larger cities, where, rooting into the close-quartered population, it abated during the winter, only to reappear in spring and rage for another six months.

In 1349 it resumed in Paris, spread to Picardy, Flanders, and the Low Countries, and from England to Scotland and Ireland as well as to Norway, where a ghost ship with a cargo of wool and a dead crew drifted offshore until it ran aground near Bergen. From there the plague passed into Sweden, Denmark, Prussia, Iceland, and as far as Greenland. Leaving a strange pocket of immunity in Bohemia, and Russia unattacked until 1351, it had passed from most of Europe by mid-1350. Although the mortality rate was erratic, ranging from one fifth in some places to nine tenths or almost total elimination in others, the overall estimate of modern demographers has settled—for the area extending from India to Iceland—around the same figure expressed in Froissart's casual words: "a third of the world died." His estimate, the common one at the time, was not an inspired guess but a borrowing of St. John's figure for mortality from plague in Revelation, the favorite guide to human affairs of the Middle Ages.

8   A third of Europe would have meant about 20 million deaths. No one knows in truth how many died. Contemporary reports were an awed impression, not an accurate count. In crowded Avignon, it was said, 400 died daily; 7,000 houses emptied by death were shut up; a single graveyard received 11,000 corpses in six weeks; half the city's inhabitants reportedly died, including 9 cardinals or one third of the total, and 70 lesser prelates. Watching the endlessly passing death carts, chroniclers let normal exaggeration take wings and put the Avignon death toll at 62,000 and even at 120,000, although the city's total population was probably less than 50,000.

9   When graveyards filled up, bodies at Avignon were thrown into the Rhône until mass burial pits were dug for dumping the corpses. In London, in such pits, corpses piled up in layers until they overflowed. Everywhere reports speak of the sick dying too fast for the living to bury. Corpses were dragged out of homes and left in front of doorways. Morning light revealed new piles of bodies. In Florence the dead were gathered up by the Compagnia della Misericordia—founded in 1244 to care for the sick—whose members wore red robes and hoods masking the face except for the eyes. When their efforts failed, the dead lay putrid in the streets for days at a time. When no coffins were to be had, the bodies were laid on boards, two or three at once, to be carried to graveyards or common pits. Families dumped their own relatives into the pits, or buried them so hastily and thinly "that dogs dragged them forth and devoured their bodies."

10   Amid accumulating death and fear of contagion, people died without last rites and were buried without prayers, a prospect that terrified the last hours of the stricken. A bishop in England gave permission to laymen to make confession to each other as was done by the Apostles, "or if no man is present then even to a woman," and if no priest could be found to administer extreme unction, "then faith must suffice." Clement VI found it necessary to grant remissions of sin to all who died of the plague because so many were unattended by priests. "And no bells tolled," wrote

a chronicler of Siena, "and nobody wept no matter what his loss because almost everyone expected death. . . . And people said and believed, 'This is the end of the world.'?"

In Paris, where the plague lasted through 1349, the reported 11 death rate was 800 a day, in Pisa 500, in Vienna 500 to 600. The total dead in Paris numbered 50,000 or half the population. Florence, weakened by the famine of 1347, lost three to four fifths of its citizens, Venice two thirds, Hamburg and Bremen, though smaller in size, about the same proportion. Cities, as centers of transportation, were more likely to be affected than villages, although once a village was infected, its death rate was equally high. At Givry, a prosperous village in Burgundy of 1,200 to 1,500 people, the parish register records 615 deaths in the space of fourteen weeks, compared to an average of thirty deaths a year in the previous decade. In three villages of Cambridgeshire, manorial records show a death rate of 47 percent, 57 percent, and in one case 70 percent. When the last survivors, too few to carry on, moved away, a deserted village sank back into the wilderness and disappeared from the map altogether, leaving only a grass-covered ghostly outline to show where mortals once had lived.

In enclosed places such as monasteries and prisons, the 12 infection of one person usually meant that of all, as happened in the Franciscan convents of Carcassonne and Marseille, where every inmate without exception died. Of the 140 Dominicans at Montpellier only seven survived. Petrarch's brother Gherardo, member of a Carthusian monastery, buried the prior and 34 fellow monks one by one, sometimes three a day, until he was left alone with his dog and fled to look for a place that would take him in. Watching every comrade die, men in such places could not but wonder whether the strange peril that filled the air had not been sent to exterminate the human race. In Kilkenny, Ireland, Brother John Clyn of the Friars Minor, another monk left alone among dead men, kept a record of what had happened lest "things which should be remembered perish with time and vanish from the memory of those who come after us." Sensing "the whole world, as it were, placed within the grasp of the Evil One," and waiting for death to visit him too, he wrote, "I leave parchment to continue this work, if perchance any man survive and any of the race of Adam escape this pestilence and carry on the work which I have begun." Brother John, as noted by another hand, died of the pestilence, but he foiled oblivion.

13   The largest cities of Europe, with populations of about 100,000, were Paris and Florence, Venice and Genoa. At the next level, with more than 50,000, were Ghent and Bruges in Flanders, Milan, Bologna, Rome, Naples, and Palermo, and Cologne. London hovered below 50,000, the only city in England except York with more than 10,000. At the level of 20,000 to 50,000 were Bordeaux, Toulouse, Montpellier, Marseille, and Lyon in France, Barcelona, Seville, and Toledo in Spain, Siena, Pisa, and other secondary cities in Italy, and the Hanseatic trading cities of the Empire. The plague raged through them all, killing anywhere from one third to two thirds of their inhabitants. Italy, with a total population of 10 to 11 million, probably suffered the heaviest toll. Following the Florentine bankruptcies, the crop failures and workers' riots of 1346–47, the revolt of Cola di Rienzi that plunged Rome into anarchy, the plague came as the peak of successive calamities. As if the world were indeed in the grasp of the Evil One, its first appearance on the European mainland in January 1348 coincided with a fearsome earthquake that carved a path of wreckage from Naples up to Venice. Houses collapsed, church towers toppled, villages were crushed, and the destruction reached as far as Germany and Greece. Emotional response, dulled by horrors, underwent a kind of atrophy epitomized by the chronicler who wrote, "And in these days was burying without sorrowe and wedding without friendschippe."

14   In Siena, where more than half the inhabitants died of the plague, work was abandoned on the great cathedral, planned to be the largest in the world, and never resumed, owing to loss of workers and master masons and "the melancholy and grief" of the survivors. The cathedral's truncated transept still stands in permanent witness to the sweep of death's scythe. Agnolo di Tura, a chronicler of Siena, recorded the fear of contagion that froze every other instinct. "Father abandoned child, wife husband, one brother another," he wrote, "for this plague seemed to strike through the breath and sight. And so they died. And no one could be found to bury the dead for money or friendship. . . . And

I, Agnolo di Tura, called the Fat, buried my five children with my own hands, and so did many others likewise."

There were many to echo his account of inhumanity and few to balance it, for the plague was not the kind of calamity that inspired mutual help. Its loathsomeness and deadliness did not herd people together in mutual distress, but only prompted their desire to escape each other. "Magistrates and notaries refused to come and make the wills of the dying," reported a Franciscan friar of Piazza in Sicily; what was worse, "even the priests did not come to hear their confessions." A clerk of the Archbishop of Canterbury reported the same of English priests who "turned away from the care of their benefices from fear of death." Cases of parents deserting children and children their parents were reported across Europe from Scotland to Russia. The calamity chilled the hearts of men, wrote Boccaccio in his famous account of the plague in Florence that serves as introduction to the *Decameron*. "One man shunned another...kinsfolk held aloof, brother was forsaken by brother, oftentimes husband by wife; nay, what is more, and scarcely to be believed, fathers and mothers were found to abandon their own children to their fate, untended, unvisited as if they had been strangers." Exaggeration and literary pessimism were common in the 14th century, but the Pope's physician, Guy de Chauliac, was a sober, careful observer who reported the same phenomenon: "A father did not visit his son, nor the son his father. Charity was dead."

Yet not entirely. In Paris, according to the chronicler Jean de Venette, the nuns of the Hôtel Dieu or municipal hospital, "having no fear of death tended the sick with all sweetness and humility." New nuns repeatedly took the places of those who died, until the majority "many times renewed by death now rest in peace with Christ as we may piously believe."

When the plague entered northern France in July 1348, it settled first in Normandy and, checked by winter, gave Picardy a deceptive interim until the next summer. Either in mourning or warning, black flags were flown from church towers of the worst-stricken villages of Normandy. "And in that time," wrote a monk of the abbey of Fourcarment, "the mortality was so great among the people of Normandy that those of Picardy mocked them."

The same unneighborly reaction was reported of the Scots, separated by a winter's immunity from the English. Delighted to hear
of the disease that was scourging the "southrons," they gathered
forces for an invasion, "laughing at their enemies." Before they
could move, the savage mortality fell upon them too, scattering
some in death and the rest in panic to spread the infection as they
fled.

18   In Picardy in the summer of 1349 the pestilence penetrated
the castle of Coucy to kill Enguerrand's mother, Catherine, and
her new husband. Whether her nine-year-old son escaped by
chance or was perhaps living elsewhere with one of his guardians
is unrecorded. In nearby Amiens, tannery workers, responding
quickly to losses in the labor force, combined to bargain for higher
wages. In another place villagers were seen dancing to drums and
trumpets, and on being asked the reason, answered that, seeing their neighbors die day by day while their village remained
immune, they believed they could keep the plague from entering
"by the jollity that is in us. That is why we dance." Further north
in Tournai on the border of Flanders, Gilles li Muisis, Abbot of
St. Martin's, kept one of the epidemic's most vivid accounts. The
passing bells rang all day and all night, he recorded, because
sextons were anxious to obtain their fees while they could. Filled
with the sound of mourning, the city became oppressed by fear,
so that the authorities forbade the tolling of bells and the wearing of black and restricted funeral services to two mourners. The
silencing of funeral bells and of criers' announcements of deaths
was ordained by most cities. Siena imposed a fine on the wearing
of mourning clothes by all except widows.

19   Flight was the chief recourse of those who could afford it or
arrange it. The rich fled to their country places like Boccaccio's
young patricians of Florence, who settled in a pastoral palace
"removed on every side from the roads" with "wells of cool
water and vaults of rare wines." The urban poor died in their
burrows, "and only the stench of their bodies informed neighbors of their death." That the poor were more heavily afflicted
than the rich was clearly remarked at the time, in the north as
in the south. A Scottish chronicler, John of Fordun, stated flatly
that the pest "attacked especially the meaner sort and common

people—seldom the magnates." Simon de Covino of Montpellier made the same observation. He ascribed it to the misery and want and hard lives that made the poor more susceptible, which was half the truth. Close contact and lack of sanitation was the unrecognized other half. It was noticed too that the young died in greater proportion than the old; Simon de Covino compared the disappearance of youth to the withering of flowers in the fields.

In the countryside peasants dropped dead on the roads, in 20 the fields, in their houses. Survivors in growing helplessness fell into apathy, leaving ripe wheat uncut and livestock untended. Oxen and asses, sheep and goats, pigs and chickens ran wild and they too, according to local reports, succumbed to the pest. English sheep, bearers of the precious wool, died throughout the country. The chronicler Henry Knighton, canon of Leicester Abbey, reported 5,000 dead in one field alone, "their bodies so corrupted by the plague that neither beast nor bird would touch them," and spreading an appalling stench. In the Austrian Alps wolves came down to prey upon sheep and then, "as if alarmed by some invisible warning, turned and fled back into the wilderness." In remote Dalmatia bolder wolves descended upon a plague-stricken city and attacked human survivors. For want of herdsmen, cattle strayed from place to place and died in hedgerows and ditches. Dogs and cats fell like the rest.

The dearth of labor held a fearful prospect because the 14th 21 century lived close to the annual harvest both for food and for next year's seed. "So few servants and laborers were left," wrote Knighton, "that no one knew where to turn for help." The sense of a vanishing future created a kind of dementia of despair. A Bavarian chronicler of Neuberg on the Danube recorded that "Men and women . . . wandered around as if mad" and let their cattle stray "because no one had any inclination to concern themselves about the future." Fields went uncultivated, spring seed unsown. Second growth with nature's awful energy crept back over cleared land, dikes crumbled, salt water reinvaded and soured the lowlands. With so few hands remaining to restore the work of centuries, people felt, in Walsingham's words, that "the world could never again regain its former prosperity."

22   Though the death rate was higher among the anonymous poor, the known and the great died too. King Alfonso XI of Castile was the only reigning monarch killed by the pest, but his neighbor King Pedro of Aragon lost his wife, Queen Leonora, his daughter Marie, and a niece in the space of six months. John Cantacuzene, Emperor of Byzantium, lost his son. In France the lame Queen Jeanne and her daughter-in-law Bonne de Luxemburg, wife of the Dauphin, both died in 1349 in the same phase that took the life of Enguerrand's mother. Jeanne, Queen of Navarre, daughter of Louis X, was another victim. Edward III's second daughter, Joanna, who was on her way to marry Pedro, the heir of Castile, died in Bordeaux. Women appear to have been more vulnerable than men, perhaps because, being more housebound, they were more exposed to fleas. Boccaccio's mistress Fiammetta, illegitimate daughter of the King of Naples, died, as did Laura, the beloved—whether real or fictional—of Petrarch. Reaching out to us in the future, Petrarch cried, "Oh happy posterity who will not experience such abysmal woe and will look upon our testimony as a fable."

23   In Florence Giovanni Villani, the great historian of his time, died at 68 in the midst of an unfinished sentence: ". . .*e dure questo pistolenza fino a* . . . (in the midst of this pestilence there came to an end . . .)." Siena's master painters, the brothers Ambrogio and Pietro Lorenzetti, whose names never appear after 1348, presumably perished in the plague, as did Andrea Pisano, architect and sculptor of Florence. William of Ockham and the English mystic Richard Rolle of Hampole both disappear from mention after 1349. Francisco Datini, merchant of Prato, lost both his parents and two siblings. Curious sweeps of mortality afflicted certain bodies of merchants in London. All eight wardens of the Company of Cutters, all six wardens of the Hatters, and four wardens of the Goldsmiths died before July 1350. Sir John Pulteney, master draper and four times Mayor of London, was a victim, likewise Sir John Montgomery, Governor of Calais.

24   Among the clergy and doctors the mortality was naturally high because of the nature of their professions. Out of 24 physicians in Venice, 20 were said to have lost their lives in the plague, although, according to another account, some were believed

to have fled or to have shut themselves up in their houses. At Montpellier, site of the leading medieval medical school, the physician Simon de Covino reported that, despite the great number of doctors, "hardly one of them escaped." In Avignon, Guy de Chauliac confessed that he performed his medical visits only because he dared not stay away for fear of infamy, but "I was in continual fear." He claimed to have contracted the disease but to have cured himself by his own treatment; if so, he was one of the few who recovered.

Clerical mortality varied with rank. Although the one-third 25 toll of cardinals reflects the same proportion as the whole, this was probably due to their concentration in Avignon. In England, in strange and almost sinister procession, the Archbishop of Canterbury, John Stratford, died in August 1348, his appointed successor died in May 1349, and the next appointee three months later, all three within a year. Despite such weird vagaries, prelates in general managed to sustain a higher survival rate than the lesser clergy. Among bishops the deaths have been estimated at about one in twenty. The loss of priests, even if many avoided their fearful duty of attending the dying, was about the same as among the population as a whole.

Government officials, whose loss contributed to the general 26 chaos, found, on the whole, no special shelter. In Siena four of the nine members of the governing oligarchy died, in France one third of the royal notaries, in Bristol 15 out of the 52 members of the Town Council or almost one third. Tax collecting obviously suffered, with the result that Philip VI was unable to collect more than a fraction of the subsidy granted him by the Estates in the winter of 1347–48.

Lawlessness and debauchery accompanied the plague as they 27 had during the great plague of Athens of 430 B.C., when according to Thucydides, men grew bold in the indulgence of pleasure: "For seeing how the rich died in a moment and those who had nothing immediately inherited their property, they reflected that life and riches were alike transitory and they resolved to enjoy themselves while they could." Human behavior is timeless. When St. John had his vision of plague in Revelation, he knew from some experience or race memory that those who survived "repented not of the work of their hands. . . . Neither repented they of their murders, nor of their sorceries, nor of their fornication, nor of their thefts."

28   Ignorance of the cause augmented the sense of horror. Of the real carriers, rats and fleas, the 14th century had no suspicion, perhaps because they were so familiar. Fleas, though a common household nuisance, are not once mentioned in contemporary plague writings, and rats only incidentally, although folklore commonly associated them with pestilence. The legend of the Pied Piper arose from an outbreak of 1284. The actual plague bacillus, *Pasturella pestis*, remained undiscovered for another 500 years. Living alternately in the stomach of the flea and the bloodstream of the rat who was the flea's host, the bacillus in its bubonic form was transferred to humans and animals by the bite of either rat or flea. It traveled by virtue of *Rattus rattus*, the small medieval black rat that lived on ships, as well as by the heavier brown or sewer rat. What precipitated the turn of the bacillus from innocuous to virulent form is unknown, but the occurrence is now believed to have taken place not in China but somewhere in central Asia and to have spread along the caravan routes. Chinese origin was a mistaken notion of the 14th century based on real but belated reports of huge death tolls in China from drought, famine, and pestilence, which have since been traced to the 1330s, too soon to be responsible for the plague that appeared in India in 1346.

29   The phantom enemy had no name. Called the Black Death only in later recurrences, it was known during the first epidemic simply as the Pestilence or Great Mortality. Reports from the East, swollen by fearful imaginings, told of strange tempests and "sheets of fire" mingled with huge hailstones that "slew almost all," or a "vast rain of fire" that burned up men, beasts, stones, trees, villages, and cities. In another version, "foul blasts of wind" from the fires carried the infection to Europe "and now as some suspect it cometh round the seacoast." Accurate observation in this case could not make the mental jump to ships and rats because no idea of animal- or insect-borne contagion existed.

30   The earthquake was blamed for releasing sulfurous and foul fumes from the earth's interior, or as evidence of a titanic struggle of planets and oceans causing waters to rise and vaporize until

fish died in masses and corrupted the air. All these explanations had in common a factor of poisoned air, of miasmas and thick, stinking mists traced to every kind of natural or imagined agency from stagnant lakes to malign conjunction of the planets, from the hand of the Evil One to the wrath of God. Medical thinking, trapped in the theory of astral influences, stressed air as the communicator of disease, ignoring sanitation or visible carriers. The existence of two carriers confused the trail, the more so because the flea could live and travel independently of the rat for as long as a month and, if infected by the particularly virulent septicemic form of the bacillus, could infect humans without reinfecting itself from the rat. The simultaneous presence of the pneumonic form of the disease, which was indeed communicated through the air, blurred the problem further.

The mystery of the contagion was "the most terrible of all 31 the terrors," as an anonymous Flemish cleric in Avignon wrote to a correspondent in Bruges. Plagues had been known before, from the plague of Athens (believed to have been typhus) to the prolonged epidemic of the 6th century A.D., to the recurrence of sporadic outbreaks in the 12th and 13th centuries, but they had left no accumulated store of understanding. That the infection came from contact with the sick or with their houses, clothes, or corpses was quickly observed but not comprehended. Gentile da Foligno, renowned physician of Perugia and doctor of medicine at the universities of Bologna and Padua, came close to respiratory infection when he surmised that poisonous material was "communicated by means of air breathed out and in." Having no idea of microscopic carriers, he had to assume that the air was corrupted by planetary influences. Planets, however, could not explain the ongoing contagion. The agonized search for an answer gave rise to such theories as transference by sight. People fell ill, wrote Guy de Chauliac, not only by remaining with the sick but "even by looking at them." Three hundred years later Joshua Barnes, the 17th century biographer of Edward III, could write that the power of infection had entered into beams of light and "darted death from the eyes."

Doctors struggling with the evidence could not break away 32 from the terms of astrology, to which they believed all human physiology was subject. Medicine was the one aspect of medieval life, perhaps because of its links with the Arabs, not shaped by Christian doctrine. Clerics detested astrology, but could not dislodge its influence. Guy de Chauliac, physician to three popes in succession, practiced in obedience to the zodiac. While his *Cirurgia* was the major treatise on surgery of its time, while he understood the use of anesthesia made from the juice of opium, mandrake, or hemlock, he nevertheless prescribed bleeding and purgatives by the planets and divided chronic from acute diseases on the basis of one being under the rule of the sun and the other of the moon.

33   In October 1348 Philip VI asked the medical faculty of the University of Paris for a report on the affliction that seemed to threaten human survival. With careful thesis, antithesis, and proofs, the doctors ascribed it to a triple conjunction of Saturn, Jupiter, and Mars in the 40th degree of Aquarius said to have occurred on March 20, 1345. They acknowledged, however, effects "whose cause is hidden from even the most highly trained intellects." The verdict of the masters of Paris became the official version. Borrowed, copied by scribes, carried abroad, translated from Latin into various vernaculars, it was everywhere accepted, even by the Arab physicians of Cordova and Granada, as the scientific if not the popular answer. Because of the terrible interest of the subject, the translations of the plague tracts stimulated use of national languages. In that one respect, life came from death.

34   To the people at large there could be but one explanation— the wrath of God. Planets might satisfy the learned doctors, but God was closer to the average man. A scourge so sweeping and unsparing without any visible cause could only be seen as Divine punishment upon mankind for its sins. It might even be God's terminal disappointment in his creature. Matteo Villani compared the plague to the Flood in ultimate purpose and believed he was recording "the extermination of mankind." Efforts to appease Divine wrath took many forms, as when the city of Rouen ordered that everything that could anger God, such as gambling, cursing, and drinking, must be stopped. More general were the penitent processions authorized at first by the Pope, some lasting as long as three days, some attended by as many as 2,000, which everywhere accompanied the plague and helped to spread it.

Barefoot in sackcloth, sprinkled with ashes, weeping, pray- 35
ing, tearing their hair, carrying candles and relics, sometimes with
ropes around their necks or beating themselves with whips, the
penitents wound through the streets, imploring the mercy of
the Virgin and saints at their shrines. In a vivid illustration for
the *Très Riches Heures* of the Due de Berry, the Pope is shown in a
penitent procession attended by four cardinals in scarlet from hat
to hem. He raises both arms in supplication to the angel on top of
the Castel Sant' Angelo, while white-robed priests bearing banners and relics in golden cases turn to look as one of their number, stricken by the plague, falls to the ground, his face contorted
with anxiety. In the rear, a gray-clad monk falls beside another
victim already on the ground as the townspeople gaze in horror.
(Nominally the illustration represents a 6th century plague in the
time of Pope Gregory the Great, but as medieval artists made no
distinction between past and present, the scene is shown as the
artist would have seen it in the 14th century.) When it became evident that these processions were sources of infection, Clement VI
had to prohibit them.

In Messina, where the plague first appeared, the people 36
begged the Archbishop of neighboring Catania to lend them
the relics of St. Agatha. When the Catanians refused to let the
relics go, the Archbishop dipped them in holy water and took
the water himself to Messina, where he carried it in a procession
with prayers and litanies through the streets. The demonic, which
shared the medieval cosmos with God, appeared as "demons
in the shape of dogs" to terrify the people. "A black dog with a
drawn sword in his paws appeared among them, gnashing his
teeth and rushing upon them and breaking all the silver vessels
and lamps and candlesticks on the altars and casting them hither
and thither. . . . So the people of Messina, terrified by this prodigious vision, were all strangely overcome by fear."

The apparent absence of earthly cause gave the plague a 37
supernatural and sinister quality. Scandinavians believed that a
Pest Maiden emerged from the mouth of the dead in the form
of a blue flame and flew through the air to infect the next house.
In Lithuania the Maiden was said to wave a red scarf through
the door or window to let in the pest. One brave man, according

to legend, deliberately waited at his open window with drawn sword and, at the fluttering of the scarf, chopped off the hand. He died of his deed, but his village was spared and the scarf long preserved as a relic in the local church.

38   Beyond demons and superstition the final hand was God's. The Pope acknowledged it in a Bull of September 1348, speaking of the "pestilence with which God is afflicting the Christian people." To the Emperor John Cantacuzene it was manifest that a malady of such horrors, stenches, and agonies, and especially one bringing the dismal despair that settled upon its victims before they died, was not a plague "natural" to mankind but "a chastisement from Heaven." To Piers Plowman "these pestilences were for pure sin."

39   The general acceptance of this view created an expanded sense of guilt, for if the plague were punishment there had to be terrible sin to have occasioned it. What sins were on the 14th century conscience? Primarily greed, the sin of avarice, followed by usury, worldliness, adultery, blasphemy, falsehood, luxury, irreligion. Giovanni Villani, attempting to account for the cascade of calamity that had fallen upon Florence, concluded that it was retribution for the sins of avarice and usury that oppressed the poor. Pity and anger about the condition of the poor, especially victimization of the peasantry in war, was often expressed by writers of the time and was certainly on the conscience of the century. Beneath it all was the daily condition of medieval life, in which hardly an act or thought, sexual, mercantile, or military, did not contravene the dictates of the Church. Mere failure to fast or attend mass was sin. The result was an underground lake of guilt in the soul that the plague now tapped.

40   That the mortality was accepted as God's punishment may explain in part the vacuum of comment that followed the Black Death. An investigator has noticed that in the archives of Périgord references to the war are innumerable, to the plague few. Froissart mentions the great death but once, Chaucer gives it barely a glance. Divine anger so great that it contemplated the extermination of man did not bear close examination.

Description

Fifth Avenue, Uptown

James Baldwin

There is a housing project standing now where the house in 1
which we grew up once stood, and one of those stunted city
trees is snarling where our doorway used to be. This is on the
rehabilitated side of the avenue. The other side of the avenue—
for progress takes time—has not been rehabilitated yet and it
looks exactly as it looked in the days when we sat with our
noses pressed against the windowpane, longing to be allowed to
go "across the street." The grocery store which gave us credit is
still there, and there can be no doubt that it is still giving credit.
The people in the project certainly need it—far more, indeed,
than they ever needed the project. The last time I passed by, the
Jewish proprietor was still standing among his shelves, looking sadder and heavier but scarcely any older. Farther down
the block stands the shoe-repair store in which our shoes were
repaired until reparation became impossible and in which, then,
we bought all our "new" ones. The Negro proprietor is still in
the window, head down, working at the leather.

These two, I imagine, could tell a long tale if they would 2
(perhaps they would be glad to if they could), having watched so
many, for so long, struggling in the fishhooks, the barbed wire, of
this avenue.

The avenue is elsewhere the renowned and elegant Fifth. The 3
area I am describing, which, in today's gang parlance, would
be called "the turf," is bounded by Lenox Avenue on the west,

the Harlem River on the east, 135th Street on the north, and 130th Street on the south. We never lived beyond these boundaries; this is where we grew up. Walking along 145th Street—for example—familiar as it is, and similar, does not have the same impact because I do not know any of the people on the block. But when I turn east on 131st Street and Lenox Avenue, there is first a soda-pop joint, then a shoeshine "parlor," then a grocery store, then a dry cleaners', then the houses. All along the street there are people who watched me grow up, people who grew up with me, people I watched grow up along with my brothers and sisters; and, sometimes in my arms, sometimes underfoot, sometimes at my shoulder—or on it—their children, a riot, a forest of children, who include my nieces and nephews.

4   When we reach the end of this long block, we find ourselves on wide, filthy, hostile Fifth Avenue, facing that project which hangs over the avenue like a monument to the folly, and the cowardice, of good intentions. All along the block, for anyone who knows it, are immense human gaps, like craters. These gaps are not created merely by those who have moved away, inevitably into some other ghetto; or by those who have risen, almost always into a greater capacity for self-loathing and self-delusion; or yet by those who, by whatever means—World War II, the Korean war, a policeman's gun or billy, a gang war, a brawl, madness, an overdose of heroin, or, simply, unnatural exhaustion—are dead. I am talking about those who are left, and I am talking principally about the young. What are they doing? Well, some, a minority, are fanatical churchgoers, members of the more extreme of the Holy Roller sects. Many, many more are "moslems," by affiliation or sympathy, that is to say that they are united by nothing more—and nothing less—than a hatred of the white world and all its works. They are present, for example, at every Buy Black street-corner meeting—meetings in which the speaker urges his hearers to cease trading with white men and establish a separate economy. Neither the speaker nor his hearers can possibly do this, of course, since Negroes do not own General Motors or RCA or the A & P, nor, indeed, do they own more than a wholly insufficient fraction of anything else in Harlem (those who *do* own anything are more interested in

their profits than in their fellows). But these meetings neverthe-less keep alive in the participators a certain pride of bitterness without which, however futile this bitterness may be, they could scarcely remain alive at all. Many have given up. They stay home and watch the TV screen, living on the earnings of their parents, cousins, brothers, or uncles, and only leave the house to go to the movies or to the nearest bar. "How're you making it?" one may ask, running into them along the block, or in the bar. "Oh, I'm TV-ing it"; with the saddest, sweetest, most shamefaced of smiles, and from a great distance. This distance one is com-pelled to respect; anyone who has traveled so far will not easily be dragged again into the world. There are further retreats, of course, than the TV screen or the bar. There are those who are simply sitting on their stoops, "stoned," animated for a moment only, and hideously, by the approach of someone who may lend them the money for a "fix." Or by the approach of someone from whom they can purchase it, one of the shrewd ones, on the way to prison or just coming out.

And the others, who have avoided all of these deaths, get 5 up in the morning and go downtown to meet "the man." They work in the white man's world all day and come home in the evening to this fetid block. They struggle to instill in their chil-dren some private sense of honor or dignity which will help the child to survive. This means, of course, that they must struggle, stolidly, incessantly, to keep this sense alive in themselves, in spite of the insults, the indifference, and the cruelty they are cer-tain to encounter in their working day. They patiently browbeat the landlord into fixing the heat, the plaster, the plumbing; this demands prodigious patience; nor is patience usually enough. In trying to make their hovels habitable, they are perpetu-ally throwing good money after bad. Such frustration, so long endured, is driving many strong, admirable men and women whose only crime is color to the very gates of paranoia.

One remembers them from another time—playing handball 6 in the playground, going to church, wondering if they were going to be promoted at school. One remembers them going off to war—gladly, to escape this block. One remembers their return. Perhaps one remembers their wedding day. And one sees where the girl is now—vainly looking for salvation from some other embittered, trussed, and struggling boy—and sees the all-but-abandoned children in the streets.

1948

Once More to the Lake
E. B. White

AUGUST 1941

1   One summer, along about 1904, my father rented a camp on a lake in Maine and took us all there for the month of August. We all got ringworm from some kittens and had to rub Pond's Extract on our arms and legs night and morning, and my father rolled over in a canoe with all his clothes on; but outside of that the vacation was a success and from then on none of us ever thought there was any place in the world like that lake in Maine. We returned summer after summer—always on August 1 for one month. I have since become a salt-water man, but sometimes in summer there are days when the restlessness of the tides and the fearful cold of the sea water and the incessant wind that blows across the afternoon and into the evening make me wish for the placidity of a lake in the woods. A few weeks ago this feeling got so strong I bought myself a couple of bass hooks and a spinner and returned to the lake where we used to go, for a week's fishing and to revisit old haunts.

2   I took along my son, who had never had any fresh water up his nose and who had seen lily pads only from train windows. On the journey over to the lake I began to wonder what it would be like. I wondered how time would have marred this unique, this holy spot—the coves and streams, the hills that the sun set behind, the camps and the paths behind the camps. I was sure that the tarred road would have found it out, and I wondered in what other ways

it would be desolated. It is strange how much you can remember about places like that once you allow your mind to return into the grooves that lead back. You remember one thing, and that suddenly reminds you of another thing. I guess I remembered clearest of all the early mornings, when the lake was cool and motionless, remembered how the bedroom smelled of the lumber it was made of and of the wet woods whose scent entered through the screen. The partitions in the camp were thin and did not extend clear to the top of the rooms, and as I was always the first up I would dress softly so as not to wake the others, and sneak out into the sweet outdoors and start out in the canoe, keeping close along the shore in the long shadows of the pines. I remembered being very careful never to rub my paddle against the gunwale for fear of disturbing the stillness of the cathedral.

The lake had never been what you would call a wild lake. 3 There were cottages sprinkled around the shores, and it was in farming country although the shores of the lake were quite heavily wooded. Some of the cottages were owned by nearby farmers, and you would live at the shore and eat your meals at the farmhouse. That's what our family did. But although it wasn't wild, it was a fairly large and undisturbed lake and there were places in it that, to a child at least, seemed infinitely remote and primeval.

I was right about the tar: it led to within half a mile of the 4 shore. But when I got back there, with my boy, and we settled into a camp near a farmhouse and into the kind of summertime I had known, I could tell that it was going to be pretty much the same as it had been before—I knew it, lying in bed the first morning smelling the bedroom and hearing the boy sneak quietly out and go off along the shore in a boat. I began to sustain the illusion that he was I, and therefore, by simple transposition, that I was my father. This sensation persisted, kept cropping up all the time we were there. It was not an entirely new feeling, but in this setting it grew much stronger. I seemed to be living a dual existence. I would be in the middle of some simple act, I would be picking up a bait box or laying down a table fork, or I would be saying something and suddenly it would be not I but my father who was saying the words or making the gesture. It gave me a creepy sensation.

5   We went fishing the first morning. I felt the same damp moss covering the worms in the bait can, and saw the dragonfly alight on the tip of my rod as it hovered a few inches from the surface of the water. It was the arrival of this fly that convinced me beyond any doubt that everything was as it always had been, that the years were a mirage and that there had been no years. The small waves were the same, chucking the rowboat under the chin as we fished at anchor, and the boat was the same boat, the same color green and the ribs broken in the same places, and under the floorboards the same fresh water leavings and debris—the dead hellgrammite, the wisps of moss, the rusty discarded fishhook, the dried blood from yesterday's catch. We stared silently at the tips of our rods, at the dragonflies that came and went. I lowered the tip of mine into the water, tentatively, pensively dislodging the fly, which darted two feet away, poised, darted two feet back, and came to rest again a little farther up the rod. There had been no years between the ducking of this dragonfly and the other one—the one that was part of memory. I looked at the boy, who was silently watching his fly, and it was my hands that held his rod, my eyes watching. I felt dizzy and didn't know which rod I was at the end of.

6   We caught two bass, hauling them in briskly as though they were mackerel, pulling them over the side of the boat in a businesslike manner without any landing net, and stunning them with a blow on the back of the head. When we got back for a swim before lunch, the lake was exactly where we had left it, the same number of inches from the dock, and there was only the merest suggestion of a breeze. This seemed an utterly enchanted sea, this lake you could leave to its own devices for a few hours and come back to, and find that it had not stirred, this constant and trustworthy body of water. In the shallows, the dark, water-soaked sticks and twigs, smooth and old, were undulating in clusters on the bottom against the clean ribbed sand, and the track of the mussel was plain. A school of minnows swam by, each minnow with its small individual shadow, doubling the attendance, so clear and sharp in the sunlight. Some of the other campers were in swimming, along the shore, one of them with a cake of soap, and the water felt thin and clear and unsubstantial.

Over the years there had been this person with the cake of soap, this cultist, and here he was. There had been no years.

Up to the farmhouse to dinner through the teeming dusty 7 field, the road under our sneakers was only a two-track road. The middle track was missing, the one with the marks of the hooves and the splotches of dried, flaky manure. There had always been three tracks to choose from in choosing which track to walk in; now the choice was narrowed down to two. For a moment I missed terribly the middle alternative. But the way led past the tennis court, and something about the way it lay there in the sun reassured me; the tape had loosened along the backline, the alleys were green with plantains and other weeds, and the net (installed in June and removed in September) sagged in the dry noon, and the whole place steamed with midday heat and hunger and emptiness. There was a choice of pie for dessert, and one was blueberry and one was apple, and the waitresses were the same country girls, there having been no passage of time, only the illusion of it as in a dropped curtain—the waitresses were still fifteen; their hair had been washed, that was the only difference—they had been to the movies and seen the pretty girls with the clean hair.

Summertime, oh, summertime, pattern of life indelible with 8 fade-proof lake, the wood unshatterable, the pasture with the sweetfern and the juniper forever and ever, summer without end; this was the background, and the life along the shore was the design, the cottages with their innocent and tranquil design, their tiny docks with the flagpole and the American flag floating against the white clouds in the blue sky, and little paths over the roots of the trees leading from camp to camp and the paths leading back to the outhouses and the can of lime for sprinkling, and at the souvenir counters at the store the miniature birch-bark canoes and the postcards that showed things looking a little better than they looked. This was the American family at play, escaping the city heat, wondering whether the newcomers in the camp at the head of the cove were "common" or "nice," wondering whether it was true that the people who drove up for Sunday dinner at the farmhouse were turned away because there wasn't enough chicken.

9   It seemed to me, as I kept remembering all this, that those times and those summers had been infinitely precious and worth saving. There had been jollity and peace and goodness. The arriving (at the beginning of August) had been so big a business in itself, at the railway station the farm wagon drawn up, the first smell of the pine-laden air, the first glimpse of the smiling farmer, and the great importance of the trunks and your father's enormous authority in such matters, and the feel of the wagon under you for the long ten-mile haul, and at the top of the last long hill catching the first view of the lake after eleven months of not seeing this cherished body of water. The shouts and cries of the other campers when they saw you, and the trunks to be unpacked, to give up their rich burden. (Arriving was less exciting nowadays, when you sneaked up in your car and parked it under a tree near the camp and took out the bags and in five minutes it was all over, no fuss, no loud wonderful fuss about trunks.)

10   Peace and goodness and jollity. The only thing that was wrong now, really, was the sound of the place, an unfamiliar nervous sound of the outboard motors. This was the note that jarred, the one thing that would sometimes break the illusion and set the years moving. In those other summertimes all motors were inboard; and when they were at a little distance, the noise they made was a sedative, an ingredient of summer sleep. They were one-cylinder and two-cylinder engines, and some were make-and-break and some were jump-spark, but they all made a sleepy sound across the lake. The one-lungers throbbed and fluttered, and the twin-cylinder ones purred and purred, and that was a quiet sound, too. But now the campers all had outboards. In the daytime, in the hot mornings, these motors made a petulant, irritable sound; at night in the still evening when the afterglow lit the water, they whined about one's ears like mosquitoes. My boy loved our rented outboard, and his great desire was to achieve single-handed mastery over it, and authority, and he soon learned the trick of choking it a little (but not too much), and the adjustment of the needle valve. Watching him I would remember the things you could do with the old one-cylinder engine with the

heavy flywheel, how you could have it eating out of your hand if you got really close to it spiritually. Motorboats in those days didn't have clutches, and you would make a landing by shutting off the motor at the proper time and coasting in with a dead rudder. But there was a way of reversing them, if you learned the trick, by cutting the switch and putting it on again exactly on the final dying revolution of the flywheel, so that it would kick back against compression and begin reversing. Approaching a dock in a strong following breeze, it was difficult to slow up sufficiently by the ordinary coasting method, and if a boy felt he had complete mastery over his motor, he was tempted to keep it running beyond its time and then reverse it a few feet from the dock. It took a cool nerve, because if you threw the switch a twentieth of a second too soon you would catch the flywheel when it still had speed enough to go up past center, and the boat would leap ahead, charging bull-fashion at the dock.

We had a good week at the camp. The bass were biting well 11 and the sun shone endlessly, day after day. We would be tired at night and lie down in the accumulated heat of the little bedrooms after the long hot day and the breeze would stir almost imperceptibly outside and the smell of the swamp drifted in through the rusty screens. Sleep would come easily and in the morning the red squirrel would be on the roof, tapping out his gay routine. I kept remembering everything, lying in bed in the mornings—the small steamboat that had a long rounded stern like the lip of a Ubangi, and how quietly she ran on the moonlight sails, when the older boys played their mandolins and the girls sang and we ate doughnuts dipped in sugar, and how sweet the music was on the water in the shining night, and what it had felt like to think about girls then. After breakfast we would go up to the store and the things were in the same place—the minnows in a bottle, the plugs and spinners disarranged and pawed over by the youngsters from the boys' camp, the Fig Newtons and the Beeman's gum. Outside, the road was tarred and cars stood in front of the store. Inside, all was just as it had always been, except there was more Coca-Cola and not so much Moxie and root beer and birch beer and sarsaparilla. We would walk out with a bottle of pop apiece and sometimes the pop would backfire up our noses and hurt. We explored the streams, quietly, where the turtles slid off the sunny logs and dug their way into the soft bottom; and we lay on the town wharf and fed worms to the tame bass. Everywhere we went I had trouble making out which was I, the one walking at my side, the one walking in my pants.

12   One afternoon while we were at that lake, a thunderstorm came up. It was like the revival of an old melodrama that I had seen long ago with childish awe. The second-act climax of the drama of the electrical disturbance over a lake in America had not changed in any important respect. This was the big scene, still the big scene. The whole thing was so familiar, the first feeling of oppression and heat and a general air around camp of not wanting to go very far away. In mid-afternoon (it was all the same) a curious darkening of the sky, and a lull in everything that had made life tick; and then the way the boats suddenly swung the other way at their moorings with the coming of a breeze out of the new quarter, and the premonitory rumble. Then the kettle drum, then the snare, then the bass drum and cymbals, then crackling light against the dark, and the gods grinning and licking their chops in the hills. Afterward the calm, the rain steadily rustling in the calm lake, the return of light and hope and spirits, and the campers running out in joy and relief to go swimming in the rain, their bright cries perpetuating the deathless joke about how they were getting simply drenched, and the children screaming with delight at the new sensation of bathing in the rain, and the joke about getting drenched linking the generations in a strong indestructible chain. And the comedian who waded in carrying an umbrella.

13   When the others went swimming my son said he was going in, too. He pulled his dripping trunks from the line where they had hung all through the shower and wrung them out. Languidly, and with no thought of going in, I watched him, his hard little body, skinny and bare, saw him wince slightly as he pulled up around his vitals the small, soggy, icy garment. As he buckled the swollen belt, suddenly my groin felt the chill of death.

1939

Marrying Absurd

Joan Didion

To be married in Las Vegas, Clark County, Nevada, a bride must swear that she is eighteen or has parental permission and a bridegroom that he is twenty-one or has parental permission. Someone must put up five dollars for the license. (On Sundays and holidays, fifteen dollars. The Clark County Courthouse issues marriage licenses at any time of the day or night except between noon and one in the afternoon, between eight and nine in the evening, and between four and five in the morning.) Nothing else is required. The State of Nevada, alone among these United States, demands neither a premarital blood test nor a waiting period before or after the issuance of a marriage license. Driving in across the Mojave from Los Angeles, one sees the signs way out on the desert, looming up from that moonscape of rattlesnakes and mesquite, even before the Las Vegas lights appear like a mirage on the horizon: "GETTING MARRIED? Free License Information First Strip Exit." Perhaps the Las Vegas wedding industry achieved its peak operational efficiency between 9:00 P.M. and midnight of August 26, 1965, an otherwise unremarkable Thursday which happened to be, by Presidential order, the last day on which anyone could improve his draft status merely by getting married. One hundred and seventy-one couples were pronounced man and wife in the name of Clark County and the State of Nevada that night, sixty-seven of them by a single justice of the peace, Mr. James A. Brennan. Mr. Brennan did one wedding at the Dunes and the other sixty-six in his office, and charged each couple eight dollars. One bride lent her veil to six others. "I got it down from five to three minutes," Mr. Brennan said later of his feat. "I could've married them *en masse*, but they're people, not cattle. People expect more when they get married."

What people who get married in Las Vegas actually do expect—what, in the largest sense, their "expectations" are—strikes one as a curious and self-contradictory business. Las Vegas is the most extreme and allegorical of American settlements, bizarre and beautiful in its venality and in its devotion to immediate gratification, a place the tone of which is set by mobsters and call girls and ladies' room attendants with amyl nitrite poppers in their uniform pockets. Almost everyone notes that there is no "time" in Las Vegas, no night and no day and no past and no future (no Las Vegas casino, however, has taken the obliteration of the ordinary time sense quite so far as Harold's Club in Reno, which for a while issued, at odd intervals in the day and night, mimeographed "bulletins" carrying news from the world outside); neither is there any logical sense of where one is. One is standing on a highway in the middle of a vast hostile desert looking at an eighty-foot sign which blinks "STARDUST" or "CAESAR'S PALACE." Yes, but what does that explain? This geographical implausibility reinforces the sense that what happens there has no connection with "real" life; Nevada cities like Reno and Carson City are ranch towns, Western towns, places behind which there is some historical imperative. But Las Vegas seems to exist only in the eye of the beholder. All of which makes it an extraordinarily stimulating and interesting place, but an odd one in which to want to wear a candlelight satin Priscilla of Boston wedding dress with Chantilly lace insets, tapered sleeves and a detachable modified train.

3   And yet the Las Vegas wedding business seems to appeal to precisely that impulse. "Sincere and Dignified Since 1954," one wedding chapel advertises. There are nineteen such wedding chapels in Las Vegas, intensely competitive, each offering better, faster, and, by implication, more sincere services than the next: Our Photos Best Anywhere, Your Wedding on A Phonograph Record, Candlelight with Your Ceremony, Honeymoon Accommodations, Free Transportation from Your Motel to Courthouse to Chapel and Return to Motel, Religious or Civil Ceremonies, Dressing Rooms, Flowers, Rings, Announcements, Witnesses Available, and Ample Parking. All of these services, like most others in Las Vegas (sauna baths, payroll-check cashing, chinchilla coats for sale or rent) are offered twenty-four hours a day, seven days a week, presumably on the premise that marriage, like craps, is a game to be played when the table seems hot.

4   But what strikes one most about the Strip chapels, with their wishing wells and stained-glass paper windows and their artificial bouvardia, is that so much of their business is by no means a

matter of simple convenience, of late-night liaisons between show girls and baby Crosbys. Of course there is some of that. (One night about eleven o'clock in Las Vegas I watched a bride in an orange minidress and masses of flame-colored hair stumble from a Strip chapel on the arm of her bridegroom, who looked the part of the expendable nephew in the movies like *Miami Syndicate*. "I gotta get the kids," the bride whimpered. "I gotta pick up the sitter, I gotta get to the midnight show." "What you gotta get," the bridegroom said, opening the door of a Cadillac Coupe de Ville and watching her crumple on the seat, "is sober.") But Las Vegas seems to offer something other than "convenience"; it is merchandising "niceness," the facsimile of proper ritual, to children who do not know how else to find it, how to make the arrangements, how to do it "right." All day and evening long on the Strip, one sees actual wedding parties, waiting under the harsh lights at a crosswalk, standing uneasily in the parking lot of the Frontier while the photographer hired by The Little Church of the West ("Wedding Place of the Stars") certifies the occasion, takes the picture: the bride in a veil and white satin pumps, the bridegroom usually in a white dinner jacket, and even an atten-dant or two, a sister or a best friend in hot-pink *peau de soie*, a flirtation veil, a carnation nosegay. "When I Fall in Love It Will Be Forever," the organist plays, and then a few bars of Lohengrin. The mother cries; the stepfather, awkward in his role, invites the chapel hostess to join them for a drink at the Sands. The hostess declines with a professional smile; she has already transferred her interest to the group waiting outside. One bride out, another in, and again the sign goes up on the chapel door: "One moment please—Wedding."

I sat next to one such wedding party in a Strip restaurant the ⁵ last time I was in Las Vegas. The marriage had just taken place; the bride still wore her dress, the mother her corsage. A bored waiter poured out a few swallows of pink champagne ("on the house") for everyone but the bride, who was too young to be served. "You'll need something with more kick than that," the bride's father said with heavy jocularity to his new son-in-law; the ritual jokes about the wedding night had a certain Panglossian charac-ter, since the bride was clearly several months pregnant. Another round of pink champagne, this time not on the house, and the bride began to cry. "It was just as nice," she sobbed, "as I hoped and dreamed it would be."

1967

A Partial Remembrance of a Puerto Rican Childhood

Judith Ortiz Cofer

1   At three or four o'clock in the afternoon, the hour of *café con leche*, the women of my family gathered in Mamá's living room to speak of important things and retell familiar stories meant to be overheard by us young girls, their daughters. In Mamá's house (everyone called my grandmother Mamá) was a large parlor built by my grandfather to his wife's exact specifications so that it was always cool, facing away from the sun. The doorway was on the side of the house so no one could walk directly into her living room. First they had to take a little stroll through and around her beautiful garden where prize-winning orchids grew in the trunk of an ancient tree she had hollowed out for that purpose. This room was furnished with several mahogany rocking chairs, acquired at the births of her children, and one intricately carved rocker that had passed down to Mamá at the death of her own mother.

2   It was on these rockers that my mother, her sisters, and my grandmother sat on these afternoons of my childhood to tell their stories, teaching each other, and my cousin and me, what it was like to be a woman, more specifically, a Puerto Rican woman. They talked about life on the island, and life in *Los Nueva Yores*, their way of referring to the United States from New York City to California: the other place, not home, all the same. They told

real-life stories though, as I later learned, always embellishing them with a little or a lot of dramatic detail. And they told *cuentos*, the morality and cautionary tales told by the women in our family for generations: stories that became a part of my subconscious as I grew up in two worlds, the tropical island and the cold city, and that would later surface in my dreams and in my poetry.

One of these tales was about the woman who was left at 3 the altar. Mamá liked to tell that one with histrionic intensity. I remember the rise and fall of her voice, the sighs, and her constantly gesturing hands, like two birds swooping through her words. This particular story usually would come up in a conversation as a result of someone mentioning a forthcoming engagement or wedding. The first time I remember hearing it, I was sitting on the floor at Mamá's feet, pretending to read a comic book. I may have been eleven or twelve years old, at that difficult age when a girl was no longer a child who could be ordered to leave the room if the women wanted freedom to take their talk into forbidden zones, nor really old enough to be considered a part of their conclave. I could only sit quietly, pretending to be in another world, while absorbing it all in a sort of unspoken agreement of my status as silent auditor. On this day, Mamá had taken my long, tangled mane of hair into her ever-busy hands. Without looking down at me and with no interruption of her flow of words, she began braiding my hair, working at it with the quickness and determination that characterized all her actions. My mother was watching us impassively from her rocker across the room. On her lips played a little ironic smile. I would never sit still for *her* ministrations, but even then, I instinctively knew that she did not possess Mamá's matriarchal power to command and keep everyone's attention. This was never more evident than in the spell she cast when telling a story.

"It is not like it used to be when I was a girl," Mamá 4 announced. "Then a man could leave a girl standing at the church altar with a bouquet of fresh flowers in her hands and disappear off the face of the earth. No way to track him down if he was from another town. He could be a married man, with maybe even two or three families all over the island. There was no way to know.

And there were men who did this. Hombres with the devil in their flesh who would come to a pueblo, like this one, take a job at one of the haciendas, never meaning to stay, only to have a good time and to seduce the women."

5   The whole time she was speaking, Mamá would be weaving my hair into a flat plait that required pulling apart the two sections of hair with little jerks that made my eyes water; but knowing how grandmother detested whining and *boba* (sissy) tears, as she called them, I just sat up as straight and stiff as I did at La Escuela San José, where the nuns enforced good posture with a flexible plastic ruler they bounced off of slumped shoulders and heads. As Mamá's story progressed, I noticed how my young Aunt Laura lowered her eyes, refusing to meet Mamá's meaningful gaze. Laura was seventeen, in her last year of high school, and already engaged to a boy from another town who had staked his claim with a tiny diamond ring, then left for Los Nueva Yores to make his fortune. They were planning to get married in a year. Mamá had expressed serious doubts that the wedding would ever take place. In Mamá's eyes, a man set free without a legal contract was a man lost. She believed that marriage was not something men desired, but simply the price they had to pay for the privilege of children and, of course, for what no decent (synonymous with "smart") woman would give away for free.

6   "María La Loca was only seventeen when *it* happened to her." I listened closely at the mention of this name. María was a town character, a fat middle-aged woman who lived with her old mother on the outskirts of town. She was to be seen around the pueblo delivering the meat pies the two women made for a living. The most peculiar thing about María, in my eyes, was that she walked and moved like a little girl though she had the thick body and wrinkled face of an old woman. She would swing her hips in an exaggerated, clownish way, and sometimes even hop and skip up to someone's house. She spoke to no one. Even if you asked her a question, she would just look at you and smile, showing her yellow teeth. But I had heard that if you got close enough, you could hear her humming a tune without words. The kids yelled out nasty things to her, calling her *La Loca*, and the

men who hung out at the bodega playing dominoes sometimes whistled mockingly as she passed by with her funny, outlandish walk. But María seemed impervious to it all, carrying her basket of *pasteles* like a grotesque Little Red Riding Hood through the forest.

María La Loca interested me, as did all the eccentrics and 7 crazies of our pueblo. Their weirdness was a measuring stick I used in my serious quest for a definition of normal. As a Navy brat shuttling between New Jersey and the pueblo, I was constantly made to feel like an oddball by my peers, who made fun of my two-way accent: a Spanish accent when I spoke English, and when I spoke Spanish I was told that I sounded like a *Gringa*. Being the outsider had already turned my brother and me into cultural chameleons. We developed early on the ability to blend into a crowd, to sit and read quietly in a fifth story apartment building for days and days when it was too bitterly cold to play outside, or, set free, to run wild in Mamá's realm, where she took charge of our lives, releasing Mother for a while from the intense fear for our safety that our father's absences instilled in her. In order to keep us from harm when Father was away, Mother kept us under strict surveillance. She even walked us to and from Public School No. 11, which we attended during the months we lived in Paterson, New Jersey, our home base in the states. Mamá freed all three of us like pigeons from a cage. I saw her as my liberator and my model. Her stories were parables from which to glean the *Truth*.

"María La Loca was once a beautiful girl. Everyone thought 8 she would marry the Méndez boy." As everyone knew, Rogelio Méndez was the richest man in town. "But," Mamá continued, knitting my hair with the same intensity she was putting into her story, "this *macho* made a fool out of her and ruined her life." She paused for the effect of her use of the word *macho*, which at that time had not yet become a popular epithet for an unliberated man. This word had for us the crude and comical connotation of "male of the species," stud; a *macho* was what you put in a pen to increase your stock.

I peeked over my comic book at my mother. She too was 9 under Mamá's spell, smiling conspiratorially at this little swipe at men. She was safe from Mamá's contempt in this area. Married at an early age, an unspotted lamb, she had been accepted by a good family of strict Spaniards whose name was old and respected, though their fortune had been lost long before my birth. In a rocker Papá had painted sky blue sat Mamá's oldest child, Aunt Nena. Mother of three children, step-mother of two more, she was a quiet woman who liked books but had married an ignorant and abusive widower whose main interest in life was accumulating wealth. He too was in the mainland working on his dream of returning home rich and triumphant to buy the *finca* of his dreams. She was waiting for him to send for her. She would leave her children with Mamá for several years while the two of them slaved away in factories. He would one day be a rich man, and she a sadder woman. Even now her life-light was dimming. She spoke little, an aberration in Mamá's house, and she read avidly, as if storing up spiritual food for the long winters that awaited her in Los Nueva Yores without her family. But even Aunt Nena came alive to Mamá's words, rocking gently, her hands over a thick book in her lap.

10   Her daughter, my cousin Sara, played jacks by herself on the tile porch outside the room where we sat. She was a year older than I. We shared a bed and all our family's secrets. Collaborators in search of answers, Sara and I discussed everything we heard the women say, trying to fit it all together like a puzzle that, once assembled, would reveal life's mysteries to us. Though she and I still enjoyed taking part in boys' games—chase, volleyball and even *vaqueros*, the island version of cowboys and Indians involving capgun battles and violent shoot-outs under the mango tree in Mamá's backyard—we loved best the quiet hours in the afternoon when the men were still at work and the boys had gone to play serious baseball at the park. Then Mamá's house belonged only to us women. The aroma of coffee perking in the kitchen, the mesmerizing creaks and groans of the rockers, and the women telling their lives in *cuentos* are forever woven into the fabric of my imagination, braided like my hair that day I felt my grandmother's hands teaching me about strength, her voice convincing me of the power of storytelling.

That day Mamá told how the beautiful María had fallen prey 11
to a man whose name was never the same in subsequent versions
of the story; it was Juan one time, José, Rafael, Diego, another.
We understood that neither the name nor any of the *facts* were
important, only that a woman had allowed love to defeat her.
Mamá put each of us in María's place by describing her wedding
dress in loving detail: how she looked like a princess in her lace
as she waited at the altar. Then, as Mamá approached the tragic
denouement of her story, I was distracted by the sound of my
Aunt Laura's violent rocking. She seemed on the verge of tears.
She knew the fable was intended for her. That week she was
going to have her wedding gown fitted, though no firm date
had been set for the marriage. Mamá ignored Laura's obvious
discomfort, digging out a ribbon from the sewing basket she
kept by her rocker while describing María's long illness, "a fever
that would not break for days." She spoke of a mother's despair:
"that woman climbed the church steps on her knees every morning, wore only black as a *promesa* to the Holy Virgin in exchange
for her daughter's health." By the time María returned from her
honeymoon with death, she was ravished, no longer young or
sane. "As you can see, she is almost as old as her mother already,"
Mamá lamented while tying the ribbon to the ends of my hair,
pulling it back with such force that I just knew I would never be
able to close my eyes completely again.

"That María is getting crazier every day." Mamá's voice 12
would take a lighter tone now, expressing satisfaction, either for
the perfection of my braid, or for a story well told—it was hard
to tell. "You know that tune María is always humming?" Carried
away by her enthusiasm, I tried to nod, but Mamá still had me
pinned between her knees.

"Well, that's the wedding march." Surprising us all, Mamá 13
sang out, "Da, da, dara. . .da, da, dara." Then lifting me off the
floor by my skinny shoulders, she would lead me around the
room in an impromptu waltz—another session ending with the
laughter of women, all of us caught up in the infectious joke of
our lives.

1990

Monuments to Our Better Nature

Michael Byers

1 Growing up in the seventies in Bethesda, Maryland, a suburb of Washington, D.C., I had the good fortune to be taken regularly to the National Mall by my mother. She was a scientist, and in the aftermath of the Vietnam War she found much to be disheartened by. The immense Smithsonian museums on the Mall acted, for her, as repositories of truth and exactitude in an age of cupidity, paranoia, and evasion; they were her solace.

2 In the National Museum of Natural History, the gargantuan blue whale hanging above us with its great grooved throat was a *fact* about the world that could not be denied. The stuffed African elephant on its circular dais in the rotunda was composed of billions of skin cells and tiny cilia, and its ivory tusks wore an unfalsifiable brown patina of age. The chambered skull of the brontosaurus, the irrefutable chain of his vertebrae, his ponderous thighbones, and his sculpted metatarsals—each the size and heft of an anchor—had been painstakingly recovered from a stony Canadian grave, cleaned, and finally pieced together again, eons after the original owner had ceased to have any use for them.

3 Certain truths, the museums assured us, were undeniable. The meteorites upstairs had roamed the vacuum of space for billions of years until at last, following the Keplerian laws of orbit and velocity, they had collided with Earth, their nickel cores becoming polished by the final scalding plunge through the atmosphere. What a wonder it all was, and how true. And how could anyone not grasp that these truths were, in so many cases, utterly beautiful? This was the sort of thing my young mother wanted to be reassured of in those days, and it was an idea she wanted me to appreciate, too.

4 But my secret love was not the museums themselves but their grand exteriors and their placement among the other monuments and memorials. Looking ghostly in the distance, these stone structures spoke of a grandeur whose reach and glory had no measure. While for my mother these temples were tainted by chauvinism—in them she saw the young, rough-edged country

trying to polish its image—for me they were transcendent. Even as a very young boy I knew they had the power to draw me across the grass, and they still do.

Washington, particularly the vast, open Mall, is the place where I first felt like a *citizen*. Standing in front of this monument or that memorial, I understood what it meant to belong to a country so populous as this one. This is the first purpose of these places, it seems to me: to inform citizens of the nation's collective character. They are massive, and beside them we are tiny. So it is politically. Alone, each of us is almost without value, but in the aggregate we are the point of the whole improbable enterprise. One is lost in the multitude, but the multitude itself is essential. It is no mistake that the White House—often the scene of great reputations made and lost—is on the back of the twenty-dollar bill, while Lincoln and his memorial find themselves on the penny. You are only a penny, the monuments tell us, but you are dearly counted.

And in life, while the White House may resemble an over-built embassy, the Lincoln Memorial is sublime. What American can approach Henry Bacon's temple to the humble son of Illinois and not feel his own soul beginning to rise eerily through the top of his head? What a glory to mount the broad stairs; what a thrilling incantation to count the thirty-six Doric columns, one for every state of the Union in 1864. And what a pleasure it is to call out the rank of states whose names, inscribed here above the entrance—VIRGINIA TENNESSEE GEORGIA—bring to mind not demagogic governors or backward pockets of creation science but ideal, benign subrepublics run by citizens much like ourselves. All around us, as we climb the stairs, fellow Americans are dressed in logo-covered T-shirts and careless blue jeans, and many are young, and loud. But there they are beside us anyhow, and at the top of the stairs we all stop and turn—we cannot help ourselves—to see where we have come from. And how far indeed it is that we, as a people, have traveled. Below us lie the steps where in Easter of 1939 the contralto Marian Anderson, black daughter of a coal dealer, sang "America" and "Nobody Knows the Trouble I've Seen," as seventy-five thousand looked on in the April cold. On these steps, Martin Luther King, Jr., shrugged himself away from his prepared text and in that extemporaneous moment produced a supreme example of American oratory—his long Whitmanesque lines echoing with the names of the states carved high on the temple's walls behind him: "Let freedom ring from the snowcapped Rockies of Colorado! Let freedom ring from the curvaceous peaks of California! But not only that; let freedom ring from Stone Mountain of Georgia! Let freedom ring from Lookout Mountain of Tennessee! Let freedom ring from every hill and every molehill of Mississippi!"

7   What a glory it is to stand where Anderson sang and King spoke—and what a glory to have been permitted to climb these steps unwatched, unquestioned, without a ticket of admission, and at last to arrive at the portico, where the simple Indiana limestone pillars are much larger than they appeared from below, and where the Tennessee pink marble floor is scuffed with millions of our footsteps, and where, as we pass inside, the Alabama marble ceiling—soaked in paraffin to make it translucent—casts a pale light. Hushed, we stop. There he is, Lincoln, on his throne, looking down at us all, while at the other end of the Mall the messy business of the Capitol goes on under his tireless, admonitory gaze.

8   Americans are not known for good behavior in public, but here we become subdued, reflective. It is a long way to the ceiling, and our voices fade. Who is not moved by the sentences carved into the walls? "With malice toward none; with charity for all; with firmness in the right . . . Let us strive on to finish the work we are in; to bind up the nation's wounds . . . to do all which may achieve and cherish a just and lasting peace, among ourselves, and with all nations." At this, who does not feel grateful, and feel a lump in the throat? And even those few of us who are ignorant, or disdainful, who choose to snap gum or answer cell phones— well, we are Americans, and this is our monument, and whatever we do here is by definition permissible because it is ours.

9   Everyone goes to the Lincoln Memorial. Not everyone goes to the Jefferson. You can drive there and park, but from the Lincoln Memorial you must walk along the Tidal Basin and cross a busy bridge. The monument faces the water, so you must approach it obliquely, or from the back. Jefferson stands, bronze, his coattails flared, his proud calves on display, his handsome head erect. Under the dome, pigeons flutter from place to place like thoughts moving in a great curved brain. The building, designed by John

Russell Pope, is modeled after the Pantheon in Rome, but where is the dramatic soaring reach of the ceiling? Jefferson seems too large for his temple.

Disappointment may come from our feelings about Jefferson 10 himself: we appreciate the need for him, but still we do not much like him. Surely we take him too much for granted. He is remote, a rationalist. And what are we to make of the arcane inscriptions? "I am not an advocate for frequent changes in laws and constitution, but laws and institutions go hand in hand with the progress of the human mind. . . . We might as well require a man to wear the same coat that fitted him when he was a boy." All right, but where is the poetry? We have left it over there across the water, in the big rough hands of Lincoln.

We approach the third great presidential monument, Robert 11 Mills's stark tribute to George Washington, without much excitement. It is the Mall's least lovely structure, and its most primitive. Thirty-seven years in the making, and what do we have? An obelisk, which seems to the eye not quite vertical as it rises above the city. But maybe it is fitting that this most distant figure of the American pantheon should have this least expressive tower built in his name: the first president as Zoroaster, a demigod whose name we have heard but whom we do not know personally. This monument seems Egyptian, and as such out of place here on the green among the more welcoming Greek and Roman temples. But this is fitting too. Washington, we know, was himself somewhat uncomfortable in civilian life, by turns noble, humble, and clumsy. Like some of the other lifelong military men who would later find themselves in the presidency, he was never quite sure where he stood. At the top of his monument, people shove their way to the windows. If we swoon at the drop and step back from the glass, our place is quickly taken.

There is no shoving at the Vietnam Veterans Memorial. 12 Behavior here is impeccable, and we have its intuitive, minimalist design by Maya Lin to thank. This monument is public architecture at its finest: open, instructive, and moving. The ambivalent descent, deeper and deeper, along a sinister black wall, exactly mimics the national experience of the war: the early trickle of bad news, the growing sense of obligation, the gradual realization that we are in over our heads, and at its nadir, the dark hopelessness from which there seems no escaping. We catch our breath as we descend. We are silent, knowing that some of the visitors here will have lost a brother, son, father, friend.

13   Adults climb out of this hole sadder and wiser. But do the twelve-year-olds also behave well here only because of the crying man in the army fatigues? Or do they, like their parents, feel that something terrible has happened, and been preserved somehow in black marble? And will their children feel the same way, or will they need to learn the lessons of Vietnam again?

14   At the top of the ramp we are released again onto the green. We walk to the Korean War Veterans Memorial but leave with a bad taste. It tries too hard to move us, and it fails. And so we look suspiciously at the construction under way at the foot of the Reflecting Pool where the World War II Memorial is at last taking shape. We are willing to suspend judgment, but we are concerned about the loss of open space.

15   Because ultimately the defined space of the Mall is its greatest asset. It is one of America's most venerable and trafficked pedestrian public spaces, where you can fly a kite alone or stand among a hundred thousand and hear a speech being given half a mile away by a barely discernible figure. It is the *distance* between monuments that I find myself appreciating every time I visit. The buildings appear on the horizon and resolve, slowly, as you approach them on foot across the grass. In this way the Mall itself functions like an enormous museum, and these imperfect places are what we have so far in our national display case, laid out on the green velvet of the enormous lawn.

16   As adults, we eventually learn that the brontosaurus is now called apatosaurus, and half of its bones are informed reconstructions. We discover there were ten million African elephants in 1930, and that now there are only thirty-five thousand. We see that government is bought and paid for, no matter what party is in power. But still: Who can stand on the top step of the Lincoln Memorial and not think. *I am a participant in a world civilization, I have history entrusted to me, we are all in this together*—and feel it, for a minute or two, as the simple, honest truth?

2003

Beneath My House

Louise Erdrich

It was as if the house itself had given birth. One day the floor 1
cried where I stepped on it, and I jumped back. I was near a
heating vent, and when I bent and pried the cover off and thrust
my hand in, I briefly grabbed a ball of fur that hissed and spat. I
heard the kitten scrambling away, the tin resounding like small
thunder along the length of its flight.

I went down to the basement, looking for it with a flash- 2
light, but, of course, at my step the untamed creature fled from
the concrete-floored area and off into the earthen crawl space—
draped with spiderwebs as thick as cotton, a place of unpeeled
log beams, the underside of the house. I put out milk in a saucer.
I crouched on the other side of the furnace, and I waited until I fell
half-asleep. But the kitten was too young to drink from a dish and
never came. Instead, she set up, from just beyond where I could
catch her, a piteous crying that I could hardly stand to hear.

I went after her. The earth was moldy, a dense clay. No sun had 3
fallen here for over two centuries. I climbed over the brick retaining wall and crawled toward the sound of the kitten. As I neared,
as it sensed my presence was too large to be its mother, it went
silent and scrabbled away from the reach of my hand. I brushed
fur, though, and that slight warmth filled me with what must
have been a mad calm because when the creature squeezed into a
bearing wall of piled stones, I inched forward on my stomach. My
back was now scraping along the beams that bore the weight of
the whole house above me. Tons and tons of plaster, boards, appli-
ances, and furniture, this was no crawl space anymore. I could
hardly raise my shoulders to creep forward, could move only by
shifting my hips up and down. On the edge of panic—I had never
before been in a space so tight—one thought pressed in: if I heard
the house creak, if it settled very suddenly upon my back, my last
crushed words would be, "Shit! I don't even like cats." Because I
don't like cats, just find their silken ways irresistible.

Its face popped out right in front of me, and vanished. How 4
far back did the piled rock go? If I moved a rock, would the whole

house fall on me? I reached for the kitten, missed, reached again, missed. I tried to breathe, to be patient. Then, after a time, the kitten backed toward me, away from a clump of dirt I managed to throw at the far wall. Its tail flicked through a space in the rocks, and I snatched it. Held it, drew it toward me. Out it came with a squeak of terror, a series of panting comic hisses, and a whirl of claws and teeth, tiny needles it didn't yet know how to use.

5   She is a pretty cat, a calico marbled evenly with orange and black. Rocky. She sits near as I write, leaps into the warmth of my chair when I leave, and is jealous of the baby.

6   The night after I pulled her from the house, the darkness pressed down on me until I woke. I'd swum weightlessly into a smaller and smaller space. What the body remembers of birth it anticipates as death. In the house of my dreams the basement is the most fearful: the awful place filled with water, the place of both comfort and death. I fear in particular the small space, the earth closing in on me, the house like a mother settling its cracked bones and plumbing.

7   That afternoon, from underneath, I had heard the house all around me like an old familiar body. I hadn't told anybody else that I was going after the kitten, so nobody knew I was below. The normal sounds of my family's daily life were magnified. Their steps trailed and traveled around me, boomed in my ears. Their voices jolted me, their words loud but meaningless, warped by their travel through the walls and beams. Water flowed through invisible pipes around me, hitched and gurgled. It was like being dead, or unborn. I hadn't thought about it then, but now I could clearly see part of me, the husk of myself, still buried against the east wall: a person sacrificed to ensure the good luck of a temple, a kind of house god, a woman lying down there, still, an empty double.

3

Process Analysis

Why Leaves Turn Color in the Fall

Diane Ackerman

The stealth of autumn catches one unaware. Was that a goldfinch 1 perching in the early September woods, or just the first turning leaf? A red-winged blackbird or a sugar maple closing up shop for the winter? Keen-eyed as leopards, we stand still and squint hard, looking for signs of movement. Early morning frost sits heavily on the grass, and turns barbed wire into a string of stars. On a distant hill, a small square of yellow appears to be a lighted stage. At last the truth dawns on us: Fall is staggering in, right on schedule, with its baggage of chilly nights, macabre holidays, and spectacular, heart-stoppingly beautiful leaves. Soon the leaves will start cringing on the trees, and roll up in clenched fists before they actually fall off. Dry seedpods will rattle like tiny gourds. But first there will be weeks of gushing color so bright, so pastel, so confettilike, that people will travel up and down the East Coast just to stare at it—a whole season of leaves.

Where do the colors come from? Sunlight rules most living 2 things with its golden edicts. When the days begin to shorten, soon after the summer solstice on June 21, a tree reconsiders its leaves. All summer it feeds them so they can process sunlight, but in the dog days of summer the tree begins pulling nutrients back into its trunk and roots, pares down, and gradually chokes off its leaves. A corky layer of cells forms at the leaves' slender petioles, then scars over. Undernourished, the leaves stop producing the pigment chlorophyll, and photosynthesis ceases. Animals can migrate, hibernate, or store food to prepare for winter. But where can a tree go? It survives by dropping its leaves, and by the end of autumn only a few fragile threads of fluid-carrying xylem hold leaves to their stems.

3   A turning leaf stays partly green at first, then reveals splotches of yellow and red as the chlorophyll gradually breaks down. Dark green seems to stay longest in the veins, outlining and defining them. During the summer, chlorophyll dissolves in the heat and light, but it is also being steadily replaced. In the fall, on the other hand, no new pigment is produced, and so we notice the other colors that were always there, right in the leaf, although chlorophyll's shocking green hid them from view. With their camouflage gone, we see these colors for the first time all year, and marvel, but they were always there, hidden like a vivid secret beneath the hot glowing greens of summer.

4   The most spectacular range of fall foliage occurs in the northeastern United States and in eastern China, where the leaves are robustly colored, thanks in part to a rich climate. European maples don't achieve the same flaming reds as their American relatives, which thrive on cold nights and sunny days. In Europe, the warm, humid weather turns the leaves brown or mildly yellow. Anthocyanin, the pigment that gives apples their red and turns leaves red or red-violet, is produced by sugars that remain in the leaf after the supply of nutrients dwindles. Unlike the carotenoids, which color carrots, squash, and corn, and turn leaves orange and yellow, anthocyanin varies from year to year, depending on the temperature and amount of sunlight. The fiercest colors occur in years when the fall sunlight is strongest and the nights are cool and dry (a state of grace scientists find vexing to forecast). This is also why leaves appear dizzyingly bright and clear on a sunny fall day: The anthocyanin flashes like a marquee.

5   Not all leaves turn the same colors. Elms, weeping willows, and the ancient ginkgo all grow radiant yellow, along with hickories, aspens, bottlebrush buckeyes, cottonweeds, and tall, keening poplars. Basswood turns bronze, birches bright gold. Water-loving maples put on a symphonic display of scarlets. Sumacs turn red,

too, as do flowering dogwoods, black gums, and sweet gums. Though some oaks yellow, most turn a pinkish brown. The farmlands also change color, as tepees of cornstalks and bales of shredded-wheat-textured hay stand drying in the fields. In some spots, one slope of a hill may be green and the other already in bright color, because the hillside facing south gets more sun and heat than the northern one.

An odd feature of the colors is that they don't seem to 6 have any special purpose. We are predisposed to respond to their beauty, of course. They shimmer with the colors of sunset, spring flowers, the tawny buff of a colt's pretty rump, the shuddering pink of a blush. Animals and flowers color for a reason—adaptation to their environment—but there is no adaptive reason for leaves to color so beautifully in the fall any more than there is for the sky or ocean to be blue. It's just one of the haphazard marvels the planet bestows every year. We find the sizzling colors thrilling, and in a sense they dupe us. Colored like living things, they signal death and disintegration. In time, they will become fragile and, like the body, return to dust. They are as we hope our own fate will be when we die: Not to vanish, just to sublime from one beautiful state into another. Though leaves lose their green life, they bloom with urgent colors, as the woods grow mummified day by day, and Nature becomes more carnal, mute, and radiant.

We call the season "fall," from the Old English *feallan*, to fall, 7 which leads back through time to the Indo-European *phol*, which also means to fall. So the word and the idea are both extremely ancient, and haven't really changed since the first of our kind needed a name for fall's leafy abundance. As we say the word, we're reminded of that other Fall, in the garden of Eden, when fig leaves never withered and scales fell from our eyes. Fall is the time when leaves fall from the trees, just as spring is when flowers spring up, summer is when we simmer, and winter is when we whine from the cold.

Children love to play in piles of leaves, hurling them into the 8 air like confetti, leaping into soft unruly mattresses of them. For children, leaf fall is just one of the odder figments of Nature, like hailstones or snowflakes. Walk down a lane overhung with trees in the never-never land of autumn, and you will forget about time and death, lost in the sheer delicious spill of color. Adam and Eve concealed their nakedness with leaves, remember? Leaves have always hidden our awkward secrets.

9   But how do the colored leaves fall? As a leaf ages, the growth hormone, auxin, fades, and cells at the base of the petiole divide. Two or three rows of small cells, lying at right angles to the axis of the petiole, react with water, then come apart, leaving the petioles hanging on by only a few threads of xylem. A light breeze, and the leaves are airborne. They glide and swoop, rocking in invisible cradles. They are all wing and may flutter from yard to yard on small whirlwinds or updrafts, swiveling as they go. Firmly tethered to earth, we love to see things rise up and fly—soap bubbles, balloons, birds, fall leaves. They remind us that the end of a season is capricious, as is the end of life. We especially like the way leaves rock, careen, and swoop as they fall. Everyone knows the motion. Pilots sometimes do a maneuver called a "falling leaf," in which the plane loses altitude quickly and on purpose, by slipping first to the right, then to the left. The machine weighs a ton or more, but in one pilot's mind it is a weightless thing, a falling leaf. She has seen the motion before, in the Vermont woods where she played as a child. Below her the trees radiate gold, copper, and red. Leaves are falling, although she can't see them fall, as she falls, swooping down for a closer view.

10   At last the leaves leave. But first they turn color and thrill us for weeks on end. Then they crunch and crackle underfoot. They *shush*, as children drag their small feet through leaves heaped along the curb. Dark, slimy mats of leaves cling to one's heels after a rain. A damp, stuccolike mortar of semidecayed leaves protects the tender shoots with a roof until spring, and makes a rich humus. An occasional bulge or ripple in the leafy mounds signals a shrew or a field mouse tunneling out of sight. Sometimes one finds in fossil stones the imprint of a leaf, long since disintegrated whose outlines remind us how detailed, vibrant, and alive are the things of this earth that perish.

1990

Writing Drafts

Richard Marius

Finally the moment comes when you sit down to begin your 1
first draft. It is always a good idea at the start to list the points
you want to cover. A list is not as elaborate as a formal outline.
In writing your first list, don't bother to set items down in the
order of importance. List your main points and trust your mind
to organize them. You will probably make one list, study it, make
another, study it, and perhaps make another. You can organize
each list more completely than the last. This preliminary process
may save you hours of starting and stopping.

Write with your list outline in front of you. Once you begin 2
to write, commit yourself to the task at hand. Do not get up until
you have written for an hour. Write your thoughts quickly. Let one
sentence give you an idea to develop in the next. Organization,
grammar, spelling, and even clarity of sentences are not nearly as
important as getting the first draft together. No matter how desperate you feel, keep going.

Always keep your mind open to new ideas that pop into 3
your head as you write. Let your list outline help you, but don't
become a slave to it. Writers often start an essay with one topic in
mind only to discover that another pushes the first one aside as
they work. Ideas you had not even thought of before you began
to write may pile onto your paper, and five or six pages into your
first draft you may realize that you are going to write about something you did not imagine when you started.

If such a revelation comes, be grateful and accept it. But don't 4
immediately tear up or erase your draft and start all over again.
Make yourself keep on writing, developing these new ideas as
they come. If you suddenly start all over again, you may break
the train of thought that has given you the new topic. Let your
thoughts follow your new thesis, sailing on that tack until the
wind changes.

When you have said everything you can say in this draft, 5
print it out if you are working on a computer. Get up from your
desk and go sit in a chair somewhere else to read it without

correcting anything. Then put it aside, preferably overnight. If possible, read your rough draft just before you go to sleep. Many psychological tests have shown that our minds organize and create while we sleep if we pack them full before bedtime. Study a draft just before sleep, and you may discover new ideas in the morning.

6   Be willing to make radical changes in your second draft. If your thesis changed while you were writing your first draft, you will base your second draft on this new subject. Even if your thesis has not changed, you may need to shift paragraphs around, eliminate paragraphs, or add new ones. Inexperienced writers often suppose that revising a paper means changing only a word or two or adding a sentence or two. This kind of editing is part of the writing process, but it is not the most important part. The most important part of rewriting is a willingness to turn the paper upside down, to shake out of it those ideas that interest you most, to set them in a form where they will interest the reader, too.

7   I mentioned earlier that some writers cut up their first drafts with a pair of scissors. They toss some paragraphs into the trash; others they paste up with rubber cement in the order that seems most logical and coherent. Afterward they type the whole thing through again, smoothing out the transitions, adding new material, getting new ideas as they work. The translation of the first draft into the second nearly always involves radical cutting and shifting around. Now and then you may firmly fix the order of your thoughts in your first draft, but I find that the order of my essays is seldom established until the second draft.

8   With the advent of computers the shifting around of parts of the essays has become easy. We can cut and paste electronically with a few strokes of the keyboard. We can also make back-up copies of our earlier drafts so we can go back to them if we wish. But as I said earlier, computers do not remove from us the necessity to think hard about revising.

9   Always be firm enough with yourself to cut out thoughts or stories that have nothing to do with your thesis, even if they are interesting. Cutting is the supreme test of a writer. You may create a smashing paragraph or sentence only to discover later that it

does not help you make your point. You may develop six or seven examples to illustrate a point and discover you need only one.

Now and then you may digress a little. If you digress too [10] often or too far, readers will not follow you unless your facts, your thoughts, and your style are so compelling that they are somehow driven to follow you. Not many writers can pull such digressions off, and most editors will cut out the digressions even when they are interesting. In our hurried and harried time, most readers get impatient with the rambling scenic route. They want to take the most direct way to their destination. To appeal to most of them, you must cut things that do not apply to your main argument.

In your third draft, you can sharpen sentences, add informa- [11] tion here and there, cut some things, and attend to other details to heighten the force of your writing. In the third draft, writing becomes a lot of fun (for most of us). By then you have usually decided what you want to say. You can now play a bit, finding just the right word, choosing just the right sentence form, com- pressing here, expanding there.

I find it helpful to put a printed draft down beside my key- [12] board and type the whole thing through again as a final draft, letting all the words run through my mind and fingers one more time rather than merely deleting and inserting on the computer screen. I wrote four drafts of the first edition of this book; I have preserved the final draft of that edition on computer diskettes. But I am writing this draft by propping the first edition up here beside me and typing it all over again. By comparing the first draft and the second draft, one can see how many changes I have made, most of them unforeseen until I sat down here to work.

I have outlined here my own writing process. It works for me. [13] You must find the process that works for you. It may be different from mine. A friend tells me that his writing process consists of writing a sentence, agonizing over it, walking around the room, thinking, sitting down, and writing the next sentence. He does not revise very much. I think it unnecessarily painful to bleed out prose that way, but he bleeds out enough to write what he needs to write. Several of my friends tell me they cannot compose at a typewriter; they must first write with a pencil on a yellow pad. These are the people most likely to cut up their drafts with scissors and paste them together in a different form. They also tend to be older. Most young writers are learning to compose at a keyboard, and they cannot imagine another way to write. Neither can I—though on occasion yet I go back to my pencil for pages at a time.

14   The main thing is to keep at it. B. F. Skinner has pointed out that if you write only fifty words a night, you will produce a good-sized book every two or three years. That's not a bad record for any writer. William Faulkner outlined the plot of his Nobel Prize–winning novel *A Fable* on a wall inside his house near Oxford, Mississippi. You can see it there to this day. Once he got the outline on the wall, he sat down with his typewriter and wrote, following the outline to the end. If writing an outline on a kitchen wall does the trick for you, do it. You can always repaint the wall if you must.

15   Think of writing as a process making its way toward a product—sometimes painfully. Don't imagine you must know everything you are going to say before you begin. Don't demean yourself and insult your readers by letting your first draft be your final draft. Don't imagine that writing is easy or that you can do it without spending time on it. And don't let anything stand in your way of doing it. Let your house get messy. Leave your magazines unread and your mail unanswered. Put off getting up for a drink of water or a cup of tea. (Never mix alcohol with your writing; true, lots of writers have become alcoholics, but it has not helped their writing.) Don't make a telephone call. Don't straighten up your desk. Sit down and write. And write, and write, and write.

1988

Alone on the Hilltop

John (Fire) Lame Deer and Richard Erdoes

1   I was all alone on the hilltop. I sat there in the vision pit, a hole dug into the hill, my arms hugging my knees as I watched old man Chest, the medicine man who had brought me there,

disappear far down in the valley. He was just a moving black dot among the pines, and soon he was gone altogether.

Now I was all by myself, left on the hilltop for four days ₂ and nights without food or water until he came back for me. You know, we Indians are not like some white folks—a man and a wife, two children, and one baby sitter who watches the TV set while the parents are out visiting somewhere.

Indian children are never alone. They are always surrounded ₃ by grandparents, uncles, cousins, relatives of all kinds, who fondle the kids, sing to them, tell them stories. If the parents go someplace, the kids go along.

But here I was, crouched in my vision pit, left alone by ₄ myself for the first time in my life. I was sixteen then, still had my boy's name and, let me tell you, I was scared. I was shivering and not only from the cold. The nearest human being was many miles away, and four days and nights is a long, long time. Of course, when it was all over, I would no longer be a boy, but a man. I would have had my vision. I would be given a man's name.

Sioux men are not afraid to endure hunger, thirst and loneli- ₅ ness, and I was only ninety-six hours away from being a man. The thought was comforting. Comforting, too, was the warmth of the star blanket which old man Chest had wrapped around me to cover my nakedness. My grandmother had made it especially for this, my first *hanblechia*, my first vision-seeking. It was a beautifully designed quilt, white with a large morning star made of many pieces of brightly colored cloth. That star was so big it covered most of the blanket. If Waken Tanka, the Great Spirit, would give me the vision and the power, I would become a medicine man and perform many ceremonies wrapped in that quilt. I am an old man now and many times a grandfather, but I still have that star blanket my grandmother made for me. I treasure it; some day I shall be buried in it.

The medicine man had also left a peace pipe with me, ₆ together with a bag of *kinnickinnick*—our kind of tobacco made of red willow bark. This pipe was even more of a friend to me than my star blanket. To us the pipe is like an open Bible. White people need a church house, a preacher and a pipe organ to get into a praying mood. There are so many things to distract you: who else is in the church, whether the other people notice that you have come, the pictures on the wall, the sermon, how much money you should give and did you bring it with you. We think you can't have a vision that way.

7   For us Indians there is just the pipe, the earth we sit on and the open sky. The spirit is everywhere. Sometimes it shows itself through an animal, a bird or some trees and hills. Sometimes it speaks from the Badlands, a stone, or even from the water. That smoke from the peace pipe, it goes straight up to the spirit world. But this is a two-way thing. Power flows down to us through that smoke, through the pipe stem. You feel that power as you hold your pipe; it moves from the pipe right into your body. It makes your hair stand up. That pipe is not just a thing; it is alive. Smoking this pipe would make me feel good and help me to get rid of my fears.

8   As I ran my fingers along its bowl of smooth red pipestone, red like the blood of my people, I no longer felt scared. That pipe had belonged to my father and to his father before him. It would someday pass to my son and, through him, to my grandchildren. As long as we had the pipe there would be a Sioux nation. As I fingered the pipe, touched it, felt its smoothness that came from long use, I sensed that my forefathers who had once smoked this pipe were with me on the hill, right in the vision pit. I was no longer alone.

9   Besides the pipe the medicine man had also given me a gourd. In it were forty small squares of flesh which my grandmother had cut from her arm with a razor blade. I had seen her do it. Blood had been streaming down from her shoulder to her elbow as she carefully put down each piece of skin on a handkerchief, anxious not to lose a single one. It would have made those anthropologists mad. Imagine, performing such an ancient ceremony with a razor blade instead of a flint knife! To me it did not matter. Someone dear to me had undergone pain, given me something of herself, part of her body, to help me pray and make me stronghearted. How could I be afraid with so many people—living and dead—helping me?

One thing still worried me. I wanted to become a medicine 10 man, a *yuwipi*, a healer carrying on the ancient ways of the Sioux nation. But you cannot learn to be a medicine man like a white man going to medical school. An old holy man can teach you about herbs and the right ways to perform a ceremony where everything must be in its proper place, where every move, every word has its own, special meaning. These things you can learn— like spelling, like training a horse. But by themselves these things mean nothing. Without the vision and the power this learning will do no good. It would not make me a medicine man.

What if I failed, if I had no vision? Or if I dreamed of the 11 Thunder Beings, or lightning struck the hill? That would make me at once into a *heyoka*, a contrarywise, an upside-down man, a clown. "You'll know it, if you get the power," my Uncle Chest had told me. "If you are not given it, you won't lie about it, you won't pretend. That would kill you, or kill somebody close to you, somebody you love."

Night was coming on. I was still lightheaded and dizzy from 12 my first sweat bath in which I had purified myself before going up the hill. I had never been in a sweat lodge before. I had sat in the little beehive-shaped hut made of bent willow branches and covered with blankets to keep the heat in. Old Chest and three other medicine men had been in the lodge with me. I had my back against the wall, edging as far away as I could from the red-hot stones glowing in the center. As Chest poured water over the rocks, hissing white steam enveloped me and filled my lungs. I thought the heat would kill me, burn the eyelids off my face! But right in the middle of all this swirling steam I heard Chest singing. So it couldn't be all that bad. I did not cry out "All my relatives!"—which would have made him open the flap of the sweat lodge to let in some cool air—and I was proud of this. I heard him praying for me: "Oh, holy rocks, we receive your white breath, the steam. It is the breath of life. Let this young boy inhale it. Make him strong."

The sweat bath had prepared me for my vision-seeking. Even 13 now, an hour later, my skin still tingled. But it seemed to have made my brains empty. Maybe that was good, plenty of room for new insights.

14   Darkness had fallen upon the hill. I knew that *hanhepiwi* had risen, the night sun, which is what we call the moon. Huddled in my narrow cave, I did not see it. Blackness was wrapped around me like a velvet cloth. It seemed to cut me off from the outside world, even from my own body. It made me listen to the voices within me. I thought of my forefathers who had crouched on this hill before me, because the medicine men in my family had chosen this spot for a place of meditation and vision-seeking ever since the day they had crossed the Missouri to hunt for buffalo in the White River country some two hundred years ago. I thought that I could sense their presence right through the earth I was leaning against. I could feel them entering my body, feel them stirring in my mind and heart.

15   Sounds came to me through the darkness: the cries of the wind, the whisper of the trees, the voices of nature, animal sounds, the hooting of an owl. Suddenly I felt an overwhelming presence. Down there with me in my cramped hole was a big bird. The pit was only as wide as myself, and I was a skinny boy, but that huge bird was flying around me as if he had the whole sky to himself. I could hear his cries, sometimes near and sometimes far, far away. I felt feathers or a wing touching my back and head. This feeling was so overwhelming that it was just too much for me. I trembled and my bones turned to ice. I grasped the rattle with the forty pieces of my grandmother's flesh. It also had many little stones in it, tiny fossils picked up from an ant heap. Ants collect them. Nobody knows why. These little stones are supposed to have a power in them. I shook the rattle and it made a soothing sound, like rain falling on rock. It was talking to me, but it did not calm my fears. I took the sacred pipe in my other hand and began to sing and pray: "Tunkashila, grandfather spirit, help me." But this did not help. I don't know what got into me, but I was no longer myself. I started to cry. Crying, even my voice was different. I sounded like an older man, I couldn't even recognize this strange voice. I used long-ago words in my prayer, words no longer used nowadays. I tried to wipe away my tears, but they wouldn't stop. In the end I just pulled that quilt over me, rolled myself up in it. Still I felt the bird wings touching me.

Slowly I perceived that a voice was trying to tell me some- 16
thing. It was a bird cry, but I tell you, I began to understand some
of it. That happens sometimes. I know a lady who had a butterfly
sitting on her shoulder. That butterfly told her things. This made
her become a great medicine woman.

I heard a human voice too, strange and high-pitched, a voice 17
which could not come from an ordinary, living being. All at once
I was way up there with the birds. The hill with the vision pit
was way above everything. I could look down even on the stars,
and the moon was close to my left side. It seemed as though the
earth and the stars were moving below me. A voice said, "You are
sacrificing yourself here to be a medicine man. In time you will be
one. You will teach other medicine men. We are the fowl people,
the winged ones, the eagles and the owls. We are a nation and
you shall be our brother. You will never kill or harm any one of
us. You are going to understand us whenever you come to seek a
vision here on this hill. You will learn about herbs and roots, and
you will heal people. You will ask them for nothing in return. A
man's life is short. Make yours a worthy one."

I felt that these voices were good, and slowly my fear left me. 18
I had lost all sense of time. I did not know whether it was day or
night. I was asleep, yet wide awake. Then I saw a shape before
me. It rose from the darkness and the swirling fog which penetrated my earth hole. I saw that this was my great-grandfather,
Tahca Ushte, Lame Deer, old man chief of the Minneconjou. I
could see the blood dripping from my great-grandfather's chest
where a white soldier had shot him. I understood that my great-
grandfather wished me to take his name. This made me glad
beyond words.

We Sioux believe that there is something within us that 19
controls us, something like a second person almost. We call it
nagi, what other people might call soul, spirit or essence. One
can't see it, feel it or taste it, but that time on the hill—and only
that once—I knew it was there inside of me. Then I felt the
power surge through me like a flood. I cannot describe it, but
it filled all of me. Now I knew for sure that I would become
a *wicasa wakan*, a medicine man. Again I wept, this time with
happiness.

20   I didn't know how long I had been up there on that hill—one minute or a lifetime. I felt a hand on my shoulder gently shaking me. It was old man Chest, who had come for me. He told me that I had been in the vision pit four days and four nights and that it was time to come down. He would give me something to eat and water to drink and then I was to tell him everything that had happened to me during my *hanblechia*. He would interpret my visions for me. He told me that the vision pit had changed me in a way that I would not be able to understand at that time. He told me also that I was no longer a boy, that I was a man now. I was Lame Deer.

1972

Chronicles of Ice

Gretel Ehrlich

1 A trapped turbulence—as if wind had solidified. Then noise: timpani and a hard crack, the glacier's internal heat spilling out as an ice stream far below. I've come on a bus from El Calafate, Argentina, to visit the World Heritage glacier Perito Moreno, to see its bowls, lips, wombs, fenders, gravelly elbows, ponds, and ice streams, and to learn whatever lessons a glacier has to teach.

2   Some glaciers retreat, some surge, some do both, advancing and retreating even as the climate warms. Perito Moreno is 257 square kilometers across. It advances two meters a day at the center. From where I'm standing, I can look directly down on the glacier's snout. Two spires tilt forward, their lips touching. They meet head to head, but their bodies are hollow. Sun scours them as they twist toward light.

3   I walk down stairs to a platform that gives me a more intimate view. A row of ice teeth is bent sideways, indicating basal movement. Out of the corner of my eye I see something fall. A spectator gasps. An icy cheekbone crumbles. People come here

to see only the falling and failings, not the power it takes for the glacier to stay unified.

A glacier is not static. Snow falls, accretes, and settles until 4 finally its own weight presses it down. The flakes become deformed. They lose coherence and pattern, become something crystalline called *firn* which then turns to ice. As an ice mountain grows, its weight displaces its bulk and it spreads outward, filling whole valleys, hanging off mountains, running toward seas.

There are warm glaciers and cold glaciers, depending on 5 latitude and altitude. Cold glaciers don't slide easily; they're fixed and frozen to rock. They move like men on stilts—all awkwardness, broken bones of sheared rock. Internal deformation affects flow patterns; melting occurs faster at the margins than in the center. Warm glaciers have internal melt-streams at every level and torrents of water flow out from under the ice at the glacier's foot. The "sole" of the glacier is close to the melting point and slides easily over rock. Friction creates heat, heat increases sole-melt, slipperiness, and speed. The quasi-liquid surface that results is a disordered layer, a complicated boundary where heat and cold, melting and freezing, play off each other and are inextricably bound, the way madness and sanity, cacophony and stillness, are.

Because ice melts as it moves and moves as it melts, a glacier 6 is always undermining itself. It lives by giving itself away.

A glacier balances its gains and losses like a banker. 7 Accumulation has to exceed ablation for a glacier to grow. At the top, snow stacks up and does not melt. Midway down, the area of "mass balance" is where the profits and losses of snow can go either way. Surface melting can mean that water percolates down, refreezes, melts, and freezes again, creating a lens of ice. Below this region of equilibrium, ablation occurs. Profits are lost when the rate of melting exceeds the rate of accumulation. But a glacier will still advance if enough snow falls at the top and stays. . . .

A glacier is an archivist and historian. It registers every fluc- 8 tuation of weather. It saves everything no matter how small or big, including pollen, dust, heavy metals, bugs, and minerals. As snow becomes firn and then ice, oxygen bubbles are trapped in the glacier, providing samples of ancient atmosphere: carbon dioxide and methane. Records of temperatures and levels of atmospheric gases from before industrialization can be compared with those after—a mere 150 years. We can now see that the steady gains in greenhouse gases and air and water temperatures have occurred only since the rise of our smokestack and tailpipe society.

9   A glacier is time incarnate. When we lose a glacier—and we are losing most of them—we lose history, an eye into the past; we lose stories of how living beings evolved, how weather vacillated, why plants and animals died. The retreat and disappearance of glaciers—there are only 160,000 left—means we're burning libraries and damaging the planet, possibly beyond repair. Bit by bit glacier by glacier, rib by rib, we're living the Fall. . . .

10   Twenty thousand years ago temperatures plummeted and ice grew from the top of the world like vines and ground covers. Glaciers sprouted and surged, covering 10 million square miles—more than thirteen times what they cover now. As a result of their worldwide retreat and a global decrease in winter snow cover, the albedo effect—the ability of ice and snow to deflect heat back into space—is quickly diminishing. Snow and ice are the Earth's built-in air conditioner—crucial to the health of the planet. Without winter's white mantle, Earth will become a heat sponge. As heat escalates, all our sources of fresh water will disappear.

11   Already, warmer temperatures are causing meltwater to stream into oceans, changing temperature and salinity; sea ice and permafrost are thawing, pulsing methane into the air; seawater is expanding, causing floods and intrusions. Islands are disappearing, and vast human populations in places like Bangladesh are in grave danger. The high-mountain peoples of Peru, Chile, and Bolivia who depend on meltwater from snowpack are at risk; the Inuit cultures in Alaska, Arctic Canada, Siberia, and Greenland that depend on ice for transportation, and live on a diet of marine mammals, could disappear.

12   In temperate climates everywhere, the early onset of spring and the late arrival of winter are creating ecosystem pandemonium. It is not unreasonable to think that a whole season can become extinct, at least for a time. Winter might last only one

day—minor punctuation in a long sentence of heat. Mirages rising from shimmering heat waves would be the only storms. . . .

The bus takes me back to town. I get out near a grove of 13 trees where loose horses wander. It's good to be in a place where there are such freedoms. All over the world the life of rocks, ice, mountains, snow, oceans, islands, albatross, sooty gulls, whales, crabs, limpets, and guanaco once flowed up into the bodies of the people who lived in small hunting groups and villages, and out came killer-whale prayers, condor chants, crab feasts, and guanaco songs. Life went where there was food. Food occurred in places of great beauty, and the act of living directly fueled people's movements, thoughts, and lives.

Everything spoke. Everything made a sound—birds, ghosts, 14 animals, oceans, bogs, rocks, humans, trees, flowers, and rivers— and when they passed each other a third sound occurred. That's why weather, mountains, and each passing season were so noisy. Song and dance, sex and gratitude, were the season-sensitive ceremonies linking the human psyche to the larger, wild, weather-ridden world.

Now, the enterprise we human beings in the "developed 15 world" have engaged in is almost too darkly insane to contemplate. Our bent has been to "improve" on nature and local culture, which has meant that we've reduced the parallel worlds of spirit, imagination, and daily life to a single secularized pile. The process of empire-building is a kind of denigration. Nothing that's not nuts and bolts and money-making is allowed in. Our can-do optimism and our head-in-the-sand approach to economics—one that takes only profit, and not the biological health of our planet, into account—has left us one-sided.

When did we begin thinking that weather was something to 16 be rescued from? Why did we trade in our ceremonial lives for the workplace? Is this a natural progression or a hiccup in human civilization that we'll soon renounce?

I eat at a rustic bar with other travelers. It's late when night 17 comes, maybe 10:30. In the darkness, Perito Moreno is still calving and moving, grabbing snowflakes, stirring weather, spitting out ice water, and it makes me smile.

Desperation Writing

Peter Elbow

1 I know I am not alone in my recurring twinges of panic that I won't be able to write something when I need to, I won't be able to produce coherent speech or thought. And that lingering doubt is a great hindrance to writing. It's a constant fog or static that clouds the mind. I never got out of its clutches till I discovered that it was possible to write something–not something great or pleasing but at least something usable, workable–when my mind is out of commission. The trick is that you have to do all your cooking out on the table: your mind is incapable of doing any inside. It means using symbols and pieces of paper not as a crutch but as a wheelchair.

2   The first thing is to admit your condition: because of some mood or event or whatever, your mind is incapable of anything that could be called thought. It can put out a babbling kind of speech utterance, it can put a simple feeling, perception or sort-of-thought into understandable (though terrible) words. But it is incapable of considering anything in relation to anything else. The moment you try to hold that thought or feeling up against some other to see the relationship, you simply lose the picture– you get nothing but buzzing lines or waving colors.

3   So admit this. Avoid anything more than one feeling, perception, or thought. Simply write as much as possible. Try simply to steer your mind in the direction or general vicinity of the thing you are trying to write about and start writing and keep writing.

4   Just write and keep writing. (Probably best to write on only one side of the paper in case you should want to cut parts out with scissors–but you probably won't.) Just write and keep writing. It will probably come in waves. After a flurry, stop and take a brief rest. But don't stop too long. Don't think about what you are writing or what you have written or else you will overload the circuit again. Keep writing as though you are drugged or drunk. Keep doing this till you feel you have a lot of material that might be useful; or, if necessary, till you can't stand it any more–even if you doubt that there's anything useful there.

Then take a pad of little pieces of paper-or perhaps 3 x 5 cards- 5 and simply start at the beginning of what you were writing, and as you read over what you wrote, every time you come to any thought, feeling, perception, or image that could be gathered up into one sentence or one assertion, do so and write it by itself on a little sheet of paper. In short, you are trying to turn, say, ten or twenty pages of wandering mush into twenty or thirty hard little crab apples. Sometimes there won't be many on a page. But if it seems to you that there are none on a page, you are making a serious error–the same, foolish, worthless ideas for no ideas at all. Your job is not to pick out good ideas but to pick out ideas. As long as you were conscious, your words will be full of things that could be called feelings, utterances, ideas–things that can be squeezed into one simple sentence. This is your job. Don't ask for too much.

After you have done this, take those little slips or cards, 6 read through them a number of times–not struggling with them, simply wandering and mulling through them; perhaps shifting them around and looking through them in various sequences. In a sense these are cards you are playing solitaire with, and the rules of this particular game permit shuffling the unused pile.

The goal of this procedure with the cards is to get them to dis- 7 tribute themselves in two or three or ten or fifteen different piles on your desk. You can get them to do this almost by themselves if you simply keep reading through them in different orders; certain cards will begin to feel like they go with other cards. I emphasize this passive, thoughtless mode because I want to talk about desperation writing in its pure state. In practice, almost invariably at some point in the procedure, your sanity begins to return. It is often at this point. You actually are moved to have thoughts or–and the difference between active and passive is crucial here– to *exert* thought; to hold two cards together and *build* or *assert* a relationship. It is a matter of bringing energy to bear.

So you may start to be able to do something active with 8 these cards, and begin actually to think. But if not, just allow the cards to find their own piles with each other by feel, by drift, by intuition, by mindlessness.

You have now engaged in the two main activities that will 9 permit you to get something cooked out on the table rather than in your brain: writing out into messy words, summing up into a single assertions, and even sensing relationships between assertions. You can simply continue to deploy these two activities.

10   If, for example, after the first round of writing, assertion-making, and pile-making, your piles feel as though they are useful and satisfactory for what you are writing–paragraphs or sections or trains of thought–then you can carry on from there. See if you can gather each pile up into a single assertion. When you can, then put the subsidiary assertions of that pile into their best order to fit with that single unifying one. If you *can't* get the pile into one assertion, then take the pile as the basis for doing some more writing out into words. In the course of this writing, you may produce for yourself the single unifying assertion you were looking for; or you may have to go through the cycle of turning the writing into assertions and piles and so forth. Perhaps more than once. The pile may turn out to want to be two or more piles itself; or it may want to become part of a pile you already have. This is natural. This kind of meshing into one configuration, then coming apart, then coming together and meshing into a different configuration–this is growing and cooking. It makes a terrible mess, but if you can't do it in your head, you have to put up with a cluttered desk and a lot of confusion.

11   If, on the other hand, all that writing didn't have useful material in it, it means that your writing wasn't loose, drifting, quirky, jerky, associative enough. This time try especially to let things simply remind you of things that are seemingly crazy or unrelated. Follow these old associations. Make as many metaphors as you can–be as nutty as possible–and explore the metaphors themselves–open them out. You may have all your energy tied up in some area of your experience that you are leaving out. Don't refrain from writing about whatever else is on your mind: how you feel at the moment, what you are losing your mind over, randomness that intrudes itself on your consciousness, the pattern on the wallpaper, what those people you see out the window have on their minds–though keep coming back to the wateveritis you are supposed to be writing about. Treat it, in short, like ten-minute writing exercises. Your best perceptions and thoughts are always going to be tied up in whatever is really occupying you,

and that is also where your energy is. You may end up writing a love poem–or a hate poem–in one of those little piles while the other piles will finally turn into a lab report on data processing or whatever you have to write about. But you couldn't, in your present state of having your head shot off, have written that report without also writing the poem. And the report will have some of the juice of the poem in it and vice versa.

Chapter

Definition

What Is Poverty?

Jo Goodwin Parker

1   You ask me what is poverty? Listen to me. Here I am, dirty, smelly, and with no "proper" underwear on and with the stench of my rotting teeth near you. I will tell you. Listen to me. Listen without pity. I cannot use your pity. Listen with understanding. Put yourself in my dirty, worn out, ill-fitting shoes, and hear me.

2   Poverty is getting up every morning from a dirt- and illness-stained mattress. The sheets have long since been used for diapers. Poverty is living in a smell that never leaves. This is a smell of urine, sour milk, and spoiling food sometimes joined with the strong smell of long-cooked onions. Onions are cheap. If you have smelled this smell, you did not know how it came. It is the smell of the outdoor privy. It is the smell of young children who cannot walk the long dark way in the night. It is the smell of the mattresses where years of "accidents" have happened. It is the smell of the milk which has gone sour because the refrigerator long has not worked, and it costs money to get it fixed. It is the smell of rotting garbage. I could bury it, but where is the shovel? Shovels cost money.

3   Poverty is being tired. I have always been tired. They told me at the hospital when the last baby came that I had chronic anemia caused from poor diet, a bad case of worms, and that I needed a corrective operation. I listened politely—the poor are always polite. The poor always listen. They don't say that there is no money for iron pills, or better food, or worm medicine. The

idea of an operation is frightening and costs so much that, if I had dared, I would have laughed. Who takes care of my children? Recovery from an operation takes a long time. I have three children. When I left them with "Granny" the last time I had a job, I came home to find the baby covered with fly specks, and a diaper that had not been changed since I left. When the dried diaper came off, bits of my baby's flesh came with it. My other child was playing with a sharp bit of broken glass, and my oldest was playing alone at the edge of a lake. I made twenty-two dollars a week, and a good nursery school costs twenty dollars a week for three children. I quit my job.

Poverty is dirt. You can say in your clean clothes coming 4 from your clean house, "Anybody can be clean." Let me explain about housekeeping with no money. For breakfast I give my children grits with no oleo or cornbread without eggs and oleo. This does not use up many dishes. What dishes there are, I wash in cold water and with no soap. Even the cheapest soap has to be saved for the baby's diapers. Look at my hands, so cracked and red. Once I saved for two months to buy a jar of Vaseline for my hands and the baby's diaper rash. When I had saved enough, I went to buy it and the price had gone up two cents. The baby and I suffered on. I have to decide every day if I can bear to put my cracked sore hands into the cold water and strong soap. But you ask, why not hot water? Fuel costs money. If you have a wood fire it costs money. If you burn electricity, it costs money. Hot water is a luxury. I do not have luxuries. I know you will be surprised when I tell you how young I am. I look so much older. My back has been bent over the wash tubs every day for so long. I cannot remember when I ever did anything else. Every night I wash every stitch my school age child has on and just hope her clothes will be dry by morning.

Poverty is staying up all night on cold nights to watch the fire 5 knowing one spark on the newspaper covering the walls means your sleeping child dies in flames. In summer, poverty is watching gnats and flies devour your baby's tears when he cries. The screens are torn and you pay so little rent you know they will never be fixed. Poverty means insects in your food, in your nose, in your eyes, and crawling over you when you sleep. Poverty is hoping it never rains because diapers won't dry when it rains and soon you are using newspapers. Poverty is seeing your children forever with runny noses. Paper handkerchiefs cost money and all your rags you need for other things. Even more costly are antihistamines. Poverty is cooking without food and cleaning without soap.

6   Poverty is asking for help. Have you ever had to ask for help, knowing your children will suffer unless you get it? Think about asking for a loan from a relative, if this is the only way you can imagine asking for help. I will tell you how it feels. You find out where the office is that you are supposed to visit. You circle that block four or five times. Thinking of your children, you go in. Everyone is very busy. Finally, someone comes out and you tell her that you need help. That never is the person you need to see. You go see another person, and after spilling the whole shame of your poverty all over the desk between you, you find that this isn't the right office after all—you must repeat the whole process, and it never is any easier at the next place.

7   You have asked for help, and after all it has a cost. You are again told to wait. You are told why, but you don't really hear because of the red cloud of shame and the rising cloud of despair.

8   Poverty is remembering. It is remembering quitting school in junior high because "nice" children had been so cruel about my clothes and my smell. The attendance officer came. My mother told him I was pregnant. I wasn't, but she thought that I could get a job and help out. I had jobs off and on, but never long enough to learn anything. Mostly I remember being married. I was so young then. I am still young. For a time, we had all the things you have. There was a little house in another town, with hot water and everything. Then my husband lost his job. There was unemployment insurance for a while and what few jobs I could get. Soon, all our nice things were repossessed and we moved back here. I was pregnant then. This house didn't look so bad when we first moved in. Every week it gets worse. Nothing is ever fixed. We now had no money. There were a few odd jobs for my husband, but everything went for food then, as it does now. I don't know how we lived through three years and three babies, but we did. I'll tell you something, after the last baby I destroyed my marriage. It had been a good one, but could you keep on bringing

children in this dirt? Did you ever think how much it costs for any kind of birth control? I knew my husband was leaving the day he left, but there were no goodbyes between us. I hope he has been able to climb out of this mess somewhere. He never could hope with us to drag him down.

That's when I asked for help. When I got it, you know how 9 much it was? It was, and is, seventy-eight dollars a month for the four of us; that is all I ever can get. Now you know why there is no soap, no needles and thread, no hot water, no aspirin, no worm medicine, no hand cream, no shampoo. None of these things forever and ever and ever. So that you can see clearly, I pay twenty dollars a month rent, and most of the rest goes for food. For grits and cornmeal, and rice and milk and beans. I try my best to use only the minimum electricity. If I use more, there is that much less for food.

Poverty is looking into a black future. Your children won't 10 play with my boys. They will turn to other boys who steal to get what they want. I can already see them behind the bars of their prison instead of behind the bars of my poverty. Or they will turn to the freedom of alcohol or drugs, and find themselves enslaved. And my daughter? At best, there is for her a life like mine.

But you say to me, there are schools. Yes, there are schools. 11 My children have no extra books, no magazines, no extra pencils, or crayons, or paper and most important of all, they do not have health. They have worms, they have infections, they have pink-eye all summer. They do not sleep well on the floor, or with me in my one bed. They do not suffer from hunger, my seventy-eight dollars keeps us alive, but they do suffer from malnutrition. Oh yes, I do remember what I was taught about health in school. It doesn't do much good. In some places there is a surplus commodities program. Not here. The county said it costs too much. There is a school lunch program. But I have two children who will already be damaged by the time they get to school.

But, you say to me, there are health clinics. Yes, there are 12 health clinics and they are in the towns. I live out here eight miles from town. I can walk that far (even if it is sixteen miles both ways), but can my little children? My neighbor will take me when he goes; but he expects to get paid, *one way or another*. I bet you know my neighbor. He is that large man who spends his time at the gas station, the barbershop, and the corner store complaining about the government spending money on the immoral mothers of illegitimate children.

13   Poverty is an acid that drips on pride until all pride is worn away. Poverty is a chisel that chips on honor until honor is worn away. Some of you say that you would do *something* in my situation, and maybe you would, for the first week or the first month, but for year after year after year?

14   Even the poor can dream. A dream of a time when there is money. Money for the right kinds of food, for worm medicine, for iron pills, for toothbrushes, for hand cream, for a hammer and nails and a bit of screening, for a shovel, for a bit of paint, for some sheeting, for needles and thread. Money to pay *in money* for a trip to town. And, oh, money for hot water and money for soap. A dream of when asking for help does not eat away the last bit of pride. When the office you visit is as nice as the offices of other governmental agencies, when there are enough workers to help you quickly, when workers do not quit in defeat and despair. When you have to tell your story to only one person, and that person can send you for other help and you don't have to prove your poverty over and over and over again.

15   I have come out of my despair to tell you this. Remember I did not come from another place or another time. Others like me are all around you. Look at us with an angry heart, anger that will help you help me. Anger that will let you tell of me. The poor are always silent. Can you be silent too?

1971

The Company Man

Ellen Goodman

1 He worked himself to death, finally and precisely, at 3:00 A.M. Sunday morning.

The obituary didn't say that, of course. It said that he died of a ₂ coronary thrombosis—I think that was it—but everyone among his friends and acquaintances knew it instantly. He was a perfect Type A, a workaholic, a classic, they said to each other and shook their heads—and thought for five or ten minutes about the way they lived.

This man who worked himself to death finally and precisely at ₃ 3:00 A.M. Sunday morning—on his day off—was fifty-one years old and a vice-president. He was, however, one of six vice-presidents, and one of three who might conceivably—if the president died or retired soon enough—have moved to the top spot. Phil knew that.

He worked six days a week, five of them until eight or nine ₄ at night, during a time when his own company had begun the four-day week for everyone but the executives. He worked like the Important People. He had no outside "extracurricular interests," unless, of course, you think about a monthly golf game that way. To Phil, it was work. He always ate egg salad sandwiches at his desk. He was, of course, overweight, by 20 or 25 pounds. He thought it was okay, though, because he didn't smoke.

On Saturdays, Phil wore a sports jacket to the office instead ₅ of a suit, because it was the weekend.

He had a lot of people working for him, maybe sixty, and ₆ most of them liked him most of the time. Three of them will be seriously considered for his job. The obituary didn't mention that.

But it did list his "survivors" quite accurately. He is survived ₇ by his wife, Helen, forty-eight years old, a good woman of no particular marketable skills, who worked in an office before marrying and mothering. She had, according to her daughter, given up trying to compete with his work years ago, when the children were small. A company friend said, "I know how much you will miss him." And she answered, "I already have."

"Missing him all these years," she must have given up part ₈ of herself which had cared too much for the man. She would be "well taken care of."

His "dearly beloved" eldest of the "dearly beloved" children ₉ is a hard-working executive in a manufacturing firm down South. In the day and a half before the funeral, he went around the neighborhood researching his father, asking the neighbors what he was like. They were embarrassed.

10   His second child is a girl, who is twenty-four and newly married. She lives near her mother and they are close, but whenever
she was alone with her father, in a car driving somewhere, they
had nothing to say to each other.

11   The youngest is twenty, a boy, a high-school graduate who
has spent the last couple of years, like a lot of his friends, doing
enough odd jobs to stay in grass and food. He was the one who
tried to grab at his father, and tried to mean enough to him to
keep the man at home. He was his father's favorite. Over the last
two years, Phil stayed up nights worrying about the boy.

12   The boy once said, "My father and I only board here." At the
funeral, the sixty-year-old company president told the forty-eight-
year-old widow that the fifty-one-year-old deceased had meant
much to the company and would be missed and would be hard
to replace. The widow didn't look him in the eye. She was afraid
he would read her bitterness and, after all, she would need him to
straighten out the finances—the stock options and all that.

13   Phil was overweight and nervous and worked too hard. If he
wasn't at the office, he was worried about it. Phil was a Type A, a
heart-attack natural. You could have picked him out in a minute
from a lineup.

14   So when he finally worked himself to death, at precisely
3:00 A.M. Sunday morning, no one was really surprised.

15   By 5:00 P.M. the afternoon of the funeral, the company president had begun, discreetly of course, with care and taste, to make
inquiries about his replacement. One of three men. He asked
around: "Who's been working the hardest?"

1981

Meanings of a Word

Gloria Naylor

1 Language is the subject. It is the written form with which I've
managed to keep the wolf away from the door and, in diaries,
to keep my sanity. In spite of this, I consider the written word

inferior to the spoken, and much of the frustration experienced by novelists is the awareness that whatever we manage to capture in even the most transcendent passages falls far short of the richness of life. Dialogue achieves its power in the dynamics of a fleeting moment of sight, sound, smell and touch.

I'm not going to enter the debate here about whether it is 2 language that shapes reality or vice versa. That battle is doomed to be waged whenever we seek intermittent reprieve from the chicken and egg dispute. I will simply take the position that the spoken word, like the written word, amounts to a nonsensical arrangement of sounds or letters without a consensus that assigns "meaning." And building from the meanings of what we hear, we order reality. Words themselves are innocuous; it is the consensus that gives them true power.

I remember the first time I heard the word nigger. In my third- 3 grade class, our math tests were being passed down the rows, and as I handed the papers to a little boy in back of me, I remarked that once again he had received a much lower mark than I did. He snatched his test from me and spit out that word. Had he called me a nymphomaniac or a necrophiliac, I couldn't have been more puzzled. I didn't know what a nigger was, but I knew that whatever it meant, it was something he shouldn't have called me. This was verified when I raised my hand, and in a loud voice repeated what he had said and watched the teacher scold him for using a "bad" word. I was later to go home and ask the inevitable question that every black parent must face—"Mommy, what does 'nigger' mean?"

And what exactly did it mean? Thinking back, I realize that 4 this could not have been the first time the word was used in my presence. I was part of a large extended family that had migrated from the rural South after World War II and formed a close-knit network that gravitated around my maternal grandparents. Their ground-floor apartment in one of the buildings they owned in Harlem was a weekend mecca for my immediate family, along with countless aunts, uncles and cousins who brought along assorted friends. It was a bustling and open house with assorted neighbors and tenants popping in and out to exchange bits of gossip, pick up an old quarrel or referee the ongoing checkers game in which my grandmother cheated shamelessly. They were all there to let down their hair and put up their feet after a week of labor in the factories, laundries and shipyards of New York.

5   Amid the clamor, which could reach deafening proportions—two or three conversations going on simultaneously, punctuated by the sound of a baby's crying somewhere in the back rooms or out on the street—there was still a rigid set of rules about what was said and how. Older children were sent out of the living room when it was time to get into the juicy details about "you-know-who" up on the third floor who had gone and gotten herself "p-r-e-g-n-a-n-t!" But my parents, knowing that I could spell well beyond my years, always demanded that I follow the others out to play. Beyond sexual misconduct and death, everything else was considered harmless for our young ears. And so among the anecdotes of the triumphs and disappointments in the various workings of their lives, the word nigger was used in my presence, but it was set within contexts and inflections that caused it to register in my mind as something else.

6   In the singular, the word was always applied to a man who had distinguished himself in some situation that brought their approval for his strength, intelligence or drive:

7   "Did Johnny really do that?"

8   "I'm telling you, that nigger pulled in $6,000 of overtime last year. Said he got enough for a down payment on a house."

9   When used with a possessive adjective by a woman—"my nigger"—it became a term of endearment for husband or boyfriend. But it could be more than just a term applied to a man. In their mouths it became the pure essence of manhood—a disembodied force that channeled their past history of struggle and present survival against the odds into a victorious statement of being: "Yeah, that old foreman found out quick enough—you don't mess with a nigger."

10   In the plural, it became a description of some group within the community that had overstepped the bounds of decency as my family defined it: Parents who neglected their children, a drunken couple who fought in public, people who simply refused to look for work, those with excessively dirty mouths or unkempt households were all "trifling niggers." This particular circle could forgive hard times, unemployment, the occasional

bout of depression—they had gone through all of that them-selves—but the unforgivable sin was lack of self-respect.

A woman could never be a "nigger" in the singular, with its 11 connotation of confirming worth. The noun "girl" was its closest equivalent in that sense, but only when used in direct address and regardless of the gender doing the addressing. "Girl" was a token of respect for a woman. The one-syllable word was drawn out to sound like three in recognition of the extra ounce of wit, nerve or daring that the woman had shown in the situation under discussion.

"G-i-r-l, stop. You mean you said that to his face?" 12

But if the word was used in a third-person reference or 13 shortened so that it almost snapped out of the mouth, it always involved some element of communal disapproval. And age became an important factor in these exchanges. It was only between individuals of the same generation, or from an older person to a younger (but never the other way around), that "girl" would be considered a compliment.

I don't agree with the argument that use of the word nigger 14 at this social stratum of the black community was an internaliza-tion of racism. The dynamics were the exact opposite: the people in my grandmother's living room took a word that whites used to signify worthlessness or degradation and rendered it impotent. Gathering there together, they transformed "nigger" to signify the varied and complex human beings they knew themselves to be. If the word was to disappear totally from the mouths of even the most racist of white society, no one in that room was naïve enough to believe it would disappear from white minds. Meeting the word head on, they proved it had absolutely nothing to do with the way they were determined to live their lives.

So there must have been dozens of times that the word "nig- 15 ger" was spoken in front of me before I reached the third grade. But I didn't "hear" it until it was said by a small pair of lips that had already learned it could be a way to humiliate me. That was the word I went home and asked my mother about. And since she knew that I had to grow up in America, she took me in her lap and explained.

1986

The Green-Eyed Monster: Envy Is Nothing to Be Jealous Of

Joseph Epstein

1   Of the seven deadly sins, only envy is no fun at all. Sloth may not seem that enjoyable, nor anger either, but giving way to deep laziness has its pleasures, and the expression of anger entails a release that is not without its small delights. In recompense, envy may be the subtlest—perhaps I should say the most insidious—of the seven deadly sins. Surely it is the one that people are least likely to want to own up to, for to do so is to admit that one is probably ungenerous, mean, small-hearted. It may also be the most endemic. Apart from Socrates, Jesus, Marcus Aurelius, Saint Francis, Mother Teresa, and only a few others, at one time or another, we have all felt flashes of envy, even if in varying intensities, from its minor pricks to its deep, soul-destroying, lacerating stabs. So widespread is it—a word for envy, I have read, exists in all known languages—that one is ready to believe it is the sin for which the best argument can be made that it is part of human nature.

2   In politics, envy, or at any rate the hope of eliminating it, is said to be the reigning principle of socialism, as greed is said to be that of capitalism (though modern capitalist advertising is about few things more than the regular stimulation of envy). On the international scene, many if not most wars have been fought because of one nation's envy of another's territory and all they derive from it, or out of jealously guarded riches that a nation feels are endangered by those less rich who are likely to be envious of their superior position. In this connection, it is difficult not to feel that, at least in part, much of the anti-American feeling that arose after September 11, 2001, had envy, some of it fairly rancorous, at its heart. In the magazine *Granta*, the Indian writer Ramachandra Guha wrote that "historically, anti-Americanism in India was shaped by an aesthetic distaste for America's greatest gift—the making of money." But can "aesthetic distaste" here be any more than a not-very-well-disguised code word for envy?

Is envy a "feeling," an "emotion," a "sin," a "temperamental 3 disposition," or a "world-view"? Might it also be a Rorschach test: Tell what you envy, and you reveal a great deal about yourself. It can be all of these things—and more. No one would doubt that, whatever else it is, envy is certainly a charged, indeed a supercharged, word: One of the few words left in the English language that retains the power to scandalize. Most of us could still sleep decently if accused of any of the other six deadly sins; but to be accused of envy would be seriously distressing, so clearly does such an accusation go directly to character. The other deadly sins, though all have the disapproval of religion, do not so thoroughly, so deeply demean, diminish, and disqualify a person. Not the least of its stigmata is the pettiness implicit in envy.

The *Webster's* definition of the word won't quite do: "(1) 4 *Obs*. malice; (2) painful or resentful awareness of the advantage enjoyed by another joined with a desire to possess the same advantage." The *Oxford English Dictionary* is rather better: It defines envy first as "malignant or hostile feeling; ill-will, malice, enmity," and then as "active evil, harm, mischief," both definitions accounted *Obscure*. But the great *OED* only gets down to serious business in its third definition, where it defines envy as "the feeling of mortification and ill-will occasioned by the contemplation of superior advantages possessed by another," in which usage the word envy first pops up around 1500. It adds a fourth definition, one in which the word is used without "notions of malevolence," and has to do with the (a) "desire to equal another in achievement, or excellence; emulation," and (b) speaks to "a longing for the advantages enjoyed by another person." Aristotle, in *The Rhetoric*, writes of emulation as good envy, or envy ending in admiration and thus in the attempt to imitate the qualities one began by envying. Yet it must be added that envy doesn't generally work this way. Little is good about envy, except shaking it off, which, as any of us who have felt it deeply knows, is not so easily done.

Both the *OED* and *Webster's* definitions are inattentive to 5 the crucial distinction between envy and jealousy. Most people, failing to pick up the useful distinction, mistakenly use the two words interchangeably. I suspect people did not always do so.

H. W. Fowler, in his splendid *Modern English Usage* of 1926, carries no entry on either word, suggesting that formerly there was no confusion. Bryan A. Garner, in his 1998 *Dictionary of Modern American Usage*, says that "the careful writer distinguishes between these terms," but does not himself do so sufficiently. He writes that *"jealousy* is properly restricted to contexts involving affairs of the heart, *envy* is used more broadly of resentful contemplation of a more fortunate person."

6   With the deep pedantic delight one takes in trumping a recognized usage expert, it pleases me to say, "Not quite so." The real distinction is that *one is jealous of what one has, envious of what other people have.* Jealousy is not always pejorative; one can after all be jealous of one's dignity, civil rights, honor. Envy, except when used in the emulative sense mentioned by Aristotle, is always pejorative. If jealousy is, in cliché parlance, spoken of as the "green-eyed monster," envy is cross-, squinty-, and blearily red-eyed. Never, to put it very gently, a handsome or good thing, envy. Although between jealousy and envy, jealousy is often the more intensely felt of the two, it can also be the more realistic: One is, after all, sometimes correct to feel jealousy. And not all jealousy plays the familiar role of sexual jealousy. One may be jealous—again, rightly—of one's reputation, integrity, and other good things. One is almost never right to feel envy: To be envious is to be, *ipso facto*, wrong.

7   Apart from emulative envy, the only aspect of envy that does not seem to me pejorative is a form of envy I have myself felt, as I suspect have others who are reading this article: the envy that I think of as faith envy. This is the envy one feels for those who have the true and deep and intelligent religious faith that sees them through the darkest of crises, death among them. If one is oneself without faith and wishes to feel this emotion, I cannot recommend a better place to find it than in the letters of Flannery O'Connor. There one will discover a woman still in her thirties, who, after coming into her radiant talent, knows she is going to die well before her time and, fortified by her Catholicism, faces her end without voicing complaint or fear. I not long ago heard, in Vienna, what seemed to me a perfect rendering of Beethoven's *Ninth Symphony*, and was hugely moved by it, but how much

more would I have been moved, I could not help wonder, if I were in a state of full religious belief, since the *Ninth Symphony* seems to me in many ways a religious work. Faith envy is envy, alas, about which one can do nothing but quietly harbor it.

Envy must also be distinguished from general yearning. One sees people at great social ease and wishes to be more like them; or feels keenly how good it would be once more to be young; or longs to be wealthier; or pines to be taller, thinner, more muscular, less awkward, more beautiful generally. All this is yearning. Envy is never general, but always very particular—at least envy of the kind one feels strongly.

The envious tend to be injustice collectors. "Envy, among other ingredients, has a love of justice in it," William Hazlitt wrote. "We are more angry at undeserved than at deserved good fortune." Something to it, but, my sense is, not all that much. Much more often than not, envy expresses feelings more personal than the love of justice. In another useful distinction, Kierkegaard in *The Sickness Unto Death* wrote that "admiration is happy self-surrender; envy is unhappy self-satisfaction." Envy asks one leading question: What about me? Why does he or she have beauty, talent, wealth, power, the world's love, and other gifts, or at any rate a larger share of them than I? Why not me? Dorothy Sayers, in a little book on the seven deadly sins, writes: "Envy is the great leveler: if it cannot level things up, it will level them down…. At its best, envy is a climber and a snob; at its worst it is a destroyer—rather than have anyone happier than itself, it will see us all miserable together." A self-poisoning of the mind, envy is usually less about what one lacks than about what other people have. A strong element of the begrudging resides in envy, thus making the envious, as Immanuel Kant remarked in *The Metaphysics of Morals*, "intent on the destruction of the happiness of others."

One might call someone or something—another's family life, health, good fortune—"enviable" without intending rancor. In the same way, one might say, "I envy you your two-month holiday in the south of France," without, in one's mind, plotting how to do the person out of it. Or one might say, "I don't envy him the responsibilities of his job," by which one merely means that one is pleased not to have another's worries. There probably ought to be a word falling between envy and admiration, as there ought to be a word that falls between talent and genius. Yet there isn't. The language is inept. Nor ought envy to be confused with open conflict. Someone has something that one feels one wants—customers, a high ranking or rating, government office, a position of power—and one contends for it, more or less aggressively, but out in the open. The openness changes the nature of the game. Envy is almost never out in the open; it is secretive, plotting, behind the scenes. Helmut Schoeck, who in *Envy: A Theory of Social Behavior* has written the most comprehensive book on the subject, notes that it "is a silent, secretive process and not always verifiable." Envy, to qualify as envy, has to have a strong touch—sometimes more than a touch—of malice behind it. Malice that cannot speak its name, cold-blooded but secret hostility, impotent desire, hidden rancor, and spite all cluster at the center of envy. La Rochefoucauld opened the subject of envy nicely with a silver stiletto, when he wrote: "In the misfortune of our best friends, we always find something that is not displeasing to us." Yes, really not displeasing at all. Dear old envy.

2003

Pride

Dagoberto Gilb

1   It's almost time to close at the northwest corner of Altura and Copia in El Paso. That means it is so dark that it is as restful as the deepest un-remembering sleep, dark as the empty space around this spinning planet, as a black star. Headlights that beam a little cross-eyed from a fatso American car are feeling around the asphalt road up the hill toward the Good Time Store, its yellow

plastic smiley face bright like a sugary suck candy. The loose muffler holds only half the misfires, and, dry springs squeaking, the automobile curves slowly into the establishment's lot, swerving to avoid the new self-serve gas pump island. Behind it, across the street, a Texas flag—out too late this and all the nights—pops and slaps in a summer wind that finally is cool.

A good man, gray on the edges, an assistant manager in a 2 brown starched and ironed uniform, is washing the glass windows of the store, lit up by as many watts as Venus, with a roll of paper towels and the blue liquid from a spray bottle. Good night, m'ijo! he tells a young boy coming out after playing the video game, a Grande Guzzler the size of a wastebasket balanced in one hand, an open bag of Flaming Hot Cheetos, its red dye already smearing his mouth and the hand not carrying the weight of the soda, his white T-shirt, its short sleeves reaching halfway down his wrists, the whole XXL of it billowing and puffing in the outdoor gust.

A plump young woman steps out of that car. She's wearing a 3 party dress, wide scoops out of the top, front, and back, its hemline way above the knees.

Did you get a water pump? the assistant manager asks her. 4 Are you going to make it to Horizon City? He's still washing the glass of the storefront, his hand sweeping in small hard circles.

The young woman is patient and calm like a loving mother. I 5 don't know yet, she tells him as she stops close to him, thinking. I guess I should make a call, she says, and her thick-soled shoes, the latest fashion, slap against her heels to one of the pay phones at the front of the store.

Pride is working a job like it's as important as art or war, is 6 the happiness of a new high score on a video arcade game, of a pretty new black dress and shoes. Pride is the deaf and blind confidence of the good people who are too poor but don't notice.

A son is a long time sitting on the front porch where he 7 played all those years with the squirmy dog who still licks his face, both puppies then, even before he played on the winning teams of Little League baseball and City League basketball. They sprint down the sidewalk and across streets, side by side, until they stop to rest on the park grass, where a red ant, or a spider, bites the son's calf. It swells, but he no longer thinks to complain to his mom about it—he's too old now—when he comes home. He gets ready, putting on the shirt and pants his mom would have ironed but he wanted to iron himself. He takes the ride with his best friend since first grade. The hundreds of moms and dads, abuelos y abuelitas, the tios and primos, baby brothers and older married sisters, all are at the Special Events Center for the son's high school graduation. His dad is a man bigger than most, and when he walks in his dress eel-skin boots down the cement stairs to get as close to the hardwood basketball-court floor and ceremony to see—m'ijo!—he feels an embarrassing sob bursting from his eyes and mouth. He holds it back, and with his hands, hides the tears that do escape, wipes them with his fingers, because the chavalitos in his aisle are playing and laughing and they are so small and he is so big next to them. And when his son walks to the stage to get his high school diploma and his dad wants to scream his name, he hears how many others, from the floor in caps and gowns and from around the arena, are already screaming it—could be any name, it could be any son's or daughter's: Alex! Vanessa! Carlos! Veronica! Ricky! Tony! Estella! Isa!—and sees his boy waving back to all of them.

8   Pride hears gritty dirt blowing against an agave whose stiff fertile stalk, so tall, will not bend—the love of land, rugged like the people who live on it. Pride sees the sunlight on the Franklin Mountains in the first light of morning and listens to a neighbor's gallo—the love of culture and history. Pride smells a sweet, musky drizzle of rain and eats huevos con chile in corn tortillas heated on a cast-iron pan—the love of heritage.

9   Pride is the fearless reaction to disrespect and disregard. It is knowing the future will prove that wrong.

10   Seeing the beauty: Look out there from a height of the mountain and on the north and south of the Rio Grande, to the far away and close, the so many miles more of fuzz on the wide horizon, knowing how many years the people have passed and have stayed, the ancestors, the ones who have medaled, limped back on crutches or died or were heroes from wars in the Pacific or Europe or Korea or Vietnam or the Persian Gulf, the ones who have raised the fist and dared to defy, the ones who wash

the clothes and cook and serve the meals, who stitch the factory shoes and the factory slacks, who assemble and sort, the ones who laugh and the ones who weep, the ones who care, the ones who want more, the ones who try, the ones who love, those ones with shameless courage and hardened wisdom, and the old ones still so alive, holding their grandchildren, and the young ones in their glowing prime, strong and gorgeous, holding each other, the ones who will be born from them. The desert land is rock-dry and ungreen. It is brown. Brown like the skin is brown. Beautiful brown.

"Blaxicans" and Other Reinvented Americans

Richard Rodriguez

There is something unsettling about immigrants because . . . well, because they chatter incomprehensibly, and they get in everyone's way. Immigrants seem to be bent on undoing America. Just when Americans think we know who we are—we are Protestants, culled from Western Europe, are we not? —then new immigrants appear from Southern Europe or from Eastern Europe. We—we who are already here—we don't know exactly what the latest comers will mean to our community. How will they fit in with us? Thus we—we who were here first—we begin to question our own identity. 1

After a generation or two, the grandchildren or the great-grandchildren of immigrants to the United States and the grandchildren of those who tried to keep immigrants out of the United States will romanticize the immigrant, will begin to see the immigrant as the figure who teaches us most about what it means to be an American. The immigrant, in mythic terms, travels from the outermost rind of America to the very center of American mythology. None of this, of course, can we admit to 2 the Vietnamese immigrant who served us our breakfast at the hotel this morning. In another 40 years, we will be prepared to say to the Vietnamese immigrant that he, with his breakfast tray, with his intuition for travel, with his memory of tragedy, with his recognition of peerless freedoms, he fulfills the meaning of America.

3   In 1997, Gallup conducted a survey on race relations in America, but the poll was concerned only with white and black Americans. No question was put to the aforementioned Vietnamese man. There was certainly no question for the Chinese grocer, none for the Guatemalan barber, none for the tribe of Mexican Indians who reroofed your neighbor's house.

4   The American conversation about race has always been a black-and-white conversation, but the conversation has become as bloodless as badminton.

5   I have listened to the black-and-white conversation for most of my life. I was supposed to attach myself to one side or the other, without asking the obvious questions: What is this perpetual dialectic between Europe and Africa? Why does it admit so little reference to anyone else?

6   I am speaking to you in American English that was taught me by Irish nuns—immigrant women. I wear an Indian face; I answer to a Spanish surname as well as this California first name, Richard. You might wonder about the complexity of historical factors, the collision of centuries, that creates Richard Rodriguez. My brownness is the illustration of that collision, or the bland memorial of it. I stand before you as an Impure-American, an Ambiguous-American.

7   In the 19th century, Texans used to say that the reason Mexicans were so easily defeated in battle was because we were so dilute, being neither pure Indian nor pure Spaniard. Yet, at the same time, Mexicans used to say that Mexico, the country of my ancestry, joined two worlds, two competing armies. José Vasconcelos, the Mexican educator and philosopher, famously described Mexicans as *la raza cósmica,* the cosmic race. In Mexico what one finds as early as the 18th century is a predominant population of mixed-race people. Also, once the slave had been freed in Mexico, the incidence of marriage between Indian and

African people there was greater than in any other country in the Americas and has not been equaled since.

Race mixture has not been a point of pride in America. 8 Americans speak more easily about "diversity" than we do about the fact that I might marry your daughter; you might become we; we might become us. America has so readily adopted the Canadian notion of multiculturalism because it preserves our preference for thinking ourselves separate—our elbows need not touch, thank you. I would prefer that table. I can remain Mexican, whatever that means, in the United States of America.

I would propose that instead of adopting the Canadian model 9 of multiculturalism, America might begin to imagine the Mexican alternative—that of a mestizaje society.

Because of colonial Mexico, I am mestizo. But I was rein- 10 vented by President Richard Nixon. In the early 1970s, Nixon instructed the Office of Management and Budget to identify the major racial and ethnic groups in the United States. OMB came up with five major ethnic or racial groups. The groups are white, black, Asian/Pacific Islander, American Indian/Eskimo, and Hispanic.

It's what I learned to do when I was in college: to call myself a 11 Hispanic. At my university we even had separate cafeteria tables and "theme houses," where the children of Nixon could gather — of a feather. Native Americans united. African Americans. Casa Hispanic.

The interesting thing about Hispanics is that you will never 12 meet us in Latin America. You may meet Chileans and Peruvians and Mexicans. You will not meet Hispanics. If you inquire in Lima or Bogotá about Hispanics, you will be referred to Dallas. For "Hispanic" is a gringo contrivance, a definition of the world according to European patterns of colonization. Such a definition suggests I have more in common with Argentine Italians than with American Indians; that there is an ineffable union between the white Cuban and the mulatto Puerto Rican because of Spain. Nixon's conclusion has become the basis for the way we now organize and understand American society.

The Census Bureau foretold that by the year 2003, Hispanics 13 would outnumber blacks to become the largest minority in the

United States. And, indeed, the year 2003 has arrived and the proclamation of Hispanic ascendancy has been published far and wide. While I admit a competition has existed—does exist—in America between Hispanic and black people, I insist that the comparison of Hispanics with blacks will lead, ultimately, to complete nonsense. For there is no such thing as a Hispanic race. In Latin America, one sees every race of the world. One sees white Hispanics, one sees black Hispanics, one sees brown Hispanics who are Indians, many of whom do not speak Spanish because they resist Spain. One sees Asian-Hispanics. To compare blacks and Hispanics, therefore, is to construct a fallacious equation.

14   Some Hispanics have accepted the fiction. Some Hispanics have too easily accustomed themselves to impersonating a third race, a great new third race in America. But Hispanic is an ethnic term. It is a term denoting culture. So when the Census Bureau says by the year 2060 one-third of all Americans will identify themselves as Hispanic, the Census Bureau is not speculating in pigment or quantifying according to actual historical narratives, but rather is predicting how by the year 2060 one-third of all Americans will identify themselves culturally. For a country that traditionally has taken its understandings of community from blood and color, the new circumstance of so large a group of Americans identifying themselves by virtue of language or fashion or cuisine or literature is an extraordinary change, and a revolutionary one.

15   People ask me all the time if I envision another Quebec forming in the United States because of the large immigrant movement from the south. Do I see a Quebec forming in the Southwest, for example? No, I don't see that at all. But I do notice the Latin American immigrant population is as much as 10 years younger than the U.S. national population. I notice the Latin American immigrant population is more fertile than the U.S. national population. I see the movement of the immigrants from south to north as a movement of youth—like approaching spring! —into a country that is growing middle-aged. I notice immigrants are the archetypal Americans at a time when we— U.S. citizens—have become post-Americans, most concerned with subsidized medications.

I was at a small Apostolic Assembly in East Palo Alto a few years ago—a mainly Spanish-speaking congregation in an area along the freeway, near the heart of the Silicon Valley. This area used to be black East Palo Alto, but it is quickly becoming an Asian and Hispanic Palo Alto neighborhood. There was a moment in the service when newcomers to the congregation were introduced. Newcomers brought letters of introduction from sister evangelical churches in Latin America. The minister read out the various letters and pronounced the names and places of origin to the community. The congregation applauded. And I thought to myself: It's over. The border is over. These people were not being asked whether they had green cards. They were not being asked whether they arrived here legally or illegally. They were being welcomed within a new community for reasons of culture. There is now a north-south line that is theological, a line that cannot be circumvented by the U.S. Border Patrol.

I was on a British Broadcasting Corporation interview show, and a woman introduced me as being "in favor" of assimilation. I am not in favor of assimilation any more than I am in favor of the Pacific Ocean or clement weather. If I had a bumper sticker on the subject, it might read something like ASSIMILATION HAPPENS. One doesn't get up in the morning, as an immigrant child in America, and think to oneself, "How much of an American shall I become today?" One doesn't walk down the street and decide to be 40 percent Mexican and 60 percent American. Culture is fluid. Culture is smoke. You breathe it. You eat it. You can't help hearing it—Elvis Presley goes in your ear, and you cannot get Elvis Presley out of your mind.

I am in favor of assimilation. I am not in favor of assimilation. I recognize assimilation. A few years ago, I was in Merced, Calif. —a town of about 75,000 people in the Central Valley where the two largest immigrant groups at that time (California is so fluid, I believe this is no longer the case) were Laotian Hmong and Mexicans. Laotians have never in the history of the world, as far as I know, lived next to Mexicans. But there they were in Merced, and living next to Mexicans. They don't like each other. I was talking to the Laotian kids about why they don't like the Mexican kids. They were telling me that the Mexicans do this and the

Mexicans don't do that, when I suddenly realized that they were speaking English with a Spanish accent.

19   On his interview show, Bill Moyers once asked me how I thought of myself. As an American? Or Hispanic? I answered that I am Chinese, and that is because I live in a Chinese city and because I want to be Chinese. Well, why not? Some Chinese American people in the Richmond and Sunset districts of San Francisco sometimes paint their houses (so many qualifiers!) in colors I would once have described as garish: lime greens, rose reds, pumpkin. But I have lived in a Chinese city for so long that my eye has taken on that palette, has come to prefer lime greens and rose reds and all the inventions of this Chinese Mediterranean. I see photographs in magazines or documentary footage of China, especially rural China, and I see what I recognize as home. Isn't that odd?

20   I do think distinctions exist. I'm not talking about an America tomorrow in which we're going to find that black and white are no longer the distinguishing marks of separateness. But many young people I meet tell me they feel like Victorians when they identify themselves as black or white. They don't think of themselves in those terms. And they're already moving into a world in which tattoo or ornament or movement or commune or sexuality or drug or rave or electronic bombast are the organizing principles of their identity. The notion that they are white or black simply doesn't occur.

21   And increasingly, of course, one meets children who really don't know how to say what they are. They simply are too many things. I met a young girl in San Diego at a convention of mixed-race children, among whom the common habit is to define one parent over the other—black over white, for example. But this girl said that her mother was Mexican and her father was African. The girl said "Blaxican." By reinventing language, she is reinventing America.

22   America does not have a vocabulary like the vocabulary the Spanish empire evolved to describe the multiplicity of racial possibilities in the New World. The conversation, the interior monologue of America cannot rely on the old vocabulary—black, white. We are no longer a black-white nation.

So, what myth do we tell ourselves? The person who got 23
closest to it was Karl Marx. Marx predicted that the discovery of
gold in California would be a more central event to the Americas
than the discovery of the Americas by Columbus—which was
only the meeting of two tribes, essentially, the European and the
Indian. But when gold was discovered in California in the 1840s,
the entire world met. For the first time in human history, all of
the known world gathered. The Malaysian stood in the gold
fields alongside the African, alongside the Chinese, alongside the
Australian, alongside the Yankee.

That was an event without parallel in world history and the 24
beginning of modern California—why California today provides
the mythological structure for understanding how we might talk
about the American experience: not as biracial, but as the recreation of the known world in the New World.

Sometimes truly revolutionary things happen without regard. 25
I mean, we may wake up one morning and there is no black race.
There is no white race either. There are mythologies, and—as
I am in the business, insofar as I am in any business at all, of
demythologizing such identities as black and white—I come to
you as a man of many cultures. I come to you as Chinese. Unless
you understand that I am Chinese, then you have not understood
anything I have said.

Chapter

5

Division and Classification

Predictable Crises of Adulthood

Gail Sheehy

1 We are not unlike a particularly hardy <u>crustacean</u>. The lobster grows by developing and shedding a series of hard, protective shells. Each time it expands from within, the confining shell must be s<u>loughe</u>d off. It is left exposed and vulnerable until, in time, a new covering grows to replace the old.

2 With each passage from one stage of human growth to the next we, too, must shed a protective structure. We are left exposed and vulnerable—but also y<u>east</u>y and embryonic again, capable of stretching in ways we hadn't known before. These sheddings may take several years or more. Coming out of each passage, though, we enter a longer and more stable period in which we can expect relative tranquility and a sense of equilibrium regained. . . .

3 As we shall see, each person engages the steps of development in his or her own characteristic *step-style*. Some people never complete the whole sequence. And none of us "solves" with one step—by jumping out of the parental home into a job or marriage, for example—the problems in separating from the caregivers of childhood. Nor do we "achieve" autonomy once and for all by converting our dreams into concrete goals, even when we attain those goals. The central issues or tasks of one period are never fully completed, tied up, and cast aside. But when they lose their

primacy and the current life structure has served its purpose, we are ready to move on to the next period.

Can one catch up? What might look to others like listless- 4 ness, contrariness, a maddening refusal to face up to an obvious task may be a person's own unique detour that will bring him out later on the other side. Developmental gains won can later be lost—and rewon. It's plausible, though it can't be proven, that the mastery of one set of tasks fortifies us for the next period and the next set of challenges. But it's important not to think too mechanistically. Machines work by units. The bureaucracy (supposedly) works step by step. Human beings, thank God, have an individual inner dynamic that can never be precisely coded.

Although I have indicated the ages when Americans are 5 likely to go through each stage, and the differences between men and women where they are striking, do not take the ages too seriously. The stages are the thing, and most particularly the sequence.

Here is the briefest outline of the developmental ladder.   6

PULLING UP ROOTS

Before 18, the motto is loud and clear: "I have to get away from 7 my parents." But the words are seldom connected to action. Generally still safely part of our families, even if away at school, we feel our autonomy to be subject to erosion from moment to moment.

After 18, we begin Pulling Up Roots in earnest. College, 8 military service, and short-term travels are all customary vehicles our society provides for the first round-trips between family and a base of one's own. In the attempt to separate our view of the world from our family's view, despite vigorous protestations to the contrary—"I know exactly what I want!"—we cast about for any beliefs we can call our own. And in the process of testing those beliefs we are often drawn to fads, preferably those most mysterious and inaccessible to our parents.

Whatever tentative memberships we try out in the world, 9 the fear haunts us that we are really kids who cannot take care of ourselves. We cover that fear with acts of defiance and mimicked confidence. For allies to replace our parents, we turn to our contemporaries. They become conspirators. So long as their perspective meshes with our own, they are able to substitute for the sanctuary of the family. But that doesn't last very long. And the instant they diverge from the shaky ideals of "our group," they are seen as betrayers. Rebounds to the family are common between the ages of 18 and 22.

10   The tasks of this passage are to locate ourselves in a peer group role, a sex role, an anticipated occupation, an ideology or world view. As a result, we gather the impetus to leave home physically and the identity to *begin* leaving home emotionally.

11   Even as one part of us seeks to be an individual, another part longs to restore the safety and comfort of merging with another. Thus one of the most popular myths of this passage is: We can piggyback our development by attaching to a Stronger One. But people who marry during this time often prolong financial and emotional ties to the family and relatives that impede them from becoming self-sufficient.

12   A stormy passage through the Pulling Up Roots years will probably facilitate the normal progression of the adult life cycle. If one doesn't have an identity crisis at this point, it will erupt during a later transition, when the penalties may be harder to bear.

THE TRYING TWENTIES

13 The Trying Twenties confront us with the question of how to take hold in the adult world. Our focus shifts from the interior turmoils of late adolescence—"Who am I?" "What is truth?"—and we become almost totally preoccupied with working out the externals. "How do I put my aspirations into effect?" "What is the best way to start?" "Where do I go?" "Who can help me?" "How did you do it?"

14   In this period, which is longer and more stable compared with the passage that leads to it, the tasks are as enormous as they are exhilarating: To shape a Dream, that vision of ourselves which will generate energy, aliveness, and hope. To prepare for a

lifework. To find a mentor if possible. And to form the capacity for intimacy without losing in the process whatever consistency of self we have thus far mustered. The first test structure must be erected around the life we choose to try.

Doing what we "should" is the most pervasive theme of the 15 twenties. The "shoulds" are largely defined by family models, the press of the culture, or the prejudices of our peers. If the prevailing cultural instructions are that one should get married and settle down behind one's own door, a nuclear family is born. If instead the peers insist that one should do one's own thing, the 25-year-old is likely to harness himself onto a Harley-Davidson and burn up Route 66 in the commitment to have no commitments.

One of the terrifying aspects of the twenties is the inner 16 conviction that the choices we make are irrevocable. It is largely a false fear. Change is quite possible, and some alteration of our original choices is probably inevitable.

Two impulses, as always, are at work. One is to build a firm, 17 safe structure for the future by making strong commitments, to "be set." Yet people who slip into a readymade form without much self-examination are likely to find themselves *locked* in.

The other urge is to explore and experiment, keeping any 18 structure tentative and therefore easily reversible. Taken to the extreme, these are people who skip from one trial job and one limited personal encounter to another, spending their twenties in the *transient* state.

Although the choices of our twenties are not irrevocable, 19 they do set in motion a Life Pattern. Some of us follow the lock-in pattern, others the transient pattern; the wunderkind pattern, the caregiver pattern, and there are a number of others. Such patterns strongly influence the particular questions raised for each person during each passage. . . .

Buoyed by powerful illusions and belief in the power of 20 the will, we commonly insist in our twenties that what we have chosen to do is the one true course in life. Our backs go up at the merest hint that we are like our parents, that two decades of parental training might be reflected in our current actions and attitudes.

"Not me," is the motto, "I'm different."   21

CATCH-30

22   Impatient with devoting ourselves to the "shoulds," a new vitality springs from within as we approach 30. Men and women alike speak of feeling too narrow and restricted. They blame all sorts of things, but what the restrictions boil down to are the outgrowth of career and personal choices of the twenties. They may have been choices perfectly suited to that stage. But now the fit feels different. Some inner aspect that was left out is striving to be taken into account. Important new choices must be made, and commitments altered or deepened. The work involves great change, turmoil, and often crisis—a simultaneous feeling of rock bottom and the urge to bust out.

23   One common response is the tearing up of the life we spent most of our twenties putting together. It may mean striking out on a secondary road toward a new vision or converting a dream of "running for president" into a more realistic goal. The single person feels a push to find a partner. The woman who was previously content at home with children chafes to venture into the world. The childless couple reconsiders children. And almost everyone who is married, especially those married for seven years, feels a discontent.

24   If the discontent doesn't lead to a divorce, it will, or should, call for a serious review of the marriage and of each partner's aspirations in their Catch-30 condition. The gist of that condition was expressed by a 29-year-old associate with a Wall Street law firm:

25   "I'm considering leaving the firm. I've been there four years now; I'm getting good feedback, but I have no clients of my own. I feel weak. If I wait much longer, it will be too late, too close to that fateful time of decision on whether or not to become a partner. I'm success-oriented. But the concept of being 55 years old and stuck in a monotonous job drives me wild. It drives me crazy now, just a little bit. I'd say that 85 percent of the time I thoroughly enjoy my work. But when I get a screwball case, I come away from court saying, 'What am I doing here?' It's a _visceral_ reaction that I'm wasting my time. I'm trying to find some way to make a social contribution or a slot in city government. I keep saying, 'There's something more.'"

Besides the push to broaden himself professionally, there is 26 a wish to expand his personal life. He wants two or three more children. "The concept of a home has become very meaningful to me, a place to get away from troubles and relax. I love my son in a way I could not have anticipated. I never could live alone."

Consumed with the work of making his own critical life- 27 steering decisions, he demonstrates the essential shift at this age: An absolute requirement to be more self-concerned. The self has new value now that his competency has been proved.

His wife is struggling with her own age-30 priorities. She 28 wants to go to law school, but he wants more children. If she is going to stay home, she wants him to make more time for the family instead of taking on even wider professional commit- ments. His view of the bind, of what he would most like from his wife, is this:

"I'd like not to be bothered. It sounds cruel, but I'd like not to 29 have to worry about what she's going to do next week. Which is why I've told her several times that I think she should do some- thing. Go back to school and get a degree in social work or geog- raphy or whatever. Hopefully that would fulfill her, and then I wouldn't have to worry about her line of problems. I want her to be decisive about herself."

The trouble with his advice to his wife is that it comes out of 30 concern with *his* convenience, rather than with *her* development. She quickly picks up on this lack of goodwill: He is trying to dispose of her. At the same time, he refuses her the same latitude to be "selfish" in making an independent decision to broaden her horizons. Both perceive a lack of mutuality. And that is what Catch-30 is all about for the couple.

ROOTING AND EXTENDING

Life becomes less provisional, more rational and orderly in the 31 early thirties. We begin to settle down in the full sense. Most of us begin putting down roots and sending out new shoots. People buy houses and become very earnest about climbing career lad- ders. Men in particular concern themselves with "making it."

Satisfaction with marriage generally goes downhill in the thirties (for those who have remained together) compared with the highly valued, vision-supporting marriage of the twenties. This coincides with the couple's reduced social life outside the family and the inturned focus on raising their children.

THE DEADLINE DECADE

32   In the middle of the thirties we come upon a crossroads. We have reached the halfway mark. Yet even as we are reaching our prime, we begin to see there is a place where it finishes. Time starts to squeeze.

33   The loss of youth, the faltering of physical powers we have always taken for granted, the fading purpose of stereotyped roles by which we have thus far identified ourselves, the spiritual dilemma of having no absolute answers—any or all of these shocks can give this passage the character of crisis. Such thoughts usher in a decade between 35 and 45 that can be called the Deadline Decade. It is a time of both danger and opportunity. All of us have the chance to rework the narrow identity by which we defined ourselves in the first half of life. And those of us who make the most of the opportunity will have a full-out authenticity crisis.

34   To come through this authenticity crisis, we must reexamine our purposes and reevaluate how to spend our resources from now on. "Why am I doing all this? What do I really believe in?" No matter what we have been doing, there will be parts of ourselves that have been suppressed and now need to find expression. "Bad" feelings will demand acknowledgment along with the good.

35   It is frightening to step off onto the treacherous footbridge leading to the second half of life. We can't take everything with us on this journey through uncertainty. Along the way, we discover that we are alone. We no longer have to ask permission because we are the providers of our own safety. We must learn to give ourselves permission. We stumble upon feminine or masculine aspects of our natures that up to this time have usually been masked. There is grieving to be done because an old self

is dying. By taking in our suppressed and even our unwanted parts, we prepare at the gut level for the reintegration of an identity that is ours and ours alone—not some artificial form put together to please the culture or our mates. It is a dark passage at the beginning. But by disassembling ourselves, we can glimpse the light and gather our parts into a renewal.

Women sense this inner crossroads earlier than men do. The 36 time pinch often prompts a woman to stop and take an all-points survey at age 35. Whatever options she has already played out, she feels a "my last chance" urgency to review those options she has set aside and those that aging and biology will close off in the now *foreseeable* future. For all her qualms and confusion about where to start looking for a new future, she usually enjoys an exhilaration of release. Assertiveness begins rising. There are so many firsts ahead.

Men, too, feel the time push in the mid-thirties. Most men 37 respond by pressing down harder on the career accelerator. It's "my last chance" to pull away from the pack. It is no longer enough to be the loyal junior executive, the promising young novelist, the lawyer who does a little *pro bono* work on the side. He wants now to become part of top management, to be recognized as an established writer, or an active politician with his own legislative program. With some chagrin, he discovers that he has been too anxious to please and too vulnerable to criticism. He wants to put together his own ship.

During this period of intense concentration on external 38 advancement, it is common for men to be unaware of the more difficult, gut issues that are propelling them forward. The survey that was neglected at 35 becomes a crucible at 40. Whatever rung of achievement he has reached, the man of 40 usually feels stale, restless, burdened, and unappreciated. He worries about his health. He wonders, "Is this all there is?" He may make a series of departures from well-established lifelong base lines, including marriage. More and more men are seeking second careers in midlife. Some become self-destructive. And many men in their forties experience a major shift of emphasis away from pouring all their energies into their own advancement. A more tender, feeling side comes into play. They become interested in developing an ethical self.

RENEWAL OR RESIGNATION

39   Somewhere in the mid-forties, equilibrium is regained. A new stability is achieved, which may be more or less satisfying.

40   If one has refused to budge through the midlife transition, the sense of staleness will calcify into resignation. One by one, the safety and supports will be withdrawn from the person who is standing still. Parents will become children; children will become strangers; a mate will grow away or go away; the career will become just a job—and each of these events will be felt as an abandonment. The crisis will probably emerge again around 50. And although its wallop will be greater, the jolt may be just what is needed to prod the resigned middle-ager toward seeking revitalization.

41   On the other hand . . .

42   If we have confronted ourselves in the middle passage and found a renewal of purpose around which we are eager to build a more authentic life structure, these may well be the best years. Personal happiness takes a sharp turn upward for partners who can now accept the fact: "I cannot expect *anyone* to fully understand me." Parents can be forgiven for the burdens of our childhood. Children can be let go without leaving us in collapsed silence. At 50, there is a new warmth and mellowing. Friends become more important than ever, but so does privacy. Since it is so often proclaimed by people past midlife, the motto of this stage might be "No more bullshit."

1976

Growing Up Asian in America

Kesaya E. Noda

1   Sometimes when I was growing up, my identity seemed to hurtle toward me and paste itself right to my face. I felt that way, encountering the stereotypes of my race perpetuated by

non-Japanese people (primarily white) who may or may not have had contact with other Japanese in America. "You don't like cheese, do you?" someone would ask. "I know your people don't like cheese." Sometimes questions came making allusions to history. That was another aspect of the identity. Events that had happened quite apart from the me who stood silent in that moment connected my face with an incomprehensible past. "Your parents were in California? Were they in those camps during the war?" And sometimes there were phrases or nicknames: "Lotus Blossom." I was sometimes addressed or referred to as racially Japanese, sometimes as Japanese-American, and sometimes as an Asian woman. Confusions and distortions abounded.

How is one to know and define oneself? From the inside— 2 within a context that is self-defined, from a grounding in community and a connection with culture and history that are comfortably accepted? Or from the outside—within terms or messages received from the media and people who are often ignorant? Even as an adult I can still see two sides of my face and past. I can see from the inside out, in freedom. And I can see from the outside in, driven by the old voices of childhood and lost in anger and fear.

I AM RACIALLY JAPANESE

A voice from my childhood says: "You are other. You are less 3 than. You are unalterably alien." This voice has its own history. We have indeed been seen as other and alien since the early years of our arrival in the United States. The very first immigrants were welcomed and sought as laborers to replace the dwindling numbers of Chinese, whose influx had been cut off by the Chinese Exclusion Act of 1882. The Japanese fell natural heir to the same anti-Asian prejudice that had arisen against the Chinese. As soon as they began striking for better wages, they were no longer welcomed.

I can see myself today as a person historically defined by law 4 and custom as being forever alien. Being neither "free white," nor "African," our people in California were deemed "aliens, ineligible for citizenship," no matter how long they intended to stay here. Aliens ineligible for citizenship were prohibited from owning, buying, or leasing land. They did not and could not belong here. The voice in me remembers that I am always a *Japanese*-American in the eyes of many. A third-generation German-American is an American. A third-generation Japanese-American is a Japanese-American. Being Japanese means being a danger to the country during the war and knowing how to use chopsticks. I wear this history on my face.

5   I move to the other side. I see a different light and claim a different context. My race is a line that stretches across ocean and time to link me to the shrine where my grandmother was raised. Two high, white banners lift in the wind at the top of the stone steps leading to the shrine. It is time for the summer festival. Black characters are written against the sky as boldly as the clouds, as lightly as kites, as sharply as the big black crows I used to see above the fields in New Hampshire. At festival time there is liquor and food, ritual, discipline, and abandonment. There is music and drunkenness and invocation. There is hope. Another season has come. Another season has gone.

6   I am racially Japanese. I have a certain claim to this crazy place where the prayers intoned by a neighboring Shinto priest (standing in for my grandmother's nephew who is sick) are drowned out by the rehearsals for the pop singing contest in which most of the villagers will compete later that night. The village elders, the priest, and I stand respectfully upon the immaculate, shining wooden floor of the outer shrine, bowing our heads before the hidden powers. During the patchy intervals when I can hear him, I notice the priest has a stutter. His voice flutters up to my ears only occasionally because two men and a woman are singing gustily into a microphone in the compound, testing the sound system. A pre-recorded tape of guitars, samisens, and drums accompanies them. Rock music and Shinto prayers. That night, to loud applause and cheers, a young man is given the award for the most *netsuretsu*—passionate, burning—rendition of a song. We roar our approval of the reward. Never mind that his voice had wandered and slid, now slightly above, now slightly below the given line of the melody. Netsuretsu. Netsuretsu.

In the morning, my grandmother's sister kneels at the foot of 7 the stone stairs to offer her morning prayers. She is too crippled to climb the stairs, so each morning she kneels here upon the path. She shuts her eyes for a few seconds, her motions as matter of fact as when she washes rice. I linger longer than she does, so reluctant to leave, savoring the connection I feel with my grandmother in America, the past, and the power that lives and shines in the morning sun.

Our family has served this shrine for generations. The fam- 8 ily's need to protect this claim to identity and place outweighs any individual claim to any individual hope. I am Japanese.

I AM A JAPANESE-AMERICAN

"Weak." I hear the voice from my childhood years. "Passive," I hear. 9 Our parents and grandparents were the ones who were put into those camps. They went without resistance; they offered cooperation as proof of loyalty to America. "Victim," I hear. And, "Silent."

Our parents are painted as hard workers who were socially 10 uncomfortable and had difficulty expressing even the smallest opinion. Clean, quiet, motivated, and determined to match the American way; that is us, and that is the story of our time here.

"Why did you go into those camps?" I raged at my parents, 11 frightened by my own inner silence and timidity. "Why didn't you do anything to resist? Why didn't you name it the injustice it was?" Couldn't our parents even think? Couldn't they? Why were we so passive?

I shift my vision and my stance. I am in California. My uncle 12 is in the midst of the sweet potato harvest. He is pressed, trying to get the harvesting crews onto the field as quickly as possible, worried about the flow of equipment and people. His big pickup is pulled off to the side, motor running, door ajar. I see two tractors in the yard in front of an old shed; the flatbed harvesting platform on which the workers will stand has already been brought over from the other field. It's early morning. The workers stand loosely grouped and at ease, but my uncle looks as harried and tense as a police officer trying to unsnarl a New York City traffic jam.

Driving toward the shed, I pull my car off the road to make way for an approaching tractor. The front wheels of the car sink luxuriously into the soft, white sand by the roadside and the car slides to a dreamy halt, tail still on the road. I try to move forward. I try to move back. The front bites contentedly into the sand, the back lifts itself at a jaunty angle. My uncle sees me and storms down the road, running. He is shouting before he is even near me.

13   "What's the matter with you?" he screams. "What the hell are you doing?" In his frenzy, he grabs his hat off his head and slashes it through the air across his knee. He is beside himself. "Don't you know how to drive in sand? What's the matter with you? You've blocked the whole roadway. How am I supposed to get my tractors out of here? Can't you use your head? You've cut off the whole roadway, and we've got to get out of here."

14   I stand on the road before him helplessly thinking. "No, I don't know how to drive in sand. I've never driven in sand."

15   "I'm sorry, uncle," I say, burying a smile beneath a look of sincere apology. I notice my deep amusement and my affection for him with great curiosity. I am usually devastated by anger. Not this time.

16   During the several years that follow I learn about the people and the place, and much more about what has happened in this California village where my parents grew up. The issei, our grandparents, made this settlement in the desert. Their first crops were eaten by rabbits and ravaged by insects. The land was so barren that men walking from house to house sometimes got lost. Women came here too. They bore children in 114-degree heat, then carried the babies with them into the fields to nurse when they reached the end of each row of grapes or other truck-farm crops.

17   I had had no idea what it meant to buy this kind of land and make it grow green. Or how, when the war came, there was no space at all for the subtlety of being who we were—Japanese-Americans. Either/or was the way. I hadn't understood that people were literally afraid for their lives then, that their money had been frozen in banks; that there was a five-mile travel limit; that when the early evening curfew came and they were inside their houses, some of them watched helplessly as people they knew went into their barns to steal their belongings. The police were patrolling the road, interested only in violators of curfew.

There was no help for them in the face of thievery. I had not been able to imagine before what it must have felt like to be an American—to know absolutely that one is an American—and yet to have almost everyone else deny it. Not only deny it, but challenge that identity with machine guns and troops of white American soldiers. In those circumstances it was difficult to say, "I'm a Japanese-American." "American" had to do.

But now I can say that I am a Japanese-American. It means I 18 have a place here in this country, too. I have a place here on the East Coast, where our neighbor is so much a part of our family that my mother never passes her house at night without glancing at the lights to see if she is home and safe; where my parents have hauled hundreds of pounds of rocks from fields and arduously planted Christmas trees and blueberries, lilacs, asparagus, and crab apples; where my father still dreams of angling a stream to a new bed so that he can dig a pond in the field and fill it with water and fish. "The neighbors already came for their Christmas tree?" he asks in December. "Did they like it? Did they like it?"

I have a place on the West Coast where my relatives still farm, 19 where I heard the stories of feuds and backbiting, and where I saw that people survived and flourished because fundamentally they trusted and relied upon one another. A death in the family is not just a death in a family; it is a death in the community. I saw people help each other with money, materials, labor, attention, and time. I saw men gather once a year, without fail, to clean the grounds of a ninety-year-old woman who had helped the community before, during, and after the war. I saw her remembering them with birthday cards sent to each of their children.

I come from a people with a long memory and a distinctive 20 grace. We live our thanks. And we are Americans. Japanese-Americans.

I AM A JAPANESE-AMERICAN WOMAN

Woman. The last piece of my identity. It has been easier by far for 21 me to know myself in Japan and to see my place in America than it has been to accept my line of connection with my own mother.

She was my dark self, a figure in whom I thought I saw all that I feared most in myself. Growing into womanhood and looking for some model of strength, I turned away from her. Of course, I could not find what I sought. I was looking for a black feminist or a white feminist. My mother is neither white nor black.

22 My mother is a woman who speaks with her life as much as with her tongue. I think of her with her own mother. Grandmother had Parkinson's disease and it had frozen her gait and set her fingers, tongue, and feet jerking and trembling in a terrible dance. My aunts and uncles wanted her to be able to live in her own home. They fed her, bathed her, dressed her, awoke at midnight to take her for one last trip to the bathroom. My aunts (her daughters-in-law) did most of the care, but my mother went from New Hampshire to California each summer to spend a month living with Grandmother, because she wanted to and because she wanted to give my aunts at least a small rest. During those hot summer days, mother lay on the couch watching the television or reading, cooking foods that Grandmother liked, and speaking little. Grandmother thrived under her care.

23 The time finally came when it was too dangerous for Grandmother to live alone. My relatives kept finding her on the floor beside her bed when they went to wake her in the mornings. My mother flew to California to help clean the house and make arrangements for Grandmother to enter a local nursing home. On her last day at home, while Grandmother was sitting in her big, overstuffed armchair, hair combed and wearing a green summer dress, my mother went to her and knelt at her feet. "Here, Mamma," she said. "I've polished your shoes." She lifted Grandmother's legs and helped her into the shiny black shoes. My Grandmother looked down and smiled slightly. She left her house walking, supported by her children, carrying her pocket-book, and wearing her polished black shoes. "Look, Mamma," my mom had said, kneeling. "I've polished your shoes."

24 Just the other day, my mother came to Boston to visit. She had recently lost a lot of weight and was pleased with her new shape and her feeling of good health. "Look at me, Kes," she exclaimed, turning toward me, front and back, as naked as the day she was born. I saw her small breasts and the wide, brown scar, belly

button to pubic hair, that marked her because my brother and I were both born by Caesarean section. Her hips were small. I was not a large baby, but there was so little room for me in her that when she was carrying me she could not even begin to bend over toward the floor. She hated it, she said.

"Don't I look good? Don't you think I look good?"   25

I looked at my mother, smiling and as happy as she, thinking   26 of all the times I have seen her naked. I have seen both my parents naked throughout my life, as they have seen me. From childhood through adulthood we've had our naked moments, sharing baths, idle conversations picked up as we moved between showers and closets, hurried moments at the beginning of days, quiet moments at the end of days.

I know this to be Japanese, this ease with the physical, and   27 it makes me think of an old Japanese folk song. A young nursemaid, a fifteen-year-old girl, is singing a lullaby to a baby who is strapped to her back. The nursemaid has been sent as a servant to a place far from her own home. "We're the beggars," she says, "and they are the nice people. Nice people wear fine sashes. Nice clothes."

> If I should drop dead,
> bury me by the roadside!
> I'll give a flower to
> everyone who passes.
>
> What kind of flower?
> The cam-cam-camellia [tsun-tsun-tsubaki]
> watered by Heaven:
> alms water.

The nursemaid is the intersection of heaven and earth, the   28 intersection of the human, the natural world, the body, and the soul. In this song, with clear eyes, she looks steadily at life, which is sometimes so very terrible and sad. I think of her while looking at my mother, who is standing on the red and purple carpet before me, laughing, without any clothes.

I am my mother's daughter. And I am myself.   29

I am a Japanese-American woman.   30

EPILOGUE

31   I recently heard a man from West Africa share some memories of his childhood. He was raised Muslim, but when he was a young man, he found himself deeply drawn to Christianity. He struggled against his inner impulse for years, trying to avoid the church yet feeling pushed to return to it again and again. "I would have done anything to avoid the change," he said. At last, he became Christian. Afterwards he was afraid to go home, fearing that he would not be accepted. The fear was groundless, he discovered, when at last he returned—he had separated himself, but his family and friends (all Muslim) had not separated themselves from him.

32   The man, who is now a professor of religion, said that in the Africa he knew as a child and a young man, pluralism was embraced rather than feared. There was "a kind of tolerance that did not deny your particularity," he said. He alluded to zestful, spontaneous debates that would sometimes loudly erupt between Muslims and Christians in the village's public spaces. His memories of an atheist who harangued the villagers when he came to visit them once a week moved me deeply. Perhaps the man was an agricultural advisor or inspector. He harassed the women. He would say: "Don't go to the fields! Don't even bother to go to the fields. Let God take care of you. He'll send you the food. If you believe in God, why do you need to work? You don't need to work! Let God put the seeds in the ground. Stay home."

33   The professor said, "The women laughed, you know? They just laughed. Their attitude was, 'Here is a child of God. When will he come home?'"

34   The storyteller, the professor of religion, smiled a most fantastic tender smile as he told this story. "In my country, there is a deep affirmation of the oneness of God," he said. "The atheist and the women were having quite different experiences in their encounter, though the atheist did not know this. He saw himself as quite separate from the women. But the women did not see themselves as being separate from him. 'Here is a child of God,' they said. 'When will he come home?'"

1989

The Truth about Lying

Judith Viorst

I've been wanting to write on a subject that intrigues and chal- 1
lenges me: The subject of lying. I've found it very difficult to
do. Everyone I've talked to has a quite intense and personal but
often rather intolerant point of view about what we can—and can
never *never*—tell lies about. I've finally reached the conclusion
that I can't present any ultimate conclusions, for too many people
would promptly disagree. Instead, I'd like to present a series of
moral puzzles, all concerned with lying. I'll tell you what I think
about them. Do you agree?

SOCIAL LIES

Most of the people I've talked with say that they find social lying 2
acceptable and necessary. They think it's the civilized way for folks
to behave. Without these little white lies, they say, our relationships
would be short and brutish and nasty. It's arrogant, they say, to
insist on being so incorruptible and so brave that you cause other
people unnecessary embarrassment or pain by compulsively assail-
ing them with your honesty. I basically agree. What about you?

Will you say to people, when it simply isn't true, "I like your 3
new hairdo," "You're looking much better," "It's so nice to see
you," "I had a wonderful time"?

Will you praise hideous presents and homely kids?   4

Will you decline invitations with "We're busy that night—so 5
sorry we can't come," when the truth is you'd rather stay home
than dine with the So-and-sos?

And even though, as I do, you may prefer the polite evasion 6
of "You really cooked up a storm" instead of "The soup"—which
tastes like warmed-over coffee—"is wonderful," will you, if you
must, proclaim it wonderful?

There's one man I know who absolutely refuses to tell social 7
lies. "I can't play that game," he says; "I'm simply not made that
way." And his answer to the argument that saying nice things

to someone doesn't cost anything is, "Yes, it does—it destroys your credibility." Now, he won't, unsolicited, offer his views on the painting you just bought, but you don't ask his frank opinion unless you want *frank*, and his silence at those moments when the rest of us liars are muttering, "Isn't it lovely?" is, for the most part, eloquent enough. My friend does not indulge in what he calls "flattery, false praise and mellifluous comments." When others tell fibs he will not go along. He says that social lying is lying, that little white lies are still lies. And he feels that telling lies is morally wrong. What about you?

PEACE-KEEPING LIES

8 Many people tell peace-keeping lies; lies designed to avoid irritation or argument; lies designed to shelter the liar from possible blame or pain; lies (or so it is rationalized) designed to keep trouble at bay without hurting anyone.

9   I tell these lies at times, and yet I always feel they're wrong. I understand why we tell them, but still they feel wrong. And whenever I lie so that someone won't disapprove of me or think less of me or holler at me, I feel I'm a bit of a coward, I feel I'm dodging responsibility, I feel . . . guilty. What about you?

10   Do you, when you're late for a date because you overslept, say that you're late because you got caught in a traffic jam?

11   Do you, when you forget to call a friend, say that you called several times but the line was busy?

12   Do you, when you didn't remember that it was your father's birthday, say that his present must be delayed in the mail?

13   And when you're planning a weekend in New York City and you're not in the mood to visit your mother, who lives there, do you conceal—with a lie, if you must—the fact that you'll be in New York? Or do you have the courage—or is it the cruelty?—to say, "I'll be in New York, but sorry—I don't plan on seeing you"?

14   (Dave and his wife Elaine have two quite different points of view on this very subject. He calls her a coward. She says she's being wise. He says she must assert her right to visit New York sometimes and not see her mother. To which she always patiently

replies: "Why should we have useless fights? My mother's too old to change. We get along much better when I lie to her.")

Finally, do you keep the peace by telling your husband lies 15 on the subject of money? Do you reduce what you really paid for your shoes? And in general do you find yourself ready, willing and able to lie to him when you make absurd mistakes or lose or break things?

"I used to have a romantic idea that part of intimacy was con- 16 fessing every dumb thing that you did to your husband. But after a couple of years of that," says Laura, "have I changed my mind!"

And having changed her mind, she finds herself telling 17 peace-keeping lies. And yes, I tell them too. What about you?

PROTECTIVE LIES

Protective lies are lies folks tell—often quite serious lies—because 18 they're convinced that the truth would be too damaging. They lie because they feel there are certain human values that supersede the wrong of having lied. They lie, not for personal gain, but because they believe it's for the good of the person they're lying to. They lie to those they love, to those who trust them most of all, on the grounds that breaking this trust is justified.

They may lie to their children on money or marital matters.   19

They may lie to the dying about the state of their health.   20

They may lie about adultery, and not—or so they insist—to 21 save their own hide, but to save the heart and the pride of the men they are married to.

They may lie to their closest friend because the truth about 22 her talents or son or psyche would be—or so they insist—utterly devastating.

I sometimes tell such lies, but I'm aware that it's quite pre- 23 sumptuous to claim I know what's best for others to know. That's called playing God. That's called manipulation and control. And we never can be sure, once we start to juggle lies, just where they'll land, exactly where they'll roll.

And furthermore, we may find ourselves lying in order to 24 back up the lies that are backing up the lie we initially told.

25 And furthermore—let's be honest—if conditions were reversed, we certainly wouldn't want anyone lying to us.

26 Yet, having said all that, I still believe that there are times when protective lies must nonetheless be told. What about you?

27 If your Dad had a very bad heart and you had to tell him some bad family news, which would you choose: To tell him the truth or to lie?

28 If your former husband failed to send his monthly child support check and in other ways behaved like a total rat, would you allow your children—who believed he was simply wonderful— to continue to believe that he was wonderful?

29 If your dearly beloved brother selected a wife whom you deeply disliked, would you reveal your feelings or would you fake it?

30 And if you were asked, after making love, "And how was that for you?" would you reply, if it wasn't too good, "Not too good"?

31 Now, some would call a sex lie unimportant, little more than social lying, a simple act of courtesy that makes all human intercourse run smoothly. And some would say all sex lies are bad news and unacceptably protective. Because, says Ruth, "a man with an ego that fragile doesn't need your lies—he needs a psychiatrist." Still others feel that sex lies are indeed protective lies, more serious than simple social lying, and yet at times they tell them on the grounds that when it comes to matters sexual, everybody's ego is somewhat fragile.

32 "If most of the time things go well in sex," says Sue, "I think you're allowed to dissemble when they don't. I can't believe it's good to say, 'Last night was four stars, darling, but tonight's performance rates only a half.'"

33 I'm inclined to agree with Sue. What about you?

TRUST-KEEPING LIES

34 Another group of lies are trust-keeping lies, lies that involve triangulation, with A (that's you) telling lies to B on behalf of C (whose trust you'd promised to keep). Most people concede that

once you've agreed not to betray a friend's confidence, you can't betray it, even if you must lie. But I've talked with people who don't want you telling them anything that they might be called on to lie about.

"I don't tell lies for myself," says Fran, "and I don't want to have to tell them for other people." Which means, she agrees, that if her best friend is having an affair, she absolutely doesn't want to know about it. 35

"Are you saying," her best friend asks, "that if I went off with a lover and I asked you to tell my husband I'd been with you, that you wouldn't lie for me, that you'd betray me?" 36

Fran is very pained but very adamant. "I wouldn't want to betray you, so . . . don't ask me." 37

Fran's best friend is shocked. What about you? 38

Do you believe you can have close friends if you're not prepared to receive their deepest secrets? 39

Do you believe you must always lie for your friends? 40

Do you believe, if your friend tells a secret that turns out to be quite immoral or illegal, that once you've promised to keep it, you must keep it? 41

And what if your friend were your boss—if you were perhaps one of the President's men—would you betray or lie for him over, say, Watergate? 42

As can see, these issues get terribly sticky. 43

It's my belief that once we've promised to keep a trust, we must tell lies to keep it. I also believe that we can't tell Watergate lies. And if these two statements strike you as quite contradictory, you're right—they're quite contradictory. But for now they're the best I can do. What about you? 44

Some say that truth will out and thus you might as well tell the truth. Some say you can't regain the trust that lies lose. Some say that even though the truth may never be revealed, our lies pervert and damage our relationships. Some say . . . well, here's what some of them have to say. 45

"I'm a coward," says Grace, "about telling close people important, difficult truths. I find that I'm unable to carry it off. And so if something is bothering me, it keeps building up inside till I end up just not seeing them any more." 46

47   "I lie to my husband on sexual things, but I'm furious," says Joyce, "that he's too insensitive to know I'm lying."

48   "I suffer most from the misconception that children can't take the truth," says Emily. "But I'm starting to see that what's harder and more damaging for them is being told lies, is *not* being told the truth."

49   "I'm afraid," says Joan, "that we often wind up feeling a bit of contempt for the people we lie to."

50   And then there are those who have no talent for lying.

51   "Over the years, I tried to lie," a friend of mine explained, "but I always got found out and I always got punished. I guess I gave myself away because I feel guilty about any kind of lying. It looks as if I'm stuck with telling the truth."

52   For those of us, however, who are good at telling lies, for those of us who lie and don't get caught, the question of whether or not to lie can be a hard and serious moral problem. I liked the remark of a friend of mine who said, "I'm willing to lie. But just as a last resort—the truth's always better."

53   "Because," he explained, "though others may completely accept the lie I'm telling, I don't."

54   I tend to feel that way too.

55   What about you?

1981

Doublespeak

William Lutz

1   There are no potholes in the streets of Tucson, Arizona, just "pavement deficiencies." The Reagan Administration didn't propose any new taxes, just "revenue enhancement" through new "user's fees." Those aren't bums on the street, just "non-goal-oriented members of society." There are no more poor people, just

"fiscal underachievers." There was no robbery of an automatic teller machine, just an "unauthorized withdrawal." The patient didn't die because of medical malpractice, it was just a "diagnostic misadventure of a high magnitude." The U.S. Army doesn't kill the enemy anymore, it just "services the target." And the doublespeak goes on.

Doublespeak is language that pretends to communicate but 2 really doesn't. It is language that makes the bad seem good, the negative appear positive, the unpleasant appear attractive or at least tolerable. Doublespeak is language that avoids or shifts responsibility, language that is at variance with its real or purported meaning. It is language that conceals or prevents thought; rather than extending thought, doublespeak limits it. . . .

HOW TO SPOT DOUBLESPEAK

How can you spot doublespeak? Most of the time you will recog- 3 nize doublespeak when you see or hear it. But, if you have any doubts, you can identify doublespeak just by answering these questions: Who is saying what to whom, under what conditions and circumstances, with what intent, and with what results? Answering these questions will usually help you identify as doublespeak language that appears to be legitimate or that at first glance doesn't even appear to be doublespeak.

First Kind of Doublespeak

There are at least four kinds of doublespeak. The first is the 4 euphemism, an inoffensive or positive word or phrase used to avoid a harsh, unpleasant, or distasteful reality. But a euphemism can also be a tactful word or phrase which avoids directly mentioning a painful reality, or it can be an expression used out of concern for the feelings of someone else, or to avoid directly discussing a topic subject to a social or cultural taboo.

When you use a euphemism because of your sensitivity for 5 someone's feelings or out of concern for a recognized social or cultural taboo, it is not doublespeak. For example, you express your condolences that someone has "passed away" because you do not want to say to a grieving person, "I'm sorry your father is dead." When you use the euphemism "passed away," no one is misled. Moreover, the euphemism functions here not just to protect the feelings of another person, but to communicate also your concern for that person's feelings during a period of mourning. When you excuse yourself to go to the "restroom," or you mention that someone is "sleeping with" or "involved with" someone else, you do not mislead anyone about your meaning, but you do respect the social taboos about discussing bodily functions and sex in direct terms. You also indicate your sensitivity to the feelings of your audience, which is usually considered a mark of courtesy and good manners.

6   However, when a euphemism is used to mislead or deceive, it becomes doublespeak. For example, in 1984 the U.S. State Department announced that it would no longer use the word "killing" in its annual report on the status of human rights in countries around the world. Instead, it would use the phrase "unlawful or arbitrary deprivation of life," which the department claimed was more accurate. Its real purpose for using this phrase was simply to avoid discussing the embarrassing situation of government-sanctioned killings in countries that are supported by the United States and have been certified by the United States as respecting the human rights of their citizens. This use of a euphemism constitutes doublespeak, since it is designed to mislead, to cover up the unpleasant. Its real intent is at variance with its apparent intent. It is language designed to alter our perception of reality.

7   The Pentagon, too, avoids discussing unpleasant realities when it refers to bombs and artillery shells that fall on civilian targets as "incontinent ordnance." And in 1977 the Pentagon tried to slip funding for the neutron bomb unnoticed into an appropriations bill by calling it a "radiation enhancement device."

Second Kind of Doublespeak

8 A second kind of doublespeak is jargon, the specialized language of a trade, profession, or similar group, such as that used by doctors, lawyers, engineers, educators, or car mechanics. Jargon can

serve an important and useful function. Within a group, jargon functions as a kind of verbal shorthand that allows members of the group to communicate with each other clearly, efficiently, and quickly. Indeed, it is a mark of membership in the group to be able to use and understand the group's jargon.

But jargon, like the euphemism, can also be doublespeak. It 9 can be—and often is—pretentious, obscure, and esoteric terminology used to give an air of profundity, authority, and prestige to speakers and their subject matter. Jargon as doublespeak often makes the simple appear complex, the ordinary profound, the obvious insightful. In this sense it is used not to express but impress. With such doublespeak, the act of smelling something becomes "organoleptic analysis," glass becomes "fused silicate," a crack in a metal support beam becomes a "discontinuity," conservative economic policies become "distributionally conservative notions."

Lawyers, for example, speak of an "involuntary conversion" 10 of property when discussing the loss or destruction of property through theft, accident, or condemnation. If your house burns down or if your car is stolen, you have suffered an involuntary conversion of your property. When used by lawyers in a legal situation, such jargon is a legitimate use of language, since lawyers can be expected to understand the term.

However, when a member of a specialized group uses its jar- 11 gon to communicate with a person outside the group, and uses it knowing that the nonmember does not understand such language, then there is doublespeak. For example, on May 9, 1978, a National Airlines 727 airplane crashed while attempting to land at the Pensacola, Florida, airport. Three of the fifty-two passengers aboard the airplane were killed. As a result of the crash, National made an after-tax insurance benefit of $1.7 million, or an extra 18¢ a share dividend for its stock-holders. Now National Airlines had two problems: It did not want to talk about one of its airplanes crashing, and it had to account for the $1.7 million when it issued its annual report to its stockholders. National solved the problem by inserting a footnote in its annual report which explained that the $1.7 million income was due to "the involuntary conversion of a 727." National thus acknowledged the crash of its airplane and the subsequent profit it made from the crash, without once mentioning the accident or the deaths. However, because airline officials knew that most stockholders in the company, and indeed most of the general public, were not familiar with legal jargon, the use of such jargon constituted doublespeak.

Third Kind of Doublespeak

12   A third kind of doublespeak is gobbledygook or bureaucratese. Basically, such doublespeak is simply a matter of piling on words, of overwhelming the audience with words, the bigger the words and the longer the sentences the better. Alan Greenspan, then chair of President Nixon's Council of Economic Advisors, was quoted in *The Philadelphia Inquirer* in 1974 as having testified before a Senate committee that "It is a tricky problem to find the particular calibration in timing that would be appropriate to stem the acceleration in risk premiums created by falling incomes without prematurely aborting the decline in the inflation-generated risk premiums."

13   Nor has Mr. Greenspan's language changed since then. Speaking to the meeting of the Economic Club of New York in 1988, Mr. Greenspan, now Federal Reserve chair, said, "I guess I should warn you, if I turn out to be particularly clear, you've probably misunderstood what I've said." Mr. Greenspan's doublespeak doesn't seem to have held back his career.

14   Sometimes gobbledygook may sound impressive, but when the quote is later examined in print it doesn't even make sense. During the 1988 presidential campaign, vice-presidential candidate Senator Dan Quayle explained the need for a strategic defense initiative by saying, "Why wouldn't an enhanced deterrent, a more stable peace, a better prospect to denying the ones who enter conflict in the first place to have a reduction of offensive systems and an introduction to defense capability? I believe this is the route the country will eventually go."

15   The investigation into the *Challenger* disaster in 1986 revealed the doublespeak of gobbledygook and bureaucratese used by too many involved in the shuttle program. When Jesse Moore, NASA's associate administrator, was asked if the performance of the shuttle program had improved with each launch or if it had

remained the same, he answered, "I think our performance in terms of the liftoff performance and in terms of the orbital performance, we knew more about the envelope we were operating under, and we have been pretty accurately staying in that. And so I would say the performance has not by design drastically improved. I think we have been able to characterize the performance more as a function of our launch experience as opposed to it improving as a function of time." While this language may appear to be jargon, a close look will reveal that it is really just gobbledygook laced with jargon. But you really have to wonder if Mr. Moore had any idea what he was saying.

Fourth Kind of Doublespeak

The fourth kind of doublespeak is inflated language that is 16 designed to make the ordinary seem extraordinary; to make everyday things seem impressive; to give an air of importance to people, situations, or things that would not normally be considered important; to make the simple seem complex. Often this kind of doublespeak isn't hard to spot, and it is usually pretty funny. While car mechanics may be called "automotive internists," elevator operators members of the "vertical transportation corps," used cars "pre-owned" or "experienced cars," and black-and-white television sets described as having "nonmulticolor capability," you really aren't misled all that much by such language.

However, you may have trouble figuring out that, when 17 Chrysler "initiates a career alternative enhancement program," it is really laying off five thousand workers; or that "negative patient care outcome" means the patient died; or that "rapid oxidation" means a fire in a nuclear power plant.

The doublespeak of inflated language can have serious conse- 18 quences. In Pentagon doublespeak, "pre-emptive counterattack" means that American forces attacked first; "engaged the enemy on all sides" means American troops were ambushed; "backloading of augmentation personnel" means a retreat by American troops. In the doublespeak of the military, the 1983 invasion of Grenada was conducted not by the U.S. Army, Navy, Air Force, and Marines, but by the "Caribbean Peace Keeping Forces." But then, according to the Pentagon, it wasn't an invasion, it was a "predawn vertical insertion." . . .

THE DANGERS OF DOUBLESPEAK

19 These . . . examples of doublespeak should make it clear that double-speak is not the product of carelessness or sloppy thinking. Indeed, most doublespeak is the product of clear thinking and is carefully designed and constructed to appear to communicate when in fact it doesn't. It is language designed not to lead but mislead. It is language designed to distort reality and corrupt thought. . . . When a fire in a nuclear reactor building is called "rapid oxidation," an explosion in a nuclear power plant is called an "energetic disassembly," the illegal overthrow of a legitimate government is termed "destabilizing a government," and lies are seen as "inoperative statements," we are hearing doublespeak that attempts to avoid responsibility and make the bad seem good, the negative appear positive, something unpleasant appear attractive; and which seems to communicate but doesn't. It is language designed to alter our perception of reality and corrupt our thinking. Such language does not provide us with the tools we need to develop, advance, and preserve our culture and our civilization. Such language breeds suspicion, cynicism, distrust, and, ultimately, hostility.

1989

What Secrets Tell

Luc Sante

1 Secrets are a permanent feature of the human condition. We need secrets the way we need black holes, for their mystery; the way we need landspeed records, for their enlargement of scale; the way we need sexy models in advertisements, for their seductively false

promises; the way we need lotteries, for their vague possibility. We also need them the way we need bank vaults and sock drawers and glove compartments. Anybody who doesn't carry around one or two secrets probably has all the depth of a place mat.

But then the word *secret* conceals under its mantle a teeming 2 and motley population of types. Secrets cater to the entire range of human susceptibilities, from the laughably trivial to the terrifyingly fundamental. Principal landmarks along the way include:

Personal Secrets   In other words, those secrets that are chiefly 3 of interest to the persons who carry them around. You know the sort: You pick your nose when no one's looking; your real first name is Eustace; you wear a truss for nonmedical reasons. If such things were revealed, your ego might take a beating and your intimates could gain a weapon for use in squabbles or extortions, but the foundations of your house would not be shaken.

Romantic Secrets   They run the gamut. That interval of pas- 4 sion you once shared with your dentist when the two of you were stuck in an elevator with a bottle of Cherry Kijafa may remain swathed in gauze for all eternity, although your partner might eventually demand to know the identity of this "Shirley" whose name you utter in your sleep. That you enjoy above all the erotic sensation of being pinched with tweezers until you bleed might not matter a whole lot to anyone, unless you decide to run for office, and then you will find yourself sending discreet sums of money to people you haven't thought of in years. Couples often tacitly erect a whole edifice of secrets, based on real or imagined causes for jealousy. This can be relatively harmless, or it can be a symptom of the relationship's becoming a regime.

Secrets in Gossip   That is, the wheat left over when gossip's 5 chaff is sifted out. Secrets that surface as gossip are usually of the mildest sort, personal eccentricities and romantic peccadilloes not of much interest outside a closed circle. (It is understood that there is a direct correlation between the degree of triviality of the secret transmitted as gossip and the rank of the gossip's subject within that circle.) Gossip, though, demonstrates how secrets can become currency, as the teller invests the hearer with power in exchange for esteem. The possession of a secret concerning another is, like all forms of power, something of a burden, a weight pressing one's lips together, which can be relieved only by telling someone else. This, added to a hunger for knowledge on the part of all within the gossip circle, keeps the wheel of the secret-fueled gossip economy turning.

6   **Trade Secrets**   The monetary economy, meanwhile, revolves around a wide and diverse range of secrets. A business strategy is a secret until it becomes a fait accompli. The details of the financial health of a company are kept as secret as the law allows. Anyone with a degree of power in the market is continually keeping secrets—from competitors, from the press, from anyone who is an outsider, including friends and family, but sometimes from colleagues and office mates. The reasons are obvious: Everyone is naked in a cutthroat world, and secrets are clothing. It goes without saying that secrets protect innovations and that they also hide various extralegal undertakings—the ostensibly respectable bank that takes in laundry on the side, for example. Business also employs secrets strategically, as secrets qua secrets, usually painting the word *secret* in letters ten stories tall. Naturally the new car model will differ little from the previous year's, but a bit of cloak-and-dagger about it will increase public interest. The "secret recipe" is on a par with "new and improved" as a carny barker's hook. The cake mix or soft drink or laundry soap may, of course, actually include a secret ingredient, known only to staff chemists and highly placed executives, but very often a "secret ingredient" is rumored or bruited about primarily as a lure to the gulls of the public.

7   **Secret Formulas**   The public hunger for secrets is primordial. It is first and foremost a matter of curiosity, but it also springs from a painful awareness of rank and a belief that things are different upstairs, with a more or less fanciful idea of the specifics. These days, with fortune-building running at a pitch not seen since the 1920s, there is widespread demand for financial folklore. You can make a lot of money catering to the suspicion that there exist shortcuts known only to a few. That some people are richer, thinner, more charismatic or whiter of teeth may be a result of a variety of imponderable factors, but for everyone who in moments of desperation has imagined that there must be some simple trick, some formula or high sign or investment

routine or hidden spa, there is an author with a book aimed at the exact combination of vulnerability and prurient imagination. Such publications run along the entire span of implied legitimacy based upon demographics, from the crudities aimed at the super-market-tabloid constituency (diets centered on junk food named in the Bible, for instance) to the overpriced hardcover pamphlets catering to the anxieties of the managerial class by dressing up received ideas with slogans and numbered lists. For centuries, the secret has been a sure-fire sales gimmick. All you have to do is combine the banal and the esoteric.

Secret Societies   There are probably a lot fewer than there 8 once were, but somewhere in America, no doubt, insurance adjusters and trophy engravers still gather once a month in acrylic gowns and button-flap underwear to exchange phrases in pseudobiblical double Dutch and then get down to the business of drinking beer. It helps them feel special to be the only ones in town who know the three-finger handshake. The setup descends from the heresies of the Middle Ages by the way of the pecking order of the playground. We can laugh at them, now that they are so enfeebled, but there was a time not long ago when they domi-nated the social life of male middle-class America, and in many ways their pretensions are not so far removed from those of the Mafia or the CIA.

Mystical Secrets   The secret is bait. The secret leads votaries 9 by the nose through a maze of connected chambers, in each of which they must ante up. Only when they have finally tumbled to there being no secret (and they have run through the better part of their inheritances) can they truly be counted as initiates. But few have the stamina to get that far, and most instead spend their spare afternoons consuming one tome after another pro-moting the secrets of, variously, the pyramids, the Templars, the ascended masters, the elders of Mu, the Essene scrolls, and so on through greater and lesser degrees of perceived legitimacy, all of which flutter around the edges of the secret, none of which make so bold as to suggest what it might consist of.

State Secrets   "Our laws are not generally known; they are 10 kept secret by the small group of nobles who rule us," wrote Kafka in one of his miniature stories. "We are convinced that these ancient laws are scrupulously administered; nevertheless it is an extremely painful thing to be ruled by laws that one does not know." This is the essence of state secrets. A government does not have to be totalitarian, particularly, to possess a stratum of laws whose existence cannot be generally known because they describe the limits of the knowable. It is forbidden for unauthorized persons to possess certain kinds of information. What kinds of information? Well, that's the trouble; if you knew that, you would already know too much. State secrets range all the way from banal prohibitions on photographing customs booths and power plants to the highest levels of technical esoterica.

11   **Atomic Secrets**   "Stop me if you've heard this atomic secret," cracked William Burroughs in *Naked Lunch*. Atomic secrets may be the world's most famous class of secret, an oxymoron, surely, but for the fact that few enough people would recognize or understand an atomic secret if it landed in their mailboxes. The workaday state secret may be a matter of mere protocol or protection of resources, not unlike industries safeguarding the peculiarities of their production methods. The atomic secret, however, ascends to the level of the sacred because it manifests in concrete form the terror that mystics can only suggest: the end of the world. The secret of life may be an empty proposition, but the secret of death is actually legible to those who possess the language and the tools. . . .

12   People need secrets because they need the assurance that there is something left to discover, that they have not exhausted the limits of their environment, that a prize might lie in wait like money in the pocket of an old jacket, that the existence of things beyond their ken might propose as a corollary that their own minds contain unsuspected corridors. People need uncertainty and destabilization the way they need comfort and security. It's not that secrets make them feel small but that they make the world seem bigger—a major necessity these days, when sensations need to be extreme to register at all. Secrets reawaken that feeling from childhood that the ways of the world were infinitely mysterious, unpredictable and densely packed, and that someday you might come to know and master them. Secrets purvey affordable glamour, suggest danger without presenting an actual threat. If there were no more secrets,

an important motor of life would be stopped, and the days would merge into a continuous blur. Secrets hold out the promise, false but necessary, that death will be deferred until their unveiling.

The 12 Most Annoying Types of Facebookers

Brandon Griggs

Facebook, for better or worse, is like being at a big party with all your friends, family, acquaintances and co-workers. 1

There are lots of fun, interesting people you're happy to talk to when they stroll up. Then there are the other people, the ones who make you cringe when you see them coming. This article is about those people. 2

Sure, Facebook can be a great tool for keeping up with folks who are important to you. Take the status update, the 160-character message that users post in response to the question, "What's on your mind?" An artful, witty or newsy status update is a pleasure—a real-time, tiny window into a friend's life. 3

But far more posts read like navel-gazing diary entries, or worse, spam. A recent study categorized 40 percent of Twitter tweets as "pointless babble," and it wouldn't be surprising if updates on Facebook, still a fast-growing social network, break down in a similar way. Combine dull status updates with shameless self-promoters, "friend-padders" and that friend of a friend who sends you quizzes every day, and Facebook becomes a daily reminder of why some people can get on your nerves. 4

Here are 12 of the most annoying types of Facebook users: 5

The Let-Me-Tell-You-Every-Detail-of-My-Day Bore. "I'm waking up." "I had Wheaties for breakfast." "I'm bored at work." "I'm stuck in traffic." You're kidding! How fascinating! No moment is too mundane for some people to broadcast unsolicited to the world. Just because you have 432 Facebook friends doesn't mean we all want to know when you're waiting for the bus. 6

7   **The Self-Promoter.** OK, so we've probably all posted at least once about some achievement. And sure, maybe your friends really do want to read the fascinating article you wrote about beet farming. But when almost EVERY update is a link to your blog, your poetry reading, your 10k results or your art show, you sound like a bragger or a self-centered careerist.

8   **The Friend-Padder.** The average Facebook user has 120 friends on the site. Schmoozers and social butterflies—you know, the ones who make lifelong pals on the subway—might reasonably have 300 or 400. But 1,000 "friends?" Unless you're George Clooney or just won the lottery, no one has that many. That's just showing off.

9   **The Town Crier.** "Michael Jackson is dead!!!" You heard it from me first! Me, and the 213,000 other people who all saw it on TMZ. These Matt Drudge wannabes are the reason many of us learn of breaking news not from TV or news sites but from online social networks. In their rush to trumpet the news, these people also spread rumors, half-truths and innuendo. No, Jeff Goldblum did not plunge to his death from a New Zealand cliff.

10   **The TMIer.** "Brad is heading to Walgreens to buy something for these pesky hemorrhoids." Boundaries of privacy and decorum don't seem to exist for these too-much-information updaters, who unabashedly offer up details about their sex lives, marital troubles and bodily functions. Thanks for sharing.

11   **The Bad Grammarian.** "So sad about Fara Fauset but Im so gladd its friday yippe." Yes, I know the punctuation rules are different in the digital world. And, no, no one likes a spelling-Nazi schoolmarm. But you sound like a moron.

12   **The Sympathy-Baiter.** "Barbara is feeling sad today." "Man, am I glad that's over." "Jim could really use some good news about now." Like anglers hunting for fish, these sad sacks cast out their hooks—baited with vague tales of woe—in the hopes of landing concerned responses. Genuine bad news is one thing, but these manipulative posts are just pleas for attention.

13   **The Lurker.** The Peeping Toms of Facebook, these voyeurs are too cautious, or maybe too lazy, to update their status or write on your wall. But once in a while, you'll be talking to them and

they'll mention something you posted, so you know they're on your page, hiding in the shadows. It's just a little creepy.

The Crank. These curmudgeons, like the trolls who spew 14 hate in blog comments, never met something they couldn't complain about. "Carl isn't really that impressed with idiots who don't realize how idiotic they are." [Actual status update.] Keep spreading the love.

The Paparazzo. Ever visit your Facebook page and discover 15 that someone's posted a photo of you from last weekend's party—a photo you didn't authorize and haven't even seen? You'd really rather not have to explain to your mom why you were leering like a drunken hyena and French-kissing a bottle of Jagermeister.

The Obscurist. "If not now then when?" "You'll see..." 16 "Grist for the mill." "John is, small world." "Dave thought he was immune, but no. No, he is not." [Actual status updates, all.] Sorry, but you're not being mysterious—just nonsensical.

The Chronic Inviter. "Support my cause. Sign my petition. 17 Play Mafia Wars with me. Which 'Star Trek' character are you? Here are the 'Top 5 cars I have personally owned.' Here are '25 Things About Me.' Here's a drink. What drink are you? We're related! I took the 'What President Are You?' quiz and found out I'm Millard Fillmore! What president are you?"

You probably mean well, but stop. Just stop. I don't care what 18 president I am—can't we simply be friends? Now excuse me while I go post the link to this story on my Facebook page.

6

Comparison and Contrast

Grant and Lee: A Study in Contrasts

Bruce Catton

1   When Ulysses S. Grant and Robert E. Lee met in the parlor of a modest house at Appomattox Court House, Virginia, on April 9, 1865, to work out the terms for the surrender of Lee's Army of Northern Virginia, a great chapter in American life came to a close, and a great new chapter began.

2   These men were bringing the Civil War to its virtual finish. To be sure, other armies had yet to surrender, and for a few days the fugitive Confederate government would struggle desperately and vainly, trying to find some way to go on living now that its chief support was gone. But in effect it was all over when Grant and Lee signed the papers. And the little room where they wrote out the terms was the scene of one of the poignant, dramatic contrasts in American history.

3   They were two strong men, these oddly different generals, and they represented the strengths of two conflicting currents that, through them, had come into final collision.

4   Back of Robert E. Lee was the notion that the old aristocratic concept might somehow survive and be dominant in American life.

5   Lee was tidewater Virginia, and in his background were family, culture, and tradition...the age of chivalry transplanted to a New World which was making its own legends and its own myths. He embodied a way of life that had come down through the age of

knighthood and the English country squire. America was a land that was beginning all over again, dedicated to nothing much more complicated than the rather hazy belief that all men had equal rights, and should have an equal chance in the world. In such a land Lee stood for the feeling that it was somehow of advantage to human society to have a pronounced inequality in the social structure. There should be a leisure class, backed by ownership of land; in turn, society itself should be keyed to the land as the chief source of wealth and influence. It would bring forth (according to this ideal) a class of men with a strong sense of obligation to the community; men who lived not to gain advantage for themselves, but to meet the solemn obligations which had been laid on them by the very fact that they were privileged. From them the country would get its leadership; to them it could look for the higher values—of thought, of conduct, of personal deportment—to give it strength and virtue.

Lee embodied the noblest elements of this aristocratic ideal. 6 Through him, the landed nobility justified itself. For four years, the Southern states had fought a desperate war to uphold the ideals for which Lee stood. In the end, it almost seemed as if the Confederacy fought for Lee; as if he himself was the Confederacy . . . the best thing that the way of life for which the Confederacy stood could ever have to offer. He had passed into legend before Appomattox. Thousands of tired, underfed, poorly clothed Confederate soldiers, long-since past the simple enthusiasm of the early days of the struggle, somehow considered Lee the symbol of everything for which they had been willing to die. But they could not quite put this feeling into words. If the Lost Cause, sanctified by so much heroism and so many deaths, had a living justification, its justification was General Lee.

Grant, the son of a tanner on the Western frontier, was every- 7 thing Lee was not. He had come up the hard way, and embodied nothing in particular except the eternal toughness and sinewy fiber of the men who grew up beyond the mountains. He was one of a body of men who owed reverence and obeisance to no one, who were self-reliant to a fault, who cared hardly anything for the past but who had a sharp eye for the future.

These frontier men were the precise opposites of the tidewater 8 aristocrats. Back of them, in the great surge that had taken people over the Alleghenies and into the opening Westerncountry, there was a deep, implicit dissatisfaction with a past that had settled into grooves. They stood for democracy, not from any reasoned conclusion about the proper ordering of human society, but simply because they had grown up in the middle of democracy and knew how it worked. Their society might have privileges, but they would be privileges each man had won for himself. Forms and patterns meant nothing. No man was born to anything, except perhaps to a chance to show how far he could rise. Life was competition.

9   Yet along with this feeling had come a deep sense of belonging to a national community. The Westerner who developed a farm, opened a shop or set up in business as a trader, could hope to prosper only as his own community prospered—and his community ran from the Atlantic to the Pacific and from Canada down to Mexico. If the land was settled, with towns and highways and accessible markets, he could better himself. He saw his fate in terms of the nation's own destiny. As its horizons expanded, so did his. He had, in other words, an acute dollars-and-cents stake in the continued growth and development of his country.

10   And that, perhaps, is where the contrast between Grant and Lee becomes most striking. The Virginia aristocrat, inevitably, saw himself in relation to his own region. He lived in a static society which could endure almost anything except change. Instinctively, his first loyalty would go to the locality in which that society existed. He would fight to the limit of endurance to defend it, because in defending it he was defending everything that gave his own life its deepest meaning.

11   The Westerner, on the other hand, would fight with an equal tenacity for the broader concept of society. He fought so because everything he lived by was tied to growth, expansion, and a constantly widening horizon. What he lived by would survive or fall with the nation itself. He could not possibly stand by unmoved in the face of an attempt to destroy the Union. He would combat it with everything he had, because he could only see it as an effort to cut the ground out from under his feet.

12   So Grant and Lee were in complete contrast, representing two diametrically opposed elements in American life. Grant was the

modern man emerging; beyond him, ready to come on the stage, was the great age of steel and machinery, of crowded cities and a restless, burgeoning vitality. Lee might have ridden down from the old age of chivalry, lance in hand, silken banner fluttering over his head. Each man was the perfect champion of his cause, drawing both his strengths and his weaknesses from the people he led.

Yet it was not all contrast, after all. Different as they were—in background, in personality, in underlying aspiration—these two great soldiers had much in common. Under everything else, they were marvelous fighters. Furthermore, their fighting qualities were really very much alike. 13

Each man had, to begin with, the great virtue of utter tenacity and fidelity. Grant fought his way down the Mississippi Valley in spite of acute personal discouragement and profound military handicaps. Lee hung on in the trenches at Petersburg after hope itself had died. In each man there was an indomitable quality . . . the born fighter's refusal to give up as long as he can still remain on his feet and lift his two fists. 14

Daring and resourcefulness they had, too; the ability to think faster and move faster than the enemy. These were the qualities which gave Lee the dazzling campaigns of Second Manassas and Chancellorsville and won Vicksburg for Grant. 15

Lastly, and perhaps greatest of all, there was the ability, at the end, to turn quickly from war to peace once the fighting was over. Out of the way these two men behaved at Appomattox came the possibility of a peace of reconciliation. It was a possibility not wholly realized, in the years to come, but which did, in the end, help the two sections to become one nation again . . . after a war whose bitterness might have seemed to make such a reunion wholly impossible. No part of either man's life became him more than the part he played in their brief meeting in the McLean house at Appomattox. Their behavior there put all succeeding generations of Americans in their debt. Two great Americans, Grant and Lee—very different, yet under everything very much alike. Their encounter at Appomattox was one of the great moments of American history. 16

1958

Two Views of the Mississippi

Mark Twain

1 Now when I had mastered the language of this water, and had come to know every trifling feature that bordered the great river as familiarly as I knew the letters of the alphabet, I had made a valuable acquisition. But I had lost something, too. I had lost something which could never be restored to me while I lived. All the grace, the beauty, the poetry, had gone out of the majestic river! I still keep in mind a certain wonderful sunset which I witnessed when steamboating was new to me. A broad expanse of the river was turned to blood; in the middle distance the red hue brightened into gold, through which a solitary log came floating black and conspicuous; in one place a long, slanting mark lay sparkling upon the water; in another the surface was broken by boiling, tumbling rings, that were as many-tinted as an opal; where the ruddy flush was faintest, was a smooth spot that was covered with graceful circles and radiating lines, ever so delicately traced; the shore on our left was densely wooded, and the somber shadow that fell from this forest was broken in one place by a long, ruffled trail that shone like silver; and high above the forest wall a cleanstemmed dead tree waved a single leafy bough that glowed like a flame in the unobstructed splendor that was flowing from the sun. There were graceful curves, reflected images, woody heights, soft distances; and over the whole scene, far and near, the dissolving lights drifted steadily, enriching it every passing moment with new marvels of coloring.

2 I stood like one bewitched. I drank it in, in a speechless rapture. The world was new to me, and I had never seen anything like this at home. But as I have said, a day came when I began to cease from noting the glories and the charms which the moon and the sun and the twilight wrought upon the river's face; another day came when I ceased altogether to note them. Then, if that sunset scene had been repeated, I should have looked upon it without rapture, and should have commented upon it, inwardly, after this fashion: "This sun means that we are going to have wind tomorrow; that floating log means that the river is rising, small thanks

to it; that slanting mark on the water refers to a bluff reef which is going to kill somebody's steamboat one of these nights, if it keeps on stretching out like that; those tumbling 'boils' show a dissolving bar and a changing channel there; the lines and circles in the slick water over yonder are a warning that that troublesome place is shoaling up dangerously; that silver streak in the shadow of the forest is the 'break' from a new snag, and he has located himself in the very best place he could have found to fish for steamboats; that tall dead tree, with a single living branch, is not going to last long, and then how is a body ever going to get through this blind place at night without the friendly old landmark?"

No, the romance and beauty were all gone from the river. All the value any feature of it had for me now was the amount of usefulness it could furnish toward compassing the safe piloting of a steamboat. Since those days, I have pitied doctors from my heart. What does the lovely flush in a beauty's cheek mean to a doctor but a "break" that ripples above some deadly disease? Are not all her visible charms sown thick with what are to him the signs and symbols of hidden decay? Does he ever see her beauty at all, or doesn't he simply view her professionally, and comment upon her unwholesome condition all to himself? And doesn't he sometimes wonder whether he has gained most or lost most by learning his trade?

1883

The Men We Carry in Our Minds

Scott Russell Sanders

The first men, besides my father, I remember seeing were black convicts and white guards, in the cottonfield across the road from our farm on the outskirts of Memphis. I must have been three or four. The prisoners wore dingy gray-and-black zebra suits, heavy as canvas, sodden with sweat. Hatless, stooped, they chopped weeds in the fierce heat, row after row, breathing the acrid dust of boll-weevil poison. The overseers wore dazzling white shirts and broad shadowy hats. The oiled barrels of their shotguns flashed in the sunlight. Their faces in memory are utterly blank. Of course those men, white and black, have become for me an emblem of racial hatred. But they have also come to stand for the twin poles of my early vision of manhood—the brute toiling animal and the boss.

2   When I was a boy, the men I knew labored with their bodies. They were marginal farmers, just scraping by, or welders, steel workers, carpenters; they swept floors, dug ditches, mined coal, or drove trucks, their forearms ropy with muscle; they trained horses, stoked furnaces, built tires, stood on assembly lines wrestling parts onto cars and refrigerators. They got up before light, worked all day long whatever the weather, and when they came home at night they looked as though somebody had been whipping them. In the evenings and on weekends they worked on their own places, tilling gardens that were lumpy with clay, fixing broken-down cars, hammering on houses that were always too drafty, too leaky, too small.

3   The bodies of the men I knew were twisted and maimed in ways visible and invisible. The nails of their hands were black and split, the hands tattooed with scars. Some had lost fingers. Heavy lifting had given many of them finicky backs and guts weak from hernias. Racing against conveyor belts had given them ulcers. Their ankles and knees ached from years of standing on concrete. Anyone who had worked for long around machines was hard of hearing. They squinted, and the skin of their faces was creased like the leather of old work gloves. There were times, studying them, when I dreaded growing up. Most of them coughed, from dust or cigarettes, and most of them drank cheap wine or whiskey, so their eyes looked bloodshot and bruised. The fathers of my friends always seemed older than the mothers. Men wore out sooner. Only women lived into old age.

4   As a boy I also knew another sort of men, who did not sweat and break down like mules. They were soldiers, and so far as I could tell they scarcely worked at all. During my early school years we lived on a military base, an arsenal in Ohio, and every

day I saw GIs in the guardshacks, on the stoops of barracks, at the wheels of olive drab Chevrolets. The chief fact of their lives was boredom. Long after I left the Arsenal I came to recognize the sour smell the soldiers gave off as that of souls in limbo. They were all waiting—for wars, for transfers, for leaves, for promotions, for the end of their hitch—like so many braves waiting for the hunt to begin. Unlike the warriors of older tribes, however, they would have no say about when the battle would start or how it would be waged. Their waiting was broken only when they practiced for war. They fired guns at targets, drove tanks across the churned-up fields of the military reservation, set off bombs in the wrecks of old fighter planes. I knew this was all play. But I also felt certain that when the hour for killing arrived, they would kill. When the real shooting started, many of them would die. This was what soldiers were *for*, just as a hammer was for driving nails.

Warriors and toilers: those seemed, in my boyhood vision, to 5 be the chief destinies for men. They weren't the only destinies, as I learned from having a few male teachers, from reading books, and from watching television. But the men on television—the politicians, the astronauts, the generals, the savvy lawyers, the philosophical doctors, the bosses who gave orders to both soldiers and laborers—seemed as remote and unreal to me as the figures in tapestries. I could no more imagine growing up to become one of these cool, potent creatures than I could imagine becoming a prince.

A nearer and more hopeful example was that of my father, 6 who had escaped from a red-dirt farm to a tire factory, and from the assembly line to the front office. Eventually he dressed in a white shirt and tie. He carried himself as if he had been born to work with his mind. But his body, remembering the earlier years of slogging work, began to give out on him in his fifties, and it quit on him entirely before he turned sixty-five. Even such partial escape from man's fate as he had accomplished did not seem possible for most of the boys I knew. They joined the Army, stood in line for jobs in the smoky plants, helped build highways. They were bound to work as their fathers had worked, killing themselves or preparing to kill others.

7   A scholarship enabled me not only to attend college, a rare enough feat in my circle, but even to study in a university meant for the children of the rich. Here I met for the first time young men who had assumed from birth that they would lead lives of comfort and power. And for the first time I met women who told me that men were guilty of having kept all the joys and privileges of the earth for themselves. I was baffled. What privileges? What joys? I thought about the maimed, dismal lives of most of the men back home. What had they stolen from their wives and daughters? The right to go five days a week, twelve months a year, for thirty or forty years to a steel mill or a coal mine? The right to drop bombs and die in war? The right to feel every leak in the roof, every gap in the fence, every cough in the engine, as a wound they must mend? The right to feel, when the layoff comes or the plant shuts down, not only afraid but ashamed?

8   I was slow to understand the deep grievances of women. This was because, as a boy, I had envied them. Before college, the only people I had ever known who were interested in art or music or literature, the only ones who read books, the only ones who ever seemed to enjoy a sense of ease and grace were the mothers and daughters. Like the menfolk, they fretted about money, they scrimped and made-do. But, when the pay stopped coming in, they were not the ones who had failed. Nor did they have to go to war, and that seemed to me a blessed fact. By comparison with the narrow, ironclad days of fathers, there was an expansiveness, I thought, in the days of mothers. They went to see neighbors, to shop in town, to run errands at school, at the library, at church. No doubt, had I looked harder at their lives, I would have envied them less. It was not my fate to become a woman, so it was easier for me to see the graces. Few of them held jobs outside the home, and those who did filled thankless roles as clerks and waitresses. I didn't see, then, what a prison a house could be, since houses seemed to me brighter, handsomer places than any factory. I did not realize—because such things were never spoken of—how often women suffered from men's bullying. I did learn about the wretchedness of abandoned wives, single mothers, widows; but I also learned about the wretchedness of lone men. Even then I could see how exhausting it was for a mother to cater all day to

the needs of young children. But if I had been asked, as a boy, to choose between tending a baby and tending a machine, I think I would have chosen the baby. (Having now tended both, I know I would choose the baby.)

So I was baffled when the women at college accused me and 9 my sex of having cornered the world's pleasures. I think something like my bafflement has been felt by other boys (and by girls as well) who grew up in dirt-poor farm country, in mining country, in black ghettos, in Hispanic barrios, in the shadows of factories, in Third World nations—any place where the fate of men is as grim and bleak as the fate of women. Toilers and warriors. I realize now how ancient these identities are, how deep the tug they exert on men, the undertow of a thousand generations. The miseries I saw, as a boy, in the lives of nearly all men I continue to see in the lives of many—the body-breaking toil, the tedium, the call to be tough, the humiliating powerlessness, the battle for a living and for territory.

When the women I met at college thought about the joys and 10 privileges of men, they did not carry in their minds the sort of men I had known in my childhood. They thought of their fathers, who were bankers, physicians, architects, stockbrokers, the big wheels of the big cities. These fathers rode the train to work or drove cars that cost more than any of my childhood houses. They were attended from morning to night by female helpers, wives and nurses and secretaries. They were never laid off, never short of cash at month's end, never lined up for welfare. These fathers made decisions that mattered. They ran the world.

The daughters of such men wanted to share in this power, 11 this glory. So did I. They yearned for a say over their future, for jobs worthy of their abilities, for the right to live at peace, unmolested, whole. Yes, I thought, yes yes. The difference between me and these daughters was that they saw me, because of my sex, as destined from birth to become like their fathers, and therefore as an enemy to their desires. But I knew better. I wasn't an enemy, in fact or in feeling. I was an ally. If I had known, then, how to tell them so, would they have believed me? Would they now?

1984

Neat People vs. Sloppy People

Suzanne Britt

1   I've finally figured out the difference between neat people and sloppy people. The distinction is, as always, moral. Neat people are lazier and meaner than sloppy people.

2   Sloppy people, you see, are not really sloppy. Their sloppiness is merely the unfortunate consequence of their extreme moral rectitude. Sloppy people carry in their mind's eye a heavenly vision, a precise plan, that is so stupendous, so perfect, it can't be achieved in this world or the next.

3   Sloppy people live in Never-Never Land. Someday is their métier. Someday they are planning to alphabetize all their books and set up home catalogs. Someday they will go through their wardrobes and mark certain items for tentative mending and certain items for passing on to relatives of similar shape and size. Someday sloppy people will make family scrapbooks into which they will put newspaper clippings, postcards, locks of hair, and the dried corsage from their senior prom. Someday they will file everything on the surface of their desks, including the cash receipts from coffee purchases at the snack shop. Someday they will sit down and read all the back issues of the *New Yorker*.

4   For all these noble reasons and more, sloppy people never get neat. They aim too high and wide. They save everything, planning someday to file, order, and straighten out the world. But while these ambitious plans take clearer and clearer shape in their heads, the books spill from the shelves onto the floor, the clothes pile up in the hamper and closet, the family mementos accumulate in every drawer, the surface of the desk is buried under mounds of paper and the unread magazines threaten to reach the ceiling.

5   Sloppy people can't bear to part with anything. They give loving attention to every detail. When sloppy people say they're going to tackle the surface of the desk, they really mean it. Not a paper will go unturned; not a rubber band will go unboxed. Four hours or two weeks into the excavation, the desk looks exactly the same, primarily because the sloppy person is meticulously

creating new piles of papers with new headings and scrupulously stopping to read all the old book catalogs before he throws them away. A neat person would just bulldoze the desk.

Neat people are bums and clods at heart. They have cavalier attitudes toward possessions, including family heirlooms. Everything is just another dustcatcher to them. If anything collects dust, it's got to go and that's that. Neat people will toy with the idea of throwing the children out of the house just to cut down on the clutter. 6

Neat people don't care about process. They like results. What they want to do is get the whole thing over with so they can sit down and watch the rasslin' on TV. Neat people operate on two unvarying principles: Never handle any item twice, and throw everything away. 7

The only thing messy in a neat person's house is the trash can. The minute something comes to a neat person's hand, he will look at it, try to decide if it has immediate use and, finding none, throw it in the trash. 8

Neat people are especially vicious with mail. They never go through their mail unless they are standing directly over a trash can. If the trash can is beside the mailbox, even better. All ads, catalogs, pleas for charitable contributions, church bulletins and money-saving coupons go straight into the trash can without being opened. All letters from home, postcards from Europe, bills and paychecks are opened, immediately responded to, then dropped in the trash can. Neat people keep their receipts only for tax purposes. That's it. No sentimental salvaging of birthday cards or the last letter a dying relative ever wrote. Into the trash it goes. 9

Neat people place neatness above everything, even economics. They are incredibly wasteful. Neat people throw away several toys every time they walk through the den. I knew a neat person once who threw away a perfectly good dish drainer because it had mold on it. The drainer was too much trouble to wash. And neat people sell their furniture when they move. They will sell a La-Z-Boy recliner while you are reclining in it. 10

Neat people are no good to borrow from. Neat people buy everything in expensive little single portions. They get their flour 11 and sugar in two-pound bags. They wouldn't consider clipping a coupon, saving a leftover, reusing plastic nondairy whipped cream containers or rinsing off tin foil and draping it over the unmoldy dish drainer. You can never borrow a neat person's newspaper to see what's playing at the movies. Neat people have the paper all wadded up and in the trash by 7:05 A.M.

12   Neat people cut a clean swath through the organic as well as the in-organic world. People, animals, and things are all one to them. They are so insensitive. After they've finished with the pantry, the medicine cabinet, and the attic, they will throw out the red geranium (too many leaves), sell the dog (too many fleas), and send the children off to boarding school (too many scuffmarks on the hardwood floors).

1983

Two Ways to Belong in America

Bharati Mukherjee

1   This is a tale of two sisters from Calcutta, Mira and Bharati, who have lived in the United States for some 35 years, but who find themselves on different sides in the current debate over the status of immigrants. I am an American citizen and she is not. I am moved that thousands of long-term residents are finally taking the oath of citizenship. She is not.

2   Mira arrived in Detroit in 1960 to study child psychology and pre-school education. I followed her a year later to study creative writing at the University of Iowa. When we left India, we were almost identical in appearance and attitude. We dressed alike, in saris; we expressed identical views on politics, social issues, love and marriage in the same Calcutta convent-school accent. We would endure our two years in America, secure our degrees, then return to India to marry the grooms of our father's choosing.

Instead, Mira married an Indian student in 1962 who was get- 3
ting his business administration degree at Wayne State University.
They soon acquired the labor certifications necessary for the
green card of hassle-free residence and employment.

Mira still lives in Detroit, works in the Southfield, Mich., 4
school system, and has become nationally recognized for her contributions in the fields of pre-school education and parent-teacher
relationships. After 36 years as a legal immigrant in this country,
she clings passionately to her Indian citizenship and hopes to go
home to India when she retires.

In Iowa City in 1963, I married a fellow student, an American 5
of Canadian parentage. Because of the accident of his North
Dakota birth, I bypassed labor-certification requirements and the
race-related "quota" system that favored the applicant's country
of origin over his or her merit. I was prepared for (and even
welcomed) the emotional strain that came with marrying outside
my ethnic community. In 33 years of marriage, we have lived in
every part of North America. By choosing a husband who was
not my father's selection, I was opting for fluidity, self-invention,
blue jeans and T-shirts, and renouncing 3000 years (at least) of
caste-observant, "pure culture" marriage in the Mukherjee family. My books have often been read as unapologetic (and in some
quarters overenthusiastic) texts for cultural and psychological
"mongrelization." It's a word I celebrate.

Mira and I have stayed sisterly close by phone. In our regular 6
Sunday morning conversations, we are unguardedly affection-
ate. I am her only blood relative on this continent. We expect
to see each other through the looming crises of aging and ill
health without being asked. Long before Vice President Gore's
"Citizenship U.S.A." drive, we'd had our polite arguments over
the ethics of retaining an overseas citizenship while expecting the
permanent protection and economic benefits that come with living and working in America.

Like well-raised sisters, we never said what was really on 7
our minds, but we probably pitied one another. She, for the lack
of structure in my life, the erasure of Indianness, the absence of
an unvarying daily core. I, for the narrowness of her perspective,
her uninvolvement with the mythic depths or the superficial pop

culture of this society. But, now, with the scapegoating of "aliens" (documented or illegal) on the increase, and the targeting of long-term legal immigrants like Mira for new scrutiny and new self-consciousness, she and I find ourselves unable to maintain the same polite discretion. We were always unacknowledged adversaries, and we are now, more than ever, sisters.

8   "I feel used," Mira raged on the phone the other night. "I feel manipulated and discarded. This is such an unfair way to treat a person who was invited to stay and work here because of her talent. My employer went to the I.N.S. and petitioned for the labor certification. For over 30 years, I've invested my creativity and professional skills into the improvement of *this* country's pre-school system. I've obeyed all the rules, I've paid my taxes, I love my work, I love my students, I love the friends I've made. How dare America now change its rules in midstream? If America wants to make new rules curtailing benefits of legal immigrants, they should apply only to immigrants who arrive after those rules are already in place."

9   To my ears, it sounded like the description of a long-enduring, comfortable yet loveless marriage, without risk or recklessness. Have we the right to demand, and to expect, that we be loved? (That, to me, is the subtext of the arguments by immigration advocates.) My sister is an expatriate, professionally generous and creative, socially courteous and gracious, and that's as far as her Americanization can go. She is here to maintain an identity, not to transform it.

10   I asked her if she would follow the example of others who have decided to become citizens because of the anti-immigration bills in Congress. And here, she surprised me. "If America wants to play the manipulative game, I'll play it too," she snapped. "I'll become a U.S. citizen for now, then change back to Indian when I'm ready to go home. I feel some kind of irrational attachment to India that I don't to America. Until all this hysteria against legal immigrants, I was totally happy. Having my green card meant I could visit any place in the world I wanted to and then come back to a job that's satisfying and that I do very well."

11   In one family, from two sisters alike as peas in a pod, there could not be a wider divergence of immigrant experience.

America spoke to me—I married it—I embraced the demotion from expatriate aristocrat to immigrant nobody, surrendering those thousands of years of "pure culture," the saris, the delightfully accented English. She retained them all. Which of us is the freak?

Mira's voice, I realize, is the voice not just of the immigrant 12 South Asian community but of an immigrant community of the millions who have stayed rooted in one job, one city, one house, one ancestral culture, one cuisine, for the entirety of their productive years. She speaks for greater numbers than I possibly can. Only the fluency of her English and the anger, rather than fear, born of confidence from her education, differentiate her from the seamstresses, the domestics, the technicians, the shop owners, the millions of hard-working but effectively silenced documented immigrants as well as their less fortunate "illegal" brothers and sisters.

Nearly 20 years ago, when I was living in my husband's 13 ancestral homeland of Canada, I was always well-employed but never allowed to feel part of the local Quebec or larger Canadian society. Then, through a Green Paper that invited a national referendum on the unwanted side effects of "nontraditional" immigration, the Government officially turned against its immigrant communities, particularly those from South Asia.

I felt then the same sense of betrayal that Mira feels now. 14 I will never forget the pain of that sudden turning, and the casual racist outbursts the Green Paper elicited. That sense of betrayal had its desired effect and drove me, and thousands like me, from the country.

Mira and I differ, however, in the ways in which we hope to 15 interact with the country that we have chosen to live in. She is happier to live in America as expatriate Indian than as an immigrant American. I need to feel like a part of the community I have adopted (as I tried to feel in Canada as well). I need to put roots down, to vote and make the difference that I can. The price that the immigrant willingly pays, and that the exile avoids, is the trauma of self-transformation.

1996

China's Biggest Gamble: Can It Have Capitalism without Democracy? A Prediction

Henry Blodget

1   On my last evening in Beijing, I walked west on the long blocks of the city's main drag toward Tiananmen Square. The sun was setting when I arrived, and, on the north side of the road, beneath the portrait of Chairman Mao on the Gate of Heavenly Peace, crowds of tourists were streaming out of the Forbidden City. On the south side, in Tiananmen Square itself, kites and flags were flying, and entrepreneurs posing as "students" were cruising around entreating foreigners to visit a nearby art "exhibit" in which their works were purportedly displayed. The students' story was clever and well-choreographed, but I'd already fallen for it once that day (enduring a guided tour of machine-made paintings being sold to fund a "trip to America"). So, I just wandered around the square and watched the sun set over the Chinese flag.

2   The story of what happened in Tiananmen in June of 1989 is different in China than the one we tell in the United States. In America, we remember the student protests as a plea for democracy, for *our* form of government (who has forgotten the students' mock-up of the Statue of Liberty?). But in China, people describe the students' goals as not *democracy*, per se, but as the end to corruption, the ability to air grievances, and the right to more control over their lives (or, as one person put it, the right to refuse to be shipped off to some dumpy factory for 40 years—a fate that would drive anyone into the streets). Although these ideals were closer to our form of government than China's was in 1989, they were not the "one man, one vote" system we hold so dear, the one that, in America, we herald the Tiananmen students as having died for. And, by local estimation, Chinese have gotten much of what the students were really hoping for 16 years ago.

3   In Beijing, as in Shanghai, the businesspeople I spoke to seemed more concerned about preserving their ability to make

money than about gaining the ability to vote leaders out of office or to express themselves however they pleased. One expects businesspeople to tend toward this end of the idealism scale, but in the U.S., democracy and freedom of speech are so fundamental to our sense of ourselves and our country that even our businesspeople can't imagine life (or economic success) without them. So, it is interesting to see China succeeding—on the surface, anyway—without them.

The question remains: Can the Chinese model—capitalism 4 without elections or free expression—succeed forever? The common Western theory is that the more China's wealth grows, the more the pressure will build, until one day, the Communist Party's chokehold on power will break and American-style freedom of speech and democracy will follow (or, alternatively, that, in a desperate attempt to preserve itself, the party will revert to Cultural Revolution–style oppression and stop the economy cold). Both theories presume that free speech and elections are high on the average Chinese citizen's agenda, but, for now, a strong economy seems to take priority. ("The average guy wants to buy a car, eat vitamins, and get his kids into Berkeley," said one Beijing entrepreneur. "As long as the government doesn't screw that up, he's willing to play along.") The Western theories also presume that the transition from socialism to capitalism inevitably includes a transition from one-party rule to elected, multi-party democracy, but perhaps this isn't so. Especially when the leaders of the one party know exactly what keeps them in power—fat consumer wallets—and are willing to go to extraordinary lengths to control the spread of potentially destabilizing ideas.

For China's economy to continue to thrive—and for its com- 5 panies to grow strong enough to compete globally on something other than price—the government will have to continue to reduce corruption, strengthen property and legal rights, and develop a more efficient capital allocation system (including a securities market in which government connections are not a prerequisite for raising cash). In a democracy with a free press, the pressure that forces such changes often comes from decision-makers' fear of being ravaged in the media and/or voted out of office. In China, the repercussions may not be so immediate and direct, but based on the government's actions over the last decade, it knows well that continued economic reform and success are not only good for the country but key to its survival. The pressure is there, in other words, with or without the media, and the government continues to make progress in reducing corruption and buttressing legal and property rights.

6   The government also seems to be deciding that, at least in the realm of business and finance, greater press freedom helps advance its economic goals and lessen its regulatory burden. Business journalism keeps companies honest and makes customers and investors comfortable that they at least have a forum in which to complain. Such freedom is not all good—in the media's eagerness to advance its own economic agenda, it often manufactures scandals where there are none and spins normal free-market processes into institutional or regulatory failures. But just as a free market is more effective than central planning at, say, managing crop production and pricing, a free press enhances the regulatory abilities of a government and creates the information flow that capitalism requires.

7   But the Chinese government will probably continue to stifle the press's freedom to criticize it. As demonstrated by the government's subtle, sophisticated control of all forms of media and its ongoing penchant for firing, beating up, jailing, and perhaps even killing journalists who cross vaguely defined lines, we won't see a Michael Moore of China anytime soon...But I doubt this will hinder the ongoing development of China's vibrant economy.

8   The key test of China's version of capitalism, of course, will be during the bust that inevitably will follow the current boom (some day). If elections were held today, many in China suggest, the current leaders would win the popular vote. On the whole, thanks to the economy, people feel they have done a good job. During the bust, the pressure for change will increase, with or without the press. If the government is to maintain control in such an environment, it will probably have to engage in a practice that has long been a fixture of oligarchies and democracies alike: blame. As long as the countrywide pain can be laid at the feet of an individual or group, instead of the system—and as long as the

scapegoats can be tossed out on their respective rears—the public pressure for revolutionary change can probably be controlled. If China can survive that inevitable economic crisis without a political uprising, we will probably be able to conclude that a dynamic free-market economy need not, in fact, go hand in hand with democracy.

Like Mexicans

Gary Soto

My grandmother gave me bad advice and good advice when I was in my early teens. For the bad advice, she said that I should become a barber because they made good money and listened to the radio all day. "Honey, they don't work *como buros*," she would say every time I visited her. She made the sound of donkeys braying: "Like that, honey!" For the good advice, she said that I should marry a Mexican girl. "No Okies, hijo"—she would say—. "Look my son. He marry one and they fight every day about I don't know what and I don't know what." For her, everyone who wasn't Mexican, black, or Asian were Okies. The French were Okies, the Italians in suits were Okies. When I asked about Jews, whom I had read about, she asked for a picture. I rode home on my bicycle and returned with a calendar depicting the important races of the world. "*Pues si, son Okies tambien!*" she said, nodding her head. She waved the calendar away and we went to the living room where she lectured me on the virtues of the Mexican girl: first, she could cook and, second, she acted like a woman, not a man, in her husband's home. She said she would tell me about a third when I got a little older.

I asked my mother about it—becoming a barber and marrying Mexican. She was in the kitchen. Steam curled from a pot of boiling beans, the radio was on, looking as squat as a loaf of bread. "Well, if you want to be a barber—they say they make good money." She slapped a round steak with a knife, her glasses slipping down with each strike. She stopped and looked up. "If you find a good Mexican girl, marry her of course." She returned to slapping the meat and I went to the backyard where my brother and David King were sitting on the lawn feeling the inside of their cheeks.

3   "This is what girls feel like," my brother said, rubbing the inside of his cheek. David put three fingers inside his mouth and scratched. I ignored them and climbed the back fence to see my best friend, Scott, a second-generation Okie. I called him and his mother pointed to the side of the house where his bedroom was a small aluminum trailer, the kind you gawk at when they're flipped over on the freeway, wheels spinning in the air. I went around to find Scott pitching horseshoes.

4   I picked up a set of rusty ones and joined him. While we played, we talked about school and friends and record albums. The horseshoes scuffed up dirt, sometimes ringing the iron that threw out a meager shadow like a sundial. After three argued-over games, we pulled two oranges a piece from his tree and started down the alley still talking school and friends and record albums. We pulled more oranges from the alley and talked about who we would marry. "No offense, Scott," I said with an orange slice in my mouth, "but I would never marry an Okie." We walked in step, almost touching, with a sled of shadows dragging behind us. "No, offense, Gary," Scott said, " but I would never marry a Mexican." I looked at him: a fang of orange slice showed from his munching mouth. I didn't think anything of it. He had his girl and I had mine. But our seventh-grade vision was the same: to marry, get jobs, buy cars and maybe a house if we had money left over.

5   We talked about our future lives until, to our surprise, we were on the downtown mall, two miles from home. We bought a bag of popcorn at Penneys and sat down on a bench near the fountain watching Mexican and Okie girls pass. "That one's mine," I pointed with my chin when a girl with eyebrows arched into black rainbows ambled by. "She's cute," Scott said about a girl with yellow hair and a mouthful of gum. We dreamed aloud, our chins busy pointing out girls. We agreed that we couldn't wait to become men and lift them onto our laps.

But the woman I married was not Mexican but Japanese. It was a surprise to me. For years, I went about wide-eyed in my search for the brown girl in a white dress at a dance. I searched the playground at the baseball diamond. When the girls raced for grounders, their hair bounced like something that couldn't be caught. When they sat together in the lunchroom, heads pressed together, I knew they were talking about us Mexican guys. I saw them and dreamed them. I threw my face into my pillow, making up sentences that were good as in the movies.

But when I was twenty, I fell in love with this other girl who worried my mother, who had my grandmother asking once again to see the calendar of the Important Races of the World. I told her I had thrown it away years before. I took a much-glanced-at snapshot from my wallet. We looked at it together, in silence. Then grandma reclined in her chair, lit a cigarette, and said, "Es pretty." She blew and asked with all her worry pushed up to her forehead: "Chinese?"

I was in love and there was no looking back. She was the one. I told my mother who was slapping hamburger into patties. "Well, sure if you want to marry her," she said. But the more I talked, the more concerned she became. Later I began to worry. Was it all a mistake? "Marry a Mexican girl," I heard my mother say in my mind. I heard it at breakfast. I heard it over math problems, between Western Civilization and cultural geography. But then one afternoon while I was hitchhiking home from school, it struck me like a baseball in the back: my mother wanted me to marry someone of my own social class—a poor girl. I considered my fiancée, Carolyn, and she didn't look poor, though I knew she came from a family of farm workers and pull-yourself-up-by-your-bootstraps ranchers. I asked my brother, who was marrying Mexican poor that fall, if I should marry a poor girl. He screamed "Yeah" above his terrible guitar playing in his bedroom. I considered my sister who had married Mexican. Cousins were dating Mexican. Uncles were remarrying poor women. I asked Scott, who was still my best friend, and he said, "She's too good for you, so you better not."

I worried about it until Carolyn took me home to meet her parents. We drove in her Plymouth until the houses gave way to farms and ranches and finally her house fifty feet from the highway. When we pulled into the drive, I panicked and begged Carolyn to make a U-turn and go back so we could talk about it over a soda. She pinched my cheek, calling me a "silly boy." I felt better, though, when I got out of the car and saw the house: the chipped paint, a cracked window, boards for a walk to the back door. There were rusting cars near the barn. A tractor with a net of spider webs under a mulberry. A field. A bale of barbed wire like children's scribbling leaning against an empty chicken coop. Carolyn took my hand and pulled me to my future mother-in-law who was coming out to greet us.

10   We had lunch: sandwiches, potato chips, and iced tea. Carolyn and her mother talked mostly about neighbors and the congregation at the Japanese Methodist Church in West Fresno. Her father, who was in khaki work clothes, excused himself with a wave that was almost a salute and went outside. I heard a truck start, a dog bark, and the truck rattle away.

11   Carolyn's mother offered another sandwich, but I declined with a shake of my head and a smile. I looked around when I could, when I was not saying over and over that I was a college student, hinting that I could take care of her daughter. I shifted my chair. I saw newspapers piled in corners, dusty cereal boxes and vinegar bottles in corners. The wallpaper was bubbled from rain that had come in from a bad roof. Dust. Dust lay on lamp shades and window sills. These people are just like Mexicans, I thought. Poor people.

12   Carolyn's mother asked me through Carolyn if I would like a sushi. A plate of black and white things were held in front of me. I took one, wide-eyed, and turned it over like a foreign coin. I was biting into one when I saw a kitten crawl up the window screen over the sink. I chewed and the kitten opened its mouth of terror as she crawled higher, wanting in to paw the leftovers from our plates. I looked at Carolyn who said that the cat was just showing off. I looked up in time to see it fall. It crawled up, then fell again.

13   We talked for an hour and had apple pie and coffee, slowly. Finally, we got up with Carolyn taking my hand. Slightly embarrassed, I tried to pull away but her grip held me. I let her have her way as she led me down the hallway with her mother right

behind me. When I opened the door, I was startled by a kitten clinging to the screen door, its mouth screaming "cat food, dog biscuits, sushi...." I opened the door and the kitten, still holding on, whined in the language of hungry animals. When I got into Carolyn's car, I looked back: the cat was still clinging. I asked Carolyn if it were possibly hungry, but she said the cat was being silly. She started the car, waved to her mother, and bounced us over the rain-poked drive, patting my thigh for being her lover baby. Carolyn waved again. I looked back, waving, then gawking at a window screen where there were now three kittens clawing and screaming to get in. Like Mexicans, I thought. I remembered the Molinas and how the cats clung to their screens—cats they shot down with squirt guns. On the highway, I felt happy, pleased by it all. I patted Carolyn's thigh. Her people were like Mexicans, only different.

7

Example and Illustration

A Few Kind Words for Superstition

Robertson Davies

1 In grave discussions of "the renaissance of the irrational" in our time, superstition does not figure largely as a serious challenge to reason or science. Parapsychology, UFOs, miracle cures, transcendental meditation and all the paths to instant enlightenment are condemned, but superstition is merely deplored. Is it because it has an unacknowledged hold on so many of us?

2 Few people will admit to being superstitious; it implies naïveté or ignorance. But I live in the middle of a large university, and I see superstition in its four manifestations, alive and flourishing among people who are indisputably rational and learned.

3 You did not know that superstition takes four forms? Theologians assure us that it does. First is what they call Vain Observances, such as not walking under a ladder, and that kind of thing. Yet I saw a deeply learned professor of anthropology, who had spilled some salt, throwing a pinch of it over his left shoulder; when I asked him why, he replied, with a wink, that it was "to hit the Devil in the eye." I did not question him further about his belief in the Devil: but I noticed that he did not smile until I asked him what he was doing.

4 The second form is Divination, or consulting oracles. Another learned professor I know, who would scorn to settle a problem by tossing a coin (which is a humble appeal to Fate to declare itself),

told me quite seriously that he had resolved a matter related to university affairs by consulting the I Ching. And why not? There are thousands of people on this continent who appeal to the I Ching, and their general level of education seems to absolve them of superstition. Almost, but not quite. The I Ching, to the embarrassment of rationalists, often gives excellent advice.

The third form is Idolatry, and universities can show plenty of that. If you have ever supervised a large examination room, you know how many jujus, lucky coins and other bringers of luck are placed on the desks of the candidates. Modest idolatry, but what else can you call it?

The fourth form is Improper Worship of the True God. A while ago, I learned that every day, for several days, a $2 bill (in Canada we have $2 bills, regarded by some people as unlucky) had been tucked under a candlestick on the altar of a college chapel. Investigation revealed that an engineering student, worried about a girl, thought that bribery of the Deity might help. When I talked with him, he did not think he was pricing God cheap, because he could afford no more. A reasonable argument, but perhaps God was proud that week, for the scientific oracle went against him.

Superstition seems to run, a submerged river of crude religion, below the surface of human consciousness. It has done so for as long as we have any chronicle of human behavior, and although I cannot prove it, I doubt if it is more prevalent today than it has always been. Superstition, the theologians tell us, comes from the Latin *supersisto*, meaning to stand in terror of the Deity. Most people keep their terror within bounds, but they cannot root it out, nor do they seem to want to do so.

The more the teaching of formal religion declines, or takes a sociological form, the less God appears to great numbers of people as a God of Love, resuming his older form of a watchful, minatory power, to be placated and cajoled. Superstition makes its appearance, apparently unbidden, very early in life, when children fear that stepping on cracks in the sidewalk will bring ill fortune. It may persist even among the greatly learned and devout, as in the case of Dr. Samuel Johnson, who felt it necessary to touch posts that he passed in the street. The psychoanalysts have their explanation, but calling a superstition a compulsion neurosis does not banish it.

9   Many superstitions are so widespread and so old that they must have risen from a depth of the human mind that is indifferent to race or creed. Orthodox Jews place a charm on their door-posts; so do (or did) the Chinese. Some peoples of Middle Europe believe that when a man sneezes, his soul, for that moment, is absent from his body, and they hasten to bless him, lest the soul be seized by the Devil. How did the Melanesians come by the same idea? Superstition seems to have a link with some body of belief that far antedates the religions we know— religions which have no place for such comforting little ceremonies and charities.

10   People who like disagreeable historical comparisons recall that when Rome was in decline, superstition proliferated wildly, and that something of the same sort is happening in our Western world today. They point to the popularity of astrology, and it is true that sober newspapers that would scorn to deal in love philters carry astrology columns and the fashion magazines count them among their most popular features. But when has astrology not been popular? No use saying science discredits it. When has the heart of man given a damn for science?

11   Superstition in general is linked to man's yearning to know his fate, and to have some hand in deciding it. When my mother was a child, she innocently joined her Roman Catholic friends in killing spiders on July 11, until she learned that this was done to ensure heavy rain the day following, the anniversary of the Battle of Boyne, when the Orangemen would hold their parade. I knew an Italian, a good scientist, who watched every morning before leaving his house, so that the first person he met would not be a priest or a nun, as this would certainly bring bad luck.

12   I am not one to stand aloof from the rest of humanity in this matter, for when I was a university student, a gypsy woman with a child in her arms used to appear every year at examination time, and ask a shilling of anyone who touched the Lucky Baby; that swarthy infant cost me four shillings altogether, and I never failed an examination. Of course, I did it merely for the joke—or so I thought then. Now, I am humbler.

1978

Black Men and Public Space

Brent Staples

My first victim was a woman—white, well dressed, probably in   1
her late twenties. I came upon her late one evening on a deserted
street in Hyde Park, a relatively affluent neighborhood in an
otherwise mean, impoverished section of Chicago. As I swung
onto the avenue behind her, there seemed to be a discreet, unin-
flammatory distance between us. Not so. She cast back a worried
glance. To her, the youngish black man—a broad six feet two
inches with a beard and billowing hair, both hands shoved into
the pockets of a bulky military jacket—seemed menacingly close.
After a few more quick glimpses, she picked up her pace and was
soon running in earnest. Within seconds, she disappeared into a
cross street.

That was more than a decade ago. I was twenty-two years   2
old, a graduate student newly arrived at the University of
Chicago. It was in the echo of that terrified woman's footfalls that
I first began to know the unwieldy inheritance I'd come into—
the ability to alter public space in ugly ways. It was clear that
she thought herself the quarry of a mugger, a rapist, or worse.
Suffering a bout of insomnia, however, I was stalking sleep, not
defenseless wayfarers. As a softy who is scarcely able to take a
knife to a raw chicken—let alone hold one to a person's throat—
I was surprised, embarrassed, and dismayed all at once. Her
flight made me feel like an accomplice in tyranny. It also made
it clear that I was indistinguishable from the muggers who occasionally seeped into the area from the surrounding ghetto. That
first encounter, and those that followed, signified that a vast,
unnerving gulf lay between nighttime pedestrians—particularly
women—and me. And I soon gathered that being perceived as
dangerous is a hazard in itself. I only needed to turn a corner
into a dicey situation, or crowd some frightened, armed person
in a foyer somewhere, or make an errant move after being pulled
over by a policeman. Where fear and weapons meet—and they
often do in urban America—there is always the possibility of
death.

3   In that first year, my first away from my hometown, I was to become thoroughly familiar with the language of fear. At dark, shadowy intersections, I could cross in front of a car stopped at a traffic light and elicit the *thunk*, thunk, thunk, thunk of the driver—black, white, male, or female—hammering down the door locks. On less traveled streets after dark, I grew accustomed to but never comfortable with people crossing to the other side of the street rather than pass me. Then there were the standard unpleasantries with policemen, doormen, bouncers, cabdrivers, and others whose business it is to screen out troublesome individuals *before* there is any nastiness.

4   I moved to New York nearly two years ago and I have remained an avid night walker. In central Manhattan, the near-constant crowd cover minimizes tense one-on-one street encounters. Elsewhere—in SoHo, for example, where sidewalks are narrow and tightly spaced buildings shut out the sky—things can get very taut indeed.

5   After dark, on the warrenlike streets of Brooklyn where I live, I often see women who fear the worst from me. They seem to have set their faces on neutral, and with their purse straps strung across their chests bandolier-style, they forge ahead as though bracing themselves against being tackled. I understand, of course, that the danger they perceive is not a hallucination. Women are particularly vulnerable to street violence, and young black males are drastically overrepresented among the perpetrators of that violence. Yet these truths are no solace against the kind of alienation that comes of being ever the suspect, a fearsome entity with whom pedestrians avoid making eye contact.

6   It is not altogether clear to me how I reached the ripe old age of twenty-two without being conscious of the lethality nighttime pedestrians attributed to me. Perhaps it was because in Chester, Pennsylvania, the small, angry industrial town where I came of age in the 1960s, I was scarcely noticeable against a backdrop of gang warfare, street knifings, and murders. I grew up one of the good boys, had perhaps a half-dozen fistfights. In retrospect, my shyness of combat has clear sources.

7   As a boy, I saw countless tough guys locked away; I have since buried several, too. They were babies, really—a teenage

cousin, a brother of twenty-two, a childhood friend in his mid-twenties—all gone down in episodes of bravado played out in the streets. I came to doubt the virtues of intimidation early on. I chose, perhaps unconsciously, to remain a shadow—timid, but a survivor.

The fearsomeness mistakenly attributed to me in public places 8 often has a perilous flavor. The most frightening of these confusions occurred in the late 1970s and early 1980s, when I worked as a journalist in Chicago. One day, rushing into the office of a magazine I was writing for with a deadline story in hand, I was mistaken for a burglar. The office manager called security and, with an ad hoc posse, pursued me through the labyrinthine halls, nearly to my editor's door. I had no way of proving who I was. I could only move briskly toward the company of someone who knew me.

Another time I was on assignment for a local paper and killing 9 time before an interview. I entered a jewelry store on the city's affluent Near North Side. The proprietor excused herself and returned with an enormous red Doberman pinscher straining at the end of a leash. She stood, the dog extended toward me, silent to my questions, her eyes bulging nearly out of her head. I took a cursory look around, nodded, and bade her good night.

Relatively speaking, however, I never fared as badly as 10 another black male journalist. He went to nearby Waukegan, Illinois, a couple of summers ago to work on a story about a murderer who was born there. Mistaking the reporter for the killer, police officers hauled him from his car at gunpoint and but for his press credentials would probably have tried to book him. Such episodes are not uncommon. Black men trade tales like this all the time.

Over the years, I learned to smother the rage I felt at so often 11 being taken for a criminal. Not to do so would surely have led to madness. I now take precautions to make myself less threatening. I move about with care, particularly late in the evening. I give a wide berth to nervous people on subway platforms during the wee hours, particularly when I have exchanged business clothes for jeans. If I happen to be entering a building behind some people who appear skittish, I may walk by, letting them clear the lobby before I return, so as not to seem to be following them.

I have been calm and extremely congenial on those rare occasions when I've been pulled over by the police.

12   And on late-evening constitutionals I employ what has proved to be an excellent tension-reducing measure: I whistle melodies from Beethoven and Vivaldi and the more popular classical composers. Even steely New Yorkers hunching toward nighttime destinations seem to relax, and occasionally they even join in the tune. Virtually everybody seems to sense that a mugger wouldn't be warbling bright, sunny selections from Vivaldi's *Four Seasons*. It is my equivalent of the cowbell that hikers wear when they know they are in bear country.

1986

Clutter

William Zinsser

1 Fighting clutter is like fighting weeds—the writer is always slightly behind. New varieties sprout overnight, and by noon they are part of American speech. Consider what President Nixon's aide John Dean accomplished in just one day of testimony on television during the Watergate hearings. The next day everyone in America was saying "at this point in time" instead of "now."

2   Consider all the prepositions that are draped onto verbs that don't need any help. We no longer head committees. We head them up. We don't face problems anymore. We face up to them when we can free up a few minutes. A small detail, you may say—not worth bothering about. It *is* worth bothering about. Writing improves in direct ratio to the number of things we can keep out of it that shouldn't be there. "Up" in "free up" shouldn't be there. Examine every word you put on paper. You'll find a surprising number that don't serve any purpose.

3   Take the adjective "personal," as in "a personal friend of mine," "his personal feeling" or "her personal physician."

It's typical of hundreds of words that can be eliminated. The personal friend has come into the language to distinguish him or her from the business friend, thereby debasing both language and friendship. Someone's feeling *is* that person's personal feeling—that's what "his" means. As for the personal physician, that's the man or woman summoned to the dressing room of a stricken actress so she won't have to be treated by the impersonal physician assigned to the theater. Someday I'd like to see that person identified as "her doctor." Physicians are physicians, friends are friends. The rest is clutter.

Clutter is the laborious phrase that has pushed out the short 4 word that means the same thing. Even before John Dean, people and businesses had stopped saying "now." They were saying "currently" ("all our operators are currently assisting other customers"), or "at the present time," or "presently" (which means "soon"). Yet the idea can always be expressed by "now" to mean the immediate moment ("Now I can see him"), or by "today" to mean the historical present ("Today prices are high"), or simply by the verb "to be" ("It is raining"). There's no need to say, "At the present time we are experiencing precipitation."

"Experiencing" is one of the worst clutterers. Even your den- 5 tist will ask if you are experiencing any pain. If he had his own kid in the chair he would say, "Does it hurt?" He would, in short, be himself. By using a more pompous phrase in his professional role he not only sounds more important, he blunts the painful edge of truth. It's the language of the flight attendant demonstrating the oxygen mask that will drop down if the plane should run out of air. "In the unlikely possibility that the aircraft should experience such an eventuality," she begins—a phrase so oxygen-depriving in itself that we are prepared for any disaster.

Clutter is the ponderous euphemism that turns a slum into 6 a depressed socioeconomic area, garbage collectors into waste-disposal personnel and the town dump into the volume reduction unit. I think of Bill Mauldin's cartoon of two hoboes riding a freight car. One of them says, "I started as a simple bum, but now I'm hard-core unemployed." Clutter is political correctness gone amok. I saw an ad for a boys' camp designed to provide "individual attention for the minimally exceptional."

7   Clutter is the official language used by corporations to hide their mistakes. When the Digital Equipment Corporation eliminated 3,000 jobs its statement didn't mention layoffs; those were "involuntary methodologies." When an Air Force missile crashed, it "impacted with the ground prematurely." When General Motors had a plant shutdown, that was a "volume-related production-schedule adjustment." Companies that go belly-up have "a negative cash-flow position."

8   Clutter is the language of the Pentagon calling an invasion a "reinforced protective reaction strike" and justifying its vast budgets on the need for "counterforce deterrence." As George Orwell pointed out in "Politics and the English Language," an essay written in 1946 but often cited during the wars in Cambodia, Vietnam and Iraq, "political speech and writing are largely the defense of the indefensible. . . . Thus political language has to consist largely of euphemism, question-begging and sheer cloudy vagueness." Orwell's warning that clutter is not just a nuisance but a deadly tool has come true in the recent decades of American military adventurism. It was during George W. Bush's presidency that "civilian casualties" in Iraq became "collateral damage."

9   Verbal camouflage reached new heights during General Alexander Haig's tenure as President Reagan's secretary of state. Before Haig nobody had thought of saying "at this juncture of maturization" to mean "now." He told the American people that terrorism could be fought with "meaningful sanctionary teeth" and that intermediate nuclear missiles were "at the vortex of cruciality." As for any worries that the public might harbor, his message was "leave it to Al," though what he actually said was: "We must push this to a lower decibel of public fixation. I don't think there's much of a learning curve to be achieved in this area of content."

10   I could go on quoting examples from various fields—every profession has its growing arsenal of jargon to throw dust in the eyes of the populace. But the list would be tedious. The point of raising it now is to serve notice that clutter is the enemy. Beware, then, of the long word that's no better than the short word: "assistance" (help), "numerous" (many), "facilitate" (ease),

"individual" (man or woman), "remainder" (rest), "initial" (first), "implement" (do), "sufficient" (enough), "attempt" (try), "referred to as" (called) and hundreds more. Beware of all the slippery new fad words: paradigm and parameter, prioritize and potentialize. They are all weeds that will smother what you write. Don't dialogue with someone you can talk to. Don't interface with anybody.

Just as insidious are all the word clusters with which we 11 explain how we propose to go about our explaining: "I might add," "It should be pointed out," "It is interesting to note." If you might add, add it. If it should be pointed out, point it out. If it is interesting to note, *make* it interesting; are we not all stupefied by what follows when someone says, "This will interest you"? Don't inflate what needs no inflating: "with the possible exception of" (except), "due to the fact that" (because), "he totally lacked the ability to" (he couldn't), "until such time as" (until), "for the purpose of" (for).

Is there any way to recognize clutter at a glance? Here's a 12 device my students at Yale found helpful. I would put brackets around every component in a piece of writing that wasn't doing useful work. Often just one word got bracketed: the unnecessary preposition appended to a verb ("order up"), or the adverb that carries the same meaning as the verb ("smile happily"), or the adjective that states a known fact ("tall skyscraper"). Often my brackets surrounded the little qualifiers that weaken any sentence they inhabit ("a bit," "sort of"), or phrases like "in a sense," which don't mean anything. Sometimes my brackets surrounded an entire sentence—the one that essentially repeats what the previous sentence said, or that says something readers don't need to know or can figure out for themselves. Most first drafts can be cut by 50 percent without losing any information or losing the author's voice.

My reason for bracketing the students' superfluous words, 13 instead of crossing them out, was to avoid violating their sacred prose. I wanted to leave the sentence intact for them to analyze. I was saying, "I may be wrong, but I think this can be deleted and the meaning won't be affected. But *you* decide. Read the sentence without the bracketed material and see if it works." In the early weeks of the term I handed back papers that were festooned with brackets. Entire paragraphs were bracketed. But soon the students learned to put mental brackets around their own clutter, and by the end of the term their papers were almost clean. Today many of those students are professional writers, and they tell me, "I still see your brackets—they're following me through life."

14   You can develop the same eye. Look for the clutter in your writing and prune it ruthlessly. Be grateful for everything you can throw away. Reexamine each sentence you put on paper. Is every word doing new work? Can any thought be expressed with more economy? Is anything pompous or pretentious or faddish? Are you hanging on to something useless just because you think it's beautiful?

15   Simplify, simplify.

2006

Forbidden Things

Bailey White

1   I was leaning over the little railing, looking down into the Devil's Millhopper, an interesting geological formation and the focal point of a Florida state park. Waterfalls plunge 120 feet down into a bowl-shaped sinkhole; maidenhair ferns and moss grow in little crevices along the steep, sloping sides of the gorge; and a beautiful mist rises up.

2   I stood there, gazing down, and feeling a reverence for these spectacles of the natural world. I felt the slow sweep of geologic time. I felt the remnants of the spiritual significance this place had had for the Indians who lived here for thousands of years. I felt the wonder and awe of the first European explorers of Florida looking down into this chasm for the first time.

3   Then another feeling crept over me, a deep, almost atavistic longing. It was the urge to throw something down into the Devil's Millhopper. I looked around. A stone or a stick would do, but what

I really wanted was a piece of food, the nibbled end of a hotdog bun or a wedge of chocolate cake without the icing. Then I noticed the sign, one of those tastefully unobtrusive state park signs:

DO NOT THROW FOOD OR TRASH IN GORGE

It was 4:00 A.M. I was at the Los Angeles, California, bus station, 4 my next-to-last stop on a dreary transcontinental bus trip—three days and three nights on a Greyhound bus. My back ached, my knees ached, my head ached. Ever since El Paso, Texas, my seat-mate had been an old man who chain-smoked Marlboro cigarettes and sucked and slobbered over a perpetual ham sandwich that kept oozing out of a greasy crumple of waxed paper.

I longed for a bath in my own bathtub, and then a deep sleep 5 in my own bed, stretched out full-length between clean sheets. But, I thought, pushing open the door of the bus station bath-room, if I just wash my feet and my hair I will be all right. I lined up my soap, my washrag, and my little bottle of shampoo on the back of the sink and took off my shoes and socks. Ahh, I thought. Then I saw the sign on the mirror:

DO NOT WASH HAIR OR FEET IN SINK

A few weeks ago I went into our little downtown restaurant 6 and saw that it had replaced its tired old salad bar with a gor-geous saltwater aquarium with sea anemones, chunks of living coral, and big slow-moving colorful fish with faces I could almost recognize. I spent my whole lunchtime staring into that tank, mesmerized by the fish as they gracefully looped and glided, sending the tentacles of the sea anemones into slow twirls and fanning out the tall grasses.

When I finished my sandwich I noticed that there were a 7 couple of crumbs left on my plate, just the size to pinch between thumb and finger. Oh, I thought, to pinch up those crumbs and dip my fingers down into the water, breaking through the smooth surface into the coolness and silence of that peaceful world. One of the fish would make a looping turn, his odd exophthalmic eyes would rotate slowly in their sockets and fix upon the crumbs in my fingers. Then he would angle up, and I would feel for just one exquisite instant those thorny fish lips rasping across my fingertips. With rising delight and anticipation, I pinched up a crumb, two crumbs. I scrabbled across the plastic top of the tank, found the little door, lifted it open—and then I saw the sign:

DO NOT FEED THE FISH
WE PROHIBIT CLIMBING IN ANY MANNER FROM OR ALONG THE CANYON RIM
DO NOT PICK FLOWERS
NO SMOKING EATING OR DRINKING
NO SWINGING FROM VINES IN TREES
NO PEDESTRIAN TRAFFIC IN WOODS
NO FISHING
NO SWIMMING
NO TRESPASSING

8   Don't get me wrong; I approve of these prohibitions. Imagine the nasty mess in the bottom of the Devil's Millhopper if every self-indulgent tourist threw a piece of food into the sinkhole. Imagine the puddles on the floor and the plumbing complications in the Los Angeles bus station if every weary transcontinental traveler washed her hair and feet in the sink. Imagine the deadly scum of grease on the surface of that saltwater aquarium if every fish-dazed diner fed the catalufa his last mayonnaise-coated crumbs.

9   But sometimes I wonder: Who makes up these necessary and useful rules, and how does he know so well the deep and touching urges of human beings to pick flowers, walk in the woods, climb canyon walls, swing from vines, and feed already well-nourished animals? I imagine with distaste a mean, sour, silent little man skulking around in public places, watching us furtively with squinny eyes while scribbling notes on his pad with a gnawed pencil. In national parks he disguises himself as a tourist in reflective sunglasses and plaid Bermuda shorts. "Bryce Canyon," he notes with a smirk, "Urinating on hoodoos and off cliffs." In zoos he wears khaki and lurks in the shadows, hiding behind a bag of peanuts. "Touching giraffe's tongue through fence wire . . . . Feeling camel's hump," he scribbles.

At night he goes home, and in his stark white workshop, illu- 10
minated with fluorescent lights, he makes those signs. Rounded
letters routed out of cypress boards for the parks: "We Prohibit. . . ,
No . . ., No . . . , and No . . ." Spiky green on white for zoos: "Do
Not . . . , . . . Not Allowed, . . . Is Prohibited." *And-we-meant* black
and white for commercial establishments: "Absolutely NO . . . ,
. . . Are Required, We Forbid . . ."

I imagine, one night, as he works late stacking and bundling 11
signs for the next day's delivery, the tendril of a grapevine creeps
in at his window. When his back is turned, its pale nose will
gently nudge itself around him.

"No Touching!" he will admonish.   12

But with a clutch and a snatch the vine will retract, and he 13
will find himself yanked through the night sky above a central
Florida state park.

"Do Not Swing from Vines!" he will shriek.   14

And with that, the vine will untwine and drop him into the 15
vortex of a limpid spring.

"No Swimming!" he will sputter as the dark, icy water closes 16
over his head. As he sinks, strange, pale-colored fish will swim
up and cock their eyes at him. "Do Not Feed the Fish," he will
squeak. But, slowly and precisely, the fish will angle up, move in,
and then, all over, he will feel the pick pick pick of those prickly
lips.

1995

Silk Parachute

John McPhee

When your mother is ninety-nine years old, you have so many 1
memories of her that they tend to overlap, intermingle, and blur.
It is extremely difficult to single out one or two, impossible to
remember any that exemplify the whole.

2   It has been alleged that when I was in college she heard that I had stayed up all night playing poker and wrote me a letter that used the word "shame" forty-two times. I do not recall this.

3   I do not recall being pulled out of my college room and into the church next door.

4   It has been alleged that on December 24, 1936, when I was five years old, she sent me to my room at or close to 7 P.M. for using four-letter words while trimming the Christmas tree. I do not recall that.

5   The assertion is absolutely false that when I came home from high school with an A-minus she demanded an explanation for the minus.

6   It has been alleged that she spoiled me with protectionism, because I was the youngest child and therefore the most vulnerable to attack from overhead—an assertion that I cannot confirm or confute, except to say that facts don't lie.

7   We lived only a few blocks from the elementary school and routinely ate lunch at home. It is reported that the following dialogue and ensuing action occurred on January 22, 1941:

8   "Eat your sandwich."

9   "I don't want to eat my sandwich."

10   "I made that sandwich, and you are going to eat it, Mister Man. You filled yourself up on penny candy on the way home, and now you're not hungry."

11   "I'm late. I have to go. I'll eat the sandwich on the way back to school."

12   "Promise?"

13   "Promise."

14   Allegedly, I went up the street with the sandwich in my hand and buried it in a snowbank in front of Dr. Wright's house. My mother, holding back the curtain in the window of the side door, was watching. She came out in the bitter cold, wearing only a light dress, ran to the snow-bank, dug out the sandwich, chased me up Nassau Street, and rammed the sandwich down my throat, snow and all. I do not recall any detail of that story. I believe it to be a total fabrication.

15   There was the case of the missing Cracker Jack at Lindel's corner store. Flimsy evidence pointed to Mrs. McPhee's smallest

child. It has been averred that she laid the guilt on with the following words: "'Like mother like son' is a saying so true, the world will judge largely of mother by you." It has been asserted that she immediately repeated that proverb three times, and also recited it on other occasions too numerous to count. I have absolutely no recollection of her saying that about the Cracker Jack or any other controlled substance.

We have now covered everything even faintly unsavory that 16 has been reported about this person in ninety-nine years, and even those items are a collection of rumors, half-truths, prevarications, false allegations, inaccuracies, innuendos, and canards.

This is the mother who—when Alfred Knopf wrote her 17 twenty-two-year-old son a letter saying, "The readers' reports in the case of your manuscript would not be very helpful, and I think might discourage you completely"—said, "Don't listen to Alfred Knopf. Who does Alfred Knopf think he is, anyway? Someone should go in there and k-nock his block off." To the best of my recollection, that is what she said.

I also recall her taking me, on or about March 8th, my 18 birthday, to the theatre in New York every year, beginning in childhood. I remember those journeys as if they were today. I remember "A Connecticut Yankee." Wednesday, March 8, 1944. Evidently, my father had written for the tickets, because she and I sat in the last row of the second balcony. Mother knew what to do about that. She gave me for my birthday an elegant spyglass, sufficient in power to bring the Connecticut Yankee back from Vermont. I sat there watching the play through my telescope, drawing as many guffaws from the surrounding audience as the comedy on the stage.

On one of those theatre days—when I was eleven or twelve— 19 I asked her if we could start for the city early and go out to LaGuardia Field to see the comings and goings of airplanes. The temperature was well below the freeze point and the March winds were so blustery that the wind-chill factor was forty below zero. Or seemed to be. My mother figured out how to take the subway to a stop in Jackson Heights and a bus from there—a feat I am unable to duplicate to this day. At LaGuardia, she accompanied me to the observation deck and stood there in the icy wind for at least an hour, maybe two, while I, spellbound, watched the DC-3s coming in on final, their wings flapping in the gusts. When we at last left the observation deck, we went downstairs into the terminal, where she bought me what appeared to be a black rubber ball but on closer inspection was a pair of hollow hemispheres hinged on one side and folded together. They contained a silk parachute. Opposite the hinge, each hemisphere had a small nib. A piece of string wrapped round and round the two nibs kept the ball closed. If you threw it high into the air, the string unwound and the parachute blossomed. If you sent it up with a tennis racquet, you could put it into the clouds. Not until the development of the ten-megabyte hard disk would the world ever know such a fabulous toy. Folded just so, the parachute never failed. Always, it floated back to you—silkily, beautifully—to start over and float back again. Even if you abused it, whacked it really hard—gracefully, lightly, it floated back to you.

1997

The Search for the World's Funniest Joke

Richard Wiseman

1   In the 1970s, Monty Python's Flying Circus created a sketch that revolved entirely around the idea of finding the world's funniest joke. In this sketch, which is set in the 1940s, a man named Ernest Scribbler thinks of the joke, writes it down, and promptly dies laughing. The joke turns out to be so funny that it kills anyone who reads it and is turned into a weapon of war.

2   In 2001 I started to think about the possibility of really searching for the world's funniest joke. I knew that there would be a firm scientific underpinning for the project, because some of the world's greatest thinkers, including Freud, Plato and Aristotle, had written extensively about humour.

I got the green light from the British Association for the 3
Advancement of Science (BAAS) for my plan for an international Internet-based project called "LaughLab." I would set up
a website that had two sections. In one part, people could input
their favourite joke. In the second section, people could answer
a few simple questions about themselves (such as their sex, age
and nationality), and then rate how funny they found various
jokes randomly selected from the archive. During the course of
the year, we would be able to discover scientifically what makes
different groups of people laugh, and which joke made the whole
world smile.

The success of the project hinged on being able to persuade 4
thousands of people worldwide to participate. To help spread the
word, we launched LaughLab with an eye-catching photograph
based on perhaps the most famous (and, as we would go on to
prove scientifically, least funny) joke in the world: "Why did the
chicken cross the road? To get to the other side."

Within a few hours of opening the website, we received more 5
than 500 jokes and 10,000 ratings. Then we hit a major problem.
Many of the jokes were rude; absolutely filthy, in fact. Other jokes
cropped up again and again ("What is brown and sticky?" "A
stick" was submitted more than 300 times).

Participants were asked to rate each joke on a five-point scale 6
ranging from "not very funny" to "very funny." Initially most
of the material was pretty poor . . . so [it] tended to obtain low
percentages. Around 25–35% of participants found the following
jokes funny, and at that point they came towards the top of the
list:

> Did you hear about the man who was proud when he com-
> pleted a jigsaw within 30 minutes, because it said 'five to six
> years' on the box?

and

> Texan: Where are you from?
>   Harvard graduate: I come from a place where we do not
> end our sentences with prepositions.
>   Texan: OK—where are you from, jackass?

7   The top jokes had one thing in common—they create a sense of superiority in the reader. The feeling arises because the person in the joke appears stupid (like the man with the jigsaw), or pricks the pomposity of another (like the Texan answering the Harvard graduate).

8   We were not the first to notice that people laugh when they feel superior. The theory was described by Plato in *The Republic*. Plato was not a fan of laughter. He thought it was wrong to laugh at the misfortune of others, and that hearty laughter involved a loss of control that resulted in people appearing to be less than fully human. In the middle ages, dwarves and hunchbacks caused much merriment. In Victorian times, people laughed at the mentally ill in psychiatric institutions.

9   Very early in LaughLab, we could see the superiority theory appearing in the age-old battle of the sexes. This joke was rated as being funny by 25% of women, but just 10% of men:

> A husband stepped onto one of those penny scales that tell you your fortune and weight, and dropped in a coin.
>
> 'Listen to this,' he said to his wife, showing her a small white card. 'It says I'm energetic, bright, resourceful and a great person.'
>
> 'Yeah,' his wife nodded, 'and it has your weight wrong, too.'

10   One obvious possibility for the difference in ratings between the sexes is that the butt of the joke is a man, and so appeals more to women. Or it could be that women generally find jokes funnier than men. A year-long study of 1200 examples of laughing in everyday conversation revealed that 71% of women laugh when a man tells a joke, but only 39% of men laugh when a woman tells a joke. To help try to tease apart these competing interpretations, we studied the LaughLab archive to find jokes that put down women, such as:

> A man driving on a highway is pulled over by a police officer. The officer asks: 'Did you know your wife and children fell out of your car a mile back?' A smile creeps onto the man's face and he exclaims: 'Thank God! I thought I was going deaf!'

On average, 15% of women rated as funny jokes putting [11] down women, compared with 50% of men.

Research suggests that men tell a lot more jokes than women. [12] People with high social status tend to tell more jokes than those lower down the pecking order. Traditionally, women have had a lower social status than men, and thus may have learned to laugh at jokes, rather than tell them. Interestingly, the only exception to this status/joke-telling relationship concerns self-disparaging humour, with people who have low social status telling more self-disparaging jokes than those with high status. Researchers examining self-disparaging humour produced by male and female professional comedians found that 12% of male scripts contained self-disparaging humour, compared with 63% of female scripts.

Quite quickly we downloaded 10,000 jokes, and the ratings [13] from 100,000 people. The top joke at that early stage had been rated as funny by 46% of participants. It involved the famous fictional detective Sherlock Holmes and his long-suffering sidekick Dr. Watson:

> Sherlock Holmes and Dr. Watson were going camping. They pitched their tent under the stars and went to sleep. Sometime in the middle of the night Holmes woke Watson up and said: 'Watson, look up at the stars, and tell me what you see.'
>
> Watson replied: 'I see millions and millions of stars.'
>
> Holmes said: 'And what do you deduce from that?'
>
> Watson replied: 'Well, if there are millions of stars, and if even a few of those have planets, it's quite likely there are some planets like earth out there. And if there are a few planets like earth out there, there might also be life.'
>
> And Holmes said: 'Watson, you idiot, it means that somebody stole our tent.'

It is a classic example of two-tiered superiority theory. We [14] laugh at Watson for missing the absence of the tent, and also at the pompous way in which Holmes delivered the news to Watson.

According to Freud, jokes act as a kind of psychological [15] release valve that helps prevent the pressure of repression from becoming too great. Many of the jokes submitted to LaughLab supported Freud's ideas. Time and again, we would get jokes about the stresses and strains of loveless marriage, inadequate sexual performance and, of course, death:

> I've been in love with the same woman for 40 years. If my wife finds out, she'll kill me.
>
> A patient says to his psychiatrist: 'Last night I made a Freudian slip. I was having dinner with my mother-in-law and wanted to say: "Could you please pass the butter." But instead I said: "You silly cow, you've completely ruined my life."'

16   We also examined another source of humour—computers. LaughLab attracted lots of jokes about this topic ("The software said it needed Windows 98 or better, so I bought a Mac."). However, it also contained a few jokes actually written by a computer.

17   We were keen to discover whether computers were funnier than humans, . . . so [we] entered into LaughLab several of the computer-composed jokes. The majority of them received some of the lowest ratings in the archive. One example of computer comedy, however, was surprisingly successful, and beat about 250 human jokes:

> What kind of murderer has fibre? A cereal killer.

18   The results from another mini-experiment we conducted during LaughLab supported the widely held theory that some words and sounds are funnier than others, notably the mysterious comedy potential of the letter "K." Early on in the experiment, we received the following submission:

> There were two cows in a field. One said: 'Moo.' The other one said: 'I was going to say that!'

19   We decided to use the joke to test the words/sounds theory. We re-entered the joke into the archive several times, using a different animal and noise: two tigers going "Gruurrr," two birds going "Cheep," two mice going "Eeek," two dogs going "Woof" and so on. At the end of the study, we examined what effect the different animals had on how funny people found the joke. In

third place came the original cow joke, second were two cats going "Meow," but the winning animal-noise joke was:

> Two ducks were sitting in a pond. One of the ducks said: 'Quack.' The other duck said: 'I was going to say that!'

By the end of the project we had received 40,000 jokes, and had them rated by more than 350,000 people from 70 countries. We identified our top joke. It had been rated as funny by 55% of the people who had taken part in the experiment:

> Two hunters are out in the woods when one of them collapses. He doesn't seem to be breathing and his eyes are glazed. The other guy whips out his phone and calls the emergency services.
> He gasps, 'My friend is dead! What can I do?'
> The operator says, 'Calm down. I can help. First, let's make sure he's dead.'
> There is silence, then a shot is heard. Back on the phone, the guy says, 'OK, now what?'

The year-long search for the world's funniest joke concluded. Did we really manage to find it? In fact, I don't believe such a thing exists. If our research into humour tells us anything, it is that people find different things funny. Women laugh at jokes in which men look stupid. The elderly laugh at jokes involving memory loss and hearing difficulties. Those who are powerless laugh at those in power. There is no one joke that will make everyone guffaw. Perhaps we uncovered the world's blandest joke—the gag that makes everyone smile but very few laugh out loud.

Five years after the study, I received a telephone call from a friend. He explained that he had just seen a television documentary film about Spike Milligan, comedian and co-founder of the Goons, and that the programme contained a very early version of our winning joke. The documentary contained a brief clip from a 1951 BBC programme called *London Entertains* with the following early Goon sketch:

> Michael Bentine: I just came in and found him lying on the carpet there.
> Peter Sellers: Oh, is he dead?

Michael Bentine: I think so.
Peter Sellers: Hadn't you better make sure?
Michael Bentine: All right. Just a minute.
(Sound of two gunshots.)
Michael Bentine: He's dead.

23   Spike Milligan died in 2002, but with the help of the
documentary-makers, I contacted his daughter Sile, and she
confirmed that it was highly likely that her father would have
written the material. We announced that we believed we had
identified the author of the world's funniest joke.

24   I am often asked what was my favourite joke from the thousands that flooded in through the year. I always give the same
reply:

> A dog goes into a telegraph office, takes a blank form and
> writes: 'Woof, Woof, Woof, Woof, Woof, Woof, Woof, Woof,
> Woof.'
>
> The clerk examines the paper and politely tells the dog:
> 'There are only nine words here. You could send another "Woof"
> for the same price.'
>
> The dog looks confused and replies, 'But that would make
> no sense at all.'

2007

Family Ghosts

Maxine Hong Kingston

1 When the thermometer in our laundry reached one hundred and
eleven degrees on summer afternoons, either my mother or my
father would say that it was time to tell another ghost story so
that we could get some good chills up our backs. My parents,
my brothers, sisters, great-uncle, and "Third Aunt," who wasn't
really our aunt but a fellow villager, someone else's third aunt,
kept the presses crashing and hissing and shouted out the stories.

Those were our successful days, when so much laundry came in, my mother did not have to pick tomatoes. For breaks we changed from pressing to sorting.

"One twilight," my mother began, and already the chills 2 travelled my back and crossed my shoulders; the air rose at the nape and the back of the legs, "I was walking home after doctoring a sick family. To get home I had to cross a footbridge. In China the bridges are nothing like the ones in Brooklyn and San Francisco. This one was made from rope, laced and knotted as if by magpies. Actually it had been built by men who had returned after harvesting sea swallow nests in Malaya. They had had to swing over the faces of the Malayan cliffs in baskets they had woven themselves. Though this bridge pitched and swayed in the updraft, no one had ever fallen into the river, which looked like a bright scratch at the bottom of the canyon, as if the Queen of Heaven had swept her great silver hairpin across the earth as well as the sky."

One twilight, just as my mother stepped on the bridge, two 3 smoky columns spiraled up taller than she. Their swaying tops hovered over her head like white cobras, one at either handrail. From stillness came a wind rushing between the smoke spindles. A high sound entered her temple bones. Through the twin whirlwinds she could see the sun and the river, the river twisting in circles, the trees upside down. The bridge moved like a ship, sickening. The earth dipped. She collapsed to the wooden slates, a ladder up the sky, her fingers so weak she could not grip the rungs. The wind dragged her hair behind her, then whipped it forward across her face. Suddenly the smoke spindles disappeared. The world righted itself, and she crossed to the other side. She looked back, but there was nothing there. She used the bridge often, but she did not encounter those ghosts again.

"They were Sit Dom Kuei," said Great-Uncle. "Sit Dom 4 Kuei."

"Yes, of course," said my mother. "Sit Dom Kuei." 5

I keep looking in dictionaries under those syllables. "Kuei" 6 means "ghost," but I don't find any other words that make sense. I only hear my great-uncle's river-pirate voice, the voice of a big man who had killed someone in New York or Cuba, make the sounds—"Sit Dom Kuei." How do they translate?

7   When the Communists issued their papers on techniques for combating ghosts, I looked for "Sit Dom Kuei." I have not found them described anywhere, although now I see that my mother won in ghost battle because she can eat anything—quick, pluck out the carp's eyes, one for Mother and one for Father. All heroes are bold toward food. In the research against ghost fear published by the Chinese Academy of Science is the story of a magistrate's servant, Kao Chung, a capable eater who in 1683 ate five cooked chickens and drank ten bottles of wine that belonged to the sea monster with branching teeth. The monster had arranged its food around a fire on the beach and started to feed when Kao Chung attacked. The swan-feather sword he wrested from this monster can be seen in the Wentung County Armory in Shantung today.

8   Another big eater was Chou Yi-han of Changchow, who fried a ghost. It was a meaty stick when he cut it up and cooked it. But before that it had been a woman out at night.

9   Chen Luan-feng, during the Yuan Ho era of the T'ang dynasty (A.D. 806-820), ate yellow croaker and pork together, which the thunder god had forbidden. But Chen wanted to incur thunderbolts during drought. The first time he ate, the thunder god jumped out of the sky, its legs like old trees. Chen chopped off the left one. The thunder god fell to the earth, and the villagers could see that it was a blue pig or bear with horns and fleshy wings. Chen leapt on it, prepared to chop its neck and bite its throat, but the villagers stopped him. After that, Chen lived apart as a rainmaker, neither relatives nor the monks willing to bring lightning upon themselves. He lived in a cave, and for years whenever there was drought the villagers asked him to eat yellow croaker and pork together, and he did.

10   The most fantastic eater of them all was Wei Pang, a scholar-hunter of the Ta Li era of the T'ang dynasty (A.D. 766-779). He shot and cooked rabbits and birds, but he could also eat scorpions, snakes, cockroaches, worms, slugs, beetles, and crickets. Once he spent the night in a house that had been abandoned because its inhabitants feared contamination from the dead man next door. A shining, twinkling sphere came flying through the darkness at

Wei. He felled it with three true arrows—the first; making the thing crackle and flame; the second dimming it; and the third putting out its lights, sputter. When his servant came running in with a lamp, Wei saw his arrows sticking in a ball of flesh entirely covered with eyes, some rolled back to show the dulling whites. He and the servant pulled out the arrows and cut up the ball into little pieces. The servant cooked the morsels in sesame oil, and the wonderful aroma made Wei laugh. They ate half, saving half to show the household, which would return now.

Big eaters win. When other passers-by stepped around the bundle wrapped in white silk, the anonymous scholar of Hanchow took it home. Inside were three silver ingots and a froglike evil, which sat on the ingots. The scholar laughed at it and chased it off. That night two frogs the size of year-old babies appeared in his room. He clubbed them to death, cooked them, and ate them with white wine. The next night a dozen frogs, together the size of a pair of year-old babies, jumped from the ceiling. He ate all twelve for dinner. The third night thirty small frogs were sitting on his mat and staring at him with their frog eyes. He ate them too. Every night for a month smaller but more numerous frogs came so that he always had the same amount to eat. Soon his floor was like the healthy banks of a pond in spring when the tadpoles, having just turned, sprang in the wet grass. "Get a hedgehog to help eat," cried him family. "I'm as good as a hedgehog," the scholar said, laughing. And at the end of the month the frogs stopped coming, leaving the scholar with the white silk and the silver ingots.

Cause and Effect

White Guilt

Shelby Steele

1   I don't remember hearing the phrase "white guilt" very much before the mid-1960s. Growing up black in the 1950s, I never had the impression that whites were much disturbed by guilt when it came to blacks. When I would stray into the wrong restaurant in pursuit of a hamburger, it didn't occur to me that the waitress was unduly troubled by guilt when she asked me to leave. I can see now that possibly she was, but then all I saw was her irritability at having to carry out so unpleasant a task. If there was guilt, it was mine for having made an imposition of myself. I can remember feeling a certain sympathy for such people, as if I was victimizing them by drawing them out of an innocent anonymity into the unasked-for role of racial policemen. Occasionally they came right out and asked me to feel sorry for them. A caddymaster at a country club told my brother and me that he was doing us a favor by not letting us caddy at this white club and that we should try to understand his position, "put yourselves in my shoes." Our color had brought this man anguish and, if a part of that anguish was guilt, it was not as immediate to me as my own guilt. I smiled at the man to let him know he shouldn't feel bad and then began my long walk home. Certainly, I also judge him a coward, but in that era his cowardice was something I had to absorb.

2   In the 1960s, particularly the black-is-beautiful late 1960s, this absorption of another's cowardice was no longer necessary. The lines of moral power, like plates in the Earth, had shifted. White

196

guilt became so palpable you could see it on people. At the time what it looked like to my eyes was a remarkable loss of authority. And what whites lost in authority, blacks gained. You cannot feel guilty about anyone without giving away power to them. Suddenly, this huge vulnerability had opened up in whites and, as a black, you had the power to step right into it. In fact, black power all but demanded that you do so. What shocked me in the late 1960s, after the helplessness I had felt in the fifties, was that guilt had changed the nature of the white man's burden from the administration of inferiors to the uplift of equals—from the obligations of dominance to the urgencies of repentance.

I think what made the difference between the fifties and six- 3 ties, at least as far as white guilt was concerned, was that whites underwent an archetypal Fall. Because of the immense turmoil of the civil rights movement, and later the black-power movement, whites were confronted for more than a decade with their willingness to participate in, or comply with, the oppression of blacks, their indifference to human suffering and denigration, their capacity to abide evil for their own benefit and in the defiance of their own sacred principles. The 1964 Civil Rights Bill that bestowed equality under the law on blacks was also, in a certain sense, an admission of white guilt. Had white society not been wrong, there would have been no need for such a bill. In this bill the nation acknowledged its fallenness, its lack of racial innocence, and confronted the incriminating self-knowledge that it had rationalized for many years a flagrant injustice. Denial is a common way of handling guilt, but in the 1960s there was little will left for denial except in the most recalcitrant whites. With this defense lost there was really only one road back to innocence—through actions and policies that would bring redemption.

In the 1960s the need for white redemption from racial guilt 4 became the most powerful, yet unspoken, element in America's social-policy-making process, first giving rise to the Great Society and then to a series of programs, policies, and laws that sought to make black equality and restitution a national mission. Once America could no longer deny its guilt, it went after redemption, or at least the look of redemption, and did so with a vengeance.

Yet today, some twenty years later, study after study tells us that by many measures the gap between blacks and whites is widening rather than narrowing. A University of Chicago study indicates that segregation is more entrenched in American cities today than ever imagined. A National Research Council study notes the "status of blacks relative to whites (in housing and education) has stagnated or regressed since the early seventies." A follow-up to the famous Kerner Commission Report warns that blacks are as much at risk today of becoming a "nation within a nation" as we were twenty years ago, when the original report was made.

5   I think the white need for redemption has contributed to this tragic situation by shaping our policies regarding blacks in ways that may deliver the look of innocence to society and its institutions but that do very little actually to uplift blacks. The specific effect of this hidden need has been to bend social policy more toward reparation for black oppression than toward the much harder and more mundane work of black uplift and development. Rather than facilitate the development of blacks to achieve parity with whites, these programs and policies—affirmative action is a good example—have tended to give blacks special entitlements that in many cases are of no use because blacks lack the development that would put us in a position to take advantage of them. I think the reason there has been more entitlement than development is (along with black power) the unacknowledged white need for redemption—not true redemption, which would have concentrated policy on black development, but the appearance of redemption, which requires only that society, in the name of development, seems to be paying back its former victims with preferences. One of the effects of entitlements, I believe, has been to encourage in blacks a dependency both on entitlements and on the white guilt that generates them. Even when it serves ideal justice, bounty from another man's guilt weakens. While this is not the only factor in black "stagnation" and "regression," I believe it is one very potent factor.

6   It is easy enough to say that white guilt too often has the effect of bending social policies in the wrong direction. But what exactly is this guilt, and how does it work in American life?

I think white guilt, in its broad sense, springs from a knowl- 7
edge of ill-gotten advantage. More precisely, it comes from the
juxtaposition of this knowledge with the inevitable gratitude
one feels for being white rather than black in America. Given the
moral instincts of human beings, it is all but impossible to enjoy
an ill-gotten advantage, much less to feel at least secretly grateful
for it, without consciously or unconsciously experiencing guilt. If,
as Kierkegaard writes, "innocence is ignorance," then guilt must
always involve knowledge. White Americans *know* that their historical advantage comes from the subjugation of an entire people.
So, even for whites today for whom racism is anathema, there is
no escape from the knowledge that makes for guilt. Racial guilt
simply accompanies the condition of being white in America.

I do not believe that this guilt is a crushing anguish for most 8
whites, but I do believe it constitutes a continuing racial vulnerability—an openness to racial culpability—that is a thread in
white life, sometimes felt, sometimes not, but ever present as a
potential feeling. In the late 1960s almost any black could charge
this vulnerability with enough current for a white person to feel
it. I had a friend who had developed this activity into a sort of
specialty. I don't think he meant to be mean, though certainly
he was mean. I think he was, in that hyperbolic era, exhilarated
by the discovery that his race, which had long been a liability,
now gave him a certain edge—that white guilt was the true force
behind black power. To feel this power he would sometimes set
up what he called "race experiments." Once I watched him stop
a white businessman in the men's room of a large hotel and convince him to increase his tip to the black attendant from one to
twenty dollars.

My friend's tactic was very simple, even corny. Out of the 9
attendant's earshot he asked the man simply to look at the
attendant, a frail, elderly, and very dark man in a starched white
smock that made the skin on his neck and face look as leathery as
a turtle's. He sat listlessly, pathetically, on a straight-backed chair
next to a small table on which sat a stack of hand towels and a
silver plate for tips. Since the attendant offered no service whatever beyond the handing out of towels, one could only conclude
the hotel management offered his lowly presence as flattery to

their patrons, as an opportunity for that easy noblesse oblige that could reassure even the harried and weary traveling salesman of his superior station. My friend was quick to make this point to the businessman and to say that no white man would do this job. But when the businessman put the single back in his wallet and took out a five, my friend only sneered. Did he understand the tragedy of a life spent this way, of what it must be like to earn one's paltry living as a symbol of inferiority? And did he realize that his privilege as an affluent white businessman (ironically he had just spent the day trying to sell a printing press to the Black Muslims for their newspaper *Mohammed Speaks*) was connected to the deprivation of this man and others like him?

10   But then my friend made a mistake that ended the game. In the heat of argument, which until then had only been playfully challenging, he inadvertently mentioned his father. This stopped the victim cold and his eyes turned inward. "What about your father?" the businessman asked. My friend replied, "He had a hard life, that's all." "How did he have a hard life?" the businessman asked. Now my friend was on the defensive. I knew he did not get along with his father, a bitter man who worked nights in a factory and demanded that the house be dark and silent all day. My friend blamed his father's bitterness on racism, but I knew he had not meant to exploit his own pain in this silly "experiment." Things had gotten too close to home, but he didn't know how to get out of the situation without losing face. Now, caught in his own trap, he did what he least wanted to do. He gave forth the rage he truly felt to a white stranger in a public men's room. "My father never had a chance," he said with the kind of anger that could easily turn to tears. "He never had a freakin' chance. Your father had all the goddamn chances, and you know he did. You sell printing presses to black people and make thousands and your father probably lives down in Fat City, Florida, all because you're white." On and on he went in this vein, using—against all that was honorable in him—his own profound racial pain to extract a flash of guilt from a white man he didn't even know.

11   He got more than a flash. The businessman was touched. His eyes became mournful, and finally he simply said, "You're right.

Your people got a raw deal." He took a twenty dollar bill from his wallet and walked over and dropped it in the old man's tip plate. When he was gone my friend and I could not look at the old man, nor could we look at each other.

It is obvious that this was a rather shameful encounter for all 12 concerned—my friend and I, as his silent accomplice, trading on our racial pain, tampering with a stranger for no reason, and the stranger then buying his way out of the situation for twenty dollars, a sum that was generous by one count and cheap by another. It was not an encounter of people but of historical grudges and guilts. Yet, when I think about it now twenty years later, I see that it had all the elements of a paradigm that I believe has been very much at the heart of racial policy-making in America since the 1960s.

My friend did two things that made this businessman vul- 13 nerable to his guilt—that brought his guilt into the situation as a force. First he put this man in touch with his own knowledge of his ill-gotten advantage as a white. The effect of this was to disallow the man any pretense of racial innocence, to let him know that, even if he was not the sort of white who used the word *nigger* around the dinner table, he still had reason to feel racial guilt. But, as disarming as this might have been, it was too abstract to do much more than crack open this man's vulnerability, to expose him to the logic of white guilt. This was the five-dollar, intellectual sort of guilt. The twenty dollars required something more visceral. In achieving this, the second thing my friend did was something he had not intended to do, something that ultimately brought him as much shame as he was doling out: He made a display of his own racial pain and anger. (What brought him shame was not the pain and anger, but his trading on them for what turned out to be a mere twenty bucks.) The effect of this display was to reinforce the man's knowledge of ill-gotten advantage, to give credibility and solidity to it by putting a face on it. Here was human testimony, a young black beside himself at the thought of his father's racially constricted life. The pain of one man evidenced the knowledge of the other. When the businessman listened to my friend's pain, his racial guilt—normally only one source of guilt lying dormant among others—was called out like a neglected debt he would finally have to settle. An ill-gotten advantage is not hard to bear—it can be marked up to fate—until it touches the genuine human pain it has brought into the world. This is the pain that hardens guilty knowledge.

14   Such knowledge is a powerful influence when it becomes conscious. What makes it so powerful is the element of fear that guilt always carries, the fear of what the guilty knowledge says about us. Guilt makes us afraid for ourselves, and thus generates as much self-preoccupation as concern for others. The nature of this preoccupation is always the redemption of innocence, the reestablishment of good feeling about oneself.

15   In this sense, the fear for the self that is buried in all guilt is a pressure toward selfishness. It can lead us to put our own need for innocence above our concern for the problem that made us feel guilt in the first place. But this fear for the self does not only inspire selfishness; it also becomes a pressure to *escape* the guilt-inducing situation. When selfishness and escapism are at work, we are no longer interested in the source of our guilt and, there-fore, no longer concerned with an authentic redemption from it. Then we only want the look of redemption, the gesture of concern that will give us the appearance of innocence and escape from the situation. Obviously the businessman did not put twenty dollars in the tip plate because he thought it would uplift black Americans. He did it selfishly for the appearance of concern and for the escape it afforded him.

16   This is not to say that guilt is never the right motive for doing good works or showing concern, only that it is a very dangerous one because of its tendency to draw us into self-preoccupation and escapism. Guilt is a civilizing emotion when the fear for the self that it carries is contained—a containment that allows guilt to be more selfless and that makes genuine concern possible. I think this was the kind of guilt that, along with the other forces, made the 1964 Civil Rights Bill possible. But since then I believe too many of our social policies related to race have been shaped by the fearful underside of guilt.

17   Black power evoked white guilt and made it a force in American institutions, very much in the same way as my friend brought it to life in the businessman. Few people volunteer for

guilt. Usually others make us feel it. It was the expression of black anger and pain that hardened the guilty knowledge of white ill-gotten advantage. And black power—whether from militant fringe groups, the civil rights establishment, or big city political campaigns—knew exactly the kind of white guilt it was after. It wanted to trigger the kind of white guilt in which whites fear for their own decency and innocence; it wanted the guilt of white self-preoccupation and escapism. Always at the heart of black power, in whatever form, has been a profound anger at what was done to blacks and an equally profound feeling that there should be reparations. But a sober white guilt (in which fear for the self is still contained) seeks a strict fairness—the 1964 Civil Rights Bill that guaranteed equality under the law. It is of little value when one is after more than fairness. So black power made its mission to have whites fear for their innocence, to feel a visceral guilt from which they would have to seek a more profound redemption. In such redemption was the possibility of black reparation. Black power upped the ante on white guilt.

With black power, all of the elements of the hidden paradigm that shape America's race-related social policy were in place. Knowledge of ill-gotten advantage could now be shown and deepened by black power into the sort of guilt from which institutions could only redeem themselves by offering more than fairness—by offering forms of reparation and compensation for past injustice. I believe this bent our policies toward racial entitlements at the expense of racial development. In 1964, one of the assurances Senator Hubert Humphrey and others had to give Congress to get the landmark Civil Rights Bill passed was that the bill would not in any way require employers to use racial preferences to rectify racial imbalances. But this was before the explosion of black power in the late 1960s, before the hidden paradigm was set in motion. After black power, racial preferences became the order of the day. [18]

If this paradigm brought blacks entitlements, it also brought the continuation of the most profound problem in American society, the invisibility of blacks as a people. The white guilt that this paradigm elicits is the kind of guilt that preoccupies whites with their own innocence and pressures them toward [19] escapism—twenty dollars in the plate and out the door. With this guilt, as opposed to the contained guilt of genuine concern, whites tend to see only their own need for quick redemption. Blacks then become a means to this redemption and, as such, they must be seen as generally "less than" others. Their needs are "special," "unique," "different." They are seen exclusively along the dimension of their victimization, so that they become "different" people with whom whites can negotiate entitlements but never fully see as people like themselves. Guilt that preoccupies people with their own innocence blinds them to those who make them feel guilty. This, of course, is not racism, and yet it has the same effect as racism since it makes blacks something of a separate species for whom normal standards and values do not automatically apply.

20   Nowhere is this more evident today than in American universities. At some of America's most elite universities administrators have granted concessions in response to black student demands (black power) that all but sanction racial separatism on campus—black "theme" dorms, black student unions, black yearbooks, homecoming dances, and so forth. I don't believe administrators sincerely believe in these separatist concessions. Most of them are liberals who see racial separatism as wrong. But black student demands pull administrators into the paradigm of self-preoccupied white guilt, whereby they seek a quick redemption by offering special entitlements that go beyond fairness. As a result, black students become all but invisible to them. Though blacks have the lowest grade point average of any racial group in American universities, administrators never sit down with them and "demand" in kind that black students bring their grades up to par. The paradigm of white guilt makes the real problems of black students secondary to the need for white redemption. It also cuts administrators off from their own values, which would most certainly discourage racial separatism and encourage higher academic performance for black students. Lastly, it makes for escapist policies. There is no difference between giving black students a separate lounge and leaving twenty dollars in the tip plate on the way out the door.

1990

Where Have All the Parents Gone?

Barbara Dafoe Whitehead

"Invest in kids," George Bush mused during his 1988 presidential 1 campaign, "I like it." Apparently so do others. A growing number of corporate CEOs and educators, elected officials and child-welfare advocates have embraced the same language. "Invest in kids" is the bumper sticker for an important new cause, aptly tagged the *kids as capital* argument. It runs as follows:

America's human capital comes in two forms: The active 2 work force and the prospective work force. The bulk of tomorrow's workers are today's children, of course. So children make up much of the stockpile of America's potential human capital.

If we look at them as tomorrow's workers, we begin to appre- 3 ciate our stake in today's children. They will determine when we can retire, how well we can live in retirement, how generous our health insurance will be, how strong our social safety net, how orderly our society. What's more, today's children will determine how successfully we compete in the global economy. They will be going head-to-head against Japanese, Korean, and West German children.

Unfortunately, American children aren't prepared to run 4 the race, let alone win it. Many are illiterate, undernourished, impaired, unskilled, poor. Consider the children who started first grade in 1986: 14 percent were illegitimate; 15 percent were physically or emotionally handicapped; 15 percent spoke another language other than English; 28 percent were poor; and fully 40 percent could be expected to live in a single-parent home before they reached eighteen. Given falling birth rates, this future work force is small—all the more reason to worry about its poor quality. So "invest in kids" is not the cry of the soft-hearted altruist but the call of the hardheaded realist.

Kids as capital has caught on because it responds to a broad set 5 of national concerns. Whether one is worried about the rise of the underclass, the decline of the family, our standing in the global economy, the nation's level of educational performance, or intergenerational conflict, kids as capital seems to offer an answer.

6 Further, *kids as capital* offers the rationale for a new coalition for child welfare programs. The argument reaches beyond the community of traditional children's advocates and draws business into the child-saving fold. American corporations clearly have a stake in tomorrow's work force as they don't have in today's children. *Kids as capital* gives the tough-minded, fifty-five-year-old CEO a reason to "care" about the eight-year-old, Hispanic school girl.

7 Nevertheless, the argument left unchallenged could easily become yet another "feel-good" formula that doesn't work. Worse, it could end up betraying those it seeks to save—the nation's children.

8 First, *kids as capital* departs from a classic American vision of the future. Most often, our history has been popularly viewed as progressive, with each generation breaking with and improving on the past. As an immigrant nation, we have always measured our progress through the progress of our children; they have been the bearers of the dream.

9 *Kids as capital* turns this optimistic view on its head. It conjures up a picture of a dark and disorderly future. Essentially, kids as capital is dystopic—closer to the spirit of *Blade Runner* and *Black Rain* than *Wizard of Oz* or *It's a Wonderful Life*. Children, in this view, do not bear the dream. They carry the seeds of our destruction. In short, *kids as capital* plays on our fears, rather than our hopes. It holds out the vision of a troubled future in order to secure a safer and more orderly present.

10 There is something troubling, too, in such an instrumental view of children. To define them narrowly as tomorrow's wonders is to strip them of their full status as humans, as children: Kids can't be kids; they can only be embryonic workers. And treating *kids as capital* makes it easier to measure them solely through IQ tests, class standing, SAT scores, drop-out ratios, physical fitness tests. This leaves no place in the society for the slow starter, the handicapped, the quirky, and the nonconforming.

11 Yet *kids as capital* has an even more serious flaw. It evades the central fact of life for American children: They have parents.

12 As we all know, virtually every child in America grows up in a family with one or more parents. Parents house children.

Parents feed children. Parents clothe children. Parents nurture and protect children. Parents instruct children in everything from using a fork to driving a car. To be sure, there have been vast changes in family life, and, increasingly, parents must depend on teachers, doctors, day-care workers, and technology to help care for and educate their children. Even so, these changes haven't altered one fundamental fact: In American society, parents still bear the primary responsibility for the material and spiritual welfare of children. As our teachers and counselors and politicians keep reminding us, everything begins at home. So, if today's children are in trouble, it's because today's parents are in trouble.

As recently as a dozen years ago, it was the central argument 13 of an ambitious report by the Carnegie Council on Children. The Council put it plainly: "The best way to help children tomorrow is to support parents today." Yet, that view has been lost. The *kids as capital* argument suppresses the connection between parents and children. It imagines that we can improve the standing of children without improving the standing of the parents. In the new rhetoric, it is hard even to find the word "parent." Increasingly, kids are portrayed as standing alone out there somewhere, cosmically parent-free.

As a result, *kids as capital* ignores rather than addresses one of 14 the most important changes in American life: The decline in the power and standing of the nation's parents.

Only a generation ago, parents stood at the center of society. 15 First of all, there were so many of them—fully half the nation's households in 1960 were parent households with one or more children under eighteen. Moreover, parents looked alike—Dad worked and Mom stayed at home. And parents marched through the stages of childbearing and child rearing in virtual lockstep: Most couples who married in the 1940s and 1950s finished having their 3.2 children by the time they were in their late twenties.

Their demographic dominance meant two things: First, it 16 made for broad common ground in child rearing. Parents could do a great deal to support each other in raising the new generation. They could, and did, create a culture hospitable to children. Secondly, it made for political clout. When so many adults were parents and so many parents were part of an expanding consumer economy, private and public interests converged. The concerns of parents—housing, health, education—easily found their way into the national agenda. Locally, too, parents were dominant. In some postwar suburbs like Levittown, Pennsylvania, three-quarters of all residents were either parents or children under ten. Not surprisingly, there was little dissent when it came to building a new junior high or establishing a summer recreation program or installing a new playground. What's more, parents and kids drove the consumer economy. Every time they bought a pair of sneakers or a new bike, they were acting in the nation's best interest.

17   Behind this, of course, lurked a powerful pronatal ideology. Parenthood was the definitive credential of adulthood. More than being married, more than getting a job, it was having a child that baptized you as an adult in postwar America. In survey after survey, postwar parents rated children above marriage itself as the greatest reward of private life. For a generation forced to make personal sacrifices during the Depression and the war, having children and pursuing a private life represented a new kind of freedom.

18   By the 1970s, parents no longer enjoyed so central a place in the society. To baby boom children, postwar family life seemed suffocating and narrow. Women, in particular, wanted room to breathe. The rights movements of the sixties and seventies overturned the pronatal ideology, replacing it with an ideology of choice. Adults were free to choose among many options: Single, married, or divorced; career-primary or career-secondary; parent, stepparent, or child-free.

19   Thus, parenthood lost its singular status. It no longer served as the definitive credential of maturity and adult achievement. In fact, as careers and personal fulfillment beckoned, parenthood seemed just the opposite: A serious limitation on personal growth and success. As Gloria Steinem put it, "I either gave birth to someone else or I gave birth to myself."

20   As the pronatal ideology vanished, so did the close connection between private families and the public interest. Raising children was no longer viewed as a valuable contribution to the society, an

activity that boosted the economy, built citizen participation, and increased the nation's confidence in the future. Instead, it became one option among many. No longer a moral imperative, child rearing was just another "lifestyle choice."

Viewed this way, raising children looked like an economic 21 disaster. Starting out, parents had to shell out $3,000 for basic prenatal care and maternity costs; $3,000–$5,000 per child for day care; and $2,500 for the basic baby basket of goods and services. Crib-to-college costs for middle-class Americans could run as high as $135,000 per child. And, increasingly, the period of economic dependency for children stretched well beyond age eighteen. College tuitions and start-up subsidies for the new college graduate became part of the economic burden of parenthood. In an ad campaign, Manufacturers Hanover Trust gave prospective parents fair warning: "If you want a bundle of joy; you'll need a bundle of money."

Hard-pressed younger Americans responded to these new 22 realities in several ways. Some simply chose not to have children. Others decided to have one or two, but only after they had a good job and solid prospects. Gradually, the number of parent households in the nation declined from one-half to one-third, and America faced a birth dearth.

For those who chose the parent option, there was only one 23 way to face up to the new economic pressures of child rearing: Work longer and harder outside the home. For all but the extremely well-off, a second income became essential. But in struggling to pay the bills, parents seemed to be short-changing their children in another way. They weren't taking their moral responsibilities seriously enough. They weren't spending enough time with their kids. They weren't reading to the children or playing with the kids or supervising homework. And, most important, they weren't teaching good values.

This emerging critique marked a dramatic change in 24 the way society viewed parents. In the postwar period, the stereotypical parent was self-sacrificing, responsible, caring, attentive—an impossible standard, to be sure, but one that lent enormous popular support and approval to adults engaged in the messy and difficult work of raising children. Cruel, abusive, self-absorbed parents might exist, but the popular culture failed to acknowledge them. It was not until parents began to lose their central place in the society that this flattering image faded. Then, quite rapidly, the dominant image of The Good Parent gave way to a new and equally powerful image—the image of The Bad Parent.

25   The shift occurred in two stages. The first-stage critique emerged in the seventies and focused on an important new figure: The working mother. Working mothers were destroying their children and the family, conservative critics charged. They weren't feeding kids wholesome meals, they weren't taking the kids to church, they weren't serving as moral exemplars. Liberals sided with working mothers, but conceded that they were struggling with some new and difficult issues: Was day care as good as mother care? Was quality time good enough? Were the rewards of twelve-hour workdays great enough to make up for the loss of sleep and leisure-time? Where did the mother of a feverish child belong—at the crib or at her desk?

26   On the whole, the first-stage critique was a sympathetic critique. In its view, parents might be affected by stress and guilt, but they weren't yet afflicted by serious pathology. After all, in the seventies, the nation's most suspect drug was laetrile, not crack or ice. Divorce was still viewed as a healthy alternative to an unhappy family life. But as the eighties began, a darker image of parents appeared. In the second-stage critique, . . . parents became toxic.

27   Day after day, throughout the eighties, Americans confronted an ugly new reality. Parents were hurting and murdering their children. Day after day, the newspapers brought yet another story of a child abandoned or battered. Day after day, the local news told of a child sexually abused by a father or a stepfather or a mother's boyfriend. Week by week, the national media brought us into courtrooms where photographs of battered children were held up to the camera. The sheer volume of stories suggested an epidemic of historic proportion. In even the most staid publications, the news was sensational. *The New York Times* carried bizarre stories usually found only in tabloids: A father who

tortured his children for years; a mother who left her baby in a suitcase in a building she then set on fire; parents who abandoned babies dead or alive, in toilets, dumpsters, and alleyways.

Drug use among parents was one clear cause of abuse. And, 28 increasingly, child abuse and drug abuse were linked in the most direct way possible. Pregnant women were battering their children in the womb, delivering drugs through their umbilical cords. Nightly images of crack-addicted babies in neonatal units destroyed any lingering public sympathy for mothers of the underclass. And as the highly publicized Joel Steinberg case made clear, middle-class parents, too, took drugs and killed babies. Even those parents who occasionally indulged were causing their children harm. The Partnership for Drug-Free America ran ads asking: "With millions of parents doing drugs, is it any wonder their kids are too?"

More than drugs, it was divorce that lay at the heart of 29 middle-class parental failure. It wasn't the crackhouse but the courthouse that was the scene of their collapse. Parents engaged in bitter custody battles. Parents kidnapped their own children. Parents used children as weapons against each other or simply walked away from their responsibilities. In an important new study on the long-term effects of divorce, Judith Wallerstein challenged the earlier notion that divorce is healthy for kids. She studied middle-class families for fifteen years after divorce and came up with some startling findings: Almost half of the children in the study entered adulthood as worried, underachieving, self-deprecating, and sometimes angry young men and women; one in four experienced a severe and enduring drop in their standard of living; three in five felt rejected by at least one parent. Her study concluded: "Divorce is almost always more devastating for children than for their parents. . . . [W]hile divorce can rescue a parent from an intolerable situation, it can fail to rescue the children."

As a group, today's parents have been portrayed as selfish 30 and uncaring: Yuppie parents abandon the children to the au pair; working parents turn their kids over to the mall and the video arcade; single parents hang a key around their kids' necks and a list of emergency numbers on the refrigerator. Even in the healthiest families, parents fail to put their children first.

31   The indictment of parents is pervasive. In a survey by the Carnegie Foundation, 90 percent of a national sample of public school teachers say a lack of parental support is a problem in their classrooms. Librarians gathered at a national convention to draft a new policy to deal with the problem of parents who send unattended children to the library after school. Daycare workers complain to Ann Landers that all too often parents hand over children with empty stomachs and full diapers. Everywhere, parents are flunking the most basic tests.

32   Declining demographically, hard-pressed economically, and disarrayed politically, parents have become part of the problem. For proponents of the *kids as capital* argument, the logic is clear: Why try to help parents—an increasingly marginal and unsympathetic bunch—when you can rescue their children?

33   To blame parents for larger social changes is nothing new. In the past, child-saving movements have depended on building a public consensus that certain parents have failed. Child reformers in the Progressive Era, for example, were able to expand the scope of public sector responsibility for the welfare of children by exploiting mainstream fears about immigrant parents and their child-rearing practices. But what is new is the sense that the majority of parents—up and down the social ladder—are failing. Even middle-class parents, once solid, dependable caretakers of the next generation, don't seem to be up to the job.

34   By leaving parents out of the picture, *kids as capital* conjures up the image of our little workers struggling against the little workers of Germany and the little workers of Japan. But this picture is obviously false. For the little workers of Germany and Japan have parents too. The difference is that their parents are strongly valued and supported by the society for their contributions *as parents*. We won't be facing up to reality until we are ready to pit our parents against their parents, and thus our family policy against theirs.

1990

If Hitler Asked You to Electrocute a Stranger, Would You? Probably

Philip Meyer

In the beginning, Stanley Milgram was worried about the Nazi 1
problem. He doesn't worry much about the Nazis anymore. He
worries about you and me, and, perhaps, himself a little bit too.

Stanley Milgram is a social psychologist, and when he began 2
his career at Yale University in 1960 he had a plan to prove, scientifically, that Germans are different. The Germans-are-different
hypothesis has been used by historians, such as William L. Shirer,
to explain the systematic destruction of the Jews by the Third Reich.

The appealing thing about this theory is that it makes those 3
of us who are not Germans feel better about the whole business.
Obviously, you and I are not Hitler, and it seems equally obvious that we would never do Hitler's dirty work for him. But
now, because of Stanley Milgram, we are compelled to wonder.
Milgram developed a laboratory experiment which provided
a systematic way to measure obedience. His plan was to try it
out in New Haven on Americans and then go to Germany and
try it out on Germans. He was strongly motivated by scientific
curiosity, but there was also some moral content in his decision
to pursue this line of research, which was, in turn, colored by his
own Jewish background. If he could show that Germans are more
obedient than Americans, he could then vary the conditions of
the experiment and try to find out just what it is that makes some
people more obedient than others. With this understanding, the
world might, conceivably, be just a little bit better.

But he never took his experiment to Germany. He never took it 4
any farther than Bridgeport. The first finding, also the most unexpected and disturbing finding, was that we Americans are an obedient people: Not blindly obedient, and not blissfully obedient, just
obedient. "I found so much obedience," says Milgram softly, a little
sadly, "I hardly saw the need for taking the experiment to Germany."

There is something of the theatre director in Milgram, and 5
his technique, which he learned from one of the old masters in

experimental psychology, Solomon Asch, is to stage a play with every line rehearsed, every prop carefully selected, and everybody an actor except one person. That one person is the subject of the experiment. The subject, of course, does not know he is in a play. He thinks he is in real life.

6   The experiment worked like this: If you were an innocent subject in Milgram's melodrama, you read an ad in the newspaper or received one in the mail asking for volunteers for an educational experiment. The job would take about an hour and pay $4.50. So you make an appointment and go to an old Romanesque stone structure on High Street with the imposing name of The Yale Interaction Laboratory. It looks something like a broadcasting studio. Inside, you meet a young, crew-cut man in a laboratory coat who says he is Jack Williams, the experimenter. There is another citizen, fiftyish, Irish face, an accountant, a little overweight, and very mild and harmless-looking. This other citizen seems nervous and plays with his hat while the two of you sit in chairs side by side and are told that the $4.50 checks are yours no matter what happens. Then you listen to Jack Williams explain the experiment.

7   It is about learning, says Jack Williams in a quiet, knowledgeable way. Science does not know much about the conditions under which people learn and this experiment is to find out about negative reinforcement. Negative reinforcement is getting punished when you do something wrong, as opposed to positive reinforcement which is getting rewarded when you do something right. The negative reinforcement in this case is electric shock.

8   Then Jack Williams takes two pieces of paper, puts them in a hat, and shakes them up. One piece of paper is supposed to say, "Teacher" and the other, "Learner." Draw one and you will see which you will be. The mild-looking accountant draws one, holds it close to his vest like a poker player, looks at it, and says, "Learner." You look at yours. It says; "Teacher." You do not know that the drawing is rigged, and both slips say "Teacher." The experimenter beckons to the mild-mannered "learner."

9   "Want to step right in here and have a seat, please?" he says. "You can leave your coat on the back of that chair . . . roll up your right sleeve, please. Now what I want to do is strap down your arms to avoid excessive movement on your part during the

experiment. This electrode is connected to the shock generator in the next room.

"And this electrode paste," he says, squeezing some stuff out of a plastic bottle and putting it on the man's arm, "is to provide a good contact and to avoid a blister or burn. Are there any questions now before we go into the next room?" 10

You don't have any, but the strapped-in "learner" does. 11

"I do think I should say this," says the learner. "About two years ago, I was at the veterans' hospital . . . they detected a heart condition. Nothing serious, but as long as I'm having these shocks, how strong are they—how dangerous are they?" 12

Williams, the experimenter, shakes his head casually. "Oh, no," he says. "Although they may be painful, they're not dangerous. Anything else?" 13

Nothing else. And so you play the game. The game is for you to read a series of word pairs: For example, blue-girl, nice-day, fat-neck. When you finish the list, you read just the first word in each pair and then a multiple-choice list of four other words, including the second word of the pair. The learner, from his remote, strapped-in position, pushes one of four switches to indicate which of the four answers he thinks is the right one. If he gets it right, nothing happens and you go on to the next one. If he gets it wrong, you push a switch that buzzes and gives him an electric shock. And then you go to the next word. You start with 15 volts and increase the number of volts by 15 for each wrong answer. The control board goes from 15 volts on one end to 450 volts on the other. So that you know what you are doing, you get a test shock yourself, at 45 volts. It hurts. To further keep you aware of what you are doing to that man in there, the board has verbal descriptions of the shock levels, ranging from "Slight Shock" at the left-hand side, through "Intense Shock" in the middle, to "Danger: Severe Shock" toward the far right. Finally, at the very end, under 435- and 450-volt switches, there are three ambiguous X's. If, at any point, you hesitate, Mr. Williams calmly tells you to go on. If you still hesitate, he tells you again. 14

Except for some terrifying details, which will be explained in a moment, this is the experiment. The object is to find the shock level at which you disobey the experimenter and refuse to pull the switch. 15

16 When Stanley Milgram first wrote this script, he took it to fourteen Yale psychology majors and asked them what they thought would happen. He put it this way: Out of one hundred persons in the teacher's predicament, how would their break-off points be distributed along the 15-to-450-volt scale? They thought a few would break off very early, most would quit someplace in the middle and a few would go all the way to the end. The highest estimate of the number out of one hundred who would go all the way to the end was three. Milgram then informally polled some of his fellow scholars in the psychology department. They agreed that very few would go to the end. Milgram thought so too.

17 "I'll tell you quite frankly," he says, "before I began this experiment, before any shock generator was built, I thought that most people would break off at 'Strong Shock' or 'Very Strong Shock.' You would get only a very, very small proportion of people going out to the end of the shock generator, and they would constitute a pathological fringe."

18 In his pilot experiments, Milgram used Yale students as subjects. Each of them pushed the shock switches, one by one, all the way to the end of the board.

19 So he rewrote the script to include some protests from the learner. At first, they were mild, gentlemanly, Yalie protests, but, "it didn't seem to have as much effect as I thought it would or should," Milgram recalls. "So we had more violent protestation on the part of the person getting the shock. All of the time, of course, what we were trying to do was not to create a macabre situation, but simply to generate disobedience. And that was one of the first findings. This was not only a technical deficiency of the experiment, that we didn't get disobedience. It really was the first finding: That obedience would be much greater than we had assumed it would be and disobedience would be much more difficult than we had assumed."

20 As it turned out, the situation did become rather macabre. The only meaningful way to generate disobedience was to have the victim protest with great anguish, noise, and vehemence. The protests were tape-recorded so that all the teachers ordinarily would hear the same sounds and nuances, and they started with

a grunt at 75 volts, proceeded through a "Hey, that really hurts," at 125 volts, got desperate with, "I can't stand the pain, don't do that," at 180 volts, reached complaints of heart trouble at 195, an agonized scream at 285, a refusal to answer at 315, and only heartrending, ominous silence after that.

Still, sixty-five percent of the subjects, twenty- to fifty-year- 21 old American males, everyday, ordinary people, like you and me, obediently kept pushing those levers in the belief that they were shocking the mild-mannered learner, whose name was Mr. Wallace, and who was chosen for the role because of his innocent appearance, all the way up to 450 volts.

Milgram was now getting enough disobedience so that he had 22 something he could measure. The next step was to vary the circumstances to see what would encourage or discourage obedience.

He put the learner in the same room with the teacher. He 23 stopped strapping the learner's hand down. He rewrote the script so that at 150 volts the learner took his hand off the shock plate and declared that he wanted out of the experiment. He rewrote the script some more so that the experimenter then told the teacher to grasp the learner's hand and physically force it down on the plate to give Mr. Wallace his unwanted electric shock.

"I had the feeling that very few people would go on at that 24 point, if any," Milgram says. "I thought that would be the limit of obedience that you would find in the laboratory."

It wasn't. 25

Although seven years have now gone by, Milgram still 26 remembers the first person to walk into the laboratory in the newly rewritten script. He was a construction worker, a very short man. "He was so small," says Milgram, "that when he sat on the chair in front of the shock generator, his feet didn't reach the floor. When the experimenter told him to push the victim's hand down and give the shock, he turned to the experimenter, and he turned to the victim, his elbow went up, he fell down on the hand of the victim, his feet kind of tugged to one side, and he said, 'Like this, boss?' ZZUMPH!"

The experiment was played out to its bitter end. Milgram 27 tried it with forty different subjects. And thirty percent of them obeyed the experimenter and kept on obeying.

28   "The protests of the victim were strong and vehement, he was screaming his guts out, he refused to participate, and you had to physically struggle with him in order to get his hand down on the shock generator," Milgram remembers. But twelve out of forty did it.

29   Milgram took his experiment out of New Haven. Not to Germany, just twenty miles down the road to Bridgeport. Maybe, he reasoned, the people obeyed because of the prestigious setting of Yale University.

30   The new setting was a suite of three rooms in a run-down office building in Bridgeport. The only identification was a sign with a fictitious name: "Research Associates of Bridgeport." Questions about professional connections got only vague answers about "research for industry."

31   Obedience was less in Bridgeport. Forty-eight percent of the subjects stayed for the maximum shock, compared to sixty-five percent at Yale. But this was enough to prove that far more than Yale's prestige was behind the obedient behavior.

32   For more than seven years now, Stanley Milgram has been trying to figure out what makes ordinary American citizens so obedient. The most obvious answer—that people are mean, nasty, brutish and sadistic—won't do. The subjects who gave the shocks to Mr. Wallace to the end of the board did not enjoy it. They groaned, protested, fidgeted, argued, and in some cases, were seized by fits of nervous, agitated giggling.

33   "They even try to get out of it," says Milgram, "but they are somehow engaged in something from which they cannot liberate themselves. They are locked into a structure, and they do not have the skills or inner resources to disengage themselves."

34   Milgram's theory assumes that people behave in two different operating modes as different as ice and water. He does not rely on Freud or sex or toilet-training hang-ups for this theory. All he says is that ordinarily we operate in a state of autonomy, which means we pretty much have and assert control over what we do. But in certain circumstances, we operate under what Milgram calls a state of agency (after agent, *n* . . . one who acts for or in the place of another by authority from him; a substitute; a deputy—*Webster's Collegiate Dictionary*). A state of agency, to Milgram, is nothing more than a frame of mind.

"There's nothing bad about it, there's nothing good about it," he says. "It's a natural circumstance of living with other people. . . . I think of a state of agency as a real transformation of a person; if a person has different properties when he's in that state, just as water can turn to ice under certain conditions of temperature, a person can move to the state of mind that I call agency . . . the critical thing is that you see yourself as the instrument of the execution of another person's wishes. You do not see yourself as acting on your own. And there's a real transformation, a real change of properties of the person."

So, for most subjects in Milgram's laboratory experiments, the act of giving Mr. Wallace his painful shock was necessary, even though unpleasant, and besides they were doing it on behalf of somebody else and it was for science.

Stanley Milgram has his problems, too. He believes that in the laboratory situation, he would not have shocked Mr. Wallace. His professional critics reply that in his real-life situation he has done the equivalent. He has placed innocent and naïve subjects under great emotional strain and pressure in selfish obedience to his quest for knowledge. When you raise this issue with Milgram, he has an answer ready. There is, he explains patiently, a critical difference between his naïve subjects and the man in the electric chair. The man in the electric chair (in the mind of the naïve subject) is helpless, strapped in. But the naïve subject is free to go at any time.

Immediately after he offers this distinction, Milgram anticipates the objection.

"It's quite true," he says, "that this is almost a philosophic position, because we have learned that some people are psychologically incapable of disengaging themselves. But that doesn't relieve them of the moral responsibility."

The parallel is exquisite. "The tension problem was unexpected," says Milgram in his defense. But he went on anyway. The naïve subjects didn't expect the screaming protests from the strapped-in learner. But they went on.

"I had to make a judgment," says Milgram. "I had to ask myself, was this harming the person or not? My judgment is that it was not. Even in the extreme cases, I wouldn't say that permanent damage results."

42   Sound familiar? "The shocks may be painful," the experimenter kept saying, "but they're not dangerous."

43   After the series of experiments was completed, Milgram sent a report of the results to his subjects and a questionnaire, asking whether they were glad or sorry to have been in the experiment. Eighty-three and seven-tenths percent said they were glad and only 1.3 percent were sorry; 15 percent were neither sorry nor glad. However, Milgram could not be sure at the time of the experiment that only 1.3 percent would be sorry.

44   Kurt Vonnegut Jr. put one paragraph in the preface to *Mother Night*, in 1966, which pretty much says it for the people with their fingers on the shock-generator switches, for you and me, and maybe even for Milgram. "If I'd been born in Germany," Vonnegut said, "I suppose I would have *been* a Nazi, bopping Jews and gypsies and Poles around, leaving boots sticking out of snow banks, warming myself with my sweetly virtuous insides. So it goes."

45   Just so. One thing that happened to Milgram back in New Haven during the days of the experiment was that he kept running into people he'd watched from behind the one-way glass. It gave him a funny feeling, seeing those people going about their everyday business in New Haven and knowing what they would do to Mr. Wallace if ordered to. Now that his research results are in and you've thought about it, you can get this funny feeling too. You don't need one-way glass. A glance in your own mirror may serve just as well.

1970

The Arrow of Time

K. C. Cole

1   It was about two months ago when I realized that entropy was getting the better of me. On the same day my car broke down (again), my refrigerator conked out and I learned that I needed root canal work in my right rear tooth. The windows in the bedroom were

still leaking every time it rained and my son's baby sitter was still failing to show up every time I really needed her. My hair was turning gray and my typewriter was wearing out. The house needed paint and I needed glasses. My son's sneakers were developing holes and I was developing a deep sense of futility.

After all, what was the point of spending half of Saturday at the Laundromat if the clothes were dirty all over again the following Friday? 2

Disorder, alas, is the natural order of things in the universe. There is even a precise measure of the amount of disorder, called entropy. Unlike almost every other physical property (motion, gravity, energy), entropy does not work both ways. It can only increase. Once it's created it can never be destroyed. The road to disorder is a one-way street. 3

Because of its unnerving irreversibility, entropy has been called the arrow of time. We all understand this instinctively. Children's rooms, left on their own, tend to get messy, not neat. Wood rots, metal rusts, people wrinkle and flowers wither. Even mountains wear down; even the nuclei of atoms decay. In the city we see entropy in the rundown subways and worn-out sidewalks and torn-down buildings, in the increasing disorder of our lives. We know, without asking, what is old. If we were suddenly to see the paint jump back on an old building, we would know that something was wrong. If we saw an egg unscramble itself and jump back into its shell, we would laugh in the same way we laugh at a movie run backward. 4

Entropy is no laughing matter, however, because with every increase in entropy energy is wasted and opportunity is lost. Water flowing down a mountainside can be made to do some useful work on its way. But once all the water is at the same level it can work no more. That is entropy. When my refrigerator was working, it kept all the cold air ordered in one part of the kitchen and warmer air in another. Once it broke down the warm and cold mixed into a lukewarm mess that allowed my butter to melt, my milk to rot and my frozen vegetables to decay. 5

Of course the energy is not really lost, but it has diffused and dissipated into a chaotic caldron of randomness that can do us no possible good. Entropy is chaos. It is loss of purpose. 6

7   People are often upset by the entropy they seem to see in the haphazardness of their own lives. Buffeted about like so many molecules in my tepid kitchen, they feel that they have lost their sense of direction, that they are wasting youth and opportunity at every turn. It is easy to see entropy in marriages, when the partners are too preoccupied to patch small things up, almost guaranteeing that they will fall apart. There is much entropy in the state of our country, in the relationships between nations— lost opportunities to stop the avalanche of disorders that seems ready to swallow us all.

8   Entropy is not inevitable everywhere, however. Crystals and snowflakes and galaxies are islands of incredibly ordered beauty in the midst of random events. If it was not for exceptions to entropy, the sky would be black and we would be able to see where the stars spend their days; it is only because air molecules in the atmosphere cluster in ordered groups that the sky is blue.

9   The most profound exception to entropy is the creation of life. A seed soaks up some soil and some carbon and some sunshine and some water and arranges it into a rose. A seed in the womb takes some oxygen and pizza and milk and transforms it into a baby.

10   The catch is that it takes a lot of energy to produce a baby. It also takes energy to make a tree. The road to disorder is all downhill but the road to creation takes work. Though combating entropy is possible, it also has its price. That's why it seems so hard to get ourselves together, so easy to let ourselves fall apart.

11   Worse, creating order in one corner of the universe always creates more disorder somewhere else. We create ordered energy from oil and coal at the price of the entropy of smog.

12   I recently took up playing the flute again after an absence of several months. As the uneven vibrations screeched through the house, my son covered his ears and said, "Mom, what's wrong with your flute?" Nothing was wrong with my flute, of course. It was my ability to play it that had atrophied, or entropied, as the case may be. The only way to stop that process was to practice every day, and sure enough my tone improved, though only at the price of constant work. Like anything else, abilities deteriorate when we stop applying our energies to them.

That's why entropy is depressing. It seems as if just breaking 13
even is an uphill fight. There's a good reason that this should be
so. The mechanics of entropy are a matter of chance. Take any ice
cold air molecule milling around my kitchen. The chances that
it will wander in the direction of my refrigerator at any point
are exactly 50-50. The chances that it will wander away from my
refrigerator are also 50-50. But take billions of warm and cold
molecules mixed together, and the chances that all the cold ones
will wander toward the refrigerator and all the warm ones will
wander away from it are virtually nil.

Entropy wins not because order is impossible but because 14
there are always so many more paths toward disorder than
toward order. There are so many more different ways to do a
sloppy job than a good one, so many more ways to make a mess
than to clean it up. The obstacles and accidents in our lives almost
guarantee that constant collisions will bounce us on to random
paths, get us off the track. Disorder is the path of least resistance,
the easy but not the inevitable road.

Like so many others, I am distressed by the entropy I see 15
around me today. I am afraid of the randomness of international
events, of the lack of common purpose in the world; I am terrified that it will lead into the ultimate entropy of nuclear war.
I am upset that I could not in the city where I live send my child
to a public school; that people are unemployed and inflation is
out of control; that tensions between sexes and races seem to be
increasing again; that relationships everywhere seem to be falling apart.

Social institutions—like atoms and stars—decay if energy is 16
not added to keep them ordered. Friendships and families and
economies all fall apart unless we constantly make an effort to
keep them working and well oiled. And far too few people, it
seems to me, are willing to contribute consistently to those efforts.

Of course, the more complex things are, the harder it is. If 17
there were only a dozen or so air molecules in my kitchen, it
would be likely—if I waited a year or so—that at some point the
six coldest ones would congregate inside the freezer. But the more
factors in the equation—the more players in the game—the less
likely it is that their paths will coincide in an orderly way. The

more pieces in the puzzle, the harder it is to put back together once order is disturbed. "Irreversibility," said a physicist, "is the price we pay for complexity."

1982

Shattered Sudan

Paul Salopek

1   The oldest civil war in the world is being fought, on one side, by men who wander like demented hospital orderlies across the primordial wastes of Africa.

2   I follow them one hot morning as they flee a government ambush in the oil fields of southern Sudan. One of their comrades has just been shot dead, his body abandoned on a parched savanna that hides nearly 20 billion dollars' worth of low-sulfur crude. We retreat for hours under a scalding sun, crossing in the process a vast, cauterized plain of cracked mud. I pause a moment to watch them: an ant-like column of rebels dressed in bizarre homemade uniforms of green cotton smocks and white plastic slippers, limping into the heat waves of distance. Five casualties bounce in stretchers. They suffer their bullet wounds in silence. A boy marching in front balances a car battery on his head. He is the radio operator's assistant. Every few hundred yards he puts the battery down and empties blood out of a shoe.

3   When we finally reach a tree line, the fighters strip off their clothes and jump into a bog. The water stinks. It is infested with larvae of guinea worms, which, once ingested, burrow painfully through the body to the legs, and are extracted by making a small incision; you reel the worm out slowly, day after day, by winding it on a small stick. All around us, half-naked people move feebly through the thorn forest: ethnic Dinka herders displaced from the contested oil fields by fighting between rebels and the central

government based in the faraway capital, Khartoum. Their children, stunted and ginger-haired from malnutrition, clamber in the trees. They are collecting leaves to eat. This awful place, I learn, is called Biem—a safe haven, such as it is, of the 40,000-strong Sudan People's Liberation Army.

"You cannot reclaim what is lost," the sweating rebel commander says, squatting in the shade of an acacia, "so you just keep fighting for what little you have left."   4

He is trying to console himself. But I see little solace for the epic tragedy of Sudan. It is April 2002, and Africa's largest country is lurching into its 19th uninterrupted year of warfare—the latest round of strife that has brutalized Sudan, off and on, for most of the past half century. More than two million Sudanese are dead. We just left the latest fatality sprawling back in the yellow grasses, a bullet through his brain. And thousands of scarecrow civilians stagger through the scrub, starving atop a lucrative sea of petroleum.   5

Numbly, I crawl inside an empty grass hut to be alone. Lying flat on my back—depressed, exhausted, stewing in my own helplessness—I try to remind myself why I have returned to Sudan: Because peace is in the air. Because oil, newly tapped by the government, is shaking up the wretched status quo in Africa's most fractured nation. Because the long nightmare of Biem—and a thousand other places like it in Sudan—may soon be over.   6

Bulging like a gigantic hornet's nest against the shores of the Red Sea, Sudan has rarely known stability. Civil war erupted even before the nation gained independence from Britain in 1956. (A frail peace lasted between 1972 and 1983.) The roots of the violence have never changed: British-ruled Sudan wasn't a country; it was two. The south is tropical, underdeveloped, and populated by Dinkas, Nuers, Azandes, and some hundred other ethnic groups of African descent. The north, by contrast, is drier, and wealthier—a Saharan world with strong links to the Muslim Middle East. Shackled together by lunatic colonial borders, these two groups—northern Arabs and southern blacks—have been at odds since the 19th century, when northern slave raiders preyed on the tribes of the south.   7

8   At present, the rebel Sudan People's Liberation Army, or SPLA, controls much of the southern third of Sudan. Its insurgents sometimes carry spears as well as Kalashnikovs and are fighting for greater autonomy. The northern government in Khartoum, now dominated by Islamic fundamentalists, drops bombs on them from old Russian-made cargo planes and employs famines and modern-day slavery as crude weapons of mass destruction. So far the death toll—mostly among southern civilians—exceeds that of many of the world's recent conflicts combined, including Rwanda, the Persian Gulf war, the Balkans, and Chechnya. Four million Sudanese have been displaced by violence and starvation. Yet the calamity of Sudan unfolds largely without witnesses—an apocalypse in a vacuum. Until now.

9   Two factors are bringing new hope to Sudan. Neither has anything to do with the suffering of millions of Sudanese. Both involve the self-interest of outsiders.

10   First, the U.S. war on terrorism appears to be pressuring reforms in the northern Islamist regime. When a military coup backed by the radical National Islamic Front toppled Sudan's last democratically elected government in 1989, the country plunged into a new dark age. Independent newspapers were banned. Labor unions suppressed. The north's moderate Islamic parties were hounded into exile. The civil war escalated to the drumbeat of jihad—holy struggle against indigenous religions and Christianity in the south. Outlaws ranging from Osama bin Laden to Carlos the Jackal settled into mansions in Khartoum's sandy outskirts. And the fundamentalists' secret police, the feared *mukhabarat*, added a new word to the lexicon of political repression—the "ghost house," or unmarked detention center.

11   Recently, however, Khartoum's extremists have begun mellowing. Chafing under U.S. economic sanctions, they have begun cooperating with the global war on terror. Desperate to shed their pariah status, they have bowed to Western pressure to enter peace negotiations in the civil war. In October 2002 the government and the SPLA signed a fragile cease-fire.

12   The second—and perhaps more profound—force of change in Sudan is less noble. It is about something the whole world wants. It is about oil.

In May 1999 engineers in Khartoum opened the tap on a new 13 thousand-mile-long pipeline that connects the Muglad Basin, a huge, petroleum-rich lowland in the south, to a gleaming new tanker terminal on the shores of the Red Sea. The Muglad Basin, a prehistoric lake bed, is said to hold some three billion barrels of crude—nearly half the amount of recoverable oil that lies under the Arctic National Wildlife Refuge in Alaska. This bonanza, pessimists say, is just one more prize for the warring parties to fight over. But oil also has fueled renewed international interest in Sudan. And diplomats are more optimistic.

"It's a no-brainer," says a U.S. expert familiar with Sudan's 14 many woes. "The rebels control much of the oil country. The government has access to the sea. They need each other to get rich."

A Canadian geologist who is mapping the Muglad Basin 15 agrees: "Every Sudanese won't be driving a Mercedes tomorrow—we're not talking about another Saudi Arabia here," he tells me, "but the reserves are big enough to transform Sudan forever."

There are good reasons for skepticism. Sudan's grievances 16 are very old and complex. They confound even the Sudanese. For many, the north-south war is rooted in the old toxic relationship between Arab master and African servant. For the religious, it is a contest between northern Islam and southern indigenous religions and Christianity. For the impoverished herdsmen on the front lines, it is a local skirmish over a water hole or favorite pastureland: Violent disputes among Sudan's hundreds of ethnic groups have been inflamed—and manipulated—by the main warring parties. Yet oil cuts, literally, across all of Sudan's overlapping wars. Better than any road, or river, or political theory, the shining new pipeline leads the way through a labyrinth of misery in the Horn of Africa that defies easy interpretation.

I have traveled before to Sudan. Like many journalists, I was 17 sent there to chronicle a freak show of human suffering: endless civil war, recurrent droughts, mass starvation, slaving raids, and epidemics of killing diseases. Today, however, I am on a different mission. I will follow the flow of Sudan's oil wealth from the implacable war zones of the south to an ultramodern export terminal on the Red Sea; to the country's future.

18   This will not be an easy journey. I will be forced to complete it
in disjointed segments, side-stepping battlefronts, accommodat-
ing roadless deserts, avoiding suspicious bureaucrats—an erratic
process that mirrors life in Sudan.

19   I pressed my ear against the pipeline once: The Nile Blend
crude oozing inside emitted a faint liquid sigh. I listened hard,
sweating under a tropical sun, trying to discern some hidden
message—a clue as to whether 33 million Sudanese will stop killing each other anytime soon.

20 We are sneaking into Unity State, the start of Sudan's pipeline,
some 450 miles northwest of the Kenyan border.

21   Flying into rebel-held southern Sudan from Kenya, you
must be prepared for certain compromises. First, the flight is
illegal. The central government in Khartoum disapproves of
independent visits to its unseen war. Then there is the question
of facilities. They simply don't exist. For almost four hours we
drone over a landscape of impressive emptiness—a sea of grass
that is burned and reburned by wildfires into a mottling of pur-
plish grays, as if the muscles of the earth itself lay exposed. Later,
a huge bruise darkens the western horizon: the famous Sudd, an
enormous swamp clogging the flow of the White Nile. When the
chartered Cessna finally touches down at a rebel airstrip, the pilot
anxiously dumps my bags in the dust and leaves immediately for
Nairobi. This is natural. His shiny airplane, a target for government bombers, stands out dangerously in the bleakest liberated
zone in the world.

22   I have come to see George Athor Deng. Deng is a Dinka
fighter, an SPLA commander of note. And he has promised, via
shortwave radio, to show me what oil is doing to his people. He
smiles sourly when I tell him what the diplomats say, that oil can
bring all the Sudanese together.

23   "When has the north ever shared anything with the south?"
he says of the government oil fields a two-day's walk across the
front lines. "In the near future we will shut them down. Shut the
oil down completely."

24   I meet Deng where he spends most of his days, issuing orders
from a folding chair under a shady acacia. His headquarters,

Biem, is like an engraving from another era—from the journals of Stanley and Livingstone. Stockades of elephant grass surround his crude huts. Food is precarious. His soldiers scavenge off the land and, when possible, skim UN rations dropped from airplanes for starving civilians. (His troops' canteens are empty plastic jugs marked "Canada-Aid Soy Milk.") There are at least 25,000 displaced people jammed into Deng's territory, virtually all of them Dinka herders fleeing the fighting in the nearby oil fields, and whenever groups of famished refugees trudge through Biem, begging for food, the commander dispatches a marksman to shoot a hippo.

According to Deng—and he is broadly backed up by human 25 rights groups—oil has sparked some of the ugliest fighting Sudan has seen in years. Deng and other SPLA commanders mortar oil rigs or shoot at oil company planes. And the Khartoum regime responds by striking back ferociously against local civilians. Government helicopters bought with new oil revenues strafe Dinka and Nuer villages. Sorghum crops are torched. And the dreaded *murahilin*, Muslim raiders armed by the Sudanese Army, sweep through porous rebel lines on horseback, sowing terror and taking slaves. Khartoum denies that it is targeting noncombatants, just as it has long rejected responsibility for slavery in Sudan; it calls these raids tribal abductions, and says they are beyond its control.

"It is simple," Deng declares. "The government is depopulat- 26 ing the area to make way for foreign oil companies."

Deng's outrage would inspire more sympathy if his own 27 forces weren't so morally tainted. Traditionally, the SPLA has mistreated as much as defended Sudan's long marginalized southern peoples. Until the south's oil wealth helped forge a common cause, various rebel factions—especially the Dinka-dominated SPLA and a variety of ethnic Nuer militias—killed each other mercilessly, often with the encouragement of government bribes. Some commanders have kept civilians malnourished in order to "farm" UN aid. And the movement's political agenda has never really solidified. The SPLA's leader, an Iowa State University doctorate named John Garang, claims he is fighting for a secular, unified Sudan (as opposed to the north's theocracy), yet almost every field commander, Deng included, is gunning for full southern independence.

28   Knowing what I do about the SPLA, I am prepared to dislike Deng. Compact, scar-faced, blinded in one eye, he promenades around the refugee lean-tos of Biem with a lackey in tow, carrying his chair. Yet there is also an ineffable sadness about him. His entire family—a wife, child, and four brothers—have been wiped out in the current phase of the civil war, which erupted in 1983. Such stupefying losses pervade life in the south. They surface all the time in small, melancholy gestures.

29   Like the way Deng announces the name of his soldier who is killed, shot down and abandoned, on the ill-fated patrol that I attempt to accompany into the oil fields. "Mayak Arop," he sighs, waving a gnarled hand over a map of the expanding government oil roads, as if wishing to wipe them away.

30   Or, in the way a bowl-bellied Dinka girl stamps out a pretty little dance on a dusty path in Biem, oblivious to the thousands of haunted figures camped in the bush around her.

31   Or, in the answers to a simple question.

32   What color is oil?

33   "It's like cow urine," says Chan Akuei, an old herder at Biem with a belly wrinkled like elephant skin. Government troops have shot his cows, an incomprehensible crime in the Dinka universe. The Dinka adore their cattle. They rarely kill them for meat, and compose songs about their favorite animals. Akuei cannot stop talking about his murdered livestock.

34   "It is as clear as water," says a boy in Koch, a nearby frontline village. He is a member of an ethnic Nuer militia. The last I see of him, he is marching off at dawn to attack an oil road along with hundreds of other rebels—many of them children.

35   Nyanayule Arop Deng (the name Deng is common among the Dinka) doesn't know the color of oil. She sits by her skeletal husband, who is dying of kala-azar, a wasting disease that has killed tens of thousands in the oil zone. "All I know is the lights," she says dully. "They appear at night. We don't go near them."

36 The tower lights of Roll'n wildcat rig number 15 click on at dusk—an unexpectedly pretty sight as the sun drops behind the

iron silhouettes of the thorn trees. The quest for oil is tireless, urgent, expensive. It is like a physical thirst—an around-the-clock obsession. Before the evening shift comes on, Terry Hoffman, a sweat-soaked driller from British Columbia, runs one last stand of pipe down into the skin of Sudan.

"Killer bees, cobras, and acid-spewing bugs that give you 37 blisters!" Hoffman hollers over the rig's noisy generator, ticking off the dangers of roughnecking in Sudan. "Boredom's the worst, though. You can't even walk around this place."

Hoffman is a prisoner of his rig. He and his crew must eat 38 their barbecued chicken and cherry pies, read their e-mail, and lift weights inside a Sudanese version of Fort Apache: a 15-foot-high berm has been bulldozed around the floodlit work site. Heavily armed government troops patrol the perimeter against the likes of George Athor Deng. Deng is doubtless out there tonight, plotting under his tree.

The idea behind rig 15—a small component in a billion-dollar 39 complex of drilling equipment, dormitories, pumping stations, new roads, and prefabricated office buildings at Heglig, Sudan's torrid version of the North Slope—is visionary in its way.

At present, none of the Western energy majors dares to drill 40 in Sudan. Chevron suspended its exploration in 1984 after three of its employees were shot dead by rebels, and pulled out of the country altogether in 1990. (All American companies abandoned Sudan once the U.S. listed it as a supporter of terrorism and imposed sanctions in the 1990s.) Yet today an improbable mix of engineers from communist China, authoritarian Malaysia, democratic Canada, and Islamist Khartoum have cobbled together an experiment in globalization on the baleful plains of the Sahel. The Greater Nile Petroleum Operating Company, as it is called, pumps 240,000 barrels of crude a day out of a war zone. Two years from now that output is projected to nearly double. It may surge even higher should lasting peace return to Sudan, and the rebels allow French, Swedish, and Austrian companies to explore their concessions in the south.

"All these stories about us pushing out local people to pump 41 for oil? A total lie," says Bill, a rig supervisor with Talisman Energy, the Canadian partner in the Heglig project.

42   Bill wears cowboy boots and doesn't share his surname. Like everyone else I meet in Heglig, he seems aggrieved. Talisman has come under fire from human rights groups for allegedly turning a blind eye to government atrocities in the oil patch. (Partly because of this bad publicity, Talisman will later sell its Sudan operation to an Indian oil company.) In response to the criticism, a wary company official in Khartoum lectures me on the value of free markets in reforming oppressive regimes. Supervisors drive me around Heglig in a pickup truck, pointing out unmolested villagers in the savanna. Few of these people are southerners. Most are Baggaras, northern Muslim pastoralists who vie with the Dinkas for grazing lands, and who have come to the oil fields to hack down trees for charcoal.

43   "TV at home shows these incredible stories—famines and war in Sudan," says Bill. "Well, let me tell you, I've been in a 200-mile radius of this place, and I haven't seen that."

44   Bill may be willfully blind. But then so are his faraway customers. The only difference is, Bill must walk past a rebel bullet hole in his trailer wall every day and not see it. This is a difficult feat. But a common one in Sudan.

45   There is no fixed front line between SPLA territory and government-controlled Sudan. No walls. No razor wire fences. No permanent Thorn Curtain. The war is fluid. One army cedes power invisibly to another, and what changes across the no-man's-land are things far subtler and more profound than claims of political control. The round grass huts of Africa give way, slowly, to the square mud houses of desert dwellers. The hot blue dome of the tropical sky recedes behind a veil of white Saharan dust. As I travel north, the 21st century begins to reappear—roads are graded by machines, and human beings once more begin to congregate into towns. Some of these towns have sidewalks. The sight—concrete poured on the ground merely to ease walking—is mesmerizing; a surreal extravagance after the utter desolation of the south.

46   The oil pipeline rockets north from Heglig and crosses the eerie rock piles of the Nuba Mountains. The Nuba people, allied with the SPLA, have been fighting their own war of autonomy

against Khartoum for years. A U.S.-brokered cease-fire is in place when I drive through. I see government trucks rolling up into the hills, loaded with satellite dishes. The equipment is meant for "peace clubs" designed to lure the stubborn Nubas down from their mountain strongholds and into areas of government control. "Many of them have never seen television before," a grinning official explains in the garrison town of Kadugli. "We give them 22 channels, including CNN. Their leaders are very irritated by this."

The pipeline burrows onward under a mound of raw earth—a monumental tribal scar creasing the barren landscape. Construction began in 1998 and was finished in 14 months by 2,000 Chinese laborers sweating through double shifts. Workers who died in Sudan were cremated on the spot, and their ashes shipped back to China. 47

I chase the 28-inch-wide steel tube on bad roads. Dilling. El Obeid. Rabak. The northern towns swell, turning into ramshackle mud cities. Two days north of Heglig, the pipeline disappears into slums. A cratered highway leads me into an enormous traffic jam that backs up for miles. Buses nudge through herds of sheep. Donkey carts jockey with taxis so battered they look like the products of junkyard crushing machines. Pedestrians step unhurriedly among the stalled vehicles. Yet no one is angry or abusive. There are no honking horns, insults, threats, or curses. Silently, patiently, the drivers creep forward. They advance, inch by inch, into a city of waiting. 48

This is Khartoum. 49

"Please put your notebook away," advises Asim el Moghraby. "We don't want any problems." 50

El Moghraby and I are perched in a borrowed motorboat, bobbing in the middle of the Nile. I have joined el Moghraby expressly to avoid problems—to admire an overlooked natural wonder of Africa: the meeting of the Blue Nile and White Nile. The two majestic streams, tributaries of the world's longest river, swirl together in a mile-wide dance of light—one the hue of an evening sky and the other the color of a milky sunrise. Yet Sudan's troubles are insistent. El Moghraby, a retired University 51 of Khartoum biologist and my unofficial guide in the city, is nervous. Western visitors are relatively rare in the city. And he worries that I will draw the attention of secret police. We are too close to shoreline government ministries. "The regime is loosening up," he says apologetically as we chug back to the marina, "but nobody knows how much."

52   Change is coming to Sudan, but few know if it is deep or real. The thinking of the small cabal of generals and fundamentalists who run the country is largely opaque. Nevertheless, the virulence of their Islamic revolution began fading even before 1998, when the Clinton Administration launched cruise missiles at a pharmaceutical plant in Khartoum in retaliation for al Qaeda's terrorist bombings of two U.S. embassies in Africa. Eager to put those years behind them, Sudan's secretive rulers claim they have expelled some 3,000 foreigners linked with terror groups (bin Laden and Carlos included) and that they have released most political prisoners. Opposition parties have been invited back in from the cold, though they often remain marginalized.

53   Driving around Khartoum with el Moghraby—a lean, balding scholar who reminds me of a patient turtle, with his wrinkled neck and watchful eyes that dart behind wire-rimmed glasses—I see a crumbling metropolis of seven million that seems to be fluttering its dusty eyelids after a long slumber beneath the sands. Young couples hold hands on the banks of the Nile, unmolested by the morality police. Flashes of oil money glint off fleets of new Korean-made cars. And freshly painted Coke signs and a new BMW dealership have popped up in the city's shabby downtown.

54   Still, it is staggering to think that this insular, puritanical city—with its turbaned Arab rulers, domed mosques, and tea shops blaring pop music—is the capital of the bleeding African south. Yet the war is here too. On a blazing afternoon I visit Wad el Bashir, one of the miserable camps where some of the nearly two million southerners are sweating away their lives in and around Khartoum. Nubas and Dinkas accost me in the maze of dirt lanes. "They are taking our children!" they whisper, describing how their young men are being yanked off sidewalks and buses to fight for the Sudanese Army against their own people in

the south. Behind their mud huts I spot my old companion, the pipeline. Its inert presence now seems malevolent.

Popular discontent—and profound war-weariness—is only 55 slightly less palpable among northerners in Khartoum. University students complain about the loss of jobs and political freedoms under the Islamists. Arab businessmen bemoan Sudan's ruinous isolation. ("Please tell the world we are not all terrorists and bullyboys," pleads one wealthy trader.) And several middle-class men openly boast of evading the draft—they aren't buying jihad's promise of a direct ticket to heaven.

"What you are seeing is the northern front in Sudan's 56 civil war," explains a human rights advocate named Osman Hummaida, when I share my surprise at the cynicism I find on Khartoum's streets. "Sudan is not just divided north-south. There is a broader struggle. It is the center against the periphery—a tiny Khartoum clique against everyone else, including fellow Arabs."

My tour guide, el Moghraby, is a casualty of this subtler 57 northern war. Bullying his Land Rover through Khartoum's downtown one day, he points to a drab building and says, "That one's mine"—meaning the old ghost house where he was detained in 1992, along with his politically active lawyer. In 1995 he was arrested with his wife for producing a documentary film critical of Sudan's environmental record. He was imprisoned yet again, in 1999, for publicly questioning the country's oil projects.

Like many disillusioned northern intellectuals, el Moghraby 58 has withdrawn from public life. He has retreated into private enthusiasms—into the past. He takes me one day to see a weathered colonial monument honoring the charge of the 21st Lancers, a once famous skirmish in the British conquest of Sudan in 1898. Wistfully, el Moghraby talks of an older, more cosmopolitan Khartoum of electric trams, midnight cafés, and clean-swept streets. This nostalgia is sad, especially given Britain's divisive legacy in Sudan.

As a young soldier, Winston Churchill participated in the 59 charge of the 21st Lancers outside Khartoum. British horsemen slammed into the ranks of defending Sudanese troops with such force, he wrote, that "for perhaps ten wonderful seconds" all sides simply staggered about in a daze. The beleaguered citizens of Sudan's capital know this feeling well. They have endured it for the better part of 50 years. It is not wonderful.

60   Where is undemocratic, underdeveloped, and oil-rich Sudan headed? For answers I must leave the periphery. I go to the center.

61   Sudan's president, Lt. Gen. Omar al-Bashir, almost never grants interviews. Hassan al-Turabi, the intellectual father of Sudan's Islamist movement, is also not available, having been put under house arrest by rivals in the government. (He has since been locked up in Kober Prison.) So the task of explaining the policies of the secretive National Islamic Front that rules Sudan falls to Hasan Makki, an Islamic academic and one of the regime's leading ideologues.

62   Makki greets me in a dazzling white djellaba, or Arab robe, in his spacious home. He is a member of the elite "riverine" Arab tribes who have monopolized power in Sudan for years. Like most of Sudan's political inner circle, he is friendly, smart, and chooses his words carefully.

63   On the war: "It is effectively over, my friend. The south already has lost. Millions of their people have moved up to join us in the north." Ignoring the detail that the refugees have not come by choice, he calls Khartoum "an American-style melting pot."

64   On Arab-black hostility: "How can there be racism? Look at my skin. No northern Sudanese is a pure Arab. For centuries our blood has mixed with Africans. We are brothers!"

65   On oil: "It is a blessing. It will hold Sudan together. Before oil, we northerners were tired of the south. Why lose our children there? Why fight for a wasteland? Oil has changed all that. Now our economic survival depends on it."

66   Regarding the unpopularity of the regime, Makki has little to say. He politely pours me another cup of tea and suggests that I go look at stones.

67   We have flown, walked, and driven more than 600 miles through Sudan.

68   The pipeline leads on—tireless and unerring, far more sure of itself in the turmoil of Sudan than I ever will be. Its oil is kept at 95 degrees Fahrenheit, the temperature required for it to be thin

enough to flow freely. It tunnels through Khartoum's bleak refugee camps, then slips beneath the Nile. Emerging from the other side, it disappears north into an ocean of light: the Nubian Desert.

There, baking under the sun, are Makki's stones. They are the 69 silent remains of ancient cities and temples.

At a city called Naga, a ruin of great beauty and stillness that 70 juts from the eroding hills east of the Nile, I see a relief carved into an imposing temple wall. It depicts a queen grasping a handful of small, doomed captives. The queen is recognizably Nubian: Chiseled in pharaonic splendor, she is a mix of Egyptian elegance and full-hipped African beauty. Her prisoners too strike me as dead ringers. They look like the far-flung citizens of Sudan's modern fringe: fierce Beja nomads from the Red Sea Hills—or even Negroid Dinkas or Nubas from the south. Blinking sweat from my eyes, I stare in amazement at this antique blueprint for governance in Sudan—a 2,000-year-old political poster advertising the power of Nile-based elites over the weak periphery.

"Some things never change," says Dietrich Wildung, head of 71 the Egyptian Museum and Papyrus Collection in Berlin and one of the sunburned archaeologists working at Naga. "The north always thinks itself supreme—Egypt over Sudan, Berlin over Munich, New York over Alabama."

Wildung, an almost dauntingly effusive man, pads briskly 72 around his digs in a flimsy pair of sneakers, pointing out details on a half-excavated temple that make him exclaim with pure delight. According to archaeologists, Sudan's northern deserts hide one of the great civilizations not only of Africa but the world. These Sudanic realms—variously known as Nubia, Kush, or Meroë—were no mere appendages of neighboring Egypt, as was sometimes thought. Their intelligentsia created an Egyptian-derived writing system, Meroitic, for a still unintelligible language. And the "black pharaohs" of Sudan and their notorious archers eventually gained such power that they briefly ruled all of Egypt some 2,700 years ago.

Proudly, Wildung shows me his latest discovery: an altar 73 excavated from beneath a fallen wall. Nile gods painted on its plaster-covered pedestal indicate Egyptian influence, and the floral designs are pure Africa—all exuberance, singing colors.

Ancient Greece reveals itself too in the classical flourishes on a figurine of the Egyptian goddess Isis. Crouched over a hole in the earth, we behold the unexpected beauty of Sudan's fractured nature, the art of a continental crossroads.

74 Can oil dilute the age-old divisiveness of Sudan? The pipeline is my guide. But it is no oracle.

75   North of the city of Atbara, the steel artery is patrolled by wild-looking men in vehicles mounted with heavy machine guns: *mujahidin*, or holy warriors, guarding the pipeline from being blown up, as it was nearby in 1999. (That act of sabotage was carried out by northern opposition forces in alliance with the SPLA.) The oil squirts across the Red Sea Hills at the pace of a fast walk. Then it races 3,000 feet down to the devastatingly hot Sudanese coast. To the Bashair Marine Terminal. To the end of the line. When I visit the high-tech export facility, a Singapore-flagged tanker is preparing to gulp a million barrels of crude.

76   "You are looking at our gateway to the world," a jumpsuited technician tells me grandly in the sleek control room, some 950 miles from the oil wells pocking the savannas of Africa.

77   I hope he is right. I hope oil helps create a new era of stability in Sudan. I hope it prods international efforts, such as those of U.S. peacemaker John Danforth, to end the terrible civil war. I hope it bribes Sudan's cruel and insulated elites into abandoning selfish power struggles that have wreaked hell on millions of ordinary people. I hope it somehow lubricates relations with Egypt, the regional superpower, which exercises powerful interests in Sudan: Egypt strongly opposes southern independence, fearing that such a development will threaten its access to the vital middle reaches of the Nile. Most of all, I hope Sudan's new oil revenues—more than two million dollars a day—do not end up stoking what one analyst calls a "perfect war," a conflict waged, at tolerable cost, indefinitely. Hope: a commodity Sudan could use more of, even, than oil.

78   Near the end of my journey, I camp for a few days in the parched wilderness of the Red Sea Hills. My host is Abu Fatna, an old Beja, a Muslim nomad whose ancestors have roamed the eastern wastes of Sudan for the past 5,000 years. His tent is pegged

only 40 miles west of the pipeline, yet his life is as detached from its power and wealth as those of the southern Dinkas dying at the opposite end of the oil trail. Drought has forced Fatna to sell his camels. Saudi hunters have slaughtered all the local wild antelope. He is skinny and poor, and he has only two teeth left in his head. But he still knows which desert stars to travel by. He can still handle a tribal broadsword.

When I leave, Fatna offers me a gift: He dances good-bye in ₇₉ the dust. The flapping of his scrawny arms, the dry snatches of song—these are meant as an honor, though they seem more like a lament. Driving back to the pipeline, I wonder if this sadness, too, somehow gets pumped out of Sudan. Along with commander Deng's bitter hand-waving over a crude map. Or el Moghraby's demoralized retreat from the world. Or the terrible absences of so many dead.

So much heartbreak, it seems, gets burned up in Sudan's oil. ₈₀

2003

Our Oceans Are Turning into Plastic . . . Are We?

Susan Casey

A vast swath of the Pacific, twice the size of Texas, is full of a plas- ₁ tic stew that is entering the food chain. Scientists say these toxins are causing obesity, infertility . . . and worse.

Fate can take strange forms, and so perhaps it does not seem ₂ unusual that Captain Charles Moore found his life's purpose in a nightmare. Unfortunately, he was awake at the time, and 800 miles north of Hawaii in the Pacific Ocean.

It happened on August 3, 1997, a lovely day, at least in the ₃ beginning: Sunny. Little wind. Water the color of sapphires.

Moore and the crew of Alguita, his 50-foot aluminum-hulled catamaran, sliced through the sea.

4   Returning to Southern California from Hawaii after a sailing race, Moore had altered Alguita's course, veering slightly north. He had the time and the curiosity to try a new route, one that would lead the vessel through the eastern corner of a 10-million-square-mile oval known as the North Pacific subtropical gyre. This was an odd stretch of ocean, a place most boats purposely avoided. For one thing, it was becalmed. "The doldrums," sailors called it, and they steered clear. So did the ocean's top predators: the tuna, sharks, and other large fish that required livelier waters, flush with prey. The gyre was more like a desert—a slow, deep, clockwise-swirling vortex of air and water caused by a mountain of high-pressure air that lingered above it.

5   The area's reputation didn't deter Moore. He had grown up in Long Beach, 40 miles south of L.A., with the Pacific literally in his front yard, and he possessed an impressive aquatic résumé: deckhand, able seaman, sailor, scuba diver, surfer, and finally captain. Moore had spent countless hours in the ocean, fascinated by its vast trove of secrets and terrors. He'd seen a lot of things out there, things that were glorious and grand; things that were ferocious and humbling. But he had never seen anything nearly as chilling as what lay ahead of him in the gyre.

6   It began with a line of plastic bags ghosting the surface, followed by an ugly tangle of junk: nets and ropes and bottles, motor-oil jugs and cracked bath toys, a mangled tarp. Tires. A traffic cone. Moore could not believe his eyes. Out here in this desolate place, the water was a stew of plastic crap. It was as though someone had taken the pristine seascape of his youth and swapped it for a landfill.

7   How did all the plastic end up here? How did this trash tsunami begin? What did it mean? If the questions seemed overwhelming, Moore would soon learn that the answers were even more so, and that his discovery had dire implications for human—and planetary—health. As Alguita glided through the area that scientists now refer to as the "Eastern Garbage Patch," Moore realized that the trail of plastic went on for hundreds of miles. Depressed and stunned, he sailed for a week through

bobbing, toxic debris trapped in a purgatory of circling currents. To his horror, he had stumbled across the 21st-century Leviathan. It had no head, no tail. Just an endless body.

"Everybody's plastic, but I love plastic. I want to be plastic." This Andy Warhol quote is emblazoned on a six-foot-long magenta and yellow banner that hangs—with extreme irony—in the solar-powered workshop in Moore's Long Beach home. The workshop is surrounded by a crazy Eden of trees, bushes, flowers, fruits, and vegetables, ranging from the prosaic (tomatoes) to the exotic (cherimoyas, guavas, chocolate persimmons, white figs the size of baseballs). This is the house in which Moore, 59, was raised, and it has a kind of open-air earthiness that reflects his '60s-activist roots, which included a stint in a Berkeley commune. Composting and organic gardening are serious business here—you can practically smell the humus—but there is also a kidney-shaped hot tub surrounded by palm trees. Two wet suits hang drying on a clothesline above it.

This afternoon, Moore strides the grounds. "How about a nice, fresh boysenberry?" he asks, and plucks one off a bush. He's a striking man wearing no-nonsense black trousers and a shirt with official-looking epaulettes. A thick brush of salt-and-pepper hair frames his intense blue eyes and serious face. But the first thing you notice about Moore is his voice, a deep, bemused drawl that becomes animated and sardonic when the subject turns to plastic pollution. This problem is Moore's calling, a passion he inherited from his father, an industrial chemist who studied waste management as a hobby. On family vacations, Moore recalls, part of the agenda would be to see what the locals threw out. "We could be in paradise, but we would go to the dump," he says with a shrug. "That's what we wanted to see."

Since his first encounter with the Garbage Patch nine years ago, Moore has been on a mission to learn exactly what's going on out there. Leaving behind a 25-year career running a furniture-restoration business, he has created the Algalita Marine Research Foundation to spread the word of his findings. He has resumed his science studies, which he'd set aside when his attention swerved from pursuing a university degree to protesting the Vietnam War. His tireless effort has placed him on the front lines of this new, more abstract battle. After enlisting scientists such as Steven B. Weisberg, Ph.D. (executive director of the Southern California Coastal Water Research Project and an expert in marine environmental monitoring), to develop methods for analyzing the gyre's contents, Moore has sailed Alguita back to the Garbage Patch several times. On each trip, the volume of plastic has grown alarmingly. The area in which it accumulates is now twice the size of Texas.

11   At the same time, all over the globe, there are signs that plastic pollution is doing more than blighting the scenery; it is also making its way into the food chain. Some of the most obvious victims are the dead seabirds that have been washing ashore in startling numbers, their bodies packed with plastic: things like bottle caps, cigarette lighters, tampon applicators, and colored scraps that, to a foraging bird, resemble baitfish. (One animal dissected by Dutch researchers contained 1603 pieces of plastic.) And the birds aren't alone. All sea creatures are threatened by floating plastic, from whales down to zooplankton. There's a basic moral horror in seeing the pictures: a sea turtle with a plastic band strangling its shell into an hourglass shape; a humpback towing plastic nets that cut into its flesh and make it impossible for the animal to hunt. More than a million seabirds, 100,000 marine mammals, and countless fish die in the North Pacific each year, either from mistakenly eating this junk or from being ensnared in it and drowning.

12   Bad enough. But Moore soon learned that the big, tentacled balls of trash were only the most visible signs of the problem; others were far less obvious, and far more evil. Dragging a fine-meshed net known as a manta trawl, he discovered minuscule pieces of plastic, some barely visible to the eye, swirling like fish food throughout the water. He and his researchers parsed, measured, and sorted their samples and arrived at the following conclusion: By weight, this swath of sea contains six times as much plastic as it does plankton.

13   This statistic is grim—for marine animals, of course, but even more so for humans. The more invisible and ubiquitous the pollution, the more likely it will end up inside us. And there's growing—and disturbing—proof that we're ingesting plastic toxins constantly, and that even slight doses of these substances

can severely disrupt gene activity. "Every one of us has this huge body burden," Moore says. "You could take your serum to a lab now, and they'd find at least 100 industrial chemicals that weren't around in 1950." The fact that these toxins don't cause violent and immediate reactions does not mean they're benign: Scientists are just beginning to research the long-term ways in which the chemicals used to make plastic interact with our own biochemistry.

In simple terms, plastic is a petroleum-based mix of mono-   14 mers that become polymers, to which additional chemicals are added for suppleness, inflammability, and other qualities. When it comes to these substances, even the syllables are scary. For instance, if you're thinking that perfluorooctanoic acid (PFOA) isn't something you want to sprinkle on your microwave popcorn, you're right. Recently, the Science Advisory Board of the Environmental Protection Agency (EPA) upped its classification of PFOA to a likely carcinogen. Yet it's a common ingredient in packaging that needs to be oil- and heat-resistant. So while there may be no PFOA in the popcorn itself, if PFOA is used to treat the bag, enough of it can leach into the popcorn oil when your butter deluxe meets your superheated microwave oven that a single serving spikes the amount of the chemical in your blood.

Other nasty chemical additives are the flame retardants   15 known as poly-brominated diphenyl ethers (PBDEs). These chemicals have been shown to cause liver and thyroid toxicity, reproductive problems, and memory loss in preliminary animal studies. In vehicle interiors, PBDEs—used in moldings and floor coverings, among other things—combine with another group called phthalates to create that much-vaunted "new-car smell." Leave your new wheels in the hot sun for a few hours, and these substances can "off-gas" at an accelerated rate, releasing noxious by-products.

It's not fair, however, to single out fast food and new cars.   16 PBDEs, to take just one example, are used in many products, incuding computers, carpeting, and paint. As for phthalates, we deploy about a billion pounds of them a year worldwide despite the fact that California recently listed them as a chemical known to be toxic to our reproductive systems. Used to make plastic soft and pliable, phthalates leach easily from millions of products—packaged food, cosmetics, varnishes, the coatings of timed-release pharmaceuticals—into our blood, urine, saliva, seminal fluid, breast milk, and amniotic fluid. In food containers and some plastic bottles, phthalates are now found with another compound called bisphenol A (BPA), which scientists are discovering can wreak stunning havoc in the body. We produce 6 billion pounds of that each year, and it shows: BPA has been found in nearly every human who has been tested in the United States. We're eating these plasticizing additives, drinking them, breathing them, and absorbing them through our skin every single day. Most alarming, these chemicals may disrupt the endocrine system—the delicately balanced set of hormones and glands that affect virtually every organ and cell—by mimicking the female hormone estrogen. In marine environments, excess estrogen has led to Twilight Zone–esque discoveries of male fish and seagulls that have sprouted female sex organs.

17   On land, things are equally gruesome. "Fertility rates have been declining for quite some time now, and exposure to synthetic estrogen— especially from the chemicals found in plastic products—can have an adverse effect," says Marc Goldstein, M.D., director of the Cornell Institute for Reproductive Medicine. Dr. Goldstein also notes that pregnant women are particularly vulnerable: "Prenatal exposure, even in very low doses, can cause irreversible damage in an unborn baby's reproductive organs." And after the baby is born, he or she is hardly out of the woods. Frederick vom Saal, Ph.D., a professor at the University of Missouri at Columbia who specifically studies estrogenic chemicals in plastics, warns parents to "steer clear of polycarbonate baby bottles. They're particularly dangerous for newborns, whose brains, immune systems, and gonads are still developing." Dr. vom Saal's research spurred him to throw out every polycarbonate plastic item in his house, and to stop buying plastic-wrapped food and canned goods (cans are plastic-lined) at the grocery store. "We now know that BPA causes prostate cancer in mice and rats, and abnormalities in the prostate's stem cell, which is the cell implicated in human prostate cancer," he says. "That's enough to scare the hell out of me." At Tufts University, Ana M. Soto, M.D., a professor of anatomy and cellular biology,

has also found connections between these chemicals and breast cancer.

As if the potential for cancer and mutation weren't enough, [18] Dr. vom Saal states in one of his studies that "prenatal exposure to very low doses of BPA increases the rate of postnatal growth in mice and rats." In other words, BPA made rodents fat. Their insulin output surged wildly and then crashed into a state of resistance—the virtual definition of diabetes. They produced bigger fat cells, and more of them. A recent scientific paper Dr. vom Saal coauthored contains this chilling sentence: "These findings suggest that developmental exposure to BPA is contributing to the obesity epidemic that has occurred during the last two decades in the developed world, associated with the dramatic increase in the amount of plastic being produced each year." Given this, it is perhaps not entirely coincidental that America's staggering rise in diabetes—a 735 percent increase since 1935—follows the same arc.

This news is depressing enough to make a person reach for [19] the bottle. Glass, at least, is easily recyclable. You can take one tequila bottle, melt it down, and make another tequila bottle. With plastic, recycling is more complicated. Unfortunately, that promising-looking triangle of arrows that appears on products doesn't always signify endless reuse; it merely identifies which type of plastic the item is made from. And of the seven different plastics in common use, only two of them—PET (labeled with #1 inside the triangle and used in soda bottles) and HDPE (labeled with #2 inside the triangle and used in milk jugs)—have much of an aftermarket. So no matter how virtuously you toss your chip bags and shampoo bottles into your blue bin, few of them will escape the landfill—only 3 to 5 percent of plastics are recycled in any way.

"There's no legal way to recycle a milk container into another [20] milk container without adding a new virgin layer of plastic," Moore says, pointing out that, because plastic melts at low temperatures, it retains pollutants and the tainted residue of its former contents. Turn up the heat to sear these off, and some plastics release deadly vapors. So the reclaimed stuff is mostly used to make entirely different products, things that don't go anywhere near our mouths, such as fleece jackets and carpeting. Therefore, unlike recycling glass, metal, or paper, recycling plastic doesn't always result in less use of virgin material. It also doesn't help that fresh-made plastic is far cheaper.

21   Moore routinely finds half-melted blobs of plastic in the ocean, as though the person doing the burning realized partway through the process that this was a bad idea, and stopped (or passed out from the fumes). "That's a concern as plastic proliferates worldwide, and people run out of room for trash and start burning plastic—you're producing some of the most toxic gases known," he says. The color-coded bin system may work in Marin County, but it is somewhat less effective in subequatorial Africa or rural Peru.

22   "Except for the small amount that's been incinerated—and it's a very small amount—every bit of plastic ever made still exists," Moore says, describing how the material's molecular structure resists biodegradation. Instead, plastic crumbles into ever-tinier fragments as it's exposed to sunlight and the elements. And none of these untold gazillions of fragments is disappearing any time soon: Even when plastic is broken down to a single molecule, it remains too tough for biodegradation.

23   Truth is, no one knows how long it will take for plastic to biodegrade, or return to its carbon and hydrogen elements. We only invented the stuff 144 years ago, and science's best guess is that its natural disappearance will take several more centuries. Meanwhile, every year, we churn out about 60 billion tons of it, much of which becomes disposable products meant only for a single use. Set aside the question of why we're creating ketchup bottles and six-pack rings that last for half a millennium, and consider the implications of it: Plastic never really goes away.

24   Ask a group of people to name an overwhelming global problem, and you'll hear about climate change, the Middle East, or AIDS. No one, it is guaranteed, will cite the sloppy transport of nurdles as a concern. And yet nurdles, lentil-size pellets of plastic in its rawest form, are especially effective couriers of waste chemicals called persistent organic pollutants, or POPs, which include known carcinogens such as DDT and PCBs.

25   The United States banned these poisons in the 1970s, but they remain stubbornly at large in the environment, where they latch on to plastic because of its molecular tendency to attract oils.

The word itself—nurdles—sounds cuddly and harmless, 26 like a cartoon character or a pasta for kids, but what it refers to is most certainly not. Absorbing up to a million times the level of POP pollution in their surrounding waters, nurdles become supersaturated poison pills. They're light enough to blow around like dust, to spill out of shipping containers, and to wash into harbors, storm drains, and creeks. In the ocean, nurdles are easily mistaken for fish eggs by creatures that would very much like to have such a snack. And once inside the body of a bigeye tuna or a king salmon, these tenacious chemicals are headed directly to your dinner table. One study estimated that nurdles now account for 10 percent of plastic ocean debris. And once they're scattered in the environment, they're diabolically hard to clean up (think wayward confetti). At places as remote as Rarotonga, in the Cook Islands, 2100 miles northeast of New Zealand and a 12-hour flight from L.A., they're commonly found mixed with beach sand. In 2004, Moore received a $500,000 grant from the state of California to investigate the myriad ways in which nurdles go astray during the plastic manufacturing process. On a visit to a polyvinyl chloride (PVC) pipe factory, as he walked through an area where railcars unloaded ground-up nurdles, he noticed that his pant cuffs were filled with a fine plastic dust. Turning a corner, he saw windblown drifts of nurdles piled against a fence. Talking about the experience, Moore's voice becomes strained and his words pour out in an urgent tumble: "It's not the big trash on the beach. It's the fact that the whole biosphere is becoming mixed with these plastic particles. What are they doing to us? We're breathing them, the fish are eating them, they're in our hair, they're in our skin."

Though marine dumping is part of the problem, escaped 27 nurdles and other plastic litter migrate to the gyre largely from land. That polystyrene cup you saw floating in the creek, if it doesn't get picked up and specifically taken to a landfill, will eventually be washed out to sea. Once there, it will have plenty of places to go: The North Pacific gyre is only one of five such high-pressure zones in the oceans. There are similar areas in the South Pacific, the North and South Atlantic, and the Indian Ocean. Each of these gyres has its own version of the Garbage

Patch, as plastic gathers in the currents. Together, these areas cover 40 percent of the sea. "That corresponds to a quarter of the earth's surface," Moore says. "So 25 percent of our planet is a toilet that never flushes."

28   It wasn't supposed to be this way. In 1865, a few years after Alexander Parkes unveiled a precursor to man-made plastic called Parkesine, a scientist named John W. Hyatt set out to make a synthetic replacement for ivory billiard balls. He had the best of intentions: Save the elephants! After some tinkering, he created celluloid. From then on, each year brought a miraculous recipe: rayon in 1891, Teflon in 1938, polypropylene in 1954. Durable, cheap, versatile—plastic seemed like a revelation. And in many ways, it was. Plastic has given us bulletproof vests, credit cards, slinky spandex pants. It has led to breakthroughs in medicine, aerospace engineering, and computer science. And who among us doesn't own a Frisbee?

29   Plastic has its benefits; no one would deny that. Few of us, however, are as enthusiastic as the American Plastics Council. One of its recent press releases, titled "Plastic Bags—A Family's Trusted Companion," reads: "Very few people remember what life was like before plastic bags became an icon of convenience and practicality—and now art. Remember the 'beautiful' [sic] swirling, floating bag in *American Beauty*?"

30   Alas, the same ethereal quality that allows bags to dance gracefully across the big screen also lands them in many less desirable places. Twenty-three countries, including Germany, South Africa, and Australia, have banned, taxed, or restricted the use of plastic bags because they clog sewers and lodge in the throats of livestock. Like pernicious Kleenex, these flimsy sacks end up snagged in trees and snarled in fences, becoming eyesores and worse: They also trap rainwater, creating perfect little breeding grounds for disease-carrying mosquitoes.

31   In the face of public outrage over pictures of dolphins choking on "a family's trusted companion," the American Plastics Council takes a defensive stance, sounding not unlike the NRA: Plastics don't pollute, people do.

32   It has a point. Each of us tosses about 185 pounds of plastic per year. We could certainly reduce that. And yet—do our products

have to be quite so lethal? Must a discarded flip-flop remain with us until the end of time? Aren't disposable razors and foam packing peanuts a poor consolation prize for the destruction of the world's oceans, not to mention our own bodies and the health of future generations? "If 'more is better' and that's the only mantra we have, we're doomed," Moore says, summing it up.

Oceanographer Curtis Ebbesmeyer, Ph.D., an expert on marine debris, agrees. "If you could fast-forward 10,000 years and do an archaeological dig . . . you'd find a little line of plastic," he told the *Seattle Times* last April. "What happened to those people? Well, they ate their own plastic and disrupted their genetic structure and weren't able to reproduce. They didn't last very long because they killed themselves."

Our oceans are turning into plastic . . . are we? Wrist-slittingly depressing, yes, but there are glimmers of hope on the horizon. Green architect and designer William McDonough has become an influential voice, not only in environmental circles but among Fortune 500 CEOs. McDonough proposes a standard known as "cradle to cradle" in which all manufactured things must be reusable, poison-free, and beneficial over the long haul. His outrage is obvious when he holds up a rubber ducky, a common child's bath toy. The duck is made of phthalate-laden PVC, which has been linked to cancer and reproductive harm. "What kind of people are we that we would design like this?" McDonough asks. In the United States, it's commonly accepted that children's teething rings, cosmetics, food wrappers, cars, and textiles will be made from toxic materials. Other countries—and many individual companies—seem to be reconsidering. Currently, McDonough is working with the Chinese government to build seven cities using "the building materials of the future," including a fabric that is safe enough to eat and a new, nontoxic polystyrene.

Thanks to people like Moore and McDonough, and media hits such as Al Gore's *An Inconvenient Truth*, awareness of just how hard we've bitch-slapped the planet is skyrocketing. After all, unless we're planning to colonize Mars soon, this is where we live, and none of us would choose to live in a toxic wasteland or to spend our days getting pumped full of drugs to deal with our haywire endocrine systems and runaway cancer.

36   None of plastic's problems can be fixed overnight, but the more we learn, the more likely that, eventually, wisdom will trump convenience and cheap disposability. In the meantime, let the cleanup begin: The National Oceanographic & Atmospheric Administration (NOAA) is aggressively using satellites to identify and remove "ghost nets," abandoned plastic fishing gear that never stops killing. (A single net recently hauled up off the Florida coast contained more than 1000 dead fish, sharks, and one loggerhead turtle.) New biodegradable starch- and corn-based plastics have arrived, and Wal-Mart has signed on as a customer. A consumer rebellion against dumb and excessive packaging is afoot. And in August 2006, Moore was invited to speak about "marine debris and hormone disruption" at a meeting in Sicily convened by the science advisor to the Vatican. This annual gathering, called the International Seminars on Planetary Emergencies, brings scientists together to discuss mankind's worst threats. Past topics have included nuclear holocaust and terrorism.

37   The gray plastic kayak floats next to Moore's catamaran, Alguita, which lives in a slip across from his house. It is not a lovely kayak; in fact, it looks pretty rough. But it's floating, a sturdy, eight-foot-long two-seater. Moore stands on Alguita's deck, hands on hips, staring down at it. On the sailboat next to him, his neighbor, Cass Bastain, does the same. He has just informed Moore that he came across the abandoned craft yesterday, floating just offshore. The two men shake their heads in bewilderment.

38   "That's probably a $600 kayak," Moore says, adding, "I don't even shop anymore. Anything I need will just float by." (In his opinion, the movie *Cast Away* was a joke—Tom Hanks could've built a village with the crap that would've washed ashore during a storm.)

39   Watching the kayak bobbing disconsolately, it is hard not to wonder what will become of it. The world is full of cooler, sexier kayaks. It is also full of cheap plastic kayaks that come in more attractive colors than battleship gray. The ownerless kayak is a lummox of a boat, 50 pounds of nurdles extruded into an object that nobody wants, but that'll be around for centuries longer than we will.

And as Moore stands on deck looking into the water, it is easy 40
to imagine him doing the same thing 800 miles west, in the gyre.
You can see his silhouette in the silvering light, caught between
ocean and sky. You can see the mercurial surface of the most
majestic body of water on earth. And then below, you can see the
half-submerged madhouse of forgotten and discarded things. As
Moore looks over the side of the boat, you can see the seabirds
sweeping overhead, dipping and skimming the water. One of the
journeying birds, sleek as a fighter plane, carries a scrap of something yellow in its beak. The bird dives low and then boomerangs
over the horizon. Gone.

2007

The Value and Price of Food

Carlo Petrini

The triumph of consumerism has seen the triumph of another 1
prejudice-cum-cliché: the idea that the price and value of food has
to be low—as low as possible, in fact.

It's natural, in a market, for us to opt for the product that 2
costs least. But we should do so when quality is equal, or at least
when we have the opportunity of choosing a standard of quality
suitable for our needs. This is no longer possible in the case of
food; it has to be cheap, period. Vegetables or pasta only have to
go up by a few cents and the papers spew indignant reactions.
Yet people don't protest the same way if their bank account or
telephone bills cost more, if a professional fleeces them for his
services, or if a television-repair call costs the equivalent of a dinner for two at a restaurant.

But food's a different matter; it isn't to be meddled with. The 3
widely held opinion is: "With a great deal of effort we managed

to beat hunger years ago. We are a rich, opulent society; food has to be available everywhere and, if possible, cost a trifle. If it's expensive, let's leave it to gluttons and guzzlers with plenty of money to spend." This is what comes of having transformed food into a consumer commodity, stripping it of all its spiritual, cultural, and material values: the system built around it or of which it is part has replaced value with price. Money has supplanted other values to become the secret of happiness.

4   Food is thus no longer produced to be eaten, but to be sold. Price becomes the principal, if not the only, choice criterion. In the global agro-industry food system, foodstuffs have become commodities just like all the others—no more, no less; just like oil, timber, or other tradable goods whose prices are established by international stock exchanges. Grain, corn, coffee, and cocoa are commodities like metals or energy, hence subject to the laws of supply and demand, distributed on the market without differentiations in quality and without a care about who produces them.

5   Subjecting food to these laws leads to a standardization of food production that tends to reduce biodiversity and increase "eco-unfriendly" monocultures. And it also causes a huge amount of injustice. Especially in the South of the world, and often on account of their colonialist or neo colonialist heritage, whole countries have become specialized in given agricultural products and promptly suffer huge upheavals when their prices plummet.

6   Mostly in countries that are experiencing rapid urbanization, the fact that food is becoming something to buy and not to produce is creating poverty, hence hunger and malnutrition. A peasant farmer in a poor country who decides to abandon the hard life of the countryside for a move to the city stops producing the meager amount of food that allowed his family to get by, albeit in poor conditions. But if he doesn't find a job with a decent wage in the city, he won't be able to buy enough food for himself and his family. In a short space of time, he will descend from poverty to nothing—to hunger and downright squalor.

7   Total commodification is the price we pay for the degeneration in the value of food in both the North and the South of the world. Yet practices exist that may not be viable in monetary

terms—think of home jam making, which certainly costs less than buying jam in a store—but which enables us to earn value in terms of conviviality, personal gratification, community service, environmental protection, and, in a word, well-being.

We have perpetrated the most appalling disasters, all for the sake of Mammon. Destitute of authenticity, food ultimately eats us. Deprived of cultural, social, and environmental values, it stops being an object of attention, care, and pride—as a true resource should be—morphing into a monster that devastates the countryside socially and ecologically, causing injustice everywhere. We may think we can nonchalantly throw away food, but we can't. 8

FOOD IS EATING THE ENVIRONMENT

Industrialization, as intense in the agri-food sector as it is in others, relegates quality to the back seat. The drivers are quantity, productivity, standardization, and homogenization. Nature, characterized by complexity, indeterminateness, diversity, and multifunctionality, is something else. 9

Industrial agriculture (what an oxymoron!), the industrial processing of food, the distribution over five continents of foodstuffs that could be cultivated in loco, low prices, and the laws of the free market—all these factors have combined to make the food sector one of the most unsustainable spheres of human activity. 10

Over the last hundred years, biodiversity has disappeared at an alarming rate: the need for vast monocultures to supply industry with large amounts of cheap food has limited people's choices to the few varieties suited to this production model—to the detriment of others. As a result, in the United States alone— the world leader in industrial agriculture—80.6 percent of all tomato varieties became extinct between 1903 and 1983, as did 92.8 percent of salad varieties, 86.2 percent of apple varieties, 90.8 percent of corn varieties, and 96.1 percent of sweet corn varieties. Of the 5,000 existing potato varieties, only 4 constitute the majority of those cultivated for commercial purposes in the 11

United States. Only 2 varieties account for 96 percent of all cultivated American peas, and 6 varieties for 71 percent of the total of all cultivated corn. These have been the results wherever the industrialization of food has had the upper hand: a triumph for standardization and homogenization, and a serious peril for two of the cornerstones of life on earth—biological diversity and the ability of species to adapt.

12   The damage that has been done has achieved biblical proportions. In just one century, we have allowed the fruits of thousands of years of evolution to vanish. Luckily, many countries that have yet to experience the agro-industry boom still enjoy a decent level of biodiversity. But if their ambition is to emulate the example of the West, the disaster will become universal. Unfortunately, we are already seeing worrying signals of how, in countries such as Mexico, India, Brazil, and China—among those boasting the most edible vegetable varieties and animal breeds, but also with galloping industrial growth rates—the phenomenon of the destruction of biodiversity is repeating itself with unprecedented intensity.

13   Furthermore, even the land is being "eaten" by food on account of production being carried out on an industrial scale. Over the last few years, the use of chemical fertilizers and pesticides has increased exponentially. The same amount of synthetic chemicals has been applied to the world's soils and introduced into its natural systems in the last ten years as was used in the whole of the preceding century. The products in question are, of course, foreign to the natural cycle, and it is no secret that they will jeopardize soil fertility in the long term. The soil is a living thing, and we are murdering it. Industrial agriculture has embraced the idea of farming without farmers, but at this rate one day we'll be forced to farm without land.

14   Damage to the environment caused by the industrial global food system is so widespread and severe that the problem is now the first item on the ecological agenda. News about what is going on has leaked from the "alternative" world of organics and environmentalism and now entered the public domain. It's no longer possible to deny the facts.

15   The countryside used to be an oasis for town dwellers keen to escape from pollution. Today many areas of the planet have

become dangerous for our health, especially places where fertil-izer is spread and pesticides are sprayed. Agriculture used to be—ought to be—an alliance between man and nature, but it has gradually become a war. It's no coincidence that the technologies used to produce pesticides all originate in the armaments indus-try. Industrial agriculture is de facto a declaration of war on the earth.

To date, environmental devastation has never been calculated as an item in food economics, even though it does represent an increasingly onerous cost.   16

I believe that we pay a low market price for food, but that we also pay a high—and hidden—price, not only in economic terms, but also in terms of the earth's capacity to produce food in the future, and in terms of the quality of our own life and health and of those of future generations, to whom we cannot deny the sacred right to enjoy well-being and happiness. The low cost of food not only devalues food itself, but also hides all the evil we are doing to the earth.   17

Sooner or later, someone will have to pay for all this, and ultimately it will be "consumers," even if they are convinced they are getting a bargain when they spend small sums of money on eating.   18

Analogy

The Myth of the Cave

Plato

1 And now, I said, let me show in a figure how far our nature is enlightened or unenlightened:—Behold! human beings living in an underground den, which has a mouth open toward the light and reaching all along the den; here they have been from their childhood, and have their legs and necks chained so that they cannot move, and can only see before them, being prevented by the chains from turning round their heads. Above and behind them a fire is blazing at a distance, and between the fire and the prisoners there is a raised way; and you will see, if you look, a low wall built along the way, like the screen which marionette players have in front of them, over which they show the puppets.

2 I see.

3 And do you see, I said, men passing along the wall carrying all sorts of vessels, and statues and figures of animals made of wood and stone and various materials, which appear over the wall? Some of them are talking, others silent.

4 You have shown me a strange image, and they are strange prisoners.

5 Like ourselves, I replied; and they see only their own shadows, or the shadows of one another, which the fire throws on the opposite wall of the cave?

6 True, he said; how could they see anything but the shadows if they were never allowed to move their heads?

256

And of the objects which are being carried in like manner 7
they would only see the shadows?

Yes, he said. 8

And if they were able to converse with one another, would 9
they not suppose that they were naming what was actually before
them?

Very true. 10

And suppose further that the prison had an echo which came 11
from the other side, would they not be sure to fancy when one of
the passers-by spoke that the voice which they heard came from
the passing shadow?

No question, he replied. 12

To them, I said, the truth would be literally nothing but the 13
shadows of the images.

That is certain. 14

And now look again, and see what will naturally follow if the 15
prisoners are released and disabused of their error. At first, when
any of them is liberated and compelled suddenly to stand up
and turn his neck round and walk and look toward the light, he
will suffer sharp pains; the glare will distress him, and he will be
unable to see the realities of which in his former state he had seen
the shadows; and then conceive someone saying to him, that what
he saw before was an illusion, but that now, when he is approaching
nearer to being and his eye is turned toward more real existence, he
has a clearer vision—what will be his reply? And you may further
imagine that his instructor is pointing to the objects as they pass and
requiring him to name them—will he not be perplexed? Will he not
fancy that the shadows which he formerly saw are truer than the
objects which are now shown to him?

Far truer. 16

And if he is compelled to look straight at the light, will he 17
not have a pain in his eyes which will make him turn away to
take refuge in the objects of vision which he can see, and which
he will conceive to be in reality clearer than the things which are
now being shown to him?

True, he said. 18

And suppose once more, that he is reluctantly dragged up a 19
steep and rugged ascent, and held fast until he is forced into the

presence of the sun himself, is he not likely to be pained and irritated? When he approaches the light his eyes will be dazzled, and he will not be able to see anything at all of what are now called realities.

20 Not all in a moment, he said.

21 He will require to grow accustomed to the sight of the upper world. And first he will see the shadows best, next the reflections of men and other objects in the water, and then the objects themselves; then he will gaze upon the light of the moon and the stars and the spangled heaven; and he will see the sky and the stars by night better than the sun or the light of the sun by day?

22 Certainly.

23 Last of all he will be able to see the sun, and not mere reflections of him in the water, but he will see him in his own proper place, and not in another; and he will contemplate him as he is.

24 Certainly.

25 He will then proceed to argue that this is he who gives the season and the years, and is the guardian of all that is in the visible world, and in a certain way the cause of all things which he and his fellows have been accustomed to behold?

26 Clearly, he said, he would first see the sun and then reason about him.

27 And when he remembered his old habitation, and the wisdom of the den and his fellow-prisoners, do you not suppose that he would felicitate himself on the change, and pity them?

28 Certainly, he would.

29 And if they were in the habit of conferring honors among themselves on those who were quickest to observe the passing shadows and to remark which of them went before, and which followed after, and which were together; and who were therefore best able to draw conclusions as to the future, do you think that he would care for such honors and glories, or envy the possessors of them? Would he not say with Homer,

Better to be the poor servant of a poor master,

and to endure anything, rather than think as they do and live after their manner?

30 Yes, he said, I think that he would rather suffer anything than entertain these false notions and live in this miserable manner.

Imagine once more, I said, such a one coming suddenly out of ³¹ the sun to be replaced in his old situation; would he not be certain to have his eyes full of darkness?

To be sure, he said. ³²

And if there were a contest, and he had to compete in measur- ³³ ing the shadows with the prisoners who had never moved out of the den, while his sight was still weak, and before his eyes had become steady (and the time which would be needed to acquire this new habit of sight might be very considerable), would he not be ridiculous? Men would say of him that up he went and down he came without his eyes; and that it was better not even to think of ascending and if anyone tried to loose another and lead him up to the light, let them only catch the offender, and they would put him to death.

No question, he said. ³⁴

This entire allegory, I said, you may now append, dear ³⁵ Glaucon, to the previous argument; the prison-house is the world of sight, the light of the fire is the sun, and you will not misap- prehend me if you interpret the journey upwards to be the ascent of the soul into the intellectual world according to my poor belief, which, at your desire, I have expressed—whether rightly or wrongly God knows. But, whether true or false, my opinion is that in the world of knowledge the idea of good appears last of all, and is seen only with an effort; and, when seen, is also inferred to be the universal author of all things beautiful and right, par- ent of light and of the lord of light in this visible world, and the immediate source of reason and truth in the intellectual; and that this is the power upon which he who would act rationally either in public or private life must have his eye fixed.

I agree, he said, as far as I am able to understand you. ³⁶

Moreover, I said, you must not wonder that those who attain ³⁷ to this beatific vision are unwilling to descend to human affairs; for their souls are ever hastening into the upper world where they desire to dwell; which desire of theirs is very natural, if our allegory may be trusted.

Yes, very natural. ³⁸

And is there anything surprising in one who passes from divine ³⁹ contemplations to the evil state of man, misbehaving himself in a ridiculous manner; if, while his eyes are blinking and before he has become accustomed to the surrounding darkness, he is compelled to fight in courts of law, or in other places, about the images or the shadows of images of justice, and is endeavoring to meet the conceptions of those who have never yet seen absolute justice?

40   Anything but surprising, he replied.

41   Anyone who has common sense will remember that the bewilderments of the eyes are of two kinds, and arise from two causes, either from coming out of the light or from going into the light, which is true of the mind's eye, quite as much as of the bodily eye; and he who remembers this when he sees anyone whose vision is perplexed and weak, will not be too ready to laugh; he will first ask whether that soul of man has come out of the brighter life, and is unable to see because unaccustomed to the dark, or having turned from darkness to the day is dazzled by excess of light. And he will count the one happy in his condition and state of being, and he will pity the other; or, if he have a mind to laugh at the soul which comes from below into the light, there will be more reason in this than in the laugh which greets him who returns from above out of the light into the den.

42   That, he said, is a very just distinction.

c. 373 B.C.

Body Ritual among the Nacirema

Horace Miner

1   The anthropologist has become so familiar with the diversity of ways in which different peoples behave in similar situations that he is not apt to be surprised by even the most exotic customs. In fact, if all of the logically possible combinations of behavior have not been found somewhere in the world, he is apt to suspect that they must be present in some yet undescribed tribe. This point has, in fact,

been expressed with respect to clan organization by Murdock.[1] In this light, the magical beliefs and practices of the Nacirema present such unusual aspects that it seems desirable to describe them as an example of the extremes to which human behavior can go.

Professor Linton first brought the ritual of the Nacirema to 2 the attention of anthropologists twenty years ago, but the culture of this people is still very poorly understood. They are a North American group living in the territory between the Canadian Cree, the Yaqui and Tarahumare of Mexico, and the Carib and Arawak of the Antilles.[2] Little is known of their origin, although tradition states that they came from the east. . . .

Nacirema culture is characterized by a highly developed market 3 economy which has evolved in a rich natural habitat. While much of the people's time is devoted to economic pursuits, a large part of the fruits of these labors and a considerable portion of the day are spent in ritual activity. The focus of this activity is the human body, the appearance and health of which loom as a dominant concern in the ethos of the people. While such a concern is certainly not unusual, its ceremonial aspects and associated philosophy are unique.

The fundamental belief underlying the whole system appears 4 to be that the human body is ugly and that its natural tendency is to debility and disease. Incarcerated in such a body, man's only hope is to avert these characteristics through the use of the powerful influences of ritual and ceremony. Every household has one or more shrines devoted to this purpose. The more powerful individuals in the society have several shrines in their houses and, in fact, the opulence of a house is often referred to in terms of the number of such ritual centers it possesses. Most houses are of wattle and daub construction, but the shrine rooms of the more wealthy are walled with stone. Poorer families imitate the rich by applying pottery plaques to their shrine walls.

While each family has at least one such shrine, the rituals asso- 5 ciated with it are not family ceremonies but are private and secret. The rites are normally only discussed with children, and then only

[1]American anthropologist George Peter Murdock, authority on primitive cultures.
[2]Native American tribes formerly inhabiting the Saskatchewan region of Canada, the Sonora region of Mexico, and the West Indies.

during the period when they are being initiated into these mysteries. I was able, however, to establish sufficient rapport with the natives to examine these shrines and to have the rituals described to me.

6   The focal point of the shrine is a box or chest which is built into the wall. In this chest are kept the many charms and magical potions without which no native believes he could live. These preparations are secured from a variety of specialized practitioners. The most powerful of these are the medicine men, whose assistance must be rewarded with substantial gifts. However, the medicine men do not provide the curative potions for their clients, but decide what the ingredients should be and then write them down in an ancient and secret language. This writing is understood only by the medicine men and by the herbalists who, for another gift, provide the required charm.

7   The charm is not disposed of after it has served its purpose, but is placed in the charm-box of the household shrine. As these magical materials are specific for certain ills, and the real or imagined maladies of the people are many, the charm-box is usually full to overflowing. The magical packets are so numerous that people forget what their purposes were and fear to use them again. While the natives are very vague on this point, we can only assume that the idea in retaining all the old magical materials is that their presence in the charm-box, before which the body rituals are conducted, will in some way protect the worshipper.

8   Beneath the charm-box is a small font. Each day every member of the family, in succession, enters the shrine room, bows his head before the charm-box, mingles different sorts of holy water in the font, and proceeds with a brief rite of ablution. The holy waters are secured from the Water Temple of the community, where the priests conduct elaborate ceremonies to make the liquid ritually pure.

9   In the hierarchy of magical practitioners, and below the medicine men in prestige, are specialists whose designation is best translated "holy-mouth-men." The Nacirema have an almost pathological horror of and fascination with the mouth, the condition of which is believed to have a supernatural influence on all social relationships. Were it not for the rituals of the mouth, they believe that their teeth would fall out, their gums bleed, their jaws shrink, their friends desert them, and their lovers reject them. They also

believe that a strong relationship exists between oral and moral characteristics. For example, there is a ritual ablution of the mouth for children which is supposed to improve their moral fiber.

The daily body ritual performed by everyone includes a mouth-rite. Despite the fact that these people are so punctilious about care of the mouth, this rite involves a practice which strikes the uninitiated stranger as revolting. It was reported to me that the ritual consists of inserting a small bundle of hog hairs into the mouth, along with certain magical powders, and then moving the bundle in a highly formalized series of gestures.

In addition to the private mouth-rite, the people seek out a holy-mouth-man once or twice a year. These practitioners have an impressive set of paraphernalia, consisting of a variety of augers, awls, probes, and prods. The use of these objects in the exorcism of the evils of the mouth involves almost unbelievable ritual torture of the client. The holy-mouth-man opens the client's mouth and, using the above mentioned tools, enlarges any holes which decay may have created in the teeth. Magical materials are put into these holes. If there are not naturally occurring holes in the teeth, large sections of one or more teeth are gouged out so that the supernatural substance can be applied. In the client's view, the purpose of these ministrations is to arrest decay and to draw friends. The extremely sacred and traditional character of the rite is evident in the fact that the natives return to the holy-mouth-men year after year, despite the fact that their teeth continue to decay.

It is to be hoped that, when a thorough study of the Nacirema is made, there will be careful inquiry into the personality structure of these people. One has but to watch the gleam in the eye of a holy-mouth-man, as he jabs an awl into an exposed nerve, to suspect that a certain amount of sadism is involved. If this can be established, a very interesting pattern emerges, for most of the population shows definite masochistic tendencies. It was to these that Professor Linton referred in discussing a distinctive part of the daily body ritual which is performed only by men. This part of the rite involves scraping and lacerating the surface of the face with a sharp instrument. Special women's rites are performed only four times during each lunar month, but what they lack in frequency is made up in barbarity. As part of this ceremony, women bake their heads in small ovens for about an hour. The theoretically interesting point is that what seems to be a preponderantly masochistic people have developed sadistic specialists.

13   The medicine men have an imposing temple, or latipso, in every community of any size. The more elaborate ceremonies required to treat very sick patients can only be performed at this temple. These ceremonies involve not only the thaumaturge but a permanent group of vestal maidens who move sedately about the temple chambers in distinctive costume and headdress.

14   The latipso ceremonies are so harsh that it is phenomenal that a fair proportion of the really sick natives who enter the temple even recover. Small children whose indoctrination is still incomplete have been known to resist attempts to take them to the temple because "that is where you go to die." Despite this fact, sick adults are not only willing but eager to undergo the protracted ritual purification, if they can afford to do so. No matter how ill the supplicant or how grave the emergency, the guardians of many temples will not admit a client if he cannot give a rich gift to the custodian. Even after one has gained admission and survived the ceremonies, the guardians will not permit the neophyte to leave until he makes still another gift.

15   The supplicant entering the temple is first stripped of all his or her clothes. In everyday life the Nacirema avoids exposure of his body and its natural functions. Bathing and excretory acts are performed only in the secrecy of the household shrine, where they are ritualized as part of the body-rites. Psychological shock results from the fact that body secrecy is suddenly lost upon entry into the latipso. A man, whose own wife has never seen him in an excretory act, suddenly finds himself naked and assisted by a vestal maiden while he performs his natural functions into a sacred vessel. This sort of ceremonial treatment is necessitated by the fact that the excreta are used by a diviner to ascertain the course and nature of the client's sickness. Female clients, on the other hand, find their naked bodies are subjected to the scrutiny, manipulation and prodding of the medicine men.

16   Few supplicants in the temple are well enough to do anything but lie on their hard beds. The daily ceremonies, like the rites of the holy-mouth-men, involve discomfort and torture. With ritual

precision, the vestals awaken their miserable charges each dawn and roll them about on their beds of pain while performing ablutions, in the formal movements of which the maidens are highly trained. At other times they insert magic wands in the supplicant's mouth or force him to eat substances which are supposed to be healing. From time to time the medicine men come to their clients and jab magically treated needles into their flesh. The fact that these temple ceremonies may not cure, and may even kill the neophyte, in no way decreases the people's faith in the medicine men.

There remains one other kind of practitioner, known as a 17 "listener." This witchdoctor has the power to exorcise the devils that lodge in the heads of people who have been bewitched. The Nacirema believe that parents bewitch their own children. Mothers are particularly suspected of putting a curse on children while teaching them the secret body rituals. The counter-magic of the witchdoctor is unusual in its lack of ritual. The patient simply tells the "listener" all his troubles and fears, beginning with the earliest difficulties he can remember. The memory displayed by the Nacirema in these exorcism sessions is truly remarkable. It is not uncommon for the patient to bemoan the rejection he felt upon being weaned as a babe, and a few individuals even see their troubles going back to the traumatic effects of their own birth.

In conclusion, mention must be made of certain practices 18 which have their base in native esthetics but which depend upon the pervasive aversion to the natural body and its functions. There are ritual fasts to make fat people thin and ceremonial feasts to make thin people fat. Still other rites are used to make women's breasts larger if they are small, and smaller if they are large. General dissatisfaction with breast shape is symbolized in the fact that the ideal form is virtually outside the range of human variation. A few women afflicted with almost inhuman hypermammary development are so idolized that they make a handsome living by simply going from village to village and permitting the natives to stare at them for a fee.

Reference has already been made to the fact that excretory 19 functions are ritualized, routinized, and relegated to secrecy. Natural reproductive functions are similarly distorted. Intercourse is taboo as a topic and scheduled as an act. Efforts are made to avoid pregnancy by the use of magical materials or by limiting intercourse to certain phases of the moon. Conception is actually very infrequent. When pregnant, women dress so as to hide their condition. Parturition takes place in secret, without friends or relatives to assist, and the majority of women do not nurse their infants.

20   Our review of the ritual life of the Nacirema has certainly shown them to be a magic-ridden people. It is hard to understand how they have managed to exist so long under the burdens which they have imposed upon themselves. But even such exotic customs as these take on real meaning when they are viewed with the insight provided by Malinowski when he wrote:

21   "Looking from far and above, from our high places of safety in the developed civilization, it is easy to see all the crudity and irrelevance of magic. But without its power and guidance early man could not have mastered his practical difficulties as he has done, nor could man have advanced to the higher stages of civilization."

1956

The Cosmic Prison

Loren Eiseley

1   "A name is a prison, God is free," once observed the Greek poet Nikos Kazantzakis. He meant, I think, that valuable though language is to man, it is by very necessity limiting, and creates for man an invisible prison. Language implies boundaries. A word spoken creates a dog, a rabbit, a man. It fixes their nature before our eyes; henceforth their shapes are, in a sense, our own creation. They are no longer part of the unnamed shifting architecture of the universe. They have been transfixed as

if by sorcery, frozen into a concept, a word. Powerful though the spell of human language has proven itself to be, it has laid boundaries upon the cosmos.

No matter how far-ranging some of the mental probes that 2 man has philosophically devised, by his own created nature he is forced to hold the specious and emerging present and transform it into words. The words are startling in their immediate effectiveness, but at the same time they are always finally imprisoning because man has constituted himself a prison keeper. He does so out of no conscious intention, but because for immediate purposes he has created an unnatural world of his own, which he calls the cultural world, and in which he feels at home. It defines his needs and allows him to lay a small immobilizing spell upon the nearer portions of his universe. Nevertheless, it transforms that universe into a cosmic prison house which is no sooner mapped than man feels its inadequacy and his own.

He seeks then to escape, and the theory of escape involves 3 bodily flight. Scarcely had the first moon landing been achieved before one U.S. senator boldly announced: "We are the masters of the universe. We can go anywhere we choose." This statement was widely and editorially acclaimed. It is a striking example of the comfort of words, also of the covert substitutions and mental projections to which they are subject. The cosmic prison is not made less so by a successful journey of some two hundred and forty thousand miles in a cramped and primitive vehicle.

To escape the cosmic prison man is poorly equipped. He has 4 to drag portions of his environment with him, and his life span is that of a mayfly in terms of the distances he seeks to penetrate. There is no possible way to master such a universe by flight alone. Indeed such a dream is a dangerous illusion. This may seem a heretical statement, but its truth is self-evident if we try seriously to comprehend the nature of time and space that I sought to grasp when held up to view the fiery messenger that flared across the zenith in 1910. "Seventy-five years," my father had whispered in my ear, "seventy-five years and it will be racing homeward. Perhaps you will live to see it again. Try to remember."

And so I remembered. I had gained a faint glimpse of the size 5 of our prison house. Somewhere out there beyond a billion miles in space, an entity known as a comet had rounded on its track in the black darkness of the void. It was surging homeward toward the sun because it was an eccentric satellite of this solar system. If I lived to see it, it would be but barely, and with the dimmed eyes of age. Yet it, too, in its long traverse, was but a flitting mayfly in terms of the universe the night sky revealed.

6   So relative is the cosmos we inhabit that, as we gaze upon the outer galaxies available to the reach of our telescopes, we are placed in about the position that a single white blood cell in our bodies would occupy, if it were intelligently capable of seeking to understand the nature of its own universe, the body it inhabits. The cell would encounter rivers ramifying into miles of distance seemingly leading nowhere. It would pass through gigantic structures whose meaning it could never grasp—the brain, for example. It could never know there was an outside, a vast being on a scale it could not conceive of and of which it formed an infinitesimal part. It would know only the pouring tumult of the creation it inhabited, but of the nature of that great beast, or even indeed that it was a beast, it could have no conception whatever. It might examine the liquid in which it floated and decide, as in the case of the fall of Lucretius's atoms, that the pouring of obscure torrents had created its world.

7   It might discover that creatures other than itself swam in the torrent. But that its universe was alive, had been born and was destined to perish, its own ephemeral existence would never allow it to perceive. It would never know the sun; it would explore only through dim tactile sensations and react to chemical stimuli that were borne to it along the mysterious conduits of the arteries and veins. Its universe would be centered upon a great arborescent tree of spouting blood. This, at best, generations of white blood cells by enormous labor and continuity might succeed, like astronomers, in charting.

8   They could never, by any conceivable stretch of the imagination, be aware that their so-called universe was, in actuality, the prowling body of a cat or the more time-enduring body of a philosopher, himself engaged upon the same quest in a more gigantic world and perhaps deceived proportionately by greater vistas. What if, for example, the far galaxies man observes make up, across void spaces of which even we are atomically composed,

some kind of enormous creature or cosmic snowflake whose exterior we will never see? We will know more than the phagocyte in our bodies, but no more than that limited creature can we climb out of our universe, or successfully enhance our size or longevity sufficiently to thrust our heads through the confines of the universe that terminates our vision.

Some further "outside" will hover elusively in our thought, 9 but upon its nature, or even its reality, we can do no more than speculate. The phagocyte might observe the salty turbulence of an eternal river system, Lucretius the fall of atoms creating momentary living shapes. We suspiciously sense, in the concept of the expanding universe derived from the primordial atom—the monobloc—some kind of oscillating universal heart. At the instant of its contraction we will vanish. It is not given us, nor can our science recapture, the state beyond the monobloc, nor whether we exist in the diastole of some inconceivable being. We know only a little more extended reality than the hypothetical creature below us. Above us may lie realms it is beyond our power to grasp.

1970

Living Like Weasels

Annie Dillard

A weasel is wild. Who knows what he thinks? He sleeps in his 1 underground den, his tail draped over his nose. Sometimes he lives in his den for two days without leaving. Outside, he stalks rabbits, mice, muskrats, and birds, killing more bodies that he can eat warm, and often dragging the carcasses home. Obedient to instinct, he bites his prey at the neck, either splitting the jugular vein at the throat or crunching the brain at the base of the skull, and he does not let go. One naturalist refused to kill a weasel who was socketed into his hand deeply as a rattlesnake. The man could in no way pry

the tiny weasel off, and he had to walk half a mile to water, the weasel dangling from his palm, and soak him off like a stubborn label.

2   And once, says Ernest Thompson Seton—once, a man shot
an eagle out of the sky. He examined the eagle and found the dry
skull of a weasel fixed by the jaws to his throat. The supposition
is that the eagle had pounced on the weasel and the weasel swiveled and bit as instinct taught him, tooth to neck, and nearly won.
I would like to have seen that eagle from the air a few weeks or
months before he was shot: was the whole weasel still attached to
his feathered throat, a fur pendant? Or did the eagle eat what he
could reach, gutting the living weasel with his talons before his
breast, bending his beak, cleaning the beautiful airborne bones?

3   I have been reading about weasels because I saw one last week. I
startled a weasel who startled me, and we exchanged a long glance.

4   Twenty minutes from my house, through the woods by the
quarry and across the highway, is Hollins Pond, a remarkable piece
of shallowness, where I like to go at sunset and sit on a tree trunk.
Hollins Pond is also called Murray's Pond; it covers two acres of bot-
tomland near Tinker Creek with six inches of water and six thousand
lily pads. In winter, brown-and-white steers stand in the middle of
it, merely dampening their hooves; from the distant shore they look
like miracle itself, complete with miracle's nonchalance. Now, in
summer, the steers are gone. The water lilies have blossomed and
spread to a green horizontal plane that is terra firma to plodding
blackbirds, and tremulous ceiling to black leeches, crayfish, and carp.

5   This is, mind you, suburbia. It is a five-minute walk in three
directions to rows of houses, though none is visible here. There's
a 55 mph highway at one end of the pond, and a nesting pair of
wood ducks at the other. Under every bush is a muskrat hole or a
beer can. The far end is an alternating series of fields and woods,
fields and woods, threaded everywhere with motorcycle tracks—
in whose bare clay wild turtles lay eggs.

6   So. I had crossed the highway, stepped over two low barbed-
wire fences, and traced the motorcycle path in all gratitude
through the wild rose and poison ivy of the pond's shoreline up
into high grassy fields. Then I cut down through the woods to the
mossy fallen tree where I sit. This tree is excellent. It makes a dry,

upholstered bench at the upper, marshy end of the pond, a plush jetty raised from the thorny shore between a shallow blue body of water and a deep blue body of sky.

The sun had just set. I was relaxed on the tree trunk, ensconced 7 in the lap of lichen, watching the lily pads at my feet tremble and part dreamily over the thrusting path of a carp. A yellow bird appeared to my right and flew behind me. It caught my eye; I swiveled around—and the next instant, inexplicably, I was looking down at a weasel, who was looking up at me.

Weasel! I'd never seen one wild before. He was ten inches 8 long, thin as a curve, a muscled ribbon, brown as fruitwood, soft-furred, alert. His face was fierce, small and pointed as a lizard's; he would have made a good arrowhead. There was just a dot of chin, maybe two brown hairs' worth, and then the pure white fur began that spread down his underside. He had two black eyes I didn't see, any more than you see a window.

The weasel was stunned into stillness as he was emerging 9 from beneath an enormous shaggy wild rose bush four feet away. I was stunned into stillness twisted backward on the tree trunk. Our eyes locked, and someone threw away the key.

Our look was as if two lovers, or deadly enemies, met unex- 10 pectedly on an overgrown path when each had been thinking of something else: a clearing blow to the gut. It was also a bright blow to the brain, or a sudden beating of brains, with all the charge and intimate grate of rubbed balloons. It emptied our lungs. It felled the forest, moved the fields, and drained the pond; the world dismantled and tumbled into that black hole of eyes. If you and I looked at each other that way, our skulls would split and drop to our shoulders. But we don't. We keep our skulls. So.

He disappeared. This was only last week, and already I don't 11 remember what shattered the enchantment. I think I blinked, I think I retrieved my brain from the weasel's brain, and tried to memorize what I was seeing, and the weasel felt the yank of separation, the careening splash-down into real life and the urgent current of instinct. He vanished under the wild rose. I waited motionless, my mind suddenly full of data and my spirit with pleadings, but he didn't return.

12   Please do not tell me about "approach-avoidance conflicts."
I tell you I've been in that weasel's brain for sixty seconds, and he
was in mine. Brains are private places, muttering through unique
and secret tapes—but the weasel and I both plugged into another
tape simultaneously, for a sweet and shocking time. Can I help it
if it was a blank?

13   What goes on in his brain the rest of the time? What does a
weasel think about? He won't say. His journal is tracks in clay,
a spray of feathers, mouse blood and bone: uncollected, uncon-
nected, loose-leaf, and blown.

14   I would like to learn, or remember, how to live. I come to Hollins
Pond not so much to learn how to live as, frankly, to forget about it.
That is, I don't think I can learn from a wild animal how to live in
particular—shall I suck warm blood, hold my tail high, walk with
my footprints precisely over the prints of my hands?—but I might
learn something of mindlessness, something of the purity of living in the physical senses and the dignity of living without bias or
motive. The weasel lives in necessity and we live in choice, hating
necessity and dying at the last ignobly in its talons. I would like to
live as I should, as the weasel lives as he should. And I suspect that
for me the way is like the weasel's: open to time and death painlessly,
noticing everything, remembering nothing, choosing the given with
a fierce and pointed will.

15   I missed my chance. I should have gone for the throat. I
should have lunged for that streak of white under the weasel's
chin and held, held on through mud and into the wild rose,
held on for a dearer life. We could live under the wild rose wild
as weasels, mute and uncomprehending. I could very calmly go
wild. I could live two days in the den, curled, leaning on mouse
fur, sniffing bird bones, blinking, licking, breathing musk, my
hair tangled in the roots of grasses. Down is a good place to go,
where the mind is single. Down is out, out of your ever-loving
mind and back to your careless senses. I remember muteness as a
prolonged and giddy fast, where every moment is a feast of utterance received. Time and events are merely poured, unremarked,
and ingested directly, like blood pulsed into my gut through a

jugular vein. Could two live that way? Could two live under the wild rose, and explore by the pond, so that the smooth mind of each is as everywhere present to the other, and as received and as unchallenged, as falling snow?

We could, you know. We can live any way we want. People 16 take vows of poverty, chastity, and obedience—even of silence— by choice. The thing is to stalk your calling in a certain skilled and supple way, to locate the most tender and live spot and plug into that pulse. This is yielding, not fighting. A weasel doesn't "attack" anything; a weasel lives as he's meant to, yielding at every moment to the perfect freedom of single necessity.

I think it would be well, and proper, and obedient, and pure, 17 to grasp your one necessity and not let it go, to dangle from it limp wherever it takes you. Then even death, where you're going no matter how you live, cannot you part. Seize it and let it seize you up aloft even, till your eyes burn out and drop; let your musky flesh fall off in shreds, and let your very bones unhinge and scatter, loosened over fields, over fields and woods, lightly, thoughtless, from any height at all, from as high as eagles.

1982

Extreme Reading

Rebecca Brown

You eat because you have to, it sustains you. But once you get 1 past the basics of hydration and calories, what you eat and how you eat are determined by your own peculiar, and in the most literal sense, taste, by what can satisfy your sweet tooth or your sour tooth, your savory or unsavory desires. You eat some things because they're good for you, but there are only so many hours in a day, so many days in a life, so you also consume other things solely because you want to, because you have some craving or urge or longing that only this particular thing can fulfill. To be polite you'll eat whatever the people who invited you to dinner at their house have made for you, but when you go out you won't order something you don't like, and if something shows up on your plate in some brownish sauce or gelatinous pool or that gets in your craw or goes down wrong or doesn't appeal, you turn away from it, discreetly if you can, but if you can't if push comes to shove, if spit comes to fore, you hawk it or gag it or cough it out and you don't care who's watching.

2   I can't finish books I think are bad. I can't get through somebody's prose that reads to me like Sucaryl or some brownish lumpy sauce or is salt-and-peppered or soy-sauced beyond a shadow of its former self, that's watered down or stupid or pretentious.

3   Anthropologically speaking, we all recognize there are taboos regarding what we should not eat.

4   But no one agrees about everything.

5   We're taught to read because we need to navigate our culture, to read road signs and the names of stuff at the grocery story, to sign our names on documents when we marry or when we ought to be able to marry. This kind of reading is like hydration and calories. You need it to survive. If you don't get it you get rickets. If you are illiterate you are probably poor, you're missing something basic from your diet and you'll probably die sooner than you should.

6   But then after we've taken care of our basic needs, we're taught to read in ways that are "good for us," to provide us with a grounding in the humanities, to broaden our minds, etc., then finally to give us pleasure. At this level we decide what we like: chicken or fish, poached or grilled, comics or Rilke, the *New York Times*, the Bible, Barbara Cartland, tacos, cheese.

7   Extreme reading is like cannibalism. You take a book, like a piece of food, and eat it. For sustenance, for blood, if not to ritually ingest the soul or heart or power of your enemy or someone you loved. You take it in and chew and grind and tear it down to the smallish bits, to things that you can swallow. You rid yourself of some of it and keep some of the rest. Sometimes you keep what may not be the best for you. Your body knows what's good for you, but sometimes you don't listen, The things you eat and keep

become a part of you. You re-create inside yourself, with caverns, juices, processes you can and can't control, a kind of meat.

A book is a thing that someone made from words you think ⁸ you understand. You take it in and think you are sophisticated, a connoisseur, or at least someone with manners enough to wield a knife and fork, and not talk with your mouth full. You know that whatever it is, a ham and cheese on rye, or popcorn or *foie de* something, no matter how humble or fine, you'll break it into broken things that can be used by you and your voracious flesh.

When you read a book, you read what someone else wrote, ⁹ but you also read your own book. You may read all the words or not, but the words you keep—those that stick to your ribs and keep you awake, dyspeptic, bilious, or that nourish you as if to health, become you muscle, bone or heart—are words you shape as you desire. The book you read is what you want; you will it to your own.

Every time you read a book you read what you desire.   10
Every time you read a book you make that book your own.   11

One weekend when I was a teenager, I was sitting alone on 12 a bus on my way to my first Bible Camp Youth Retreat. Most of the other kids on the bus—Texas natives or come-here from somewhere else in the Bible Belt—had been raised in Christian households, but a few of us were recent converts. Though I believed a lot of what Christians were supposed to, I had trouble with the heaven and hell thing. This may have been part of the reason I was sitting apart from the kids singing Christian songs or doing Bible study, but I was also alone because I was reading a book that was not the Bible, but something my sister had just finished reading in college, *A Portrait of the Artist as a Young Man*.[1] As our bus hurtled

---

[1]The *A Portrait of the Artist as a Young Man* I read these days is not my sister's copy, though I thank her for the loan and for a million others. (Lawrence Ferlinghetti's *A Coney Island of the Mind*, Aldous Huxley, Margaret Atwood, etc.; tons of music— the Beatles and the Rolling Stones, then Hendrix, Simon and Garfunkel, Jethro Tull.) My reading copy is, rather, included in *The Portable James Joyce* (Viking, 1966), edited and with an introduction and notes by Harry Levin, the same guy who did my Hawthorne Riverside anthology (that guy gets around!) which I purchased, used, for the pathetic sum of $6.60.

through the steamy, spice-scented night toward the East Texas piney woods, I read about Stephan Dedalus and his family and Ireland and food and I came to this:

> Now what is the meaning of this word retreat and why is it . . . a practice of all who desire to lead before God and in the eyes of men a truly Christian life? A retreat, my dear boys, signifies a withdrawal for a while from the cares of our life, the cares of this workaday world, in order to examine the state of our conscience, to reflect on the mysteries of holy religion and to understand better why we are here in this world. During these few days I intend to put before you some thoughts concerning the four last things . . . death, judgment, hell and heaven.

13   Was it a coincidence that I was reading these words about Stephen Dedalus going on a Christian retreat to learn about heaven and hell at exactly the moment as I myself was going on a Christian retreat and worried about heaven and hell? Or had God arranged for me to read these words right here and now because He was trying to tell me something?

14   A little later I read this:

> Now let us try for a moment to realize, as far as we can, the natures of that abode of the damned which the justice of an offended God has called into existence for the eternal punishment of sinners. Hell is a strait and dark and foul-smelling prison, an abode of demons and lost souls, filled with fire and smoke. The straitness of this prisonhouse is expressly designed by God to punish those who refused to be found by His laws.

15   I knew that God sometimes spoke to His children in signs. Was God using these words in this book to say something to me? Or was I only hoping or fearing that He was? I don't remember much else about that weekend besides reading those passages over and over and over to myself.

16   I do not remember what I decided.

17   When I reread *A Portrait of the Artist as a Young Man* several years later, I could hardly believe it was the same book. The words on the page hadn't changed of course, but I had. Having

abandoned my Christian faith, I read a romantic, very male tale of the self and home and family, of nostalgia, growing up and art and God and loss.

> Every book you read contains the story of your life.   18
> Every book you read you make your own.   19

I left home, read a lot and lost my faith. I became a writer and   20 hung around with artists. One time, I went with a bunch of artist pals to the town dump. My visual artist friends had to pay the dump for the things they scavenged—bedsprings and auto parts, engines and tool handles and fence posts—whereas the dump was giving away the books. They were trying to get rid of them. Unlike the materials the artists wanted, the books did not have neat little hinges or squeaky things, they only had wilted, moldy, dirty or stuck-together pages. You couldn't make something cool out of books that you could stand up in your yard or hang your coat on or put flowers in. The books were taking up room and creating a fire hazard. No one had read them for years and probably no one was ever going to read them again. These books were utterly useless. I loved them for that. I think I also felt kind of sorry for them. I took some home.

I felt sorry for some and had contempt for others. For some   21 books I felt both. I thought about how there are so many books out there and how my work would never measure up. But also how there were so many books that were just plain shitty, worse than anything I or anyone I knew would write on our very worst day, yet those shitty books got published and people even bought them, while some actually great books languished in libraries, unchecked-out for years, then got tossed into some twenty-five-cent sale bin or thrown out to the dump. Was this what I wanted my life to be about?

I got a bunch of these books and pens and glue and crayons and   22 tape and invited friends over to my apartment to mess these books up. Some of us "illuminated" our own books, and some we made together. We gave them to each other or slipped them onto the shelves of used bookstores or libraries and fantasized what would happen when someone found them. These cut-and-paste books or illuminated manuscripts or what a librarian friend of mine calls defaced books and artists call "altered text" or "erasures" are all variations of the kinds of things Orton and Halliwell[2] did and the great Tom Phillips[3] is doing. The story about Orton and Halliwell is that their defacing was prompted by trying to check out some actual literature at the Islington library and being informed that their branch didn't stock whatever they were looking for although it did have all kinds of stupid tripe. Which the couple checked out, doctored and returned. Some of the extreme reading/book demolition my friends and I enjoyed had elements of lit crit or political commentary, like bringing forward the gay subtext in the novel of a closeted writer we knew or splicing a photography book about World War II with one about Japanese flower arranging, but mostly we were just having fun while we drank.

23   One of those old books from the dump came to my rescue.

24   For a long time after my parents died I wasn't good for much. Some days I didn't get out of bed. I lost my keys a lot. I watched a lot of videos and took a lot of walks. I'd walk downtown or to the water and sometimes drive out of the city. One time I was at some pretty place—a mountain view or by the sea—and there was one of those benches people put up with a plaque on it that says, "In memory of so'n'so, who used to love this place." I'd seen those benches and read those words a million times, but this time, when I read the words, I lost it. It had never registered with me before that every one of those nice memorial benches was for someone who was dead, someone whose dying had left behind other people who were knocked out by that death. The words, the bench, the pretty place where once I would have thought, "Oh, what a nice place to sit," were all the same, but after my parents were dead, I wasn't. I just keeled over and bawled my weepy eyes out.

[2]The altered texts made by playwright Joe Orton and his lover Kenneth Halliwell are described in John Lahr's terrific biography *Prick Up Your Ears* (Knopf, 1978). Orton and Halliwell, before the one whacked the other to death with a hammer, lived in a tiny little flat in Islington, the same part of London where I lived in the '80s. I went to what had been their place and stood outside and looked at it. I went to the library too. Though the artful altering of shitting library books earned Orton time in the slammer, those same defaced books, once evidence of criminal destruction of property, are now the crown jewels of the Islington library.

[3]Tom Phillips's great and beautiful altered text, the daddy of them all, is *A Humument*, which you should look up at www.tomphillips.co.uk and humument.com.

For a long time after my parents died, I also couldn't read. [25] I could flip through magazines or stare at the backs of cereal boxes and even read liner notes, but books were too much. They took concentration and an ability to track and to remember, and if they had stories, the stories were wrong. Or perhaps I should say what the words added up to was wrong, although not every single word was wrong, because some words were right. As I tried to read, the wrong words faded or disappeared, leaving only the horrible right ones.

I picked up one of those twenty-five-cent books I had lying [26] around and, though I couldn't really read it, individual words jumped out at me. Words like "dead" or "mother" or "no." Or "gone" or "father" or "dead." I started going through the book and finding the words in it that made sense to me. I discovered that the book was, unbeknownst to itself, telling exactly the story of what I was feeling and not feeling and remembering. There were other words between, within the words that were telling something useful to me. It started in the title, *The Mortal Storm*,[4] a novel about heroic people fighting proto-Nazies in the '30s. But actually of course, *The Mortal Storm* contained a book for me, *The MortalS*, less a narrative than a collection of fragments about the deaths of my parents.

Here are my severe edits of the 1,000 or so words that make [27] up the first three pages:

a long   illness
She lay quite still
What happened to   her
mother
would lie   remembering in   the bed
mother   sick

---

[4]*The Mortal Storm* (Little, Brown, 1938) is probably the most well-known of the many, many books by Phyllis Bottome, the British daughter of an American clergyman. Bottome's output included novels, short fiction and a biography of the man with whom she studied psychoanalysis in Vienna, Alfred Adler. In 1940, the unabashedly anti-Nazi *Mortal Storm* was made into a film starring James Stewart as a good German who doesn't join the Nazis, and Margaret Sullivan as the non-German (read Jewish) girl with whom he falls in love. The movie pissed the Nazis off so much that they banned all MGM films from being shown in Germany. *The Mortal Storm* isn't banned anywhere anymore but it might as well be, in the sense that we can't find it readily because our tastes have changed and now it comes across as just a toothless bit of cinematic junk food.

it's all over now   mother
Nothing can be helped
dead   dying   dead   dead
her mother   her mother   her mother

And so on.

28   It took me a few years to cut and paste (the term I prefer to "erasure" or "altered text" because it sounds more like what you did in grade school and less like something that you are going to call Art), through the entirety of *The MortalS*, during which I got past much of my parents' deaths. I believe that being able to, however thoughtlessly or subconsciously, engage with others' words and find the words I needed in them helped me obsess over or meditate my way through my sadness.

29   A few years later, though I had stopped having cut-and-paste parties, I still kept at it on my own. The next book I completed I'd bought for a dollar at a used bookstore in Vermont. *I Want to Be a Lady* by Maximilian Foster (J.B. Lippincott Company, 1926), is a comic western romance that tells the story of an Eastern girl who, in late nineteenth-century America, goes west where she encounters a group of lovable cowboys and scrappy, "unladylike" frontier folk. Though our heroine wants to be a lady (i.e., live a genteel, back-east-style life), she realizes that the lovable cowboys and scrappy frontier fold are warm-hearted and good and she is happier being the honest frontier wife of a lovable cowboy than a proper back-east Lady. *I Want to Be a Lady*, however, contains within it an entirely other book, which I discovered through severe editing. I went through the book, page by page, for more than a year, and painted or colored or collaged over most of the words, leaving only the words that told the story I needed to tell. My book, the book I desired, contained therein, is titled, *I Want a Lady* and it is a woeful autobiography about a doomed lesbian romance I had with an older—uh—lady, when I was young and still believed the words that books and people said.

30   Every time you read a book you read what you desire.

31   Every book you read includes the story of your life.

2009

Argument and Persuasion

ARGUMENT

Texting

Tapping into Text Messaging

Janet Kornblum

It's 9:30 a.m., and Larry Blair hopes that his 16-year-old son 1
doesn't forget his orthodontist appointment after school.

So Blair, who is on a conference call in his office in Saratoga, 2
Calif., pulls out his cell phone and thumbs in a short message.
"can u b @ sasaki @ 330," he asks.

Seconds later, Aaron, sitting at his desk at Saratoga High 3
School, feels his cell phone vibrating in his pocket. He surrepti-
tiously looks at the screen and quietly pumps in a response: "can
b there @ 320."

Welcome to the future, where the family that texts together 4
stays together.

Instant, fast, fun and cheap, texting—sending and receiving 5
brief text messages on cell phones and other portable devices—
has been the rage in Europe since the late 90s. Now it's making

inroads in the USA. Early users love it, but some people worry that it will add yet another distraction to already overtasked lives.

6   Teens, techies and other early adopters leading the charge to text say it's a great way to communicate when they are too busy to talk or when making a call would be rude or impractical. Parents keep tabs on kids. Business people silently check facts in meetings. Young professionals text-flirt at concerts. And teens gossip with friends, anytime, anywhere.

7   Teens are especially ahead of the curve: 45% of Americans ages 12-19 have a cell phone, according to market research company Teenage Research Unlimited of Northbrook, Ill. And 37% of teen cell users also use text messaging, with numbers rising every year.

8   "Some people do it for eight hours at a time," says Lita Cho, 17, a Youth Radio reporter in Alameda, Calif.

9   Teens aren't the only ones. Texting in the USA has grown from 33 million messages sent in June 2001 to more than 1 billion in December 2002, says the Cellular Telecommunications & Internet Association.

10   "When I go out, I hate to be called," says Steven Chan, 30, who owns Cyber Hunt, a cyber cafe in San Francisco. "I hate people leaving voicemail. Just text me."

11   Though Yankee Group analysts estimate that only 12% of cell phone users in the USA send or receive text messages, that soon could change: 144 million people—half of all U.S. residents— have cell phones, the telecommunications association says. And 90% of those phones are digital and can at least accept text messages. About 60% also can send messages, Jupiter Research says.

12   "Texting is a small indicator that cyberspace has now arrived—not just at our desks, but in our pockets, in our hands and in our cars," says Paul Saffo, director of the Institute for the Future in Menlo Park, Calif.

13   But is adding yet another communications tool to our already stuffed belts really a good idea?

14   Some worry that texting—also known as SMS, for Short Message Service—will make people even more distracted than they already are. Instead of watching the road, will drivers be typing into their cell phones? Instead of listening to the teacher, will

kids be checking their messages? Will pedestrians watch where they're going when they walk down the street?

"I've seen a lot more people walking into parking meters," 15 Saffo says. "No joke."

People may be "physically present," but they're increasingly 16 "psychologically absent," says James Katz, a professor of communications at Rutgers University.

Katz says cell phones are largely responsible for the "ghost- 17 ing of America," his phrase for "the hollowing-out of people. They're physical ghosts involved in their messaging and talking on the mobile phones."

But others say teens and twentysomethings who grew up 18 multitasking might simply be able to handle more distractions.

"Aaron will be on the phone at home with music playing in 19 the background and doing homework. You're time-sharing your brain," says Blair, 47, vice president of a software company. Plus, "it has made both of us more accessible at times when even a cell phone couldn't have gotten to us."

People have been concerned about the adverse effects of new 20 communication tools since Plato worried that the alphabet would cause us to lose our memorization skills and cut down on our quality time together, says Howard Rheingold, a longtime technology watcher and author of *Smart Mobs: The Next Social Revolution.* And he was right. But there's always a reason you pay the price.

"Communications behavior is filling parts of our time that 21 used to be idle or devoted to talking to strangers or noticing parts of the world that we're not going to notice as much anymore. That has an impact on individuals as well as on cities. More and more, people are walking down the street communicating with people who are somewhere else."

But, he adds, "I wouldn't be so quick to judge that (teens) are 22 paying less attention than they were before. Maybe they're multiplying the amount of attention that they pay. We call it distracted. Our grandchildren will say, 'Oh, yeah, our grandparents couldn't think on more than one track at once.'"

Go to any high school and you're likely to see kids staring 23 at tiny cell phone screens, picking at tiny keypads with their thumbs.

24   Most schools ban talking and texting in the classroom. But that doesn't stop everyone.

25   Though phone calls require talking, texting can be done on the sly. Some students don't even need to look at their phones as they type.

26   "You're not allowed, but they rarely notice if you have it under the table," Aaron says. "Teachers aren't looking around for that sort of thing. You can pass notes to people in other classes."

27   Some do more than that.

28   In January, students at the University of Maryland were caught cheating on a test by sending text messages to each other.

29   Rutgers' Katz says his informal surveys show that about half the students with text-enabled phones have used them in class, and a substantial minority say they know of others who have used texting to cheat. But it's no easier than other kinds of cheating, so few expect it to take off in a big way.

30   Regardless of where teens text, debating whether they should use the new technology "is somewhat futile," Rheingold says. "They're going to do it."

31   And adults probably will continue to adopt texting as well as other new forms of communication. Why? It fulfills a deep need.

32   "We've had speech," Rheingold says. "We've had writing. We've had the alphabet. We've had the printing press. These are technologies for extending the way we think and communicate.

33   "That's what humans do: We come up with new ways to communicate and new ways to build civilizations."

2003

Texting in Class Is Rampant

Michael Rubinkam

1   When his professors drone, Dan Kautz whips out his phone.

2   Kautz, a senior at Wilkes University, might send a text message to someone across the room—"I can't wait to get out of

here"—or make plans with his roommates. He's become so adept at texting during class that he can tap out a message without even looking at the screen, making it appear as if he's paying attention to the instructor when he's really chatting with his girlfriend.

"Every single person I know texts in class at least occasionally," 3 said Kautz, a communications studies major from Pelham, N.Y.

It's no surprise that high school and college students are 4 obsessive texters. What alarms Wilkes psychology professors Deborah Tindell and Robert Bohlander is how rampant the practice has become during class: Their recent study shows that texting at the school has surpassed doodling, daydreaming and note-passing to become the top classroom distraction.

The anonymous survey of 269 Wilkes students found that 5 nine in 10 admit to sending text messages during class—and nearly half say it's easy to do so undetected. Even more troubling, 10 percent say that they have sent or received texts during exams, and that 3 percent admit to using their phones to cheat.

The phenomenon is part of a broader revolution in the way 6 young adults communicate. Most prefer texting to e-mail and certainly to talking on the phone, Tindell said.

Indeed, most view texting as their right. 7

Almost all the students surveyed by Tindell and Bohlander 8 said they should be allowed to have their phones in class. And a clear majority—62 percent—said they should be allowed to text in class as long as they're not disturbing those around them. About one in four said texting creates a distraction.

"Students these days are so used to multitasking . . . they 9 believe they are able to process information just as effectively when they are texting as when they are not," Tindell said.

Tom Markley, 21, of Lehighton, Pa., is constantly trading texts 10 with his friends and his girlfriend during class.

"If it's a really boring class, texting is a nice alternative to 11 having to sit there and focus," said Markley, a senior computer science major at Wilkes.

But, he conceded, "there are definitely times when it takes 12 away from your concentration. Suddenly you'll be at the end of the period and say, 'What did we do today?'"

13   Tindell instituted a no-texting policy as a result of the study, which has been presented at a pair of academic conferences. She tells students that if she even sees a cell phone during a test, its owner gets an automatic zero.

14   One Syracuse University professor has taken an even harsher stand.

15   Laurence Thomas, a popular philosophy professor whose courses have waiting lists, walked out on his class of nearly 400 students last week when he caught a couple of students fiddling with their phones instead of paying attention to him.

16   It wasn't the first time Thomas has cut a class short because a student broke his no-texting rule. To Thomas, texting saps the class of its intellectual energy.

17   "My job is to engage the class, to give them stuff to think about," he said. "They need to respect that."

18   While Thomas keeps his eyes peeled for illicit texters, Tindell said most professors are likely as clueless as she used to be about the ubiquity of in-class cell phone use. Many of the surveyed students said their professors would be shocked if they knew about their texting habits.

19   Kautz said most of his professors either don't notice or don't care if students text during class time. He doesn't believe a blanket prohibition is the right way to go.

20   "There are people who can text and still be focused on class," he said. "If my roommate is short on quarters for laundry and wants to borrow some, of course I'm going to want to text him back right away and not hold him back for 40 minutes."

21   But he acknowledged that some students text excessively.

22   "I know some people will sit there for the entire class just typing away," he said. "I don't even know why they bother coming."

23   Chelsea Uselding, 20, a Wilkes junior from Chicago, sends an average of 150 texts a day. But she's the rare student who doesn't text during class—viewing that hour or two as a "nice break" from the phone and its unceasing demands on her time and attention.

24   There's also a practical reason why Uselding, a dual major in psychology and international studies, idles her thumbs.

"I'm paying all this money to listen to the person speak, and 25 I figure it's a waste of my time if I'm not going to be listening," she said.

Some high school and college teachers have sought to adapt 26 text messaging to classroom use, texting assignments; asking questions of the class and having students respond via text, with the results shown on a large screen; and allowing students to text questions or comments during class.

"Our experience has shown that positive results can be 27 achieved by encouraging students to bring their mobile phones out in the open and to use them to contribute to the class, and to their own learning—that is, by joining them instead of trying to beat them," New Zealand scholars wrote in a 2009 paper published in the journal Communications of the ACM.

Tindell and Bohlander advise professors to have clear, writ- 28 ten policies on texting, to circulate around the classroom and make frequent eye contact, and to avoid focusing all their attention on their lecture notes or PowerPoint presentations.

Tindell does allow students to text before class starts—and 29 almost all of them do.

"If they are going to go through withdrawal," she quipped, 30 "they might as well get their fix."

2010

Should This Student Have Been Expelled?

Nat Hentoff

Doug Hann, a varsity football player at Brown, was also concen- 1 trating on organizational behavior and management and business economics. On the night of October 18, 1990, Hann, a junior, was celebrating his twenty-first birthday, and in the process had imbibed a considerable amount of spirits.

2   At one point, Hann shouted into the air, "Fuck you, niggers!" It was aimed at no one in particular but apparently at all black students at Brown. Or in the world. A freshman leaned out a dormitory window and asked him to stop being so loud and offensive.

3   Hann, according to reporters on the *Brown Daily Herald,* looked up and yelled, "What are you, a faggot?" Hann then noticed an Israeli flag in the dorm. "What are you, a Jew?" he shouted. "Fucking Jew!"

4   Hann had achieved the hat trick of bigotry. (In hockey, the hat trick is scoring three goals in a game.) In less than a minute, Hann had engaged in racist, anti-Semitic, and homophobic insults.

5   He wasn't through. As reported by Smita Nerula in the *Brown Daily Herald,* the freshman who had asked Hann to cool it recruited a few people from his dorm "and followed Hann and his friends."

6   "This resulted in a verbal confrontation outside of Wayland Arch. At this time, [Hann] was said to have turned to one of the freshman's friends, a black woman, and shouted, 'My parents own your people.'"

7   To the Jewish student, or the student he thought was Jewish, Hann said, "Happy Hanukkah."

8   There are reports that at this juncture Hann tried to fight some of the students who had been following him. But, the *Brown Daily Herald* reports, he "was held back by one of his friends, while [another] friend stretched his arm across the Wayland Gates to keep the students from following Hann."

9   John Howard Crouch—a student and Brown chapter secretary of the American Civil Liberties Union there—tells me that because Hann had friends restraining him, "nobody seriously expected fighting, regardless of anyone's words."

10   Anyway, there was no physical combat. Just words. Awful words, but nothing more than speech. (Nor were there any threats.)

11   This was not the first time Hann's disgraceful drunken language had surfaced at Brown. Two years before, in an argument with a black student at a fraternity bar, Hann had called the student a "nigger." Thereupon he had been ordered to attend a race

relations workshop and to get counseling for possible alcohol abuse. Obviously, he has not been rehabilitated.

Months went by after Hann's notorious birthday celebration as Brown's internal disciplinary procedures cranked away. (To steal a phrase from Robert Sherrill, Brown's way of reaching decisions in these matters is to due process as military music is to music. But that's true of any college or university I know anything about.) 12

At last, the Undergraduate Disciplinary Council (five faculty or administration members and five students) ruled that Doug Hann was to leave the university forevermore. Until two years ago, it was possible for a Brown student to be dismissed, which meant that he or she could reapply after a decent period of penance. But now, Brown has enshrined the sentence of expulsion. You may go on to assist Mother Teresa in caring for the dying or you may teach a course in feminism to 2 Live Crew, but no accomplishments, no matter how noble, will get you back into Brown once you have been expelled. 13

Doug Hann will wander the Earth without a Brown degree for the rest of his days. 14

The president of Brown, Vartan Gregorian—formerly the genial head of the New York Public Library—had the power to commute or even reverse the sentence. But the speech code under which Hann was thrown out had been proposed by Gregorian himself shortly after he was inaugurated in 1989, so he was hardly a detached magistrate. 15

On January 25, 1991, Vartan Gregorian affirmed, with vigor, the expulsion decision by the Undergraduate Disciplinary Council. 16

Hann became a historic figure. Under all the "hate speech" codes enacted around the country in recent years, he is the first student to actually be expelled for violating one of the codes. 17

The *New York Times* (February 12) reported that "Howard Ehrlich, the research director of the National Institute Against Prejudice and Violence, said that he did not know of any other such expulsions, but that he was familiar with cases in which students who had harassed others were moved to other dormitories or ordered to undergo counseling." 18

19   But that takes place in *educational* institutions, whose presidents recognize that there are students who need help, not exile.

20   At first, there didn't seem to be much protest among the student body at Brown on free speech grounds—except for members of the Brown chapter of the ACLU and some free thinkers on the student paper, as well as some unaffiliated objectors to expelling students for what they say, not for what they do. The number of these dissenters is increasing, as we shall see.

21   At the student paper, however, the official tone has changed from the libertarian approach of Vernon Silver, who was editor-in-chief last semester. A February 13 *Brown Daily Herald* editorial was headed: "*Good Riddance.*"

22   It began: "Doug Hann is gone, and the university is well to be rid of him."

23   But President Gregorian has been getting a certain amount of flack and so, smiting his critics hip and thigh, he wrote a letter to the *New York Times.* Well, that letter (printed on February 21) was actually a press release, distributed by the Brown University News Bureau to all sorts of people, including me, on February 12. There were a few changes—and that *Brown Daily Herald* editorial was attached to it—but Gregorian's declaration was clearly not written exclusively for the *Times.*

24   Is this a new policy at the *Times*—taking public relations handouts for the letters page?

25   Next week I shall include a relentlessly accurate analysis of President Gregorian's letter by the executive director of the Rhode Island ACLU. But first, an account of what Gregorian said in that letter to the *Times.*

26   President Gregorian indignantly denies that Brown has ever expelled "anyone for the exercise of free speech, nor will it ever do so." Cross his heart.

27   He then goes into self-celebration: "My commitment to free speech and condemnation of racism and homophobia are well known. . . .

28   "The university's code of conduct does not prohibit speech; it prohibits *actions.*"

29   Now watch this pitiable curve ball:

"Offense III [of the Brown code]—which deals with harass- 30 ment—prohibits inappropriate, abusive, threatening, or demean- ing actions based on race, religion, gender, handicap, ethnicity, national origin, or sexual orientation."

In the original press release, Gregorian underlined the word 31 *actions.* There, and in the letter to the *Times*—lest a dozing reader miss the point—Gregorian emphasizes that "The rules do not proscribe words, epithets, or slanders, they proscribe behavior." Behavior that "shows flagrant disrespect for the well-being of oth- ers or is unreasonably disruptive of the University community."

Consider the overbreadth and vagueness of these penalty- 32 bearing provisions. What are the definitions of "harassment," "inappropriate," "demeaning," "flagrant," "disrespect," "wellbe- ing," "unreasonably"?

Furthermore, with regard to Brown's termination of Doug Hann 33 with extreme prejudice, Gregorian is engaging in the crudest form of Orwellian newspeak. Hann was kicked out for *speech,* and only speech—not for *actions,* as Gregorian huffily insists. As for behavior, the prickly folks whose burning of the American flag was upheld by the Supreme Court were indeed engaged in behavior, but that behavior was based entirely on symbolic speech. So was Hann's. He didn't punch anybody or vandalize any property. He brayed.

Art Spitzer, legal director of the ACLU's National Capital 34 Area affiliate, wrote a personal letter to Gregorian:

"There is a very simple test for determining whether a per- 35 son is being punished for his actions or his speech. You just ask whether he would have received the same punishment if he had spoken different words while engaging in the same conduct.

"Thus, would your student have been expelled if he had got- 36 ten drunk and stood in the same courtyard at the same hour of the night, shouting at the same decibel level, 'Black is Beautiful!' 'Gay is Good!' or 'Go Brown! Beat Yale!' or even 'Nuke Baghdad! Kill Saddam!'?

"I am confident," Spitzer said, that "he would not have been 37 expelled for such 'actions.' If that is correct, it follows that *he was expelled for the unsavory content of his speech,* and not for his actions. I have no doubt that you can understand this distinction. (Emphasis added.)

38   "Now, you are certainly entitled to believe that it is appropriate to expel a student for the content of his speech when that
content is sufficiently offensive to the 'university community.' . . .

39   "If that is your position, why can't you deliver it forthrightly?
Then the university community can have an open debate about
which opinions it finds offensive, and ban them. Perhaps this
can be done once a year, so that the university's rules can keep
pace with the tenor of the times—after all, it wouldn't do to have
outmoded rules banning procommunist or blasphemous speech
still on the books, now that it's 1991. Then students and teachers
applying for admission or employment at Brown will know what
they are getting into.

40   "Your recent statements, denying the obvious, are just
hypocritical. . . ."

41   And what did the *New York Times*—in a stunningly fatuous
February 21 editorial—say of Vartan Gregorian's sending Doug
Hann into permanent exile? "A noble attempt both to govern and
teach."

42   The *Times* editorials should really be signed, so that the rest of
the editorial board isn't blamed for such embarrassments.

1991

How Much Hate to Tolerate

New York Times editorial (February 21, 1991)

1 Free speech and human relations seemed to collide last month at
Brown University when it expelled a student for racial and religious harassment. In fact, however, to judge by all that is publicly
known, the school walked a fine line with sensitivity toward its
complex mission.

2   One mission of a university is to send into the world gradu-
ates who are tolerant of many races, faiths and cultures. Another
mission is to teach the value of free expression and tolerance even
for hateful ideas. But should such tolerance cover racist, sexist or

homophobic speech that makes the learning environment intolerable for racial and religious minorities, women and other targets of abuse? Brown found a reasonable basis for saying, clearly, no.

Douglas Hann, white, a junior and a varsity football player, 3 had previously been disciplined for alcohol abuse and for racial insults against a black fellow student. Then, one evening last fall, he shouted racial insults in a university courtyard. A Jewish student who opened a dormitory window and called for quiet was answered with a religious insult. Later that evening Mr. Hann directed a racial insult at a black undergraduate.

The student-faculty discipline committee found him guilty 4 of three violations of student rules, including another count of alcohol abuse. Vartan Gregorian, the university's president, upheld the student's expulsion last month. He had a sound basis for doing so. If the facts are reported correctly, Mr. Hann crossed the line between merely hateful speech and hateful speech that directly confronted and insulted other undergraduates.

Some courts have found that public universities are bound 5 by the First Amendment's ban on state censorship and thus may not punish students for expressing politically incorrect or socially distasteful ideas. Brown, like other private schools, is less directly bound by the Constitution but committed to its precepts. It is trying to avoid censorship but draws a line between strong language and what the courts often call "fighting words."

In the adjacent Letters column today, Mr. Gregorian insists that 6 Brown does not punish unruly speech as such but will decide case-by-case whether a student has passed "the point at which speech becomes behavior" that flagrantly disregards the well-being of others or "subjects someone to abusive or demeaning actions."

That formula is a noble attempt both to govern and teach. It 7 offers a principled basis for disciplinary action against Mr. Hann for his direct, confrontational conduct.

The lines may not be so clearly drawn in other cases. There 8 may also be more of them in the present climate of evidently increasing student intolerance. But when bigots attack other students with ugly invective, universities, whether public or private, need not remain silent. Their presidents, like Mr. Gregorian, may denounce indecency and, in so doing, protect tolerance.

Brown Expulsion Not About Free Speech

New York Times letter to the editor (February 21, 1991)

To the Editor:

1   "Student at Brown Is Expelled Under a Rule Barring 'Hate Speech'" (news article, Feb. 12) suggests I have instituted "hate-speech" prohibitions at Brown University and that the expulsion of a student who shouted racial and homophobic epithets on campus last October is the first such in the nation based on restrictions of free speech. Brown University has never expelled anyone for free speech, nor will it ever do so.

2   My commitment to free speech and condemnation of racism and homophobia are well known. In April 1989, several students were subjected to a cowardly attack of racial and homophobic graffiti. The words and slogans scrawled anonymously on doors in one of our dormitories were vicious attacks threatening the well-being and security of Brown students.

3   I condemned that anonymous poisoning of our community and said I would prosecute vigorously and seek the expulsion of those who incite hatred or perpetuate such acts of vandalism. Nothing I said then or have done since should be construed as limiting anyone's freedom of speech, nor have I revised the university's code of conduct to that effect.

4   The university's code of conduct does not prohibit speech; it prohibits actions, and these include behavior that "shows flagrant disrespect for the well-being of others or is unreasonably disruptive of the university community."

5   Offense III, which deals with harassment, prohibits inappropriate, abusive, threatening or demeaning actions based on race, religion, gender, handicap, ethnicity, national origin or sexual orientation.

6   "The Tenets of Community Behavior," which outline community standards for acceptable behavior at Brown, have been read for more than 10 years by entering students, who agree in writing to abide by them.

7   The rules do not proscribe words, epithets or slanders; they proscribe behavior. The point at which speech becomes behavior

and the degree to which that behavior shows flagrant disrespect for the well-being of others (Offense II), subjects someone to abusive or demeaning actions (Offense III) or is related to drug or alcohol use (Offense IV) is determined by a hearing to consider the circumstances of each case. The student is entitled to an appeal, which includes review by a senior officer and a decision by the president.

I cannot and will not comment about any specific case. I 8 regret the release of any student's name in connection with a disciplinary hearing and the exposure any case may receive in *The Brown Herald*.

Freedom-of-speech questions lie at the heart of any academic 9 community. The very nature of the academic enterprise necessitates that universities remain partisans of heterodoxy, of a rich and full range of opinions, ideas and expression. Imposed orthodoxies of all sorts, including what is called "politically correct" speech, are anathema to our enterprise.

The university's most compelling challenge is to achieve a 10 balance between the right of its individual members to operate and speak freely, and fostering respect for and adherence to community values and standards of conduct.

VARTAN GREGORIAN
President, Brown University
Providence, R.I., Feb. 21, 1991

Shouting "Fire!"

Alan M. Dershowitz

When the Reverend Jerry Falwell learned that the Supreme Court 1 had reversed his $200,000 judgment against *Hustler* magazine for the emotional distress that he had suffered from an outrageous parody, his response was typical of those who seek to censor speech: "Just as no person may scream 'Fire!' in a crowded theater when there is no fire, and find cover under the First Amendment, likewise, no sleazy merchant like Larry Flynt should be able to use the First Amendment as an excuse for maliciously and dishonestly attacking public figures, as he has so often done."

2   Justice Oliver Wendell Holmes's classic example of unprotected speech—falsely shouting "Fire!" in a crowded theater—has been invoked so often, by so many people, in such diverse contexts, that it has become part of our national folk language. It has even appeared—most appropriately—in the theater: In Tom Stoppard's play *Rosecrantz and Guildenstern Are Dead* a character shouts at the audience, "Fire!" He then quickly explains: "It's all right—I'm demonstrating the misuse of free speech." Shouting "Fire!" in the theater may well be the only jurisprudential analogy that has assumed the status of a folk argument. A prominent historian recently characterized it as "the most brilliantly persuasive expression that ever came from Holmes's pen." But in spite of its hallowed position in both the jurisprudence of the First Amendment and the arsenal of political discourse, it is and was an inapt analogy, even in the context in which it was originally offered. It has lately become—despite, perhaps even because of, the frequency and promiscuousness of its invocation—little more than a caricature of logical argumentation.

3   The case that gave rise to the "Fire!"-in-a-crowded-theater analogy, *Schenck v. United States,* involved the prosecution of Charles Schenck, who was the general secretary of the Socialist Party in Philadelphia, and Elizabeth Baer, who was its recording secretary. In 1917 a jury found Schenck and Baer guilty of attempting to cause insubordination among soldiers who had been drafted to fight in the First World War. They and other party members had circulated leaflets urging draftees not to "submit to intimidation" by fighting in a war being conducted on behalf of "Wall Street's chosen few."

4   Schenck admitted, and the Court found, that the intent of the pamphlet's "impassioned language" was to "influence" drafters to resist the draft. Interestingly, however, Justice Holmes noted that nothing in the pamphlet suggested that the draftees should use unlawful or violent means to oppose conscription: "In form at least [the pamphlet] confined itself to peaceful measures, such

as petition for the repeal of the act" and an exhortation to exercise "your right to assert your opposition to the draft." Many of its most impassioned words were quoted directly from the Constitution.

Justice Holmes acknowledged that "in many places and in ordinary times the defendants, in saying all that was said in the circular, would have been within their constitutional rights." "But," he added, "the character of every act depends upon the circumstances in which it is done." And to illustrate that truism he went on to say:

> The most stringent protection of free speech would not protect a man in falsely shouting fire in a theater, and causing panic. It does not even protect a man from an injunction against uttering words that may have all the effect of force.

Justice Holmes then upheld the convictions in the context of a wartime draft, holding that the pamphlet created "a clear and present danger" of hindering the war effort while our soldiers were fighting for their lives and our liberty.

The example of shouting "Fire!" obviously bore little relationship to the facts of the *Schenck* case. The Schenck pamphlet contained a substantive political message. It urged its draftee readers to *think* about the message and then—if they so chose—to act on it in a lawful and nonviolent way. The man who shouts "Fire!" in a crowded theater is neither sending a political message nor inviting his listener to think about what he has said and decide what to do in a rational, calculated manner. On the contrary, the message is designed to force action *without* contemplation. The message "Fire!" is directed not to the mind and the conscience of the listener but, rather, to his adrenaline and his feet. It is a stimulus to immediate *action*, not thoughtful reflection. It is—as Justice Holmes recognized in his follow-up sentence—the functional equivalent of "uttering words that may have all the effect of force."

Indeed, in that respect the shout of "Fire!" is not even speech, in any meaningful sense of the term. It is a *clang* sound, the equivalent of setting off a nonverbal alarm. Had Justice Holmes been more honest about his example, he would have said that freedom of speech does not protect a kid who pulls a fire alarm in the absence of a fire. But that obviously would have been irrelevant to the case at hand. The proposition that pulling an alarm is not protected speech certainly leads to the conclusion that shouting the word "fire" is also not protected. But the core analogy is the nonverbal alarm, and the derivative example is the verbal shout. By cleverly substituting the derivative shout for the core alarm, Holmes made it possible to analogize one set of words to another—as he could not have done if he had begun with the self-evident proposition that setting off an alarm bell is not free speech.

9   The analogy is thus not only inapt but also insulting. Most Americans do not respond to political rhetoric with the same kind of automatic acceptance expected of schoolchildren responding to a fire drill. Not a single recipient of the Schenck pamphlet is known to have changed his mind after reading it. Indeed, one draftee, who appeared as a prosecution witness, was asked whether reading a pamphlet asserting that the draft law was unjust would make him "immediately decide that you must erase that law." Not surprisingly, he replied, "I do my own thinking." A theatergoer would probably not respond similarly if asked how he would react to a shout of "Fire!"

10   Another important reason why the analogy is inapt is that Holmes emphasizes the factual falsity of the shout "Fire!" The Schenck pamphlet, however, was not factually false. It contained political opinions and ideas about the causes of the war and about appropriate and lawful responses to the draft. As the Supreme Court recently reaffirmed (in *Falwell v. Hustler*), "The First Amendment recognizes no such thing as a 'false' idea." Nor does it recognize false opinions about the causes of or cures for war.

11   A closer analogy to the facts of the *Schenck* case might have been provided by a person's standing outside a theater, offering the patrons a leaflet advising them that in his opinion the theater was structurally unsafe, and urging them not to enter but to complain to the building inspectors. That analogy, however, would not have served Holmes's argument for punishing Schenck. Holmes needed an analogy that would appear relevant

to Schenck's political speech but that would invite the conclusion that censorship was appropriate.

Unsurprisingly, a war-weary nation—in the throes of a know-nothing hysteria over immigrant anarchists and socialists—welcomed the comparison between what was regarded as a seditious political pamphlet and a malicious shout of "Fire!" Ironically, the "Fire!" analogy is nearly all that survives from the *Schenck* case; the ruling itself is almost certainly not good law. Pamphlets of the kind that resulted in Schenck's imprisonment have been circulated with impunity during subsequent wars. [12]

Over the past several years I have assembled a collection of instances—cases, speeches, arguments—in which proponents of censorship have maintained that the expression at issue is "just like" or "equivalent to" falsely shouting "Fire!" in a crowded theater and ought to be banned, "just as" shouting "Fire!" ought to be banned. The analogy is generally invoked, often with self-satisfaction, as an absolute argument-stopper. It does, after all, claim the high authority of the great Justice Oliver Wendell Holmes. I have rarely heard it invoked in a convincing, or even particularly relevant, way. But that, too, can claim lineage from the great Holmes. [13]

Not unlike Falwell, with his silly comparison between shouting "Fire!" and publishing an offensive parody, courts and commentators have frequently invoked "Fire!" as an analogy to expression that is not an automatic stimulus to panic. A state supreme court held that "Holmes's aphorism . . . applies with equal force to pornography"—in particular to the exhibition of the movie *Carmen Baby* in a drive-in theater in close proximity to highways of a secondary boycott" to shouting "Fire!" because in both instances "speech and conduct are brigaded." In the famous Skokie case one of the judges argued that allowing Nazis to march through a city where a large number of Holocaust survivors live "just might fall into the same category as one's 'right' to cry fire in a crowded theater." [14]

Outside court the analogies become even more badly stretched. A spokesperson for the New Jersey Sports and Exposition Authority complained that newspaper reports to the effect that [15] a large number of football players had contracted cancer after playing in the Meadowlands—a stadium atop a landfill—were the "journalistic equivalent of shouting fire in a crowded theater." An insect researcher acknowledged that his prediction that a certain amusement park might become roach-infested "may be tantamount to shouting fire in a crowded theater." The philosopher Sidney Hook, in a letter to the *New York Times* bemoaning a Supreme Court decision that required a plaintiff in a defamation action to prove that the offending statement was actually false, argued that the First Amendment does not give the press carte blanche to accuse innocent persons "any more than the First Amendment protects the right of someone falsely to shout fire in a crowded theater."

16   Some close analogies to shouting "Fire!" or setting off an alarm are, of course, available: Calling in a false bomb threat; dialing 911 and falsely describing an emergency; making a loud, gun-like sound in the presence of the President; setting off a voice-activated sprinkler system by falsely shouting "Fire!" In one case in which the "Fire!" analogy was directly to the point, a creative defendant tried to get around it. The case involved a man who calmly advised an airline clerk that he was "only here to hijack the plane." He was charged, in effect, with shouting "Fire!" in a crowded theater, and his rejected defense—as quoted by the court—was as follows: "If we built fire-proof theaters and let people know about this, then the shouting of 'Fire!' would not cause panic."

17   Here are some more-distant but still related examples: The recent incident of the police slaying in which some members of an onlooking crowd urged a mentally ill vagrant who had taken an officer's gun to shoot the officer; the screaming of racial epithets during a tense confrontation; shouting down a speaker and preventing him from continuing his speech.

18   Analogies are, by their nature, matters of degree. Some are closer to the core example than others. But any attempt to analogize political ideas in a pamphlet, ugly parody in a magazine, offensive movies in a theater, controversial newspaper articles, or any of the other expressions and actions catalogued above to the very different act of shouting "Fire!" in a crowded theater is either self-deceptive or self-serving.

The government does, of course, have some arguably legiti- 19
mate bases for suppressing speech which bear no relationship to
shouting "Fire!" It may ban the publication of nuclear-weapon
codes, of information about troop movements, and of the identity
of undercover agents. It may criminalize extortion threats and
conspiratorial agreements. These expressions may lead directly
to serious harm, but the mechanisms of causation are very different from those at work when an alarm is sounded. One may also
argue—less persuasively, in my view—against protecting certain
forms of public obscenity and defamatory statements. Here, too,
the mechanisms of causation are very different. None of these
exceptions to the First Amendment's exhortation that the government "shall make no law . . . abridging the freedom of speech, or
of the press" is anything like falsely shouting "Fire!" in a crowded
theater; they all must be justified on other grounds.

A comedian once told his audience, during a stand-up rou- 20
tine, about the time he was standing around a fire with a crowd
of people and got in trouble for yelling "Theater, theater!" That,
I think, is about as clever and productive a use as anyone has
ever made of Holmes's flawed analogy.

1989

Global Warming Is Eroding Glacial Ice

Andrew C. Revkin

The recent melting of mountain glaciers indicates that contem- 1
porary global warming is largely the result of human activity.
Although natural climatic changes are partly responsible for the
rise in average temperatures over the past century, the current
rate of glacial erosion suggests that higher levels of greenhouse
gases—resulting from pollution—are contributing significantly
to global warming. Glacial melting could lead to damaging

flash floods in some locales. Other regions that depend on melting snow for hydroelectric power could run low on water after glaciers have disappeared, requiring more communities to use pollution-creating oil or coal for energy—which in turn would produce more greenhouse gases and more global warming.

2   The icecap atop Mount Kilimanjaro, which for thousands of years has floated like a cool beacon over the shimmering plain of Tanzania, is retreating at such a pace that it will disappear in less than 15 years, according to new studies.

3   The vanishing of the seemingly perpetual snows of Kilimanjaro that inspired Ernest Hemingway, echoed by similar trends on ice-capped peaks from Peru to Tibet, is one of the clearest signs that a global warming trend in the last 50 years may have exceeded typical climate shifts and is at least partly caused by gases released by human activities, a variety of scientists say.

4   Measurements taken over a year-long period on Kilimanjaro show that its glaciers are not only retreating but also rapidly thinning, with one spot having lost a yard of thickness between February 2000 and February 2001, said Dr. Lonnie G. Thompson, a senior research scientist at the Byrd Polar Research Center of Ohio State University.

5   Altogether, he said, the mountain has lost 82 percent of the icecap it had when it was first carefully surveyed, in 1912.

6   Given that the retreat started a century ago, Dr. Thompson said, it is likely that some natural changes were affecting the glacier before it felt any effect from the large, recent rise in carbon dioxide and other heat-trapping greenhouse gases from smokestacks and tailpipes. And, he noted, glaciers have grown and retreated in pulses for tens of thousands of years.

7   But the pace of change measured now goes beyond anything in recent centuries.

8   "There may be a natural part of it, but there's something else being superimposed on top of it," Dr. Thompson said. "And it matches so many other lines of evidence of warming. Whether you're talking about bore-hole temperatures, shrinking Arctic sea ice, or glaciers, they're telling the same story."

GLACIAL EROSION

Dr. Thompson presented the fresh data in February 2001 at the 9
annual meeting of the American Association for the Advancement
of Science in San Francisco.

Other recent reports of changes under way in the natural 10
world, like gaps in sea ice at the North Pole or shifts in animal
populations, can still be ascribed to other factors, many scientists
say, but many add that having such a rapid erosion of glaciers in
so many places is harder to explain except by global warming.

The retreat of mountain glaciers has been seen from Montana 11
to Mount Everest to the Swiss Alps. In the Alps, scientists have
estimated that by 2025 glaciers will have lost 90 percent of the
volume of ice that was there a century ago. (Only Scandinavia
seems to be bucking the trend, apparently because shifting storm
tracks in Europe are dumping more snow there.)

But the melting is generally quickest in and near the tropics, 12
Dr. Thompson said, with some ancient glaciers in the Andes—
and the ice on Kilimanjaro—melting fastest of all.

Separate studies of air temperature in the tropics, made 13
using high-flying balloons, have shown a steady rise of about
15 feet a year in the altitude at which air routinely stays below
the freezing point. Dr. Thompson said that other changes could
also be contributing to the glacial shrinkage, but the rising warm
zone is probably the biggest influence.

Trying to stay ahead of the widespread melting, Dr. 14
Thompson and a team of scientists have been hurriedly traveling around the tropics to extract cores of ice from a variety of
glaciers containing a record of thousands of years of climate
shifts. The data may help predict future trends.

The four-inch-thick ice cylinders are being stored in a deep- 15
frozen archive at Ohio State, he said, so that as new technologies
are developed for reading chemical clues in bubbles and water in
ancient ice, there will still be something to examine.

The sad fact, he said, is that in a matter of years, anyone want- 16
ing to study the glaciers of Africa or Peru will probably have to
travel to Columbus, Ohio, to do so.

17   Dr. Richard B. Alley, a professor of geosciences at Pennsylvania State University, said the melting trend and the link—at least partly—to human influence is "depressing," not only because of the loss of data but also because of the remarkable changes under way to such familiar landscapes.

18   "What is a snowcap worth to us?" he said. "I don't know about you, but I like the snows of Kilimanjaro."

THREATENED WATER SUPPLIES

19   The accelerating loss of mountain glaciers is also described in a scientific report on the impact of global warming, which [was] released in February 2001 in Geneva by the Intergovernmental Panel on Climate Change, an influential network of scientists advising world governments under the auspices of the United Nations. The melting is likely to threaten water supplies in places like Peru and Nepal, the report says, and could also lead to devastating flash floods.

20   Kilimanjaro, the highest point in Africa, may provide the most vivid image of the change in glaciers, but, Dr. Thompson said, the rate of retreat is far faster along the spine of the Andes, and the consequences more significant. For 25 years, he has been tracking a particular Peruvian glacier, Qori Kalis, where the pace of shrinkage has accelerated enormously just since 1998.

21   From 1998 to 2000, the glacier pulled back 508 feet a year, he said. "That's 33 times faster than the rate in the first measurement period," he said, referring to a study from 1963 to 1978.

22   In the short run, this means the hydroelectric dams and reservoirs downstream will be flush with water, he said, but in the long run the source will run dry.

23   "The whole country right now, for its hydropower, is cashing in on a bank account that was built up over thousands of years but isn't being replenished," he said.

24   Once that is gone, he added, chances are that the communities will have to turn to oil or coal for power, adding even more greenhouse gases to the air.

The changes in the character of Kilimanjaro are registering 25 beyond the ranks of climate scientists. People in the tourism business around the mountain and surrounding national park are worried that visitors will no longer be drawn to the peak once it has lost its glimmering cap.

Dr. Douglas R. Hardy, a geologist at the University of 26 Massachusetts, returned from Kilimanjaro in February 2001 with the first yearlong record of weather data collected by a probe placed near the summit.

Just before he left, he had a long conversation with the chief 27 ranger of Kilimanjaro National Park, who expressed deep concern about the trend. "That mountain is the most mystical, magical draw to people's imagination," Dr. Hardy said. "Once the ice disappears, it's going to be a very different place."

And the melting continues. When Dr. Hardy climbed the 28 mountain to retrieve the data, he discovered that the weather instruments, erected on a tall pole, had fallen over because the ice around the base was gone.

2001

Cold Comfort for 'Global Warming'

Philip Stott

Last week's dramatic demise of the Larsen B ice shelf in Antarctica 1 has been embraced by environmentalists and commentators who warn of human-induced "global warming." After all, the ice shelf was 200 meters thick, with a surface area three times the size of Hong Kong. Around 500 billion tons of ice collapsed in less than a month. How could President Bush ignore such evidence of our guilt with regard to climate change?

An ice shelf is a floating extension of the continental ice 2 that covers the landmass of Antarctica. Larsen B was one of five shelves that have been monitored by scientists. The U.S.-based

National Snow and Ice Data Center described its break-up as "the largest single event in a series of retreats by ice shelves in the peninsula over the last 30 years."

3   One worry can be dismissed immediately: Having been a shelf—a floating part of an ice sheet, rather than over land—it does not raise sea levels upon melting. Yet the collapse has proved to be a perfect natural disaster for the "Apocalypse Now" school of journalism. It is now perfectly clear that we are all doomed and that this is the wake-up call for urgent action on greenhouse gas emissions, automobiles, industry, and virtually everything else to do with economic growth.

4   Unfortunately, the story isn't quite so straightforward. Antarctica illustrates the complexities behind understanding climate change, and it provides little support for a simplistic myth of human-induced "global warming." In fact this scare is reminiscent of a much-hyped New York Times story last year that "leads" of open water in ice fields near the North Pole filled cruise passengers with a "sense of alarm" about impending climate disasters. But icebreakers are always searching for "leads" to make their way through the ice, and after a long summer of 24-hour days it is not unusual to find them all over the place, especially after strong winds break up the winter ice. Sorry, the North Pole isn't disappearing—and neither is the South Pole.

5   Research on the West Antarctic Ice Sheet has shown precisely the opposite trend seen at Larsen B, namely that this ice sheet may be getting thicker, not thinner. Most scientists think that the sheet has probably been retreating, spasmodically, for around the last 10,000 years, but instead of the rate accelerating in recent years, it now appears to have halted its retreat. There is evidence that the ice sheet in the Ross Sea area is growing by as much as 26.8 gigatons per year, particularly on a part of the ice sheet known as Stream C.

6   This demonstrates the innate complexity of Antarctica as a continent. In reality, it has many "climates," and many geomorphological and glaciological regimes. It does not respond to change, whatever the direction, in a single, unitary fashion. Geomorphological and ecological trends are thus very difficult to interpret in a linear way.

7   One trend has been toward a colder climate. Over the last 50 years, the temperatures in the interior appear to have

been falling. University of Illinois researchers have reported, in Nature, on temperature records covering a broad area of Antarctica. Their measurements show "a net cooling on the Antarctic continent between 1966 and 2000." Indeed, some regions, like the McMurdo Dry Valleys, the largest ice-free area, appear to have cooled between 1986 and 1999 by as much as two degrees centigrade per decade. As the researchers wryly comment, "Continental Antarctic cooling, especially the seasonality of cooling, poses challenges to models of climate and ecosystem change."

At the same time that parts of the continent are cooling, it's 8 hardly surprising to see some ice melting. We are currently emerging—granted in a somewhat jerky fashion—out of the Little Ice Age that ended around 1880. It's to be expected that some parts of Antarctica like Larsen B are retreating. Yet we seem to be shocked at this perfectly natural event. When will we recognize the basic truth that change, both evolutionary and catastrophic, is the norm on our ever-restless planet?

Extreme environmentalists and sensationalist journalists pre- 9 tend that every environmental event is of our own making. If only. We don't have that much control over Mother Nature. While we've been busy gabbing about global warming, the planet may be moving in the opposite direction.

Our current interglacial period is already 10,000 years old. No 10 interglacial period during the last half-million years has persisted for more than 12,000 years. Most have had life spans of only 10,000 years or less. Statistically, therefore, we are due to slither into the next glacial period.

Despite a short-term rise in temperature of around 0.6 11 degrees centigrade over the last 150 years, the long-term temperature trend remains, overall, one of cooling. It may not be too long, therefore, before we see the ice spreading again. At worst, the emission of greenhouse gases is only likely to produce a super interglacial period; at worst, withdrawing gases might help to speed the descent into the next glacial period. And what would you prefer, a warmer or a colder world?

2002

PERSUASION

A Modest Proposal

Jonathan Swift

1   It is a melancholy object to those who walk through this great town or travel in the country, when they see the streets, the roads, and cabin doors, crowded with beggars of the female sex, followed by three, four, or six children, all in rags and importuning every passenger for an alms. These mothers, instead of being able to work for their honest livelihood, are forced to employ all their time in strolling to beg sustenance for their helpless infants: Who as they grow up either turn thieves for want of work, or leave their dear native country to fight for the Pretender in Spain, or sell themselves to the Barbadoes.

2   I think it is agreed by all parties that this prodigious number of children in the arms, or on the backs, or at the heels of their mothers, and frequently of their fathers, is in the present deplorable state of the kingdom a very great additional grievance; and, therefore, whoever could find out a fair, cheap, and easy method of making these children sound, useful members of the commonwealth, would deserve so well of the public as to have his statue set up for a preserver of the nation.

3   But my intention is very far from being confined to provide only for the children of professed beggars; it is of a much greater extent, and shall take in the whole number of infants at a certain age who are born of parents in effect as little able to support them as those who demand our charity in the streets.

4   As to my own part, having turned my thoughts for many years upon this important subject, and maturely weighed the several schemes of our projectors, I have always found them grossly mistaken in their computation. It is true, a child just dropped from its dam may be supported by her milk for a solar year, with little other

nourishment; at most not above the value of 2s., which the mother may certainly get, or the value in scraps, by her lawful occupation of begging; and it is exactly at one year old that I propose to provide for them in such a manner as instead of being a charge upon their parents or the parish, or wanting food and raiment for the rest of their lives, they shall on the contrary contribute to the feeding, and partly to the clothing, of many thousands.

There is likewise another great advantage in my scheme, that 5 it will prevent those voluntary abortions, and that horrid practice of women murdering their bastard children, alas! too frequent among us! sacrificing the poor innocent babes I doubt more to avoid the expense than the shame, which would move tears and pity in the most savage and inhuman breast.

The number of souls in this kingdom being usually reckoned 6 one million and a half, of these I calculate there may be about 200,000 couples whose wives are breeders; from which number I subtract 30,000 couples who are able to maintain their own children (although I apprehend there cannot be so many, under the present distress of the kingdom); but this being granted, there will remain 170,000 breeders. I again subtract 50,000 for those women who miscarry, or whose children die by accident or disease within the year. There only remain 120,000 children of poor parents annually born. The question therefore is, how this number shall be reared and provided for? which, as I have already said, under the present situation of affairs, is utterly impossible by all the methods hitherto proposed. For we can neither employ them in handicraft or agriculture; we neither build houses (I mean live in the country) nor cultivate land; they can very seldom pick up a livelihood by stealing, till they arrive at six years old, except where they are of towardly parts; although I confess they learn the rudiments much earlier; during which time they can, however, be properly looked upon only as probationers; as I have been informed by a principal gentleman in the county of Cavan, who protested to me that he never knew above one or two instances under the age of six, even in a part of the kingdom so renowned for the quickest proficiency in that art.

I am assured by our merchants, that a boy or a girl before 7 twelve years old is no saleable commodity; and even when they come to this age they will not yield above 31. or 31.2s. 6d. at most on the exchange; which cannot turn to account either to the parents or kingdom, the charge of nutriment and rags having been at least four times that value.

8   I shall now therefore humbly propose my own thoughts, which I hope will not be liable to the least objection.

9   I have been assured by a very knowing American of my acquaintance in London, that a young healthy child well nursed is at a year old a most delicious, nourishing, and wholesome food, whether stewed, roasted, baked, or broiled; and I make no doubt that it will equally serve in a fricassee or a ragout.

10   I do therefore humbly offer it to public consideration that of the 120,000 children already computed, 20,000 may be reserved for breed, whereof only one-fourth part to be males; which is more than we allow to sheep, black cattle, or swine; and my reason is, that these children are seldom the fruits of marriage, a circumstance not much regarded by our savages; therefore one male will be sufficient to serve four females. That the remaining 100,000 may, at a year old, be offered in sale to the persons of quality and fortune through the kingdom; always advising the mother to let them suck plentifully in the last month, so as to render them plump and fat for a good table. A child will make two dishes at an entertainment for friends; and when the family dines alone, the fore or hind quarter will make a reasonable dish, and seasoned with a little pepper or salt will be very good boiled on the fourth day, especially in winter.

11   I have reckoned upon a medium that a child just born will weigh 12 pounds, and in a solar year, if tolerably nursed, will increase to 28 pounds.

12   I grant this food will be somewhat dear, and therefore very proper for landlords, who, as they have already devoured most of the parents, seem to have the best title to the children.

13   Infant's flesh will be in season throughout the year, but more plentiful in March, and a little before and after; for we are told by a grave author, an eminent French physician, that fish being a prolific diet, there are more children born in Roman Catholic countries about nine months after Lent than at any other season; therefore, reckoning a year after Lent, the markets will be more

glutted than usual, because the number of popish infants is at least three to one in this kingdom: and therefore it will have one other collateral advantage, by lessening the number of papists among us.

I have already computed the charge of nursing a beggar's 14 child (in which list I reckon all cottagers, laborers, and four-fifths of the farmers) to be about 2s. per annum, rags included; and I believe no gentleman would repine to give 10s. for the carcass of a good fat child, which, as I have said, will make four dishes of excellent nutritive meat, when he has only some particular friend or his own family to dine with him. Thus the squire will learn to be a good landlord, and grow popular among the tenants; the mother will have 8s. net profit, and be fit for work till she produces another child.

Those who are more thrifty (as I must confess the times 15 require) may flay the carcass; the skin of which artificially dressed will make admirable gloves for ladies, and summer boots for fine gentlemen.

As to our city of Dublin, shambles may be appointed for this 16 purpose in the most convenient parts of it, and butchers we may be assured will not be wanting: although I rather recommend buying the children alive, and dressing them hot from the knife as we do roasting pigs.

A very worthy person, a true lover of his country, and whose 17 virtues I highly esteem, was lately pleased in discoursing on this matter to offer a refinement upon my scheme. He said that many gentlemen of this kingdom, having of late destroyed their deer, he conceived that the want of venison might be well supplied by the bodies of young lads and maidens, not exceeding fourteen years of age nor under twelve; so great a number of both sexes in every country being now ready to starve for want of work and service; and these to be disposed of by their parents, if alive, or otherwise by their nearest relations. But with due deference to so excellent a friend and so deserving a patriot, I cannot be altogether in his sentiments; for as to the males, my American acquaintance assured me from frequent experience that their flesh was generally tough and lean, like that of our schoolboys by continual exercise, and their taste disagreeable; and to fatten them would not answer the charge. Then as to the females, it would, I think, with humble submission be a loss to the public, because they soon would become breeders themselves; and besides, it is not improbable that some scrupulous people might be apt to censure such a practice (although indeed very unjustly), as a little bordering upon cruelty; which, I confess, has always been with me the strongest objection against any project, how well so-ever intended.

18   But in order to justify my friend, he confessed that this expedient was put into his head by the famous Psalmanazar, a native of the island Formosa, who came from thence to London about twenty years ago: And in conversation told my friend, that in his country when any young person happened to be put to death, the executioner sold the carcass to persons of quality as a prime dainty; and that in his time the body of a plump girl of fifteen, who was crucified for an attempt to poison the emperor, was sold to his imperial majesty's prime minister of state, and other great mandarins of the court, in joints from the gibbet, at 400 crowns. Neither indeed can I deny, that if the same use were made of several plump young girls in this town, who without one single groat to their fortunes cannot stir without a chair, and appear at the playhouse and assemblies in foreign fineries which they never will pay for, the kingdom would not be the worse.

19   Some persons of a desponding spirit are in great concern about that vast number of poor people, who are aged, diseased, or maimed, and I have been desired to employ my thoughts what course may be taken to ease the nation of so grievous an encumbrance. But I am not in the least pain upon that matter, because it is very well known that they are every day dying and rotting by cold and famine, and filth and vermin, as fast as can be reasonably expected. And as to the young laborers, they are now in as hopeful a condition: they cannot get work, and consequently pine away for want of nourishment, to a degree that if at any time they are accidentally hired to common labor, they have not strength to perform it; and thus the country and themselves are happily delivered from the evils to come.

20   I have too long digressed, and therefore shall return to my subject. I think the advantages by the proposal which I have made are obvious and many, as well as of the highest importance.

For first, as I have already observed, it would greatly lessen [21] the number of papists, with whom we are yearly overrun, being the principal breeders of the nation as well as our most dangerous enemies; and who stay at home on purpose to deliver the kingdom to the Pretender, hoping to take their advantage by the absence of so many good Protestants, who have chosen rather to leave their country than stay at home and pay tithes against their conscience to an Episcopal curate.

Secondly, the poor tenants will have something valuable of [22] their own, which by law may be made liable to distress and help to pay their landlord's rent, their corn and cattle being already seized, and money a thing unknown.

Thirdly, whereas the maintenance of 100,000 children from [23] two years old and upward, cannot be computed at less than 10s. apiece per annum, the nation's stock will be thereby increased £50,000 per annum, beside the profit of a new dish introduced to the tables of all gentlemen of fortune in the kingdom who have any refinement in taste. And the money will circulate among ourselves, the goods being entirely of our own growth and manufacture.

Fourthly, the constant breeders beside the gain of 8s. sterling [24] per annum by the sale of their children, will be rid of the charge of maintaining them after the first year.

Fifthly, this food would likewise bring great custom to taverns, [25] where the vintners will certainly be so prudent as to procure the best recipes for dressing it to perfection, and consequently have their houses frequented by all the fine gentlemen, who justly value themselves upon their knowledge in good eating; and a skilful cook who understands how to oblige his guests, will contrive to make it as expensive as they please.

Sixthly, this would be a great inducement to marriage, which [26] all wise nations have either encouraged by rewards or enforced by laws and penalties. It would increase the care and tenderness of mothers toward their children, when they were sure of a settlement for life to the poor babes, provided in some sort by the public, to their annual profit instead of expense. We should see an honest emulation among the married women, which of them would bring the fattest child to the market. Men would become as fond of their wives during the time of their pregnancy as they are now of their mares in foal, their cows in calf, their sows when they are ready to farrow; nor offer to beat or kick them (as is too frequent a practice) for fear of a miscarriage.

27   Many other advantages might be enumerated. For instance, the addition of some thousand carcasses in our exportation of barreled beef, the propagation of swine's flesh, and improvement in the art of making good bacon, so much wanted among us by the great destruction of pigs, too frequent at our table; which are no way comparable in taste or magnificence to a well-grown, fat, yearling child, which roasted whole will make a considerable figure at a lord mayor's feast or any other public entertainment. But this and many others I omit, being studious of brevity.

28   Supposing that 1,000 families in this city would be constant customers for infants' flesh, besides others who might have it at merry-meetings, particularly at weddings and christenings, I compute that Dublin would take off annually about 20,000 carcasses; and the rest of the kingdom (where probably they will be sold somewhat cheaper) the remaining 80,000.

I can think of no one objection that will possibly be raised against this proposal, unless it should be urged that the number of people will be thereby much lessened in the kingdom. This I freely own, and it was indeed one principal design in offering it to the world. I desire the reader will observe, that I calculate my remedy for this one individual kingdom of Ireland and for no other than ever was, is, or I think ever can be upon Earth. Therefore let no man talk to me of other expedients: Of taxing our absentees at 5s. a pound: Of using neither clothes nor household furniture except what is of our own growth and manufacture: Of utterly rejecting the materials and instruments that promote foreign luxury: Of curing the expensiveness of pride, vanity, idleness, and gaming in our women: Of introducing a vein of parsimony, prudence, and temperance: Of learning to love our country, in the want of which we differ even from Laplander and the inhabitants of Topinamboo: Of quitting our animosities and factions, nor acting any longer like the Jews, who were murdering one another at the very moment their city was taken: Of being a little cautious not to sell our country and conscience for nothing:

Of teaching landlords to have at least one degree of mercy toward their tenants: Lastly, of putting a spirit of honesty, industry, and skill into our shopkeepers; who, if a resolution could now be taken to buy only our native goods, would immediately unite to cheat and exact upon us in the price, the measure, and the goodness, nor could ever yet be brought to make one fair proposal of just dealing, though often and earnestly invited to it.

Therefore I repeat, let no man talk to me of these and the like 30 expedients, till he has at least some glimpse of hope that there will be ever some hearty and sincere attempt to put them in practice.

But as to myself, having been wearied out for many years 31 with offering vain, idle, visionary thoughts, and at length utterly despairing of success, I fortunately fell upon this proposal; which, as it is wholly new, so it has something solid and real, of no expense and little trouble, full in our own power, and whereby we can incur no danger in disobliging England. For this kind of commodity will not bear exportation, the flesh being of too tender a consistence to admit a long continuance in salt, although perhaps I could name a country which would be glad to eat up our whole nation without it.

After all, I am not so violently bent upon my own opinion as to 32 reject any offer proposed by wise men, which shall be found equally innocent, cheap, easy, and effectual. But before something of that kind shall be advanced in contradiction to my scheme, and offering a better, I desire the author or authors will be pleased maturely to consider two points. First, as things now stand, how they will be able to find food and raiment for 100,000 useless mouths and backs. And secondly, there being a round million of creatures in human figure throughout this kingdom, whose subsistence put into a common stock would leave them in debt 2,000,000*l.* sterling, adding those who are beggars by profession to the bulk of farmers, cottagers, and laborers, with the wives and children who are beggars in effect; I desire those politicians who dislike my overture, and may perhaps be so bold as to attempt an answer, that they will first ask the parents of these mortals, whether they would not at this day think it a great happiness to have been sold for food at a year old in the manner I prescribe, and thereby have avoided such a perpetual scene of misfortunes as they have since gone through by the oppression of landlords, the impossibility of paying rent without money or trade, the want of common sustenance, with neither house nor clothes to cover them from the inclemencies of the weather, and the most inevitable prospect of entailing the like or greater miseries upon their breed for ever.

33   I profess, in the sincerity of my heart, that I have not the least personal interest in endeavoring to promote this necessary work, having no other motive than the public good of my country, by advancing our trade, providing for infants, relieving the poor, and giving some pleasure to the rich. I have no children by which I can propose to get a single penny; the youngest being nine years old, and my wife past childbearing.

1714

I Have a Dream

Martin Luther King, Jr.

1   Five score years ago, a great American, in whose symbolic shadow we stand, signed the Emancipation Proclamation. This momentous decree came as a great beacon light of hope to millions of Negro slaves who had been seared in the flames of withering injustice. It came as a joyous daybreak to end the long night of captivity.

2   But one hundred years later, we must face the tragic fact that the Negro is still not free. One hundred years later, the life of the Negro is still sadly crippled by the manacles of segregation and the chains of discrimination. One hundred years later, the Negro lives on a lonely island of poverty in the midst of a vast ocean of material prosperity. One hundred years later, the Negro is still languishing in the corners of American society and finds himself an exile in his own land. So we have come here today to dramatize an appalling condition.

3   In a sense we have come to our nation's capital to cash a check. When the architects of our republic wrote the magnificent words of

the Constitution and the Declaration of Independence, they were signing a promissory note to which every American was to fall heir. This note was a promise that all men would be guaranteed the unalienable rights of life, liberty, and the pursuit of happiness.

It is obvious today that America has defaulted on this prom- 4 issory note insofar as her citizens of color are concerned. Instead of honoring this sacred obligation, America has given the Negro people a bad check; a check which has come back marked "insufficient funds." But we refuse to believe that the bank of justice is bankrupt. We refuse to believe that there are insufficient funds in the great vaults of opportunity of this nation. So we have come to cash this check—a check that will give us upon demand the riches of freedom and the security of justice. We have also come to this hallowed spot to remind America of the fierce urgency of *now.* This is no time to engage in the luxury of cooling off or to take the tranquilizing drugs of gradualism. *Now* is the time to make real the promises of Democracy. *Now* is the time to rise from the dark and desolate valley of segregation to the sunlit path of racial justice. *Now* is the time to open the doors of opportunity to all of God's children. *Now* is the time to lift our nation from the quicksands of racial injustice to the solid rock of brotherhood.

It would be fatal for the nation to overlook the urgency of the 5 moment and to underestimate the determination of the Negro. This sweltering summer of the Negro's legitimate discontent will not pass until there is an invigorating autumn of freedom and equality. 1963 is not an end, but a beginning. Those who hope that the Negro needed to blow off steam and will now be content will have a rude awakening if the nation returns to business as usual. There will be neither rest nor tranquility in America until the Negro is granted his citizenship rights. The whirlwinds of revolt will continue to shake the foundations of our nation until the bright day of justice emerges.

But there is something that I must say to my people who stand 6 on the warm threshold which leads into the palace of justice. In the process of gaining our rightful place we must not be guilty of wrongful deeds. Let us not seek to satisfy our thirst for freedom by drinking from the cup of bitterness and hatred. We must forever conduct our struggle on the high plane of dignity and discipline.

We must not allow our creative protest to degenerate into physical violence. Again and again we must rise to the majestic heights of meeting physical force with soul force. The marvelous new militancy which has engulfed the Negro community must not lead us to a distrust of all white people, for many of our white brothers, as evidenced by their presence here today, have come to realize that their destiny is tied up with our destiny and their freedom is inextricably bound to our freedom. We cannot walk alone.

7   And as we walk, we must make the pledge that we shall march ahead. We cannot turn back. There are those who are asking the devotees of civil rights, "When will you be satisfied?" We can never be satisfied as long as the Negro is the victim of the unspeakable horrors of police brutality. We can never be satisfied as long as our bodies, heavy with the fatigue of travel, cannot gain lodging in the motels of the highways and the hotels of the cities. We cannot be satisfied as long as the Negro's basic mobility is from a smaller ghetto to a larger one. We can never be satisfied as long as a Negro in Mississippi cannot vote and a Negro in New York believes he has nothing for which to vote. No, no, we are not satisfied, and we will not be satisfied until justice rolls down like waters and righteousness like a mighty stream.

8   I am not unmindful that some of you have come here out of great trials and tribulations. Some of you have come fresh from narrow jail cells. Some of you have come from areas where your quest for freedom left you battered by the storms of persecution and staggered by the winds of police brutality. You have been the veterans of creative suffering. Continue to work with the faith that unearned suffering is redemptive.

9   Go back to Mississippi, go back to Alabama, go back to South Carolina, go back to Georgia, go back to Louisiana, go back to the slums and ghettos of our northern cities, knowing that somehow this situation can and will be changed. Let us not wallow in the valley of despair.

10   I say to you today, my friends, that in spite of the difficulties and frustrations of the moment I still have a dream. It is a dream deeply rooted in the American dream.

11   I have a dream that one day this nation will rise up and live out the true meaning of its creed: "We hold these truths to be self-evident; that all men are created equal."

I have a dream that one day on the red hills of Georgia the 12
sons of former slaves and the sons of former slaveowners will be
able to sit down together at the table of brotherhood.

I have a dream that one day even the state of Mississippi, a 13
desert state sweltering with the heat of injustice and oppression,
will be transformed into an oasis of freedom and justice.

I have a dream that my four little children will one day live in 14
a nation where they will not be judged by the color of their skin
but by the content of their character.

I have a dream today. 15

I have a dream that one day the state of Alabama, whose gov- 16
ernor's lips are presently dripping with the words of interposition
and nullification, will be transformed into a situation where little
black boys and black girls will be able to join hands with little white
boys and white girls and walk together as sisters and brothers.

I have a dream today. 17

I have a dream that one day every valley shall be exalted, every 18
hill and mountain shall be made low, the rough places will be made
plain, and the crooked places will be made straight, and the glory
of the Lord shall be revealed, and all flesh shall see it together.

This is our hope. This is the faith with which I return to the 19
South. With this faith we will be able to hew out of the mountain of despair a stone of hope. With this faith we will be able
to transform the jangling discords of our nation into a beautiful symphony of brotherhood. With this faith we will be able to
work together, to pray together, to struggle together, to go to jail
together, to stand up for freedom together, knowing that we will
be free one day.

This will be the day when all of God's children will be able to 20
sing with new meaning

> My country, 'tis of thee,
> Sweet land of liberty,
> > Of thee I sing:
> Land where my fathers died,
> Land of the pilgrims' pride,
> From every mountain-side
> > Let freedom ring.

21 And if America is to be a great nation this must become true. So let freedom ring from the prodigious hilltops of New Hampshire. Let freedom ring from the mighty mountains of New York. Let freedom ring from the heightening Alleghenies of Pennsylvania!

22 Let freedom ring from the snowcapped Rockies of Colorado!

23 Let freedom ring from the curvaceous peaks of California!

24 But not only that; let freedom ring from Stone Mountain of Georgia!

25 Let freedom ring from Lookout Mountain of Tennessee!

26 Let freedom ring from every hill and molehill of Mississippi. From every mountainside, let freedom ring.

27 When we let freedom ring, when we let it ring from every village and every hamlet, from every state and every city, we will be able to speed up that day when all of God's children, black men and white men, Jews and Gentiles, Protestants and Catholics, will be able to join hands and sing in the words of the old Negro spiritual, "Free at last! free at last! thank God almighty, we are free at last!"

1963

To Any Would-Be Terrorists

Naomi Shihab Nye

1 I am sorry I have to call you that, but I don't know how else to get your attention. I hate that word. Do you know how hard some of us have worked to get rid of that word, to deny its instant connection to the Middle East? And now look. Look what extra work we have. Not only did your colleagues kill thousands of innocent, international people in those buildings and scar their families forever, they wounded a huge community of people in the Middle East, in the United States, and all over the world. If that's what

they wanted to do, please know the mission was a terrible success, and you can stop now.

Because I feel a little closer to you than many Americans 2 could possibly feel, or ever want to feel, I insist that you listen to me. Sit down and listen. I know what kinds of foods you like. I would feed them to you if you were right here, because it is very very important that you listen. I am humble in my country's pain and I am furious.

My Palestinian father became a refugee in 1948. He came to 3 the United States as a college student. He is 74 years old now and still homesick. He has planted fig trees. He has invited all the Ethiopians in his neighborhood to fill their little paper sacks with his figs. He has written columns and stories saying the Arabs are not terrorists, he has worked all his life to defy that word. Arabs are businessmen and students and kind neighbors. There is no one like him and there are thousands like him—gentle Arab daddies who make everyone laugh around the dinner table, who have a hard time with headlines, who stand outside in the evenings with their hands in their pockets staring toward the far horizon.

I am sorry if you did not have a father like that. I wish every- 4 one could have a father like that.

My hard-working American mother has spent 50 years try- 5 ing to convince her fellow teachers and choir mates not to believe stereotypes about the Middle East. She always told them, there is a much larger story. If you knew the story, you would not jump to conclusions from what you see in the news. But now look at the news. What a mess has been made. Sometimes I wish everyone could have parents from different countries or ethnic groups so they would be forced to cross boundaries, to believe in mixtures, every day of their lives. Because this is what the world calls us to do. WAKE UP!

The Palestinian grocer in my Mexican-American neighbor- 6 hood paints pictures of the Palestinian flag on his empty cartons. He paints trees and rivers. He gives his paintings away. He says, "Don't insult me" when I try to pay him for a lemonade. Arabs have always been famous for their generosity. Remember? My half-Arab brother with an Arabic name looks more like an Arab than many full-blooded Arabs do and he has to fly every week.

7   My Palestinian cousins in Texas have beautiful brown little boys. Many of them haven't gone to school yet. And now they have this heavy word to carry in their backpacks along with the weight of their papers and books. I repeat, the mission was a terrible success. But it was also a complete, total tragedy and I want you to think about a few things.

8   **1.** Many people, thousands of people, perhaps even millions of people, in the United States are very aware of the long unfairness of our country's policies regarding Israel and Palestine. We talk about this all the time. It exhausts us and we keep talking. We write letters to newspapers, to politicians, to each other. We speak out in public even when it is uncomfortable to do so, because that is our responsibility. Many of these people aren't even Arabs. Many happen to be Jews who are equally troubled by the inequity. I promise you this is true. Because I am Arab-American, people always express these views to me and I am amazed how many understand the intricate situation and have strong, caring feelings for Arabs and Palestinians even when they don't have to. Think of them, please: All those people who have been standing up for Arabs when they didn't have to. But as ordinary citizens we don't run the government and don't get to make all our government's policies, which makes us sad sometimes. We believe in the power of the word and we keep using it, even when it seems no one large enough is listening. That is one of the best things about this country: the free power of free words. Maybe we take it for granted too much. Many of the people killed in the World Trade Center probably believed in a free Palestine and were probably talking about it all the time.

9   But this tragedy could never help the Palestinians. Somehow, miraculously, if other people won't help them more, they are going to have to help themselves. And it will be peace, not violence, that fixes things. You could ask any one of the kids in the Seeds of Peace organization and they would tell you that. Do you ever talk to kids? Please, please, talk to more kids.

10   **2.** Have you noticed how many roads there are? Sure you have. You must check out maps and highways and small alternate routes just like anyone else. There is no way everyone on earth could travel on the same road, or believe in exactly the same

religion. It would be too crowded, it would be dumb. I don't believe you want us all to be Muslims. My Palestinian grandmother lived to be 106 years old, and did not read or write, but even she was much smarter than that. The only place she ever went beyond Palestine and Jordan was to Mecca, by bus, and she was very proud to be called a Hajji and to wear white clothes afterward. She worked very hard to get stains out of everyone's dresses—scrubbing them with a stone. I think she would consider the recent tragedies a terrible stain on her religion and her whole part of the world. She would weep. She was scared of airplanes anyway. She wanted people to worship God in whatever ways they felt comfortable. Just worship. Just remember God in every single day and doing. It didn't matter what they called it. When people asked her how she felt about the peace talks that were happening right before she died, she puffed up like a proud little bird and said, in Arabic, "I never lost my peace inside." To her, Islam was a welcoming religion. After her home in Jerusalem was stolen from her, she lived in a small village that contained a Christian shrine. She felt very tender toward the people who would visit it. A Jewish professor tracked me down a few years ago in Jerusalem to tell me she changed his life after he went to her village to do an oral history project on Arabs. "Don't think she only mattered to you!" he said. "She gave me a whole different reality to imagine—yet it was amazing how close we became. Arabs could never be just a 'project' after that."

Did you have a grandmother or two? Mine never wanted people to be pushed around. What did yours want? Reading about Islam since my grandmother died, I note the "tolerance" that was "typical of Islam" even in the old days. The Muslim leader Khalid ibn al-Walid signed a Jerusalem treaty which declared, "In the name of God, you have complete security for your churches which shall not be occupied by the Muslims or destroyed." It is the new millennium in which we should be even smarter than we used to be, right? But I think we have fallen behind. 11

3. Many Americans do not want to kill any more innocent people anywhere in the world. We are extremely worried about military actions killing innocent people. We didn't like this in Iraq, we never liked it anywhere. We would like no more violence, from 12 us as well as from you. HEAR US! We would like to stop the terrifying wheel of violence, just stop it, right on the road, and find something more creative to do to fix these huge problems we have. Violence is not creative, it is stupid and scary and many of us hate all those terrible movies and TV shows made in our own country that try to pretend otherwise. Don't watch them. Everyone should stop watching them. An appetite for explosive sounds and toppling buildings is not a healthy thing for anyone in any country. The USA should apologize to the whole world for sending this trash out into the air and for paying people to make it.

13   But here's something good you may not know—one of the best-selling books of poetry in the United States in recent years is the Coleman Barks translation of Rumi, a mystical Sufi poet of the 13th century, and Sufism is Islam and doesn't that make you glad?

14   Everyone is talking about the suffering that ethnic Americans are going through. Many will no doubt go through more of it, but I would like to thank everyone who has sent me a consolation card. Americans are usually very kind people. Didn't your colleagues find that out during their time living here? It is hard to imagine they missed it. How could they do what they did, knowing that?

15   **4.** We will all die soon enough. Why not take the short time we have on this delicate planet and figure out some really interesting things we might do together? I promise you, God would be happier. So many people are always trying to speak for God—I know it is a very dangerous thing to do. I tried my whole life not to do it. But this one time is an exception. Because there are so many people crying and scarred and confused and complicated and exhausted right now—it is as if we have all had a giant simultaneous breakdown. I beg you, as your distant Arab cousin, as your American neighbor, listen to me. Our hearts are broken, as yours may also feel broken in some ways we can't understand, unless you tell us in words. Killing people won't tell us. We can't read that message. Find another way to live. Don't expect others to be like you. Read Rumi. Read Arabic poetry. Poetry humanizes us in a way that news, or even religion, has a harder time doing. A great Arab scholar, Dr. Salma Jayyusi, said, "If we read one

another, we won't kill one another." Read American poetry. Plant mint. Find a friend who is so different from you, you can't believe how much you have in common. Love them. Let them love you. Surprise people in gentle ways, as friends do. The rest of us will try harder too. Make our family proud.

2001

Why I Want a Wife

Judy Brady

I belong to that classification of people known as wives. I am A Wife. And, not altogether incidentally, I am a mother. 1

Not too long ago a male friend of mine appeared on the scene fresh from a recent divorce. He had one child, who is, of course, with his ex-wife. He is looking for another wife. As I thought about him while I was ironing one evening, it suddenly occurred to me that I, too, would like to have a wife. Why do I want a wife? 2

I would like to go back to school so that I can become economically independent, support myself, and, if need be, support those dependent upon me. I want a wife who will work and send me to school. And while I am going to school I want a wife to take care of my children. I want a wife to keep track of the children's doctor and dentist appointments. And to keep track of mine, too. I want a wife to make sure my children eat properly and are kept clean. I want a wife who will wash the children's clothes and keep them mended. I want a wife who is a good nurturant attendant to my children, who arranges for their school, makes sure that they have an adequate social life with their peers, takes them to the park, the zoo, etc. I want a wife who takes care of the children when they are sick, a wife who arranges to be around when the children need special care, because, of course, I cannot miss classes at school. My wife must arrange to lose time at work 3 and not lose the job. It may mean a small cut in my wife's income from time to time, but I guess I can tolerate that. Needless to say, my wife will arrange and pay for the care of the children while my wife is working.

4   I want a wife who will take care of *my* physical needs. I want a wife who will keep my house clean. A wife who will pick up after my children, a wife who will pick up after me. I want a wife who will keep my clothes clean, ironed, mended, replaced when need be, and who will see to it that my personal things are kept in their proper place so that I can find what I need the minute I need it. I want a wife who cooks the meals, a wife who is a *good* cook. I want a wife who will plan the menus, do the necessary grocery shopping, prepare the meals, serve them pleasantly, and then do the cleaning up while I do my studying. I want a wife who will care for me when I am sick and sympathize with my pain and loss of time from school. I want a wife to go along when our family takes a vacation so that someone can continue to care for me and my children when I need a rest and change of scene.

5   I want a wife who will not bother me with rambling complaints about a wife's duties. But I want a wife who will listen to me when I feel the need to explain a rather difficult point I have come across in my course of studies. And I want a wife who will type my papers for me when I have written them.

6   I want a wife who will take care of the details of my social life. When my wife and I are invited out by my friends, I want a wife who will take care of the babysitting arrangements. When I meet people at school that I like and want to entertain, I want a wife who will have the house clean, will prepare a special meal, serve it to me and my friends, and not interrupt when I talk about things that interest me and my friends. I want a wife who will have arranged that the children do not bother us. I want a wife who takes care of the needs of my guests so that they feel comfortable, who makes sure that they have an ashtray, that they are passed the hors d'oeuvres, that they are offered a second helping of the food, that their wine glasses are replenished when necessary, that the coffee is served to them as they like it. And I want a wife who knows that sometimes I need a night out by myself.

I want a wife who is sensitive to my sexual needs, a wife who makes love passionately and eagerly when I feel like it, a wife who makes sure that I am satisfied. And, of course, I want a wife who will not demand sexual attention when I am not in the mood for it. I want a wife who assumes the complete responsibility for birth control, because I do not want more children. I want a wife who will remain sexually faithful to me so that I do not have to clutter up my intellectual life with jealousies. And I want a wife who understands that *my* sexual needs may entail more than strict adherence to monogamy. I must, after all, be able to relate to people as fully as possible.

If, by chance, I find another person more suitable as a wife than the wife I already have, I want the liberty to replace my present wife with another one. Naturally, I will expect a fresh, new life; my wife will take the children and be solely responsible for them so that I am left free.

When I am through with school and have a job, I want my wife to quit working and remain at home so that my wife can more fully and completely take care of a wife's duties.

My God, who *wouldn't* want a wife?

1970

An Indian Father's Plea

Medicine Grizzlybear Lake

Dear teacher:

I would like to introduce you to my son, Wind-Wolf. He is probably what you would consider a typical Indian kid. He was born and raised on the reservation. He has black hair, dark brown eyes, and an olive complexion. And like so many Indian children his age, he is shy and quiet in the classroom. He is five years old, in kindergarten, and I cannot understand why you have already labeled him a "slow learner."

2   At the age of five, he has already had quite an education compared with his peers in Western society. As his first introduction into this world, he was bonded to his mother and to the Mother Earth in a traditional native childbirth ceremony. And he has been continuously cared for by his mother, father, sisters, cousins, aunts, uncles, grandparents, and extended tribal family since this ceremony.

3   From his mother's loving arms, Wind-Wolf was placed in a secure and specially designed Indian baby basket. His father and the medicine elders conducted another ceremony to bond him with the essence of his genetic father, the Great Spirit, the Grandfather Sun, and the Grandmother Moon. This was all done in order to introduce him into the natural world, and to protect his soul. It is our people's way of showing the newborn respect, ensuring that he starts life on the path of spirituality.

4   The traditional Indian baby basket became his "turtle's shell" and served as the first seat for this classroom. He was strapped in for safety, protected from injury by the willow roots and hazelwood construction. The basket was made by a tribal elder who had gathered her materials with prayer. It is specially designed to provide the child with the knowledge and experience he will need in order to survive in his culture and environment.

5   Wind-Wolf was strapped in snuggly with a deliberate restriction upon his arms and legs. Although you in Western society may argue that such a method serves to hinder motor-skills development and abstract reasoning, we believe it forces the child to first develop his intuitive faculties, rational intellect, symbolic thinking, and five senses. Wind-Wolf was with his mother constantly, closely bonded, as she carried him on her back or held him in front while breast feeding. She carried him everywhere she went, and every night he slept with both parents. Because of this, Wind-Wolf's educational setting was not only "secure," but also colorful, complicated, and diverse. He has been with his mother at the ocean at daybreak when she made her prayers and gathered fresh seaweed from the rocks, he has sat with his uncles in a rowboat on the river while they fished with gill nets, and he has watched and listened to elders as they told creation stories and animal legends and sang songs around the campfires.

He has attended the sacred and ancient White Deerskin 6
Dance of his people and is well acquainted with the cultures
and languages of other tribes. He has been with his mother
when she gathered herbs for healing and watched his tribal
aunts and grandmothers gather and prepare traditional foods
such as acorn, smoked salmon, eel, and deer meat. He has
played with abalone shells, pine nuts, iris grass string, and
leather while watching the women make beaded jewelry and
traditional native regalia. He has had many opportunities to
watch his father, uncles, and ceremonial leaders use different
kinds of colorful feathers and sing different kinds of songs
while preparing for the sacred dances and rituals.

As he grew older, Wind-Wolf began to crawl out of the baby 7
basket and explore the world around him. When frightened or
sleepy, he could always return to the basket, as a turtle withdraws
into its shell. Such an inward journey allows one to reflect in
privacy on what he has learned and to carry the new knowledge
deeply into the unconscious and the soul. Shapes, sizes, colors,
texture, sound, smell, feeling, taste, and the learning process
are therefore integrated—the physical and spiritual, matter and
energy, conscious and unconscious, individual and social.

Wind-Wolf was with his mother in South Dakota while she 8
danced for seven days straight in the hot sun, in the sacred Sun
Dance Ceremony of a distant tribe. He has been doctored in a
number of different healing ceremonies by medicine men and
women from places ranging from Alaska and Arizona to New
York and California. He has been in more than twenty different
sacred sweat lodge rituals—used by native tribes to purify mind,
body, and soul—since he was three years old, and he has already
been exposed to many different religions of his racial brothers:
Protestant, Catholic, Asian Buddhist, and Tibetan Lamaist.

It takes a long time to absorb and reflect on these kinds of 9
experiences, so maybe that is why you think my Indian child is
a slow learner. His aunts and grandmothers taught him to count
while they sorted out the materials used to make the abstract
designs in native baskets. He learned his basic numbers by helping his father count and sort the rocks to be used in the sweat
lodge—seven rocks for a medicine sweat, say, or thirteen for the

summer solstice ceremony. And he was taught mathematics by counting the sticks we use in our traditional native hand game. So I realize he may be slow in grasping the methods that you are now using in your classroom but I hope you will be patient with him. It takes time to adjust to a new cultural system.

10   He is not culturally "disadvantaged," but he is culturally "different." If you ask him how many months there are in a year, he will probably tell you thirteen. He will respond this way not because he doesn't know how to count properly, but because he has been taught by our traditional people that there are thirteen full moons in a year according to the native tribal calendar and thirteen tail feathers on a perfectly balanced eagle.

11   But he also knows that some eagles may only have twelve tail feathers, or seven. He knows that the flicker has exactly ten tail feathers; that they are red and black, representing east and west, life and death, and that this bird is a "fire" bird, a power used in native healing. He can probably count more than forty different kinds of birds, tell you what kind of bird each is and where it lives, the seasons in which it appears, and how it is used in a sacred ceremony. He may have trouble writing his name on a piece of paper, but he knows how to say it and many other things in several different Indian languages. He is not fluent yet because he is only five years old and required by law to attend your educational system, learn your language, your values, your ways of thinking, and your methods of teaching.

12   So you see, all of these influences together make him somewhat shy and quiet—and perhaps "slow" according to your standards. But if Wind-Wolf was not prepared for his first tentative foray into your world, neither were you appreciative of his culture. On the first day of class, you had difficulty with his name. You wanted to call him "Wind"—insisting that Wolf somehow must be his middle name. The students in the class laughed at him, causing him embarrassment.

13   While you are trying to teach him your new methods, he may be looking out the window as if daydreaming. Why? Because he has been taught to watch and study the changes in nature. It is hard for him to switch from the right to the left hemisphere of the brain when he sees the leaves turning bright colors, the geese

heading south, and the squirrels scurrying to get ready for winter. In his heart, in his young mind, and almost by instinct, he knows that this is the time of year he is supposed to be with his people gathering and preparing fish, deer meat, and plants and herbs, and learning his assigned tasks in this role. He is caught between two worlds.

Yesterday, for the third time in two weeks, he came home 14 crying and said he wanted to have his hair cut. He said he doesn't have any friends at school because they make fun of his long hair. I tried to explain to him that in our culture, long hair is a sign of masculinity and balance and is a source of power. But he remained adamant in his position.

To make matters worse, he recently encountered his first harsh 15 case of racism. Wind-Wolf had managed to adopt at least one good school friend. On the way home from school one day, he asked his new pal if he wanted to come home to play with him until supper. That was okay with Wind-Wolf's mother, who was walking with them. When they got to the friend's house, the two boys ran inside to ask permission while Wind-Wolf's mother waited. But the other boy's mother lashed out: "It is okay if you have to play with him at school, but we don't allow that kind of people in our house!" When my wife asked why not, the other boy's mother answered, "Because you are Indians and we are white, and I don't want my kids growing up with your kind of people."

So now my young Indian child does not want to go to school 16 anymore (even though his hair is cut). He feels that he does not belong. He is the only Indian child in your class, and instead of being proud of his race, heritage, and culture, he now feels ashamed. When he watches television, he asks why white people hate us so much and always kill our people in the movies and why they take everything from us. He asks why the other kids in school are not taught about the power, beauty, and essence of nature. Now he refuses to sing his native songs, play with his Indian artifacts, learn his language, or participate in his sacred ceremonies. When I ask him to go to an urban pow-wow or help me with a sacred sweat lodge ritual, he says no because "that's weird."

So, dear teacher, I want to introduce you to my son, Wind- 17 Wolf. He stems from a long line of hereditary chiefs, medicine

men and women, and ceremonial leaders whose knowledge is
still being studied and recorded in contemporary books. He has
seven different tribal systems flowing through his blood; he is
even part white. I want my child to succeed in school and in life. I
don't want him to be a dropout or to end up on drugs and alcohol
because he is made to feel inferior or because of discrimination. I
want him to be proud of his rich culture, and I would like him to
succeed in both cultures. But I need your help.

18   What you say and what you do in the classroom has a significant effect on my child. All I ask is that you work with me to help
educate my child in the best way. If you don't have the knowledge and experience to deal with culturally different children, I
am willing to help you with the few resources I have or direct you
to other resources.

19   Millions of dollars have been appropriated by Congress each
year for "Indian Education." All you have to do is encourage your
school to use these resources. My Indian child has a constitutional right to learn and maintain his culture. By the same token,
I believe that non-Indian children have a constitutional right to
learn about our Native American heritage and culture, because
Indians play a significant part in the history of Western society.

20   My son, Wind-Wolf, is not an empty glass coming into your
class to be filled. He is a full basket coming into a different society
with something special to share. Please let him share his knowledge, heritage, and culture with you and his peers.

1995

Let Them Eat Dog

Jonathan Safran Foer

1 Despite the fact that it's perfectly legal in 44 states, eating "man's
best friend" is as taboo as a man eating his best friend. Even
the most enthusiastic carnivores won't eat dogs. TV guy and

sometimes cooker Gordon Ramsay can get pretty macho with lambs and piglets when doing publicity for something he's selling, but you'll never see a puppy peeking out of one of his pots. And though he once said he'd electrocute his children if they became vegetarian, one can't help but wonder what his response would be if they poached the family pooch.

Dogs are wonderful, and in many ways unique. But they are 2 remarkably unremarkable in their intellectual and experiential capacities. Pigs are every bit as intelligent and feeling, by any sensible definition of the words. They can't hop into the back of a Volvo, but they can fetch, run and play, be mischievous and reciprocate affection. So why don't they get to curl up by the fire? Why can't they at least be spared being tossed on the fire? Our taboo against dog eating says something about dogs and a great deal about us.

The French, who love their dogs, sometimes eat their horses.
The Spanish, who love their horses, sometimes eat their cows.
The Indians, who love their cows, sometimes eat their dogs.

While written in a much different context, George Orwell's 3 words (from "Animal Farm") apply here: "All animals are equal, but some animals are more equal than others."

So who's right? What might be the reasons to exclude canine 4 from the menu? The selective carnivore suggests:

Don't eat companion animals. But dogs aren't kept as com- 5 panions in all of the places they are eaten. And what about our petless neighbors? Would we have any right to object if they had dog for dinner?

OK, then: Don't eat animals with significant mental capaci- 6 ties. If by "significant mental capacities" we mean what a dog has, then good for the dog. But such a definition would also include the pig, cow and chicken. And it would exclude severely impaired humans.

Then: It's for good reason that the eternal taboos—don't fid- 7 dle with your crap, kiss your sister, or eat your companions—are taboo. Evolutionarily speaking, those things are bad for us. But dog eating isn't a taboo in many places, and it isn't in any way bad for us. Properly cooked, dog meat poses no greater health risks than any other meat.

8   Dog meat has been described as "gamey" "complex," "buttery" and "floral." And there is a proud pedigree of eating it. Fourth-century tombs contain depictions of dogs being slaughtered along with other food animals. It was a fundamental enough habit to have informed language itself: the Sino-Korean character for "fair and proper" (yeon) literally translates into "as cooked dog meat is delicious." Hippocrates praised dog meat as a source of strength. Dakota Indians enjoyed dog liver, and not so long ago Hawaiians ate dog brains and blood. Captain Cook ate dog. Roald Amundsen famously ate his sled dogs. (Granted, he was really hungry.) And dogs are still eaten to overcome bad luck in the Philippines; as medicine in China and Korea; to enhance libido in Nigeria and in numerous places, on every continent, because they taste good. For centuries, the Chinese have raised special breeds of dogs, like the black-tongued chow, for chow, and many European countries still have laws on the books regarding postmortem examination of dogs intended for human consumption.

9   Of course, something having been done just about everywhere is no kind of justification for doing it now. But unlike all farmed meat, which requires the creation and maintenance of animals, dogs are practically begging to be eaten. Three to four million dogs and cats are euthanized annually. The simple disposal of these euthanized dogs is an enormous ecological and economic problem. But eating those strays, those runaways, those not-quite-cute-enough-to-take and not-quite-well-behaved-enough-to-keep dogs would be killing a flock of birds with one stone and eating it, too.

10   In a sense it's what we're doing already. Rendering—the conversion of animal protein unfit for human consumption into food for livestock and pets—allows processing plants to transform useless dead dogs into productive members of the food chain. In America, millions of dogs and cats euthanized in animal shelters every year become the food for our food. So let's just eliminate this inefficient and bizarre middle step.

11   This need not challenge our civility. We won't make them suffer any more than necessary. While it's widely believed that adrenaline makes dog meat taste better—hence the traditional

methods of slaughter: hanging, boiling alive, beating to death—we can all agree that if we're going to eat them, we should kill them quickly and painlessly, right? For example, the traditional Hawaiian means of holding the dog's nose shut—in order to conserve blood—must be regarded (socially if not legally) as a no-no. Perhaps we could include dogs under the Humane Methods of Slaughter Act. That doesn't say anything about how they're treated during their lives, and isn't subject to any meaningful oversight or enforcement, but surely we can rely on the industry to "self-regulate," as we do with other eaten animals.

Few people sufficiently appreciate the colossal task of feeding a world of billions of omnivores who demand meat with their potatoes. The inefficient use of dogs—conveniently already in areas of high human population (take note, local-food advocates)—should make any good ecologist blush. One could argue that various "humane" groups are the worst hypocrites, spending enormous amounts of money and energy in a futile attempt to reduce the number of unwanted dogs while at the very same time propagating the irresponsible no-dog-for-dinner taboo. If we let dogs be dogs, and breed without interference, we would create a sustainable, local meat supply with low energy inputs that would put even the most efficient grass-based farming to shame. For the ecologically-minded it's time to admit that dog is realistic food for realistic environmentalists. 12

For those already convinced, here's a classic Filipino recipe I recently came across. I haven't tried it myself, but sometimes you can read a recipe and just know. 13

Stewed Dog, Wedding Style
First, kill a medium-sized dog, then burn off the fur over a hot fire. Carefully remove the skin while still warm and set aside for later (may be used in other recipes). Cut meat into 1" cubes. Marinate meat in mixture of vinegar, peppercorn, salt, and garlic for 2 hours. Fry meat in oil using a large wok over an open fire, then add onions and chopped pineapple and sauté until tender. Pour in tomato sauce and boiling water, add green pepper, bay leaf, and Tabasco. Cover and simmer over warm coals until meat is tender. Blend in purée of dog's liver and cook for additional 5–7 minutes.

14   There is an overabundance of rational reasons to say no to factory-farmed meat: It is the No. 1 cause of global warming, it systematically forces tens of billions of animals to suffer in ways that would be illegal if they were dogs, it is a decisive factor in the development of swine and avian flus, and so on. And yet even most people who know these things still aren't inspired to order something else on the menu. Why?

15   Food is not rational. Food is culture, habit, craving and identity. Responding to factory farming calls for a capacity to care that dwells beyond information. We know what we see on undercover videos of factory farms and slaughterhouses is wrong. (There are those who will defend a system that allows for occasional animal cruelty, but no one defends the cruelty, itself.) And despite it being entirely reasonable, the case for eating dogs is likely repulsive to just about every reader of this paper. The instinct comes before our reason, and is more important.

2009

On Liberty

John Stuart Mill

1   The subject of this Essay is not the so-called Liberty of the Will, so unfortunately opposed to the misnamed doctrine of Philosophical Necessity; but Civil, or Social Liberty: the nature and limits of the power which can be legitimately exercised by society over the individual. A question seldom stated, and hardly ever discussed, in general terms, but which profoundly influences the practical controversies of the age by its latent presence, and is likely soon to make itself recognised as the vital question of the future. It is so far from being new, that, in a certain sense, it has divided mankind, almost from the remotest ages; but in the stage of progress into which the more civilized portions of the species have now

entered, it presents itself under new conditions, and requires a different and more fundamental treatment.

The struggle between Liberty and Authority is the most 2 conspicuous feature in the portions of history with which we are earliest familiar, particularly in that of Greece, Rome, and England. But in old times this contest was between subjects, or some classes of subjects, and the Government. By liberty, was meant protection against the tyranny of the political rulers. The rulers were conceived (except in some of the popular govern-ments of Greece) as in a necessarily antagonistic position to the people whom they ruled. They consisted of a governing One, or a governing tribe or caste, who derived their authority from inheritance or conquest, who, at all events, did not hold it at the pleasure of the governed, and whose supremacy men did not venture, perhaps did not desire, to contest, whatever precautions might be taken against its oppressive exercise. Their power was regarded as necessary, but also as highly dangerous; as a weapon which they would attempt to use against their subjects, no less than against external enemies. To prevent the weaker members of the community from being preyed on by innumerable vultures, it was needful that there should be an animal of prey stronger than the rest, commissioned to keep them down. But as the king of the vultures would be no less bent upon preying upon the flock than any of the minor harpies, it was indispensable to be in a perpetual attitude of defence against his beak and claws. The aim, therefore, of patriots was to set limits to the power which the ruler should be suffered to exercise over the community; and this limitation was what they meant by liberty. It was attempted in two ways. First, by obtaining a recognition of certain immunities, called political liberties or rights, which it was to be regarded as a breach of duty in the ruler to infringe, and which, if he did infringe, specific resistance, or general rebellion, was held to be justifiable. A second, and generally a later expedient, was the establishment of constitutional checks, by which the consent of the community, or of a body of some sort, supposed to represent its interests, was made a necessary condition to some of the more important acts of the governing power. To the first of these modes of limitation, the ruling power, in most European countries, was compelled, more or less, to submit. It was not so with the second; and, to attain this, or when already in some degree possessed, to attain it more completely, became everywhere the principal object of the lovers of liberty. And so long as mankind were content to combat one enemy by another, and to be ruled by a master, on condition of being guaranteed more or less efficaciously against his tyranny, they did not carry their aspirations beyond this point.

3   A time, however, came, in the progress of human affairs, when men ceased to think it a necessity of nature that their governors should be an independent power, opposed in interest to themselves. It appeared to them much better that the various magistrates of the State should be their tenants or delegates, revocable at their pleasure. In that way alone, it seemed, could they have complete security that the powers of government would never be abused to their disadvantage. By degrees this new demand for elective and temporary rulers became the prominent object of the exertions of the popular party, wherever any such party existed; and superseded, to a considerable extent, the previous efforts to limit the power of rulers. As the struggle proceeded for making the ruling power emanate from the periodical choice of the ruled, some persons began to think that too much importance had been attached to the limitation of the power itself. *That* (it might seem) was a resource against rulers whose interests were habitually opposed to those of the people. What was now wanted was, that the rulers should be identified with the people; that their interest and will should be the interest and will of the nation. The nation did not need to be protected against its own will. There was no fear of its tyrannizing over itself. Let the rulers be effectually responsible to it, promptly removable by it, and it could afford to trust them with power of which it could itself dictate the use to be made. Their power was but the nation's own power, concentrated, and in a form convenient for exercise. This mode of thought, or rather perhaps of feeling, was common among the last generation of European liberalism, in the Continental section of which it still apparently predominates. Those who admit any limit to what a government may do, except in the case of such governments as they think ought not to exist, stand out as brilliant exceptions among the political thinkers of the Continent.

A similar tone of sentiment might by this time have been prevalent in our own country, if the circumstances which for a time encouraged it, had continued unaltered.

But, in political and philosophical theories, as well as in persons, success discloses faults and infirmities which failure might have concealed from observation. The notion, that the people have no need to limit their power over themselves, might seem axiomatic, when popular government was a thing only dreamed about, or read of as having existed at some distant period of the past. Neither was that notion necessarily disturbed by such temporary aberrations as those of the French Revolution, the worst of which were the work of an usurping few, and which, in any case, belonged, not to the permanent working of popular institutions, but to a sudden and convulsive outbreak against monarchical and aristocratic despotism. In time, however, a democratic republic came to occupy a large portion of the earth's surface, and made itself felt as one of the most powerful members of the community of nations; and elective and responsible government became subject to the observations and criticisms which wait upon a great existing fact. It was now perceived that such phrases as "self-government," and "the power of the people over themselves," do not express the true state of the case. The "people" who exercise the power are not always the same people with those over whom it is exercised; and the "self-government" spoken of is not the government of each by himself, but of each by all the rest. The will of the people, moreover, practically means the will of the most numerous or the most active *part* of the people; the majority, or those who succeed in making themselves accepted as the majority; the people, consequently, *may* desire to oppress a part of their number; and precautions are as much needed against this as against any other abuse of power. The limitation, therefore, of the power of government over individuals loses none of its importance when the holders of power are regularly accountable to the community, that is, to the strongest party therein. This view of things, recommending itself equally to the intelligence of thinkers and to the inclination of those important classes in European society to whose real or supposed interests democracy is adverse, has had no difficulty in establishing itself; and in political speculations "the tyranny of the majority" is now generally included among the evils against which society requires to be on its guard.

5   Like other tyrannies, the tyranny of the majority was at first, and is still vulgarly, held in dread, chiefly as operating through the acts of the public authorities. But reflecting persons perceived that when society is itself the tyrant—society collectively, over the separate individuals who compose it—its means of tyrannizing are not restricted to the acts which it may do by the hands of its political functionaries. Society can and does execute its own mandates: and if it issues wrong mandates instead of right, or any mandates at all in things with which it ought not to meddle, it practises a social tyranny more formidable than many kinds of political oppression, since, though not usually upheld by such extreme penalties, it leaves fewer means of escape, penetrating much more deeply into the details of life, and enslaving the soul itself. Protection, therefore, against the tyranny of the magistrate is not enough: there needs protection also against the tyranny of the prevailing opinion and feeling; against the tendency of society to impose, by other means than civil penalties, its own ideas and practices as rules of conduct on those who dissent from them; to fetter the development, and, if possible, prevent the formation, of any individuality not in harmony with its ways, and compel all characters to fashion themselves upon the model of its own. There is a limit to the legitimate interference of collective opinion with individual independence: and to find that limit, and maintain it against encroachment, is as indispensable to a good condition of human affairs, as protection against political despotism.

6   But though this proposition is not likely to be contested in general terms, the practical question, where to place the limit—how to make the fitting adjustment between individual independence and social control—is a subject on which nearly everything remains to be done. All that makes existence valuable to any one, depends on the enforcement of restraints upon the actions of other people. Some rules of conduct, therefore, must be imposed, by law in the first place, and by opinion on many things which are not fit subjects for the operation of law. What these rules should be, is the principal question in human affairs; but if we except a few of the most obvious cases, it is one of those which least progress

has been made in resolving. No two ages, and scarcely any two countries, have decided it alike; and the decision of one age or country is a wonder to another. Yet the people of any given age and country no more suspect any difficulty in it, than if it were a subject on which mankind had always been agreed. The rules which obtain among themselves appear to them self-evident and self-justifying. This all but universal illusion is one of the examples of the magical influence of custom, which is not only, as the proverb says, a second nature, but is continually mistaken for the first. The effect of custom, in preventing any misgiving respecting the rules of conduct which mankind impose on one another, is all the more complete because the subject is one on which it is not generally considered necessary that reasons should be given, either by one person to others, or by each to himself. People are accustomed to believe, and have been encouraged in the belief by some who aspire to the character of philosophers, that their feelings, on subjects of this nature, are better than reasons, and render reasons unnecessary. The practical principle which guides them to their opinions on the regulation of human conduct, is the feeling in each person's mind that everybody should be required to act as he, and those with whom he sympathizes, would like them to act. No one, indeed, acknowledges to himself that his standard of judgment is his own liking; but an opinion on a point of conduct, not supported by reasons, can only count as one person's preference; and if the reasons, when given, are a mere appeal to a similar preference felt by other people, it is still only many people's liking instead of one. To an ordinary man, however, his own preference, thus supported, is not only a perfectly satisfactory reason, but the only one he generally has for any of his notions of morality, taste, or propriety, which are not expressly written in his religious creed; and his chief guide in the interpretation even of that. Men's opinions, accordingly, on what is laudable or blameable, are affected by all the multifarious causes which influence their wishes in regard to the conduct of others, and which are as numerous as those which determine their wishes on any other subject. Sometimes their reason—at other times their prejudices or superstitions: often their social affections, not seldom their antisocial ones, their envy or jealousy, their arrogance or contemptuousness:

but most commonly, their desires or fears for themselves—their legitimate or illegitimate self-interest. Wherever there is an ascendant class, a large portion of the morality of the country emanates from its class interests, and its feelings of class superiority. The morality between Spartans and Helots, between planters and negroes, between princes and subjects, between nobles and roturiers, between men and women, has been for the most part the creation of these class interests and feelings: and the sentiments thus generated, react in turn upon the moral feelings of the members of the ascendant class, in their relations among themselves. Where, on the other hand, a class, formerly ascendant, has lost its ascendancy, or where its ascendancy is unpopular, the prevailing moral sentiments frequently bear the impress of an impatient dislike of superiority. Another grand determining principle of the rules of conduct, both in act and forbearance, which have been enforced by law or opinion, has been the servility of mankind towards the supposed preferences or aversions of their temporal masters, or of their gods. This servility, though essentially selfish, is not hypocrisy; it gives rise to perfectly genuine sentiments of abhorrence; it made men burn magicians and heretics. Among so many baser influences, the general and obvious interests of society have of course had a share, and a large one, in the direction of the moral sentiments: less, however, as a matter of reason, and on their own account, than as a consequence of the sympathies and antipathies which grew out of them: and sympathies and antipathies which had little or nothing to do with the interests of society, have made themselves felt in the establishment of moralities with quite as great force.

7   The likings and dislikings of society, or of some powerful portion of it, are thus the main thing which has practically determined the rules laid down for general observance, under the penalties of law or opinion. And in general, those who have been in advance of society in thought and feeling, have left this condition of things unassailed in principle, however they may have come into conflict with it in some of its details. They have occupied themselves rather in inquiring what things society ought to like or dislike, than in questioning whether its likings or dislikings should be a law to individuals. They preferred endeavouring to

alter the feelings of mankind on the particular points on which they were themselves heretical, rather than make common cause in defence of freedom, with heretics generally. The only case in which the higher ground has been taken on principle and maintained with consistency, by any but an individual here and there, is that of religious belief: a case instructive in many ways, and not least so as forming a most striking instance of the fallibility of what is called the moral sense: for the *odium theologicum,* in a sincere bigot, is one of the most unequivocal cases of moral feeling. Those who first broke the yoke of what called itself the Universal Church, were in general as little willing to permit difference of religious opinion as that church itself. But when the heat of the conflict was over, without giving a complete victory to any party, and each church or sect was reduced to limit its hopes to retaining possession of the ground it already occupied; minorities, seeing that they had no chance of becoming majorities, were under the necessity of pleading to those whom they could not convert, for permission to differ. It is accordingly on this battle field, almost solely, that the rights of the individual against society have been asserted on broad grounds of principle, and the claim of society to exercise authority over dissentients, openly controverted. The great writers to whom the world owes what religious liberty it possesses, have mostly asserted freedom of conscience as an indefeasible right, and denied absolutely that a human being is accountable to others for his religious belief. Yet so natural to mankind is intolerance in whatever they really care about, that religious freedom has hardly anywhere been practically realized, except where religious indifference, which dislikes to have its peace disturbed by theological quarrels, has added its weight to the scale. In the minds of almost all religious persons, even in the most tolerant countries, the duty of toleration is admitted with tacit reserves. One person will bear with dissent in matters of church government, but not of dogma; another can tolerate everybody, short of a Papist or an Unitarian; another, every one who believes in revealed religion; a few extend their charity a little further, but stop at the belief in a God and in a future state. Wherever the sentiment of the majority is still genuine and intense, it is found to have abated little of its claim to be obeyed.

8   In England, from the peculiar circumstances of our political history, though the yoke of opinion is perhaps heavier, that of law is lighter, than in most other countries of Europe; and there is considerable jealousy of direct interference, by the legislative or the executive power, with private conduct; not so much from any just regard for the independence of the individual, as from the still subsisting habit of looking on the government as representing an opposite interest to the public. The majority have not yet learnt to feel the power of the government their power, or its opinions their opinions. When they do so, individual liberty will probably be as much exposed to invasion from the government, as it already is from public opinion. But, as yet, there is a considerable amount of feeling ready to be called forth against any attempt of the law to control individuals in things in which they have not hitherto been accustomed to be controlled by it; and this with very little discrimination as to whether the matter is, or is not, within the legitimate sphere of legal control; insomuch that the feeling, highly salutary on the whole, is perhaps quite as often misplaced as well grounded in the particular instances of its application. There is, in fact, no recognised principle by which the propriety or impropriety of government interference is customarily tested. People decide according to their personal preferences. Some, whenever they see any good to be done, or evil to be remedied, would willingly instigate the government to undertake the business; while others prefer to bear almost any amount of social evil, rather than add one to the departments of human interests amenable to governmental control. And men range themselves on one or the other side in any particular case, according to this general direction of their sentiments; or according to the degree of interest which they feel in the particular thing which it is proposed that the government should do, or according to the belief they entertain that the government would, or would not, do it in the manner they prefer; but very rarely on account of any opinion to which they consistently adhere, as to what things are fit to be done by a government. And it seems to me that in consequence of this absence of rule or principle, one side is at present as often wrong as the other; the interference of government is, with about equal frequency, improperly invoked and improperly condemned.

The object of this Essay is to assert one very simple principle, ⁹ as entitled to govern absolutely the dealings of society with the individual in the way of compulsion and control, whether the means used be physical force in the form of legal penalties, or the moral coercion of public opinion. That principle is, that the sole end for which mankind are warranted, individually or collectively, in interfering with the liberty of action of any of their number, is self-protection. That the only purpose for which power can be rightfully exercised over any member of a civilized community, against his will, is to prevent harm to others. His own good, either physical or moral, is not a sufficient warrant. He cannot rightfully be compelled to do or forbear because it will be better for him to do so, because it will make him happier, because, in the opinions of others, to do so would be wise, or even right. These are good reasons for remonstrating with him, or reasoning with him, or persuading him, or entreating him, but not for compelling him, or visiting him with any evil in case he do otherwise. To justify that, the conduct from which it is desired to deter him, must be calculated to produce evil to some one else. The only part of the conduct of any one, for which he is amenable to society, is that which concerns others. In the part which merely concerns himself, his independence is, of right, absolute. Over himself, over his own body and mind, the individual is sovereign.

It is, perhaps, hardly necessary to say that this doctrine is ¹⁰ meant to apply only to human beings in the maturity of their faculties. We are not speaking of children, or of young persons below the age which the law may fix as that of manhood or womanhood. Those who are still in a state to require being taken care of by others, must be protected against their own actions as well as against external injury. For the same reason, we may leave out of consideration those backward states of society in which the race itself may be considered as in its nonage. The early difficulties in the way of spontaneous progress are so great, that there is seldom any choice of means for overcoming them; and a ruler full of the spirit of improvement is warranted in the use of any expedients that will attain an end, perhaps otherwise unattainable. Despotism is a legitimate mode of government in dealing with barbarians, provided the end be their improvement, and the means justified by actually effecting that end. Liberty, as a principle, has no application to any state of things anterior to the time when mankind have become capable of being improved by free and equal discussion. Until then, there is nothing for them but implicit obedience to an Akbar or a Charlemagne, if they are so fortunate as to find one. But as soon as mankind have attained the capacity of being guided to their own improvement by conviction or persuasion (a period long since reached in all nations with whom we need here concern ourselves), compulsion, either in the direct form or in that of pains and penalties for non-compliance, is no longer admissible as a means to their own good, and justifiable only for the security of others.

11   It is proper to state that I forego any advantage which could be derived to my argument from the idea of abstract right, as a thing independent of utility. I regard utility as the ultimate appeal on all ethical questions; but it must be utility in the largest sense, grounded on the permanent interests of man as a progressive being. Those interests, I contend, authorize the subjection of individual spontaneity to external control, only in respect to those actions of each, which concern the interest of other people. If any one does an act hurtful to others, there is a *primâ facie* case for punishing him, by law, or, where legal penalties are not safely applicable, by general disapprobation. There are also many positive acts for the benefit of others, which he may rightfully be compelled to perform; such as, to give evidence in a court of justice; to bear his fair share in the common defence, or in any other joint work necessary to the interest of the society of which he enjoys the protection; and to perform certain acts of individual beneficence, such as saving a fellow-creature's life, or interposing to protect the defenceless against ill-usage, things which whenever it is obviously a man's duty to do, he may rightfully be made responsible to society for not doing. A person may cause evil to others not only by his actions but by his inaction, and in either case he is justly accountable to them for the injury. The latter case, it is true, requires a much more cautious exercise of compulsion than the former. To make any one answerable for doing evil to others, is the rule; to make him answerable for not preventing evil, is, comparatively speaking, the exception. Yet there are many

cases clear enough and grave enough to justify that exception. In all things which regard the external relations of the individual, he is *de jure* amenable to those whose interests are concerned, and if need be, to society as their protector. There are often good reasons for not holding him to the responsibility; but these reasons must arise from the special expediencies of the case: either because it is a kind of case in which he is on the whole likely to act better, when left to his own discretion, than when controlled in any way in which society have it in their power to control him; or because the attempt to exercise control would produce other evils, greater than those which it would prevent. When such reasons as these preclude the enforcement of responsibility, the conscience of the agent himself should step into the vacant judgment seat, and protect those interests of others which have no external protection; judging himself all the more rigidly, because the case does not admit of his being made accountable to the judgment of his fellow-creatures.

But there is a sphere of action in which society, as distin- 12 guished from the individual, has, if any, only an indirect interest; comprehending all that portion of a person's life and conduct which affects only himself, or if it also affects others, only with their free, voluntary, and undeceived consent and participation. When I say only himself, I mean directly, and in the first instance: for whatever affects himself, may affect others through himself; and the objection which may be grounded on this contingency, will receive consideration in the sequel. This, then, is the appropriate region of human liberty. It comprises, first, the inward domain of consciousness; demanding liberty of conscience, in the most comprehensive sense; liberty of thought and feeling; absolute freedom of opinion and sentiment on all subjects, practical or speculative, scientific, moral, or theological. The liberty of expressing and publishing opinions may seem to fall under a different principle, since it belongs to that part of the conduct of an individual which concerns other people; but, being almost of as much importance as the liberty of thought itself, and resting in great part on the same reasons, is practically inseparable from it. Secondly, the principle requires liberty of tastes and pursuits; of framing the plan of our life to suit our own character; of doing as we like, subject to such consequences as may follow: without impediment from our fellow-creatures, so long as what we do does not harm them, even though they should think our conduct foolish, perverse, or wrong. Thirdly, from this liberty of each individual, follows the liberty, within the same limits, of combination among individuals; freedom to unite, for any purpose not involving harm to others: the persons combining being supposed to be of full age, and not forced or deceived.

13   No society in which these liberties are not, on the whole, respected, is free, whatever may be its form of government; and none is completely free in which they do not exist absolute and unqualified. The only freedom which deserves the name, is that of pursuing our own good in our own way, so long as we do not attempt to deprive others of theirs, or impede their efforts to obtain it. Each is the proper guardian of his own health, whether bodily, or mental and spiritual. Mankind are greater gainers by suffering each other to live as seems good to themselves, than by compelling each to live as seems good to the rest.

1859

11

Mixed Strategies

Sex, Drugs, Disasters, and the Extinction of Dinosaurs

Stephen Jay Gould

Science, in its most fundamental definition, is a fruitful mode of 1
inquiry, not a list of enticing conclusions. The conclusions are the
consequence, not the essence.

My greatest unhappiness with most popular presenta- 2
tions of science concerns their failure to separate fascinating
claims from the methods that scientists use to establish the
facts of nature. Journalists, and the public, thrive on controversial and stunning statements. But science is, basically, a
way of knowing—in P. B. Medawar's apt words, "the art of the
soluble." If the growing corps of popular science writers would
focus on *how* scientists develop and defend those fascinating
claims, they would make their greatest possible contribution to
public understanding.

Consider three ideas, proposed in perfect seriousness to 3
explain that greatest of all titillating puzzles—the extinction of
dinosaurs. Since these three notions invoke the primally fascinating themes of our culture—sex, drugs, and violence—they surely
reside in the category of fascinating claims. I want to show why
two of them rank as silly speculation, while the other represents
science at its grandest and most useful.

Science works with testable proposals. If, after much compi- 4
lation and scrutiny of data, new information continues to affirm

a hypothesis, we may accept it provisionally and gain confidence as further evidence mounts. We can never be completely sure that a hypothesis is right, though we may be able to show with confidence that it is wrong. The best scientific hypotheses are also generous and expansive: They suggest extensions and implications that enlighten related, and even far distant, subjects. Simply consider how the idea of evolution has influenced virtually every intellectual field.

5   Useless speculation, on the other hand, is restrictive. It generates no testable hypothesis, and offers no way to obtain potentially refuting evidence. Please note that I am not speaking of truth or falsity. The speculation may well be true; still, if it provides, in principle, no material for affirmation or rejection, we can make nothing of it. It must simply stand forever as an intriguing idea. Useless speculation turns in on itself and leads nowhere; good science, containing both seeds for its potential refutation and implications for more and different testable knowledge, reaches out. But, enough preaching. Let's move on to dinosaurs, and the three proposals for their extinction.

1. **Sex:** Testes function only in a narrow range of temperature (those of mammals hang externally in a scrotal sac because internal body temperatures are too high for their proper function). A worldwide rise in temperature at the close of the Cretaceous period caused the testes of dinosaurs to stop functioning and led to their extinction by sterilization of males.

2. **Drugs:** Angiosperms (flowering plants) first evolved toward the end of the dinosaurs' reign. Many of these plants contain psychoactive agents, avoided by mammals today as a result of their bitter taste. Dinosaurs had neither means to taste the bitterness nor livers effective enough to detoxify the substances. They died of massive overdoses.

3. **Disasters:** A large comet or asteroid struck the Earth some 65 million years ago, lofting a cloud of dust into the sky and blocking sunlight, thereby suppressing photosynthesis and so drastically lowering world temperatures that dinosaurs and hosts of other creatures became extinct.

Before analyzing these three tantalizing statements, we must 6 establish a basic ground rule often violated in proposals for the dinosaurs' demise. *There is no separate problem of the extinction of dinosaurs.* Too often we divorce specific events from their wider contexts and systems of cause and effect. The fundamental fact of dinosaur extinction is its synchrony with the demise of so many other groups across a wide range of habitats, from terrestrial to marine.

The history of life has been punctuated by brief episodes 7 of mass extinction. A recent analysis by University of Chicago paleontologists Jack Sepkoski and Dave Raup, based on the best and most exhaustive tabulation of data ever assembled, shows clearly that five episodes of mass dying stand well above the "background" extinctions of normal times (when we consider all mass extinctions, large and small, they seem to fall in a regular 26-million-year cycle). The Cretaceous debacle, occurring 65 million years ago and separating the Mesozoic and Cenozoic eras of our geological time scale, ranks prominently among the five. Nearly all the marine plankton (single-celled floating creatures) died with geological suddenness; among marine invertebrates, nearly 15 percent of all families perished, including many previously dominant groups, especially the ammonites (relatives of squids in coiled shells). On land, the dinosaurs disappeared after more than 100 million years of unchallenged domination.

In this context, speculations limited to dinosaurs alone ignore 8 the larger phenomenon. We need a coordinated explanation for a system of events that includes the extinction of dinosaurs as one component. Thus it makes little sense, though it may fuel our desire to view mammals as inevitable inheritors of the Earth, to guess that dinosaurs died because small mammals ate their eggs (a perennial favorite among untestable speculations). It seems most unlikely that some disaster peculiar to dinosaurs befell these massive beasts—and that the debacle happened to strike just when one of history's five great dyings had enveloped the Earth for completely different reasons.

The testicular theory, an old favorite from the 1940s, had its 9 root in an interesting and thoroughly respectable study of temperature tolerances in the American alligator, published in the staid *Bulletin of the American Museum of Natural History* in 1946 by three experts on living and fossil reptiles—E. H. Colbert, my own first teacher in paleontology; R. B. Cowles; and C. M. Bogert.

10   The first sentence of their summary reveals a purpose beyond alligators: "This report describes an attempt to infer the reactions of extinct reptiles, especially the dinosaurs, to high temperatures as based upon reactions observed in the modern alligator." They studied, by rectal thermometry, the body temperatures of alligators under changing conditions of heating and cooling. (Well, let's face it, you wouldn't want to try sticking a thermometer under a 'gator's tongue.) The predictions under test go way back to an old theory first stated by Galileo in the 1630s—the unequal scaling of surfaces and volumes. As an animal, or any object, grows (provided its shape doesn't change), surface areas must increase more slowly than volumes—since surfaces get larger as length squared, while volumes increase much more rapidly, as length cubed. Therefore, small animals have high ratios of surface to volume, while large animals cover themselves with relatively little surface.

11   Among cold-blooded animals lacking any physiological mechanism for keeping their temperatures constant, small creatures have a hell of a time keeping warm—because they lose so much heat through their relatively large surfaces. On the other hand, large animals, with their relatively small surfaces, may lose heat so slowly that, once warm, they may maintain effectively constant temperatures against ordinary fluctuations of climate. (In fact, the resolution of the "hot-blooded dinosaur" controversy that burned so brightly a few years back may simply be that, while large dinosaurs possessed no physiological mechanism for constant temperature, and were not therefore warm-blooded in the technical sense, their large size and relatively small surface area kept them warm.)

12   Colbert, Cowles, and Bogert compared the warming rates of small and large alligators. As predicted, the small fellows heated up (and cooled down) more quickly. When exposed to a warm sun, a tiny 50-gram (1.76-ounce) alligator heated up one degree Celsius every minute and a half, while a large alligator, 260 times bigger at 13,000 grams (28.7 pounds), took seven and a half minutes to gain a degree. Extrapolating up to an adult 10-ton

dinosaur, they concluded that a one-degree rise in body temperature would take eighty-six hours. If large animals absorb heat so slowly (through their relatively small surfaces), they will also be unable to shed any excess heat gained when temperatures rise above a favorable level.

The authors then guessed that large dinosaurs lived at or 13 near their optimum temperatures; Cowles suggested that a rise in global temperatures just before the Cretaceous extinction caused the dinosaurs to heat up beyond their optimal tolerance—and, being so large, they couldn't shed the unwanted heat. (In a most unusual statement within a scientific paper, Colbert and Bogert then explicitly disavowed this speculative extension of their empirical work on alligators.) Cowles conceded that this excess heat probably wasn't enough to kill or even to enervate the great beasts, but since testes often function only within a narrow range of temperature, he proposed that this global rise might have sterilized all the males, causing extinction by natural contraception.

The overdose theory has recently been supported by UCLA 14 psychiatrist Ronald K. Siegel. Siegel has gathered, he claims, more than 2,000 records of animals who, when given access, administer various drugs to themselves—from a mere swig of alcohol to massive doses of the big H. Elephants will swill the equivalent of twenty beers at a time, but do not like alcohol in concentrations greater than seven percent. In a silly bit of anthropocentric speculation, Siegel states that "elephants drink, perhaps, to forget . . . the anxiety produced by shrinking rangeland and the competition for food."

Since fertile imaginations can apply almost any hot idea to 15 the extinction of dinosaurs, Siegel found a way. Flowering plants did not evolve until late in the dinosaurs' reign. These plants also produced an array of aromatic, amino-acid-based alkaloids—the major group of psychoactive agents. Most mammals are "smart" enough to avoid these potential poisons. The alkaloids simply don't taste good (they are bitter); in any case, we mammals have livers happily supplied with the capacity to detoxify them. But, Siegel speculates, perhaps dinosaurs could neither taste the bitterness nor detoxify the substances once ingested. He recently told members of the American Psychological Association: "I'm not suggesting that all dinosaurs OD'd on plant drugs, but it certainly was a factor." He also argued that death by overdose may help explain why so many dinosaur fossils are found in contorted positions. (Do not go gentle into that good night.)

16   Extraterrestrial catastrophes have long pedigrees in the popular literature of extinction, but the subject exploded again in 1979, after a long lull, when the father-son, physicist-geologist team of Luis and Walter Alvarez proposed that an asteroid, some 10 km in diameter, struck the Earth 65 million years ago. (Comets, rather than asteroids, have since gained favor. Good science is self-corrective.)

17   The force of such a collision would be immense, greater by far than the megatonnage of all the world's nuclear weapons. In trying to reconstruct a scenario that would explain the simultaneous dying of dinosaurs on land and so many creatures in the sea, the Alvarezes proposed that a gigantic dust cloud, generated by particles blown aloft in the impact, would so darken the Earth that photosynthesis would cease and temperatures drop precipitously. (Rage, rage against the dying of the light.) The single-celled photosynthetic oceanic plankton, with life cycles measured in weeks, would perish outright, but land plants might survive through the dormancy of their seeds. (Land plants were not much affected by the Cretaceous extinction, and any adequate theory must account for the curious pattern of differential survival.) Dinosaurs would die by starvation and freezing; small, warm-blooded mammals, with more modest requirements for food and better regulation of body temperature, would squeak through. "Let the bastards freeze in the dark," as bumper stickers of our chauvinistic neighbors in sunbelt states proclaimed several years ago during the Northeast's winter oil crisis.

18   All three theories, testicular malfunction, psychoactive overdosing, and asteroidal zapping, grab our attention mightily. As pure phenomenology, they rank about equally high on any hit parade of primal fascination. Yet one represents expansive science, the others restrictive and untestable speculation. The proper criterion lies in evidence and methodology; we must probe behind the superficial fascination of particular claims.

19   How could we possibly decide whether the hypothesis of testicular frying is right or wrong? We would have to know things

that the fossil record cannot provide. What temperatures were optimal for dinosaurs? Could they avoid the absorption of excess heat by staying in the shade, or in caves? At what temperatures did their testicles cease to function? Were late Cretaceous climates ever warm enough to drive the internal temperatures of dinosaurs close to this ceiling? Testicles simply don't fossilize, and how could we infer their temperature tolerances even if they did? In short, Cowles's hypothesis is only an intriguing speculation leading nowhere. The most damning statement against it appeared right in the conclusion of Colbert, Cowles, and Bogert's paper, when they admitted: "It is difficult to advance any definite arguments against the hypothesis." My statement may seem paradoxical—isn't a hypothesis really good if you can't devise any arguments against it? Quite the contrary. It is simply untestable and unusable.

Siegel's overdosing has even less going for it. At least Cowles extrapolated his conclusion from some good data on alligators. And he didn't completely violate the primary guideline of siting dinosaur extinction in the context of a general mass dying—for rise in temperature could be the root cause of a general catastrophe, zapping dinosaurs by testicular malfunction and different groups for other reasons. But Siegel's speculation cannot touch the extinction of ammonites or oceanic plankton. (Diatoms make their own food with good sweet sunlight; they don't OD on the chemicals of terrestrial plants.) It is simply a gratuitous, attention-grabbing guess. It cannot be tested, for how can we know what dinosaurs tasted and what their livers could do? Livers don't fossilize any better than testicles.

The hypothesis doesn't even make any sense in its own context. Angiosperms were in full flower ten million years before dinosaurs went the way of all flesh. Why did it take so long? As for the pains of a chemical death recorded in contortions of fossils, I regret to say (or rather I'm pleased to note for the dinosaurs' sake) that Siegel's knowledge of geology must be a bit deficient: Muscles contract after death and geological strata rise and fall with motions of the Earth's crust after burial—more than enough reason to distort a fossil's pristine appearance.

The impact story, on the other hand, has a sound basis in evidence. It can be tested, extended, refined, and, if wrong, disproved. The Alvarezes did not just construct an arresting guess for public consumption. They proposed their hypothesis after laborious geochemical studies with Frank Asaro and Helen Michael had revealed a massive increase of iridium in rocks deposited right at the time of extinction. Iridium, a rare metal of the platinum group, is virtually absent from indigenous rocks of the Earth's crust; most of our iridium arrives on extraterrestrial objects that strike the Earth.

23   The Alvarez hypothesis bore immediate fruit. Based originally on evidence from two European localities, it led geochemists throughout the world to examine other sediments of the same age. They found abnormally high amounts of iridium everywhere—from continental rocks of the western United States to deep sea cores from the South Atlantic.

24   Cowles proposed his testicular hypothesis in the mid-1940s. Where has it gone since then? Absolutely nowhere, because scientists can do nothing with it. The hypothesis must stand as a curious appendage to a solid study of alligators. Siegel's overdose scenario will also win a few press notices and fade into oblivion. The Alvarezes' asteroid falls into a different category altogether, and much of the popular commentary has missed this essential distinction by focusing on the impact and its attendant results, and forgetting what really matters to a scientist—the iridium. If you talk just about asteroids, dust, and darkness, you tell stories no better and no more entertaining than fried testicles or terminal trips. It is the iridium—the source of testable evidence—that counts and forges the crucial distinction between speculation and science.

25   The proof, to twist a phrase, lies in the doing. Cowles's hypothesis has generated nothing in thirty-five years. Since its proposal in 1979, the Alvarez hypothesis has spawned hundreds of studies, a major conference, and attendant publications. Geologists are fired up. They are looking for iridium at all other extinction boundaries. Every week exposes a new wrinkle in the scientific press. Further evidence that the Cretaceous iridium represents extraterrestrial impact and not indigenous volcanism continues to accumulate. As I revise this essay in November 1984 (this paragraph will be out of date when the book is published),

new data include chemical "signatures" of other isotopes indicating unearthly provenance, glass spherules of a size and sort produced by impact and not by volcanic eruptions, and high-pressure varieties of silica formed (so far as we know) only under the tremendous shock of impact.

My point is simply this: Whatever the eventual outcome (I suspect it will be positive), the Alvarez hypothesis is exciting, fruitful science because it generates tests, provides us with things to do, and expands outward. We are having fun, battling back and forth, moving toward a resolution, and extending the hypothesis beyond its original scope.

As just one example of the unexpected, distant cross-fertilization that good science engenders, the Alvarez hypothesis made a major contribution to a theme that has riveted public attention in the past few months—so-called nuclear winter. In a speech delivered in April 1982, Luis Alvarez calculated the energy that a ten-kilometer asteroid would release on impact. He compared such an explosion with a full nuclear exchange and implied that all out atomic war might unleash similar consequences.

This theme of impact leading to massive dust clouds and falling temperatures formed an important input to the decision of Carl Sagan and a group of colleagues to model the climatic consequences of nuclear holocaust. Full nuclear exchange would probably generate the same kind of dust cloud and darkening that may have wiped out the dinosaurs. Temperatures would drop precipitously and agriculture might become impossible. Avoidance of nuclear war is fundamentally an ethical and political imperative, but we must know the factual consequences to make firm judgments. I am heartened by a final link across disciplines and deep concerns—another criterion, by the way, of science at its best. A recognition of the very phenomenon that made our evolution possible by exterminating the previously dominant dinosaurs and clearing a way for the evolution of large mammals, including us, might actually help to save us from joining those magnificent beasts in contorted poses among the strata of the Earth.

1984

Mother Tongue

Amy Tan

1   I am not a scholar of English or literature. I cannot give you much more than personal opinions on the English language and its variations in this country or others.

2   I am a writer. And by that definition, I am someone who has always loved language. I am fascinated by language in daily life. I spend a great deal of my time thinking about the power of language—the way it can evoke an emotion, a visual image, a complex idea, or a simple truth. Language is the tool of my trade. And I use them all—all the Englishes I grew up with.

3   Recently, I was made keenly aware of the different Englishes I do use. I was giving a talk to a large group of people, the same talk I had already given to half a dozen other groups. The nature of the talk was about my writing, my life, and my book *The Joy Luck Club*. The talk was going along well enough, until I remembered one major difference that made the whole talk sound wrong. My mother was in the room. And it was perhaps the first time she had heard me give a lengthy speech, using the kind of English I have never used with her. I was saying things like, "The intersection of memory upon imagination" and "There is an aspect of my fiction that relates to thus-and-thus"—a speech filled with carefully wrought grammatical phrases, burdened, it suddenly seemed to me, with nominalized forms, past perfect tenses, conditional phrases, all the forms of standard English that I had learned in school and through books, the forms of English I did not use at home with my mother.

4   Just last week, I was walking down the street with my mother, and I again found myself conscious of the English I was using, the English I do use with her. We were talking about the price of new and used furniture and I heard myself saying this: "Not waste money that way." My husband was with us as well, and he didn't notice any switch in my English. And then I realized why. It's because over the twenty years we've been together I've often used that same kind of English with him, and sometimes he even uses it with me. It has become our language

of intimacy, a different sort of English that relates to family talk, the language I grew up with.

So you'll have some idea of what this family talk I heard sounds like, I'll quote what my mother said during a recent conversation which I videotaped and then transcribed. During this conversation, my mother was talking about a political gangster in Shanghai who had the same last name as her family's, Du, and how the gangster in his early years wanted to be adopted by her family, which was rich by comparison. Later, the gangster became more powerful, far richer than my mother's family, and one day showed up at my mother's wedding to pay his respects. Here's what she said in part:

"Du Yusong having business like fruit stand. Like off the street kind. He is Du like Du Zong—but not Tsung-ming Island people. The local people call putong, the river east side, he belong to that side local people. That man want to ask Du Zong father take him in like become own family. Du Zong father wasn't look down on him, but didn't take seriously, until that man big like become a mafia. Now important person, very hard to inviting him. Chinese way, came only to show respect, don't stay for dinner. Respect for making big celebration, he shows up. Mean gives lots of respect. Chinese custom. Chinese social life that way. If too important won't have to stay too long. He come to my wedding. I didn't see, I heard it. I gone to boy's side, they have YMCA dinner. Chinese age I was nineteen."

You should know that my mother's expressive command of English belies how much she actually understands. She reads the *Forbes* report, listens to *Wall Street Week*, converses daily with her stockbroker, reads all of Shirley MacLaine's books with ease— all kinds of things I can't begin to understand. Yet some of my friends tell me they understand 50 percent of what my mother says. Some say they understand 80 to 90 percent. Some say they understand none of it, as if she was speaking pure Chinese. But to me, my mother's English is perfectly clear, perfectly natural. It's my mother tongue. Her language, as I hear it, is vivid, direct, full of observation and imagery. That was the language that helped shape the way I saw things, expressed things, made sense of the world.

8   Lately, I've been giving more thought to the kind of English my mother speaks. Like others, I have described it to people as "broken" or "fractured" English. But I wince when I say that. It has always bothered me that I can think of no way to describe it other than "broken," as if it were damaged and needed to be fixed, as if it lacked a certain wholeness and soundness. I've heard other terms used, "limited English," for example. But they seem just as bad, as if everything is limited, including people's perceptions of the limited English speaker.

9   I know this for a fact, because when I was growing up, my mother's "limited" English limited *my* perception of her. I was ashamed of her English. I believed that her English reflected the quality of what she had to say. That is, because she expressed them imperfectly her thoughts were imperfect. And I had plenty of empirical evidence to support me: the fact that people in department stores, at banks, and at restaurants did not take her seriously, did not give her good service, pretended not to understand her, or even acted as if they did not hear her.

10   My mother has long realized the limitations of her English as well. When I was fifteen, she used to have me call people on the phone to pretend I was she. In this guise, I was forced to ask for information or even to complain and yell at people who had been rude to her. One time it was a call to her stockbroker in New York. She had cashed out her small portfolio and it just so happened we were going to go to New York the next week, our very first trip outside California. I had to get on the phone and say in an adolescent voice that was not very convincing, "This is Mrs. Tan."

11   And my mother was standing in the back whispering loudly, "Why he don't send me check, already two weeks late. So mad he lie to me, losing me money."

12   And then I said in perfect English, "Yes, I'm getting rather concerned. You had agreed to send the check two weeks ago, but it hasn't arrived."

13   Then she began to talk more loudly. "What he want, I come to New York tell him front of his boss, you cheating me?" And I was trying to calm her down, make her be quiet, while telling the stockbroker, "I can't tolerate any more excuses. If I don't receive the

check immediately, I am going to have to speak to your manager when I'm in New York next week." And sure enough, the following week there we were in front of this astonished stockbroker, and I was sitting there red-faced and quiet, and my mother, the real Mrs. Tan, was shouting at his boss in her impeccable broken English.

We used a similar routine just five days ago, for a situation 14 that was far less humorous. My mother had gone to the hospital for an appointment, to find out about a benign brain tumor a CAT scan had revealed a month ago. She said she had spoken very good English, her best English, no mistakes. Still, she said, the hospital did not apologize when they said they had lost the CAT scan and she had come for nothing. She said they did not seem to have any sympathy when she told them she was anxious to know the exact diagnosis, since her husband and son had both died of brain tumors. She said they would not give her any more information until the next time and she would have to make another appointment for that. So she said she would not leave until the doctor called her daughter. She wouldn't budge. And when the doctor finally called her daughter, me, who spoke in perfect English—lo and behold—we had assurances the CAT scan would be found, promises that a conference call on Monday would be held, and apologies for any suffering my mother had gone through for a most regrettable mistake.

I think my mother's English almost had an effect on limiting 15 my possibilities in life as well. Sociologists and linguists probably will tell you that a person's developing language skills are more influenced by peers. But I do think that the language spoken in the family, especially in immigrant families which are more insular, plays a large role in shaping the language of the child. And I believe that it affected my results on achievements tests, IQ tests, and the SAT. While my English skills were never judged as poor, compared to math, English could not be considered my strong suit. In grade school I did moderately well, getting perhaps Bs, sometimes B-pluses, in English and scoring perhaps in the sixtieth or seventieth percentile on achievement tests. But those scores were not good enough to override the opinion that my true abilities lay in math and science, because in those areas I achieved As and scored in the ninetieth percentile or higher.

16   This was understandable. Math is precise; there is only one correct answer. Whereas, for me at least, the answers on English tests were always a judgment call, a matter of opinion and personal experience. Those tests were constructed around items like fill-in-the-blank sentence completion, such as: "Even though Tom was _____, Mary thought he was _____." And the correct answer always seemed to be the most bland combinations of thoughts, for example, "Even though Tom was shy, Mary thought he was charming," with the grammatical structure "even though" limiting the correct answer to some sort of semantic opposites, so you wouldn't get answers like, "Even though Tom was foolish, Mary thought he was ridiculous." Well, according to my mother, there were very few limitations as to what Tom could have been and what Mary might have thought of him. So I never did well on tests like that.

17   The same was true with word analogies, pairs of words in which you were supposed to find some sort of logical, semantic relationship—for example, "*Sunset* is to *nightfall* as _____ is to _____." And here you would be presented with a list of our possible pairs, one of which showed the same kind of relationship: *red* is to *stoplight, bus* is to *arrival, chills* is to *fever, yawn* is to *boring*. Well, I could never think that way. I knew what the tests were asking, but I could not block out of my mind the images already created by the first pair, "*sunset* is to *nightfall*"—and I would see a burst of colors against a darkening sky, the moon rising, the lowering of a curtain of stars. And all the other pairs of words—red, bus, stoplight, boring—just threw up a mass of confusing images, making it impossible for me to sort out something as logical as saying: "A sunset precedes nightfall" is the same as "a chill precedes a fever." The only way I would have gotten that answer right would have been to imagine an associative situation, for example, my being disobedient and staying out past sunset, catching a chill at night, which turns into feverish pneumonia as punishment, which indeed did happen to me.

18   I have been thinking about all this lately, about my mother's English, about achievement tests. Because lately I've been asked, as a writer, why there are not more Asian Americans represented in American literature. Why are there few Asian Americans enrolled in creative writing programs? Why do so many Chinese

students go into engineering? Well, these are broad sociological questions I can't begin to answer. But I have noticed in surveys—in fact, just last week—that Asian students, as a whole, always do significantly better on math achievement tests than in English. And this makes me think that there are other Asian-American students whose English spoken in the home might also be described as "broken" or "limited." And perhaps they also have teachers who are steering them away from writing and into math and science, which is what happened to me.

Fortunately, I happen to be rebellious in nature and enjoy the   19 challenge of disproving assumptions made about me. I became an English major my first year in college, after being enrolled as premed. I started writing nonfiction as a freelancer the week after I was told by my former boss that writing was my worst skill and I should hone my talents toward account management.

But it wasn't until 1985 that I finally began to write fiction.   20 And at first I wrote using what I thought to be wittily crafted sentences, sentences that would finally prove I had mastery over the English language. Here's an example from the first draft of a story that later made its way into *The Joy Luck Club*, but without this line: "That was my mental quandary in its nascent state." A terrible line, which I can barely pronounce.

Fortunately, for reasons I won't get into today, I later decided   21 I should envision a reader for the stories I would write. And the reader I decided upon was my mother, because these were stories about mothers. So with this reader in mind—and in fact she did read my early drafts—I began to write stories using all the Englishes I grew up with: the English I spoke to my mother, which for lack of a better term might be described as "simple"; the English she used with me, which for lack of a better term might be described as "broken"; my translation of her Chinese, which could certainly be described as "watered down"; and what I imagined to be her translation of her Chinese if she could speak in perfect English, her internal language, and for that I sought to preserve the essence, but neither an English nor a Chinese structure. I wanted to capture what language ability tests can never reveal: her intent, her passion, her imagery, the rhythms of her speech and the nature of her thoughts.

22 Apart from what any critic had to say about my writing, I knew I had succeeded where it counted when my mother finished reading my book and gave me her verdict: "So easy to read."

1990

On Dumpster Diving

Lars Eighner

1 Long before I began Dumpster diving I was impressed with Dumpsters, enough so that I wrote the Merriam-Webster research service to discover what I could about the word *Dumpster*. I learned from them that it is a proprietary word belonging to the Dempster Dumpster company. Since then I have dutifully capitalized the word, although it was lowercased in almost all the citations Merriam-Webster photocopied for me. Dempster's word is too apt. I have never heard these things called anything but Dumpsters. I do not know anyone who knows the generic name for these objects. From time to time I have heard a wino or hobo give some corrupted credit to the original and call them Dipsy Dumpsters.

2 I began Dumpster diving about a year before I became homeless.

3 I prefer the word *scavenging* and use the word *scrounging* when I mean to be obscure. I have heard people, evidently meaning to be polite, use the word *foraging*, but I prefer to reserve that word for gathering nuts and berries and such, which I do also according to the season and the opportunity. *Dumpster diving* seems to me to be a little too cute and, in my case, inaccurate because I lack the athletic ability to lower myself into the Dumpsters as the true divers do, much to their increased profit.

4 I like the frankness of the word *scavenging*, which I can hardly think of without picturing a big black snail on an aquarium wall. I live from the refuse of others. I am a scavenger. I think it a sound and honorable niche, although if I could I would naturally prefer

to live the comfortable consumer life, perhaps—and only perhaps—as a slightly less wasteful consumer, owing to what I have
learned as a scavenger.

While Lizbeth [Eighner's dog] and I were still living in the 5
shack on Avenue B as my savings ran out, I put almost all my
sporadic income into rent. The necessities of daily life I began
to extract from Dumpsters. Yes, we ate from them. Except for
jeans, all my clothes came from Dumpsters. Boom boxes, candles,
bedding, toilet paper, a virgin male love doll, medicine, books, a
typewriter, dishes, furnishing, and change, sometimes amounting
to many dollars—I acquired many things from the Dumpsters.

I have learned much as a scavenger. I mean to put some of 6
what I have learned down here, beginning with the practical art
of Dumpster diving and proceeding to the abstract.

What is safe to eat?   7

After all, the finding of objects is becoming something of an 8
urban art. Even respectable employed people will sometimes
find something tempting sticking out of a Dumpster or standing
beside one. Quite a number of people, not all of them of the bohe-
mian type, are willing to brag that they found this or that piece in
the trash. But eating from Dumpsters is what separates the dilet-
tanti from the professionals. Eating safely from the Dumpsters
involves three principles: using the senses and common sense
to evaluate the condition of the found materials, knowing the
Dumpsters of a given area and checking them regularly, and seeking always to answer the question "Why was this discarded?"

Perhaps everyone who has a kitchen and a regular supply of 9
groceries has, at one time or another, made a sandwich and eaten
half of it before discovering mold on the bread or got a mouthful
of milk before realizing the milk had turned. Nothing of the sort
is likely to happen to a Dumpster diver because he is constantly
reminded that most food is discarded for a reason. Yet a lot of
perfectly good food can be found in Dumpsters.

Canned goods, for example, turn up fairly often in the 10
Dumpsters I frequent. All except the most phobic people would
be willing to eat from a can, even if it came from a Dumpster.
Canned goods are among the safest of foods to be found in
Dumpsters but are not utterly foolproof.

11   Although very rare with modern canning methods, botulism is a possibility. Most other forms of food poisoning seldom do lasting harm to a healthy person, but botulism is almost certainly fatal and often the first symptom is death. Except for carbonated beverages, all canned goods should contain a slight vacuum and suck air when first punctured. Bulging, rusty, and dented cans and cans that spew when punctured should be avoided, especially when the contents are not very acidic or syrupy.

12   Heat can break down the botulin, but this requires much more cooking than most people do to canned goods. To the extent that botulism occurs at all, of course, it can occur in cans on pantry shelves as well as in cans from Dumpsters. Need I say that home-canned goods are simply too risky to be recommended.

13   From time to time one of my companions, aware of the source of my provisions, will ask, "Do you think these crackers are really safe to eat?" For some reason it is most often the crackers they ask about.

14   This question has always made me angry. Of course I would not offer my companion anything I had doubts about. But more than that, I wonder why he cannot evaluate the condition of the crackers for himself. I have no special knowledge and I have been wrong before. Since he knows where the food comes from, it seems to me he ought to assume some of the responsibility for deciding what he will put in his mouth. For myself I have few qualms about dry foods such as crackers, cookies, cereal, chips, and pasta if they are free of visible contaminates and still dry and crisp. Most often such things are found in the original packaging, which is not so much a positive sign as it is the absence of a negative one.

15   Raw fruits and vegetables with intact skins seem perfectly safe to me, excluding of course the obviously rotten. Many are discarded for minor imperfections that can be pared away. Leafy vegetables, grapes, cauliflower, broccoli, and similar things may be contaminated by liquids and may be impractical to wash.

16   Candy, especially hard candy, is usually safe if it has not drawn ants. Chocolate is often discarded only because it has become discolored as the cocoa butter de-emulsified. Candying, after all, is one method of food preservation because pathogens do not like very sugary substances.

All of these foods might be found in any Dumpster and can 17
be evaluated with some confidence largely on the basis of appearance. Beyond these are foods that cannot be correctly evaluated without additional information.

I began scavenging by pulling pizzas out of the Dumpster 18
behind a pizza delivery shop. In general, prepared food requires caution, but in this case I knew when the shop closed and went to the Dumpster as soon as the last of the help left.

Such shops often get prank orders; both the orders and the 19
products made to fill them are called *bogus*. Because help seldom stays long at these places, pizzas are often made with the wrong topping, refused on delivery for being cold, or baked incorrectly. The products to be discarded are boxed up because inventory is kept by counting boxes: A boxed pizza can be written off; an unboxed pizza does not exist.

I never placed a bogus order to increase the supply of pizzas 20
and I believe no one else was scavenging in this Dumpster. But the people in the shop became suspicious and began to retain their garbage in the shop overnight. While it lasted I had a steady supply of fresh, sometimes warm pizza. Because I knew the Dumpster I knew the source of the pizza, and because I visited the Dumpster regularly I knew what was fresh and what was yesterday's.

The area I frequent is inhabited by many affluent college 21
students. I am not here by chance; the Dumpsters in this area are very rich. Students throw out many good things, including food. In particular they tend to throw everything out when they move at the end of a semester, before and after breaks, and around midterm, when many of them despair of college. So I find it advantageous to keep an eye on the academic calendar.

Students throw food away around breaks because they do 22
not know whether it has spoiled or will spoil before they return. A typical discard is a half jar of peanut butter. In fact, nonorganic peanut butter does not require refrigeration and is unlikely to spoil in any reasonable time. The student does not know that, and since it is Daddy's money, the student decides not to take a chance. Opened containers require caution and some attention to the question, "Why was this discarded?" But in the case of

discards from student apartments, the answer may be that the item was thrown out through carelessness, ignorance, or wastefulness. This can sometimes be deduced when the item is found with many others, including some that are obviously perfectly good.

23   Some students, and others, approach defrosting a freezer by chucking out the whole lot. Not only do the circumstances of such a find tell the story, but also the mass of frozen goods stays cold for a long time and items may be found still frozen or freshly thawed.

24   Yogurt, cheese, and sour cream are items that are often thrown out while they are still good. Occasionally I find a cheese with a spot of mold, which of course I just pare off, and because it is obvious why such a cheese was discarded, I treat it with less suspicion than an apparently perfect cheese found in similar circumstances. Yogurt is often discarded, still sealed, only because the expiration date on the carton had passed. This is one of my favorite finds because yogurt will keep for several days, even in warm weather.

25   Students throw out canned goods and staples at the end of semesters and when they give up college at midterm. Drugs, pornography, spirits, and the like are often discarded when parents are expected—Dad's Day, for example. And spirits also turn up after big party weekends, presumably discarded by the newly reformed. Wine and spirits, of course, keep perfectly well even once opened, but the same cannot be said of beer.

26   My test for carbonated soft drinks is whether they still fizz vigorously. Many juices or other beverages are too acidic or too syrupy to cause much concern, provided they are not visibly contaminated. I have discovered nasty molds in vegetable juices, even when the product was found under its original seal; I recommend that such products be decanted slowly into a clear glass. Liquids always require some care. One hot day I found a large jug of Pat O'Brien's Hurricane mix. The jug had been opened but was still ice cold. I drank three large glasses before it became apparent to me that someone had added the rum to the mix, and not a little rum. I never tasted the rum, and by the time I began to feel the effects I had already ingested a very large quantity of the

beverage. Some divers would have considered this a boon, but being suddenly intoxicated in a public place in the early afternoon is not my idea of a good time.

I have heard of people maliciously contaminating discarded 27 food and even handouts, but mostly I have heard of this from people with vivid imaginations who have had no experience with the Dumpsters themselves. Just before the pizza shop stopped discarding its garbage at night, jalapeños began showing up on most of the thrown-out pizzas. If indeed this was meant to discourage me, it was a wasted effort because I am a native Texan.

For myself, I avoid game, poultry, pork, and egg-based foods, 28 whether I find them raw or cooked. I seldom have the means to cook what I find, but when I do I avail myself of plentiful supplies of beef, which is often in very good condition. I suppose fish becomes disagreeable before it becomes dangerous. Lizbeth is happy to have any such thing that is past its prime and, in fact, does not recognize fish as food until it is quite strong.

Home leftovers, as opposed to surpluses from restaurants, 29 are very often bad. Evidently, especially among students, there is a common type of personality that carefully wraps up even the smallest leftover and shoves it into the back of the refrigerator for six months or so before discarding it. Characteristic of this type are the reused jars and margarine tubs to which the remains are committed. I avoid ethnic foods I am unfamiliar with. If I do not know what it is supposed to look like when it is good, I cannot be certain I will be able to tell if it is bad.

No matter how careful I am I still get dysentery at least once 30 a month, oftener in warm weather. I do not want to paint too romantic a picture. Dumpster diving has serious drawbacks as a way of life.

I learned to scavenge gradually, on my own. Since then I have 31 initiated several companions into the trade. I have learned that there is a predictable series of stages a person goes through in learning to scavenge.

At first the new scavenger is filled with disgust and self- 32 loathing. He is ashamed of being seen and may lurk around, trying to duck behind things, or he may try to dive at night. (In fact, most people instinctively look away from a scavenger. By skulking around, the novice calls attention to himself and arouses suspicion. Diving at night is ineffective and needlessly messy.)

33   Every grain of rice seems to be a maggot. Everything seems to stink. He can wipe the egg yolk off the found can, but he cannot erase from his mind the stigma of eating garbage.

34   That stage passes with experience. The scavenger finds a pair of running shoes that fit and look and smell brand-new. He finds a pocket calculator in perfect working order. He finds pristine ice cream, still frozen, more than he can eat or keep. He begins to understand: People throw away perfectly good stuff, a lot of perfectly good stuff.

35   At this stage, Dumpster shyness begins to dissipate. The diver, after all, has the last laugh. He is finding all manner of good things that are his for the taking. Those who disparage his profession are the fools, not he.

36   He may begin to hang on to some perfectly good things for which he has neither a use nor a market. Then he begins to take note of the things that are not perfectly good but are nearly so. He mates a Walkman with broken earphones and one that is missing a battery cover. He picks up things that he can repair.

37   At this stage he may become lost and never recover. Dumpsters are full of things of some potential value to someone and also of things that never have much intrinsic value but are interesting. All the Dumpster divers I have known come to the point of trying to acquire everything they touch. Why not take it, they reason, since it is all free? This is, of course, hopeless. Most divers come to realize that they must restrict themselves to items of relatively immediate utility. But in some cases the diver simply cannot control himself. I have met several of these pack-rat types. Their ideas of the values of various pieces of junk verge on the psychotic. Every bit of glass may be a diamond, they think, and all that glistens, gold.

38   I tend to gain weight when I am scavenging. Partly this is because I always find far more pizza and doughnuts than water-packed tuna, nonfat yogurt, and fresh vegetables. Also I have not developed much faith in the reliability of Dumpsters as a food source, although it has been proven to me many times. I tend to eat as if I have no idea where my next meal is coming from. But mostly

I just hate to see food go to waste and so I eat much more than I should. Something like this drives the obsession to collect junk.

As for collecting objects, I usually restrict myself to collect- 39 ing one kind of small object at a time, such as pocket calculators, sunglasses, or campaign buttons. To live on the street I must anticipate my needs to a certain extent: I must pick up and save warm bedding I find in August because it will not be found in Dumpsters in November. As I have no access to health care, I often hoard essential drugs, such as antibiotics and antihista- mines. (This course can be recommended only to those with some grounding in pharmacology. Antibiotics, for example, even when indicated are worse than useless if taken in insufficient amounts.) But even if I had a home with extensive storage space, I could not save everything that might be valuable in some contingency.

I have proprietary feelings about my Dumpsters. As I have 40 mentioned, it is no accident that I scavenge from ones where good finds are common. But my limited experience with Dumpsters in other areas suggests to me that even in poorer areas, Dumpsters, if attended with sufficient diligence, can be made to yield a liveli- hood. The rich students discard perfectly good kiwifruit; poorer people discard perfectly good apples. Slacks and Polo shirts are found in the one place; jeans and T-shirts in the other. The popu- lation of competitors rather than the affluence of the dumpers most affects the feasibility of survival by scavenging. The large number of competitors is what puts me off the idea of trying to scavenge in places like Los Angeles.

Curiously, I do not mind my direct competition, other scav- 41 engers, so much as I hate the can scroungers.

People scrounge cans because they have to have a little cash. 42 I have tried scrounging cans with an able-bodied companion. Afoot a can scrounger simply cannot make more than a few dollars a day. One can extract the necessities of life from the Dumpsters directly with far less effort than would be required to accumulate the equivalent value in cans. (These observations may not hold in places with container redemption laws.)

Can scroungers, then, are people who must have small 43 amounts of cash. These are drug addicts and winos, mostly the latter because the amounts are so small. Spirits and drugs do, like all other commodities, turn up in Dumpsters and the scavenger will from time to time have a half bottle of a rather good wine with his dinner. But the wino cannot survive on these occasional finds; he must have his daily dose to stave off the DTs. All the cans he can carry will buy about three bottles of Wild Irish Rose.

44   I do not begrudge them the cans, but can scroungers tend to tear up the Dumpsters, mixing the contents and littering the area. They become so specialized that they can see only cans. They earn my contempt by passing up change, canned goods, and readily hockable items.

45   There are precious few courtesies among scavengers. But it is common practice to set aside surplus items: pairs of shoes, clothing, canned goods, and such. A true scavenger hates to see good stuff go to waste, and what he cannot use he leaves in good condition in plain sight.

46   Can scroungers lay waste to everything in their path and will stir one of a pair of good shoes to the bottom of a Dumpster, to be lost or ruined in the muck. Can scroungers will even go through individual garbage cans, something I have never seen a scavenger do.

47   Individual garbage cans are set out on the public easement only on garbage days. On other days going through them requires trespassing close to a dwelling. Going through individual garbage cans without scattering litter is almost impossible. Litter is likely to reduce the public's tolerance of scavenging. Individual cans are simply not as productive as Dumpsters; people in houses and duplexes do not move so often and for some reason do not tend to discard as much useful material. Moreover, the time required to go through one garbage can that serves one household is not much less than the time required to go through a Dumpster that contains the refuse of twenty apartments.

48   But my strongest reservation about going through individual garbage cans is that this seems to me a very personal kind of invasion to which I would object if I were a householder. Although many things in Dumpsters are obviously meant never to come to light, a Dumpster is somehow less personal.

49   I avoid trying to draw conclusions about the people who dump in the Dumpsters I frequent. I think it would be unethical to do so, although I know many people will find the idea of scavenger ethics too funny for words.

Dumpsters contain bank statements, correspondence, and 50
other documents, just as anyone might expect. But there are less
obvious sources of information. Pill bottles, for example. The
labels bear the name of the patient, the name of the doctor, and
the name of the drug. AIDS drugs and antipsychotic medicines,
to name but two groups, are specific and are seldom prescribed
for any other disorders. The plastic compacts for birth-control
pills usually have complete label information.

Despite all of this sensitive information, I have had only one 51
apartment resident object to my going through the Dumpster. In
that case it turned out the resident was a university athlete who was
taking bets and who was afraid I would turn up his wager slips.

Occasionally a find tells a story. I once found a small paper 52
bag containing some unused condoms, several partial tubes of fla-
vored sexual lubricants, a partially used compact of birth-control
pills, and the torn pieces of a picture of a young man. Clearly she
was through with him and planning to give up sex altogether.

Dumpster things are often sad—abandoned teddy bears, 53
shredded wedding books, despaired-of sales kits. I find many
pets lying in state in Dumpsters. Although I hope to get off the
streets so that Lizbeth can have a long and comfortable old age,
I know this hope is not very realistic. So I suppose when her time
comes she too will go into a Dumpster. I will have no better place
for her. And after all, it is fitting, since for most of her life her livelihood has come from the Dumpster. When she finds something
I think is safe that has been spilled from a Dumpster, I let her
have it. She already knows the route around the best ones. I like
to think that if she survives me she will have a chance of evading
the dog catcher and of finding her sustenance on the route.

Silly vanities also come to rest in the Dumpsters. I am a 54
rather accomplished needleworker. I get a lot of material from
the Dumpsters. Evidently sorority girls, hoping to impress
someone, perhaps themselves, with their mastery of a womanly
art, buy a lot of embroider-by-number kits, work a few stitches
horribly, and eventually discard the whole mess. I pull out their
stitches, turn the canvas over, and work an original design. Do
not think I refrain from chuckling as I make gifts from these kits.

I find diaries and journals. I have often thought of compiling 55
a book of literary found objects. And perhaps I will one day. But

what I find is hopelessly commonplace and bad without being, even unconsciously, camp. College students also discard their papers. I am horrified to discover the kind of paper that now merits an A in an undergraduate course. I am grateful, however, for the number of good books and magazines the students throw out.

56   In the area I know best I have never discovered vermin in the Dumpsters, but there are two kinds of kitty surprise. One is alley cats whom I meet as they leap, claws first, out of Dumpsters. This is especially thrilling when I have Lizbeth in tow. The other kind of kitty surprise is a plastic garbage bag filled with some ponderous, amorphous mass. This always proves to be used cat litter.

57   City bees harvest doughnut glaze and this makes the Dumpster at the doughnut shop more interesting. My faith in the instinctive wisdom of animals is always shaken whenever I see Lizbeth attempt to catch a bee in her mouth, which she does wherever bees are present. Evidently some birds find Dumpsters profitable, for birdie surprise is almost as common as kitty surprise of the first kind. In hunting season all kinds of small game turn up in Dumpsters, some of it, sadly, not entirely dead. Curiously, summer and winter, maggots are uncommon.

58   The worst of the living and near-living hazards of the Dumpsters are the fire ants. The food they claim is not much of a loss, but they are vicious and aggressive. It is very easy to brush against some surface of the Dumpster and pick up half a dozen or more fire ants, usually in some sensitive area such as the underarm. One advantage of bringing Lizbeth along as I make Dumpster rounds is that, for obvious reasons, she is very alert to ground-based fire ants. When Lizbeth recognizes a fire-ant infestation around our feet, she does the Dance of the Zillion Fire Ants. I have learned not to ignore this warning from Lizbeth, whether I perceive the tiny ants or not, but to remove ourselves at Lizbeth's first pas de bourée. All the more so because the ants are the worst in the summer months when I wear flip-flops if I have them. (Perhaps someone will misunderstand this. Lizbeth does the Dance of the Zillion Fire Ants when she recognizes more fire ants than she cares to eat, not when she is being bitten. Since I have learned to react promptly, she does not get bitten at all. It is the isolated patrol of fire ants that falls in Lizbeth's range that deserves pity. She finds them quite tasty.)

By far the best way to go through a Dumpster is to lower 59
yourself into it. Most of the good stuff tends to settle at the bottom
because it is usually weightier than the rubbish. My more athletic
companions have often demonstrated to me that they can extract
much good material from a Dumpster I have already been over.

To those psychologically or physically unprepared to enter a 60
Dumpster, I recommend a stout stick, preferable with some barb
or hook at one end. The hook can be used to grab plastic garbage
bags. When I find canned goods or other objects loose at the bottom
of a Dumpster, I lower a bag into it, roll the desired object into the
bag, and then hoist the bag out—a procedure more easily described
than executed. Much Dumpster diving is a matter of experience for
which nothing will do except practice.

Dumpster diving is outdoor work, often surprisingly pleasant. 61
It is not entirely predictable; things of interest turn up every day and
some days there are finds of great value. I am always very pleased
when I can turn up exactly the thing I most wanted to find. Yet in
spite of the element of chance, scavenging more than most other
pursuits tends to yield returns in some proportion to the effort and
intelligence brought to bear. It is very sweet to turn up a few dollars
in change from a Dumpster that has just been gone over by a wino.

The land is now covered with cities. The cities are full of 62
Dumpsters. If a member of the canine race is ever able to know
what it is doing, then Lizbeth knows that when we go around to
the Dumpsters, we are hunting. I think of scavenging as a modern
form of self-reliance. In any event, after having survived nearly
ten years of government service, where everything is geared to the
lowest common denominator, I find it refreshing to have work that
rewards initiative and effort. Certainly I would be happy to have
a sinecure again, but I am no longer heartbroken that I left one.

I find from the experience of scavenging two rather deep les- 63
sons. The first is to take what you can use and let the rest go by.
I have come to think that there is no value in the abstract. A thing
I cannot use or make useful, perhaps by trading, has no value
however rare or fine it may be. I mean useful in a broad sense—
some art I would find useful and some otherwise.

I was shocked to realize that some things are not worth 64
acquiring, but now I think it is so. Some material things are

white elephants that eat up the possessor's substance. The second lesson is the transience of material being. This has not quite converted me to a dualist, but it has made some headway in that direction. I do not suppose that ideas are immortal, but certainly mental things are longer lived than other material things.

65   Once I was the sort of person who invests objects with sentimental value. Now I no longer have those objects, but I have the sentiments yet.

66   Many times in our travels I have lost everything but the clothes I was wearing and Lizbeth. The things I find in Dumpsters, the love letters and rag dolls of so many lives, remind me of this lesson. Now I hardly pick up a thing without envisioning the time I will cast it aside. This I think is a healthy state of mind. Almost everything I have now has already been cast out at least once, proving that what I own is valueless to someone.

67   Anyway, I find my desire to grab for the gaudy bauble has been largely sated. I think this is an attitude I share with the very wealthy—we both know there is plenty more where what we have came from. Between us are the rat-race millions who nightly scavenge the cable channels looking for they know not what.

68   I am sorry for them.

1993

Only Daughter

Sandra Cisneros

1   Once, several years ago, when I was just starting out my writing career, I was asked to write my own contributor's note for an anthology I was part of. I wrote: "I am the only daughter in a family of six sons. *That* explains everything."

2   Well, I've thought about that ever since, and yes, it explains a lot to me, but for the reader's sake I should have written: "I am

the only daughter in a *Mexican* family of six sons." Or even: "I am the only daughter of a Mexican father and a Mexican-American mother." Or: "I am the only daughter of a working-class family of nine." All of these had everything to do with who I am today.

I was/am the only daughter and *only* a daughter. Being   3 an only daughter in a family of six sons forced me by circumstance to spend a lot of time by myself because my brothers felt it beneath them to play with a *girl* in public. But that aloneness, that loneliness, was good for a would-be writer—it allowed me time to think and think, to imagine, to read and prepare myself.

Being only a daughter for my father meant my destiny would   4 lead me to become someone's wife. That's what he believed. But when I was in the fifth grade and shared my plans for college with him, I was sure he understood. I remember my father saying, "*Que bueno, mi'ja*, that's good." That meant a lot to me, especially since my brothers thought the idea hilarious. What I didn't realize was that my father thought college was good for girls—good for finding a husband. After four years in college and two more in graduate school, and still no husband, my father shakes his head even now and says I wasted all that education.

In retrospect, I'm lucky my father believed daughters were   5 meant for husbands. It meant it didn't matter if I majored in something silly like English. After all, I'd find a nice professional eventually, right? This allowed me the liberty to putter about embroidering my little poems and stories without my father interrupting with so much as a "What's that you're writing?"

But the truth is, I wanted him to interrupt. I wanted my father   6 to understand what it was I was scribbling, to introduce me as "My only daughter, the writer." Not as "This is only my daughter. She teaches." *Es maestra*—teacher. Not even *professora*.

In a sense, everything I have ever written has been for him,   7 to win his approval even though I know my father can't read English words, even though my father's only reading includes the brown-ink *Esto* sports magazine from Mexico City and the bloody ¡*Alarma!* magazines that feature yet another sighting of *La Virgen de Guadalupe* on a tortilla or a wife's revenge on her philandering husband by bashing his skull in with a *molcajete* (a kitchen mortar made of volcanic rock). Or the *fotonovelas*, the little picture paperbacks with tragedy and trauma erupting from the characters' mouths in bubbles.

8   My father represents, then, the public majority. A public who is disinterested in reading, and yet one whom I am writing about and for, and privately trying to woo.

9   When we were growing up in Chicago, we moved a lot because of my father. He suffered bouts of nostalgia. Then we'd have to let go our flat, store the furniture with mother's relatives, load the station wagon with baggage and bologna sandwiches and head south. To Mexico City.

10   We came back, of course. To yet another Chicago flat, another Chicago neighborhood, another Catholic school. Each time, my father would seek out the parish priest in order to get a tuition break, and complain or boast: "I have seven sons."

11   He meant *siete hijos*, seven children, but he translated it as "sons." "I have seven sons." To anyone who would listen. The Sears Roebuck employee who sold us the washing machine. The short-order cook where my father ate his ham-and-eggs break-fasts. "I have seven sons." As if he deserved a medal from the state.

12   My papa. He didn't mean anything by that mistranslation, I'm sure. But somehow I could feel myself being erased. I'd tug my father's sleeve and whisper: "Not seven sons. Six! and *one daughter*."

13   When my oldest brother graduated from medical school, he fulfilled my father's dream that we study hard and use this—our heads, instead of this—our hands. Even now my father's hands are thick and yellow, stubbed by a history of hammer and nails and twine and coils and springs. "Use this," my father said, tap-ping his head, "and not this," showing us those hands. He always looked tired when he said it.

14   Wasn't college an investment? And hadn't I spent all those years in college? And if I didn't marry, what was it all for? Why would anyone go to college and then choose to be poor? Especially someone who had always been poor.

15   Last year, after ten years of writing professionally, the finan-cial rewards started to trickle in. My second National Endowment

for the Arts Fellowship. A guest professorship at the University of California, Berkeley. My book, which sold to a major New York publishing house.

At Christmas, I flew home to Chicago. The house was throbbing, same as always; hot *tamales* and sweet *tamales* hissing in my mother's pressure cooker, and everybody—my mother, six brothers, wives, babies, aunts, cousins—talking too loud and at the same time, like in a Fellini film, because that's just how we are.

I went upstairs to my father's room. One of my stories had just been translated into Spanish and published in an anthology of Chicano writing, and I wanted to show it to him. Ever since he recovered from a stroke two years ago, my father likes to spend his leisure hours horizontally. And that's how I found him, watching a Pedro Infante movie on Galavisión and eating rice pudding.

There was a glass filmed with milk on the bedside table. There were several vials of pills and balled Kleenex. And on the floor, one black sock and a plastic urinal that I didn't want to look at but looked at anyway. Pedro Infante was about to burst into song, and my father was laughing.

I'm not sure if it was because my story was translated into Spanish, or because it was published in Mexico, or perhaps because the story dealt with Topeyac, the *colonia* my father was raised in and the house he grew up in, but at any rate, my father punched the mute button on his remote control and read my story.

I sat on the bed next to my father and waited. He read it very slowly. As if he were reading each line over and over. He laughed at all the right places and read lines he liked out loud. He pointed and asked questions: "Is this So-and-so?" "Yes," I said. He kept reading.

When he was finally finished, after what seemed like hours, my father looked up and asked: "Where can we get more copies of this for the relatives?"

Of all the wonderful things that happened to me last year, that was the most wonderful.

1990

Coyote v. Acme

Ian Frazier

In the United States District Court,
Southwestern District,
Tempe, Arizona
Case No. B19294,
Judge Joan Kujava, Presiding
Wile E. Coyote, Plaintiff
—v.—
Acme Company, Defendant

1   Opening Statement of Mr. Harold Schoff, attorney for Mr. Coyote:
My client, Mr. Wile E. Coyote, a resident of Arizona and contigu-
ous states, does hereby bring suit for damages against the Acme
Company, manufacturer and retail distributor of assorted mer-
chandise, incorporated in Delaware and doing business in every
state, district, and territory. Mr. Coyote seeks compensation for
personal injuries, loss of business income, and mental suffering
caused as a direct result of the actions and/or gross negligence of
said company, under Title 15 of the United States Code, Chapter
47, section 2072, subsection (a), relating to product liability.

2   Mr. Coyote states that on eighty-five separate occasions he
has purchased of the Acme Company (hereinafter, "Defendant"),
through that company's mail-order department, certain products
which did cause him bodily injury due to defects in manufacture
or improper cautionary labelling. Sales slips made out to Mr.
Coyote as proof of purchase are at present in the possession of the
Court, marked Exhibit A. Such injuries sustained by Mr. Coyote
have temporarily restricted his ability to make a living in his
profession of predator. Mr. Coyote is self-employed and thus not
eligible for Workmen's Compensation.

3   Mr. Coyote states that on December 13th he received of
Defendant via parcel post one Acme Rocket Sled. The intention of
Mr. Coyote was to use the Rocket Sled to aid him in pursuit of his
prey. Upon receipt of the Rocket Sled Mr. Coyote removed it from
its wooden shipping crate and, sighting his prey in the distance,

activated the ignition. As Mr. Coyote gripped the handlebars, the Rocket Sled accelerated with such sudden and precipitate force as to stretch Mr. Coyote's forelimbs to a length of fifty feet. Subsequently, the rest of Mr. Coyote's body shot forward with a violent jolt, causing severe strain to his back and neck and placing him unexpectedly astride the Rocket Sled. Disappearing over the horizon at such speed as to leave a diminishing jet trail along its path, the Rocket Sled soon brought Mr. Coyote abreast of his prey. At that moment the animal he was pursuing veered sharply to the right. Mr. Coyote vigorously attempted to follow this maneuver but was unable to, due to poorly designed steering on the Rocket Sled and a faulty or nonexistent braking system. Shortly thereafter, the unchecked progress of the Rocket Sled brought it and Mr. Coyote into collision with the side of a mesa.

Paragraph One of the Report of Attending Physician (Exhibit 4 B), prepared by Dr. Ernest Grosscup, M.D., D.O., details the multiple fractures, contusions, and tissue damage suffered by Mr. Coyote as a result of this collision. Repair of the injuries required a full bandage around the head (excluding the ears), a neck brace, and full or partial casts on all four legs.

Hampered by these injuries, Mr. Coyote was nevertheless 5 obliged to support himself. With this in mind, he purchased of Defendant as an aid to mobility one pair of Acme Rocket Skates. When he attempted to use this product, however, he became involved in an accident remarkably similar to that which occurred with the Rocket Sled. Again, Defendant sold over the counter, without caveat, a product which attached powerful jet engines (in this case, two) to inadequate vehicles, with little or no provision for passenger safety. Encumbered by his heavy casts, Mr. Coyote lost control of the Rocket Skates soon after strapping them on, and collided with a roadside billboard so violently as to leave a hole in the shape of his full silhouette.

Mr. Coyote states that on occasions too numerous to list in 6 this document he has suffered mishaps with explosives purchased of Defendant: the Acme "Little Giant" Firecracker, the Acme Self-Guided Aerial Bomb, etc. (For a full listing, see the Acme Mail Order Explosives Catalogue and attached deposition, entered in evidence as Exhibit C.) Indeed, it is safe to say that not once has an explosive purchased of Defendant by Mr. Coyote performed in an expected manner. To cite just one example: At the expense of much time and personal effort, Mr. Coyote constructed around the outer rim of a butte a wooden trough beginning at the top of the butte and spiralling downward around it to some few feet above a black X painted on the desert floor. The trough was designed in such a way that a spherical explosive of the type sold by Defendant would roll easily and swiftly down to the point of detonation indicated by the X. Mr. Coyote placed a generous pile of birdseed directly on the X, and then, carrying the spherical Acme Bomb (Catalogue #78–832), climbed to the top of the butte. Mr. Coyote's prey, seeing the birdseed, approached, and Mr. Coyote proceeded to light the fuse. In an instant, the fuse burned down to the stem, causing the bomb to detonate.

7   In addition to reducing all Mr. Coyote's careful preparations to naught, the premature detonation of Defendant's product resulted in the following disfigurements to Mr. Coyote:

1.   Severe singeing of the hair on the head, neck, and muzzle.
2.   Sooty discoloration.
3.   Fracture of the left ear at the stem, causing the ear to dangle in the aftershock with a creaking noise.
4.   Full or partial combustion of whiskers, producing kinking, frazzling, and ashy disintegration.
5.   Radical widening of the eyes, due to brow and lid charring.

8   We come now to the Acme Spring-Powered Shoes. The remains of a pair of these purchased by Mr. Coyote on June 23rd are Plaintiff's Exhibit D. Selected fragments have been shipped to the metallurgical laboratories of the University of California at Santa Barbara for analysis, but to date no explanation has been found for this product's sudden and extreme malfunction. As advertised by Defendant, this product is simplicity itself: two wood-and-metal sandals, each attached to milled-steel springs of high tensile strength and compressed in a tightly coiled position by a cocking device with a lanyard release. Mr. Coyote believed that this product would enable him to pounce upon his prey in the initial moments of the chase, when swift reflexes are at a premium.

To increase the shoes' thrusting power still further, Mr. 9
Coyote affixed them by their bottoms to the side of a large boulder. Adjacent to the boulder was a path which Mr. Coyote's prey was known to frequent. Mr. Coyote put his hind feet in the wood-and-metal sandals and crouched in readiness, his right forepaw holding firmly to the lanyard release. Within a short time Mr. Coyote's prey did indeed appear on the path coming toward him. Unsuspecting, the prey stopped near Mr. Coyote, well within range of the springs at full extension. Mr. Coyote gauged the distance with care and proceeded to pull the lanyard release.

At this point, Defendant's product should have thrust Mr. 10
Coyote forward and away from the boulder. Instead, for reasons yet unknown, the Acme Spring-Powered Shoes thrust the boulder away from Mr. Coyote. As the intended prey looked on unharmed, Mr. Coyote hung suspended in air. Then the twin springs recoiled, bringing Mr. Coyote to a violent feet-first collision with the boulder, the full weight of his head and forequarters falling upon his lower extremities.

The force of this impact then caused the springs to rebound, 11
whereupon Mr. Coyote was thrust skyward. A second recoil and collision followed. The boulder, meanwhile, which was roughly ovoid in shape, had begun to bounce down a hillside, the coiling and recoiling of the springs adding to its velocity. At each bounce, Mr. Coyote came into contact with the boulder, or the boulder came into contact with Mr. Coyote, or both came into contact with the ground. As the grade was a long one, this process continued for some time.

The sequence of collisions resulted in systemic physical 12
damage to Mr. Coyote, viz., flattening of the cranium, sideways displacement of the tongue, reduction of length of legs and upper body, and compression of vertebrae from base of tail to head. Repetition of blows along a vertical axis produced a series of regular horizontal folds in Mr. Coyote's body tissues—a rare and painful condition which caused Mr. Coyote to expand upward and contract downward alternately as he walked, and to emit an off-key accordionlike wheezing with every step. The distracting and embarrassing nature of this symptom has been a major impediment to Mr. Coyote's pursuit of a normal social life.

13   As the Court is no doubt aware, Defendant has a virtual monopoly of manufacture and sale of goods required by Mr. Coyote's work. It is our contention that Defendant has used its market advantage to the detriment of the consumer of such specialized products as itching powder, giant kites, Burmese tiger traps, anvils, and two-hundred-foot-long rubber bands. Much as he has come to mistrust Defendant's products, Mr. Coyote has no other domestic source of supply to which to turn. One can only wonder what our trading partners in Western Europe and Japan would make of such a situation, where a giant company is allowed to victimize the consumer in the most reckless and wrongful manner over and over again.

14   Mr. Coyote respectfully requests that the Court regard these larger economic implications and assess punitive damages in the amount of seventeen million dollars. In addition, Mr. Coyote seeks actual damages (missed meals, medical expenses, days lost from professional occupation) of one million dollars; general damages (mental suffering, injury to reputation) of twenty million dollars; and attorney's fees of seven hundred and fifty thousand dollars. Total damages: thirty-eight million seven hundred and fifty thousand dollars. By awarding Mr. Coyote the full amount, this Court will censure Defendant, its directors, officers, shareholders, successors, and assigns, in the only language they understand, and reaffirm the right of the individual predator to equal protection under the law.

1996

Test Day

Frank Bures

1 From the doorway, I can see the last of my students walking up the dirt road into the school grounds. They're late as usual, but Mr. Ndyogi isn't here to beat them, so no one is running. Their

crisp blue and white uniforms move slowly beneath the outline of Mt. Meru. I can see they're even less eager for class to begin than normal, less enthused about English grammar than ever.

They know, as they drag their feet through the dust, that ₂ today is test day.

The last students straggle into class as I write the final ques- ₃ tions on the blackboard. When the talking and the scraping of wooden chairs dies down, I tell them to put their notebooks away and begin.

Testing is a futile exercise in so many ways. For most of these ₄ students, all 47 of them on a good day, English is their third language, after Swahili and Maasai. My own Swahili is very bad and even though we've been working on prepositions for some time, I still have no idea what the Swahili word for preposition is, or if there is one.

Instead, I'm reduced to crude hand gestures and bad draw- ₅ ings on the board. Walking around the room, glancing at the papers, I can see this hasn't worked as well as I thought it would. Instead, judging from their writing, preposition roulette is the favorite strategy once again.

"Go apologize to your brother *by* punching him in the nose." ₆

"Where should I get *inward* the bus?"   ₇

"What sort of things are you interested *nothing*?"   ₈

Our school is a small one, not far from Arusha, the semi- ₉ cosmopolitan urban center of northern Tanzania. We have eight classrooms, which are staggered at intervals down a hill. The students begin at the top and after a four-year downhill slide, they end up with their "certificate." My students are about mid-slide, in Form III. I'm here for the year on a mostly self-funded teaching program, the idea being that, as an English speaker I should have enough grasp of it to pass it along. This, in other words, is test day for me too.

The walls of our classroom are whitewashed and the room is ₁₀ packed tight with desks and stools. The blackboard at the front is badly chipped and overhead are corrugated iron sheets, with one plastic panel to allow the sunshine through. Our school is called "Ekenywa," which in Maasai means "Sunrise," because (as our headmaster told us) with education, the area around the school is waking up.

11   If some of my students would wake up, they might do better on this test.

12   My only real ambition here has been to leave them with a few practical English skills—how to write a letter, for example, or what the plot of "No Longer at Ease" is. Something to help them get a job in town, or at least to pass their national exam.

13   On test day, walking between the desks, I see how far we are from such lofty goals. Take, for example, their "Letter to a friend." I don't know how many times I told them—how many times I made them write in their notebooks—to end a letter, any letter, with, "Yours sincerely."

14   Around the room, there are many interpretations of this: "Your thinthially," "you thinkfully," "Yours sincefully," "Your sincilier," "your sceneially," "Senceally," "Your friendly," "Yours be love friend." A few students do get the basics. John signs his, "Yours in the Building of the Nation," which I'm quite happy with. But mostly test day is the day I wonder why I'm here.

15   My students wonder this too. Imani even writes in his letter: "The aim of sending this letter to you is to tell you about my exam I do. The test I taking was very hard. I try to think, but I am not understand anything in this test. The teacher who make this test was not like the Form III to go in the Form IV."

16   A good effort, and not a bad letter, as they go. Rukia takes a more flattering tack.

17   "I study in Ekenywa Secondary School, and the teacher is the very good and the teacher of English is come from America so they teach very well." Or, "Frank was teach me English very well. I like it because I trie to speak English and I want to go some o my town to teach a young girl and boy, like Frenck teach me." Or, "I will get 18 points on this test are very big points."

18   Her points, I'm afraid, will be the same size as everyone else's. But they try so hard, in spite of everything working against them. At primary school everything is taught in Swahili. Then they hit secondary school and suddenly all their classes are taught in English. In this kind of immersion, most students drown. The school provides no life rafts either, such as dictionaries or grammar books or workbooks. Never mind school supplies. Some days there aren't even any teachers.

Nonetheless, the Ministry of Education sets a huge task 19 before them. Form III students, it says, should "develop the habit of reading for pleasure and for information," as well as to increase reading speed. It says they should complete 13 books during the third year.

But our school only has five of the books on the syllabus, and 20 enough copies of only three to actually use.

Of the two we finally read—"Things Fall Apart" and "No 21 Longer at Ease," both by Chinua Achebe—we had 14 and 23 copies, and only a handful in good condition. These were shared by groups of three and four students. But actually reading them would be like me reading "Don Quixote" in Spanish. Impossible.

Of course, this shows on test day. We spent several weeks 22 going over these books, and I wrote explicit outlines of everything that happened on the board, which I watched them copy down.

But on test day, students who once seemed to have mastered 23 the plot, or at least memorized the characters, answer question about Obi and his grandfather, Okonkwo, like this:

"Okonkwo Obi is falling apart." 24

"Obi is republic." 25

"Clara was very dislike because Obi's parents they don't 26 want Clara to be wife of Obi. So Clara want to kill himself for that. THIS IS NOT GOD TO WANT TO KILL YOURSELF. EVEN YOU MR. FRANK."

Hmm. The thought hadn't crossed my mind. But with many 27 more days like this, it just might.

On the other hand, sometimes on test day, a previously illiter- 28 ate student mysteriously becomes a brilliant literary critic.

"Okonkwo," writes Godson, "through his fears, becomes 29 exiled from his tribe and returns only to be forced in the ignominy of suicide to escape the results of his rash courage against the white man."

Godson is the class Rastafarian and knows the words to 30 every Bob Marley song. I know he doesn't know anything about Okonkwo.

"Obi Okonkwo," writes Tumaini in suspiciously good 31 English, "returns from his studies in England to try to live up to the expectations of his family and his tribe and at the same time to breathe the heady atmosphere of Lagos."

32   Such is the heady atmosphere of test day. Martin writes in his letter, "Just a quick note to let you know that I've had a rather serious accident in my holiday, and my leg is now in plaster. The doctor said that I've fractured it, and that I'll be laid up for about six weeks. After that I should be right as rain. I will tell you more in another letter. For now, let me end here. Yours ever, Martin Paul."

33   There are about three students in the class who might be able to write something like this. Martin is not one of them. He is one of the other 44 who come to school, sit, talk, use cheat sheets I can never find, and don't pay attention, except on days when I give up on grammar and answer questions about America.

34   "Is it true," they would ask, "that the government gives every American a gun at age 18?" "Is it true that even the poorest Americans have 12 cars?" "What's up, man?" they would ask. "Hey," I'd say. "Not much."

35   Those days were the best of all, the days when I felt that I really had something to offer, something they wanted to know. These were the days we connected. These were the days when they sat rapt, as I unlocked the secrets of America, and they, in turn, unlocked their own country, giving me all the street lingo I could use.

36   But there was no slang on the national syllabus, and it didn't help them on test day.

37   "So," I ask again as we go over the test (we've been over the material before), "Obi and Christopher went out with some Irish girls. Does anyone know what Irish means?"

38   "Irish potatoes!" someone shouts.

39   "Yes," I say, "like Irish potatoes. But what does Irish mean?"

40   "Beautiful!" someone else shouts.

41   Next question: "So, the girl tried to bribe Obi with sex. What . . . "

42   Suddenly they are all fluent. "Explain! Explain!" they yell.

43   "No!" says Seuri, "don't explain in words. Give demonstration so we can see."

44   The students hand in the tests, and the scores are abysmal again. I'm not even sure how to grade them. If I make it on a curve, it will be a very small bump. The hardest part is that I know they could do it if they had the chance, if they had some

hope. But there are too many obstacles and too few incentives. Most of my students will be married off or end up putting their certificate to work in the fields.

Yet as with so many things in Tanzania, we move on. Life is 45 hard here, but giving up is even harder, and it's not really an option. So we go forward, to the next test, the next lesson. Along the way, we look for hope and laughter and comfort where there is little, and make our own where there is none.

As class finishes, wooden chairs scrape across the floor again 46 as the students stand up to leave with their tests. I too move to the door, but accidentally step on Matthew's foot.

"Oh, sorry," I say.   47

"It's cool," he says.   48

"Where did you learn that?" I ask.   49

He looks at me and smiles.   50

"You."   51

2003

Superman and Me

Sherman Alexie

I learned to read with a Superman comic book. Simple enough, 1 I suppose. I cannot recall which particular Superman comic book I read, nor can I remember which villain he fought in that issue. I cannot remember the plot, nor the means by which I obtained the comic book. What I can remember is this: I was 3 years old, a Spokane Indian boy living with his family on the Spokane Indian Reservation in eastern Washington state. We were poor by most standards, but one of my parents usually managed to find some minimum-wage job or another, which made us middleclass by reservation standards. I had a brother and three sisters. We lived on a combination of irregular paychecks, hope, fear and government surplus food.

2   My father, who is one of the few Indians who went to Catholic school on purpose, was an avid reader of westerns, spy thrillers, murder mysteries, gangster epics, basketball player biographies and anything else he could find. He bought his books by the pound at Dutch's Pawn Shop, Goodwill, Salvation Army and Value Village. When he had extra money, he bought new novels at supermarkets, convenience stores and hospital gift shops. Our house was filled with books. They were stacked in crazy piles in the bathroom, bedrooms and living room. In a fit of unemployment-inspired creative energy, my father built a set of bookshelves and soon filled them with a random assortment of books about the Kennedy assassination, Watergate, the Vietnam War and the entire 23-book series of the Apache westerns. My father loved books, and since I loved my father with an aching devotion, I decided to love books as well.

3   I can remember picking up my father's books before I could read. The words themselves were mostly foreign, but I still remember the exact moment when I first understood, with a sudden clarity, the purpose of a paragraph. I didn't have the vocabulary to say "paragraph," but I realized that a paragraph was a fence that held words. The words inside a paragraph worked together for a common purpose. They had some specific reason for being inside the same fence. This knowledge delighted me. I began to think of everything in terms of paragraphs. Our reservation was a small paragraph within the United States. My family's house was a paragraph, distinct from the other paragraphs of the LeBrets to the north, the Fords to our south and the Tribal School to the west. Inside our house, each family member existed as a separate paragraph but still had genetics and common experiences to link us. Now, using this logic, I can see my changed family as an essay of seven paragraphs: mother, father, older brother, the deceased sister, my younger twin sisters and our adopted little brother.

4   At the same time I was seeing the world in paragraphs, I also picked up that Superman comic book. Each panel, complete with picture, dialogue and narrative was a three-dimensional paragraph. In one panel, Superman breaks through a door. His suit is red, blue and yellow. The brown door shatters into many pieces. I look at the narrative above the picture. I cannot read the words,

but I assume it tells me that "Superman is breaking down the door." Aloud, I pretend to read the words and say, "Superman is breaking down the door." Words, dialogue, also float out of Superman's mouth. Because he is breaking down the door, I assume he says, "I am breaking down the door." Once again, I pretend to read the words and say aloud, "I am breaking down the door" In this way, I learned to read.

This might be an interesting story all by itself. A little Indian 5 boy teaches himself to read at an early age and advances quickly. He reads "Grapes of Wrath" in kindergarten when other children are struggling through "Dick and Jane." If he'd been anything but an Indian boy living on the reservation, he might have been called a prodigy. But he is an Indian boy living on the reservation and is simply an oddity. He grows into a man who often speaks of his childhood in the third person, as if it will somehow dull the pain and make him sound more modest about his talents.

A smart Indian is a dangerous person, widely feared and 6 ridiculed by Indians and non-Indians alike. I fought with my classmates on a daily basis. They wanted me to stay quiet when the non-Indian teacher asked for answers, for volunteers, for help. We were Indian children who were expected to be stupid. Most lived up to those expectations inside the classroom but subverted them on the outside. They struggled with basic reading in school but could remember how to sing a few dozen powwow songs. They were monosyllabic in front of their non-Indian teachers but could tell complicated stories and jokes at the dinner table. They submissively ducked their heads when confronted by a non-Indian adult but would slug it out with the Indian bully who was 10 years older. As Indian children, we were expected to fail in the non-Indian world. Those who failed were ceremonially accepted by other Indians and appropriately pitied by non-Indians.

I refused to fail. I was smart. I was arrogant. I was lucky. 7 I read books late into the night, until I could barely keep my eyes open. I read books at recess, then during lunch, and in the few minutes left after I had finished my classroom assignments. I read books in the car when my family traveled to powwows or basketball games. In shopping malls, I ran to the bookstores and read bits and pieces of as many books as I could. I read the books my father brought home from the pawnshops and secondhand. I read the books I borrowed from the library. I read the backs of cereal boxes. I read the newspaper. I read the bulletins posted on the walls of the school, the clinic, the tribal offices, the post office. I read junk mail. I read auto-repair manuals. I read magazines. I read anything that had words and paragraphs. I read with equal parts joy and desperation. I loved those books, but I also knew that love had only one purpose. I was trying to save my life.

8   Despite all the books I read, I am still surprised I became a writer. I was going to be a pediatrician. These days, I write novels, short stories, and poems. I visit schools and teach creative writing to Indian kids. In all my years in the reservation school system, I was never taught how to write poetry, short stories or novels. I was certainly never taught that Indians wrote poetry, short stories and novels. Writing was something beyond Indians. I cannot recall a single time that a guest teacher visited the reservation. There must have been visiting teachers. Who were they? Where are they now? Do they exist? I visit the schools as often as possible. The Indian kids crowd the classroom. Many are writing their own poems, short stories and novels. They have read my books. They have read many other books. They look at me with bright eyes and arrogant wonder. They are trying to save their lives. Then there are the sullen and already defeated Indian kids who sit in the back rows and ignore me with theatrical precision. The pages of their notebooks are empty. They carry neither pencil nor pen. They stare out the window. They refuse and resist. "Books," I say to them. "Books," I say. I throw my weight against their locked doors. The door holds. I am smart. I am arrogant. I am lucky. I am trying to save our lives.

1998

Permissions Acknowledgments

Ackerman, Diane. "Where Fall Color Comes From" from *A Natural History of the Senses* by Diane Ackerman, copyright © 1990 by Diane Ackerman. Used by permission of Random House, Inc.

Alexie, Sherman. "Superman and Me" originally published in the *Los Angeles Times*, April 19, 1998, as part of a series called "The Joy of Reading and Writing."

Angelou, Maya. "Grandmother's Victory," copyright © 1969 and renewed 1997 by Maya Angelou, from *I Know Why the Caged Bird Sings* by Maya Angelou. Used by permission of Random House, Inc.

Baldwin, James. "Fifth Avenue, Uptown: A Letter from Harlem" by James Baldwin. Originally published in *Esquire*. Copyright © 1960 by James Baldwin. Copyright renewed. Collected in *Nobody Knows My Name*, published by Vintage Books. Reprinted by arrangement with the James Baldwin Estate.

Blodget, Henry. "China's Biggest Gamble: Can It Have Capitalism without Democracy? A Prediction." Copyright © 2008 by *The Washington Post*.

Brady, Judith. "Why I Want a Wife." Copyright © 1970 by Judith Brady. Reprinted by permission of the author.

Britt, Suzanne. "Neat People vs. Sloppy People" from *Show and Tell* by Suzanne Britt. Copyright © 1982 by Suzanne Britt. Reprinted by permission of the author.

Brown, Rebecca. "Extreme Reading" from *American Romances: Essays by Rebecca Brown* by Rebecca Brown. San Francisco: City Lights Books, 2009.

Bures, Frank. "Test Day" by Frank Bures as appeared in *World Hum*, September 10, 2003. Reprinted by permission of Frank Bures.

Byers, Michael. "Monuments to Our Better Nature" by Michael Byers. Originally appeared in *Preservation*, January/February 2003. Reprinted by permission of Michael Byers.

White, E. B. "Once More to the Lake" from *One Man's Meat*, text copyright 1941 by E. B. White. Copyright renewed. Reprinted by permission of Tilbury House, Publishers, Gardiner, Maine.

Whitehead, Barbara DaFoe. "Where Have All the Parents Gone?" from *New Perspectives Quarterly*, 1990, Vol. 7, pp. 30–45. Reprinted by permission of Blackwell Publishing.

Wiseman, Richard. "The Search for the World's Funniest Joke" [editors' title] from "The Truth about Lying and Laughter." Published in *The Guardian*, April 21, 2007.

X, Malcolm. "Coming to an Awareness of Language" from *The Autobiography of Malcolm X* by Malcolm X and Alex Haley, copyright © 1964 by Alex Haley and Malcolm X. Copyright © 1965 by Alex Haley and Betty Shabazz. Used by permission of Random House, Inc.

Zinsser, William. "Clutter" from *On Writing Well*, 7th Edition by William K. Zinsser. Copyright © 1976, 1980, 1985, 1988, 1990, 1994, 1998, 2006 by William K. Zinsser. Reprinted by permission of the author.

Index